You won't just qualify as a driving instructor

You'll qualify as an AA Driving Instructor

So many companies now offer driving instructor training, why choose the AA?

Well, firstly we're one of Britain's most experienced motoring organisations, with a pedigree of over 100 years.

Secondly, our comprehensive training course covers everything you need to know about becoming not just any driving instructor, but an AA Driving Instructor. This includes 60 hours of face-to-face coaching with an experienced AA trainer who will be assigned to you for the whole of your training.

All our trainers are carefully selected and the training is flexible enough to fit around your existing commitments or condense it if you need to get through the training quickly. At the same time, we train you not just to be good enough to pass, but to become a first class instructor.

When you train with us you are automatically offered an AA franchise once you achieve ADI status and obtain your green badge, the mark of being a fully qualified instructor. Start your franchise within three months of qualifying and we'll discount your fees in your first six months by £1,500 in recognition of having trained with us (subject to terms and conditions).

You will have our full support as you start and grow your new AA franchise business – beginning with a free 2-day induction course, which also includes business and marketing skills training. As you progress, you will be invited to attend our free development workshops and local meetings where you will meet fellow AA Driving Instructors to network with.

To find out more about
AA Driving Instructor Training, call 0800 072 7824
Or to apply for an AA Franchise, call 0800 3 288 288

Driving School

Why you'll find starting up with us is reassuring

At the AA we know that starting out on your own as a driving instructor can easily give you a few sleepless nights. After all, you're not just teaching people to drive, but you're also learning to run a business.

However, as an AA Driving Instructor we'll support you all the way to make sure your new career is everything you dreamt it would be. For a start, you will quickly be put at ease by our warm welcome, thorough induction process and the full support of a local AA Instructor coach to see you through your first days.

Naturally, as it is your business, you are in the driving seat in terms of where you want to operate your franchise and the hours you want to work. There is never any pressure from us to take pupils, or to work outside your area or your preferred working times.

The AA franchise fee includes the supply of a striking AA liveried Ford Focus or Ford Fiesta tuition vehicle, which is replaced every 32 weeks, and all running costs except fuel. A replacement car will be delivered within 24 hours (often sooner) in case of an emergency, to provide continuity for your pupils.

Help keep your costs down by sourcing your own pupils or use our optional Pupil Introduction service whenever you choose.

But best of all, you have the comfort of knowing there is always someone to call on for help or advice – no matter how big or small the problem.

To apply for an
AA Driving School Franchise, call 0800 3 288 288
Or for more information on AA Driving Instructor Training, call 0800 072 7824

Driving School

Bonus for driving instructors

With insurance costs for young drivers rising fast, driving instructors can help their students get the best deal possible by pointing them in the direction of cheaper premiums.

And instructors can pocket a generous £30 for themselves each time a pupil they have referred to specialist insurance broker Adrian Flux takes out a policy.

Despite rising premiums, there are still some good deals to be had for newly-qualified drivers, and the knowledgeable staff at Flux can help advise youngsters on the best ways to keep their costs down.

As well as giving instructors a bonus for successfully referring pupils on to Flux, the broker also offers a highly competitive Driving Tuition policy.

Features include:

- Comprehensive instructor insurance cover included while driving other cars under tuition
- Pupil's own cars covered
- Cover for off road tuition and under-age learners
- Legal protection and uninsured loss recovery
- Dual control courtesy vehicle following non fault accidents
- Automatic cover for banned or convicted drivers re-sitting their test

For full details visit www.adrianflux.co.uk/di or call Flux free on 0800 089 0809.
To join the pupil referral scheme, call Craig Darwin on 0844 8888 488.

The Driving Instructor's Handbook

SEVENTEENTH EDITION

The Driving Instructor's Handbook

John Miller
and Margaret Stacey

WARRINGTON BOROUGH COUNCIL	
34143100731973	
Bertrams	01/07/2011
AN	£19.99
WAR	

KoganPage

LONDON PHILADELPHIA NEW DELHI

First published in Great Britain in 1982 by Kogan Page Limited
Seventeenth edition 2011

Kogan Page Limited
120 Pentonville Road
London N1 9JN
United Kingdom
www.koganpage.com

© Autodriva Training Systems 1982, 1983, 1986, 1988

© John Miller and Margaret Stacey 1989, 1991, 1993, 1994, 1996, 1997, 1999, 2002, 2004, 2006, 2007, 2009, 2011

ISBN 978 0 7494 6319 9

British Library Cataloguing in Publication Data

A CIP record for this book is available from the British Library.

Typeset by Saxon Graphics Ltd, Derby
Print production managed by Jellyfish
Printed and bound in the UK by CPI Antony Rowe

Take control of your vehicle costs with contract hire

Looking for a cost effective way of running your vehicle? Contract hire could help.

- Fixed weekly payments for easy budgeting
- Flexible contract lengths from as little as 7 months
- Routine maintenance included
- Road fund licence included
- HE-MAN dual controls
- AA or RAC rescue and recovery
- Sign writing service
- Courtesy dual controlled vehicle if your car is off the road

Prices from as little as £49 a week*

Formerly

⊛ THE DRIVING INSTRUCTOR CENTRE ⊛

Call **01162 888 288**   Visit **www.hitachicapitaldrivinginstructorcentre.co.uk**

Owner-driver vs. contract hire: the true cost of vehicle ownership

By Candice Walters, general manager,
Hitachi Capital Driving Instructor Centre

Any prospective driving instructor needs to have a careful think about the best funding method for their school vehicle. Traditionally, driving instructors have chosen the owner-driver route. This either requires a significant outlay of cash up front to fund the acquisition, or the arrangement of a hire purchase deal before the vehicle is owned outright.

However, before choosing the ownership route, it's worth asking whether this is the most financially sound option. Funding alternatives such as contract hire could offer driving instructors more flexibility, the ability to manage costs, and the promise of a significant reduction in business downtime when the car is off the road for repair.

Ownership is commonly perceived as offering the best value, but in reality this may be far from accurate. Instructors might take some comfort in the thought that when the time comes to sell their vehicle, they'll get something back from their purchase. However, from the moment it is acquired this asset starts to depreciate, and if the car is to be replaced on a typical three year cycle, the likelihood is that more finance will be owed on the vehicle than is returned by the sale.

Driving instructors will often negotiate a hire purchase agreement over a five year term, which helps to spread the cost, but also requires a significant upfront deposit in order to secure the deal over a longer period, potentially in the region of 20-25% of the vehicle purchase price.

Conversely, contract hire deals can be secured for an administration fee of a few hundred pounds, with capped payments starting from as little as £49+ VAT per week – the cost of securing just three or four driving lessons.

The decision to become a driving instructor is often driven by a desire to change careers or to become your own boss. However, some people may find it is just not for them. Others may commit to the training and qualification process and then fall foul of the 'three strikes and you're out' rule. Contract hire offers the flexibility to adapt to a range of different outcomes, with contract lengths of as little as seven months available for instructors in training. This represents far less of a risk to a new business than having to make a financial commitment of five years or more as required by an owner-driver.

Ownership also brings with it a responsibility for maintenance and repair, which not only represents a significant ongoing cost but also considerable potential for downtime when the vehicle is off the road. Driving school vehicles accumulate mileage and suffer more than average from vehicle wear and tear. Typical yearly mileage could equate to around 30k miles which, calculated over five years, would total at least 150k.

This high mileage contributes to an accelerated parts replacement cycle on driving school vehicles, which means that at least once a year owner-drivers can expect to have to replace parts such as brake pads and discs, in addition to paying for the annual service. Factor in the 'student effect', which tends to increase the frequency of replacing parts (bumped wheels and tyres, riding the clutch etc), and the cost of maintaining a driving school vehicle soon starts to mount up.

Owner-drivers should consider the cost of replacement parts and ensure they include the cost of labour in any calculations. Many people grossly underestimate the cost of replacing an item like a clutch or accelerator, so when they realise it is going to cost at least a couple of hundred pounds it can come as quite a shock.

Driving schools running contract hire vehicles benefit from a new car at the start of each hire term, which rarely runs to any more than 18 months. This means that getting the vehicle through an MOT is not an issue, service costs are basic and many repairs will be covered under warranty. Most importantly, it provides a driving instructor with peace of mind from the ability to forward plan and anticipate expenditure.

Owner-drivers also need to consider how they will manage when their car is off the road. A specialist contract hire provider will be able to offer a replacement vehicle with dual controls, enabling the instructor to carry on teaching, uninterrupted. Most garages will just offer a standard courtesy car, which will mean lessons are cancelled at your expense until the vehicle is repaired.

Essentially, it's crucial to investigate what funding plans are out there to best suit your approach. In these uncertain economic times, when the cost of running a business is high and cash flow needs to be tightly controlled, contract hire is definitely worth careful consideration.

To find out more about contract hire on new and used vehicles, call Hitachi Capital Driving Instructor Centre on 01162 888 288.

CONTENTS

About the author xxi

Introduction 1

01 The Driving Instructor 4

The instructor's role 4
The ADI qualification 6
Selecting a course 6
ORDIT – the Official Register of Driving Instructor Training 10
Associations for driving instructors 13
The driver training industry 19
Qualities of the driver and instructor 24
Continuing professional development (CPD) 29
Code of Practice for ADIs 32

02 The ADI Register 34

Qualifications 34
Trainee licence 37
Exemptions to the ADI regulations 38
Examination structure 39
Part 1: Theory and hazard perception 39
Part 2: Driving ability 41
Part 3: Instructional ability 43
At the end of the test 45
DSA service standards 48

03 ADI Part 1: Theory and Hazard Perception 49

Theory test 49
Hazard perception test 56

04 ADI Part 2: Driving Ability 58

Application 58
The car 59
Eyesight 59
Vehicle safety questions 60

Training to be an ADI?

DeskTop Driving have all the training products to help you pass!

- Training Manuals
- Visual Aids & Cue Cards
- DSA recommended books
- 'Part 3' DVDs
- Lesson Plans & Diagrams
- DSA Question Bank books & DVDs
- Hazard Perception DVDs

Already an ADI?

Join the thousands of ADIs who are earning extra money selling driver training products to their pupils!

- Car Theory and Practical Books
- Car Theory and Practical DVDs/CDs
- All DSA Official Publications
- LGV/PCV and Motorcycle Publications
- Hazard Perception DVDs

The driving test 60
Preparation 61
Eco-safe driving 71
Marking system 72
Your driving skills 73
Profile of 'the perfect driver' 74
On the road 76
System of car control 84
Trainee licence – 'licence to instruct' 90

05   ADI Part 3: Instructional Ability 93

Application 93
The car 94
Test format 94
Structure of the test 98
Assessment of instructional ability 103
Preparation 112
The test 115
The preset tests 117
When you pass 161
If you fail 162
The ADI certificate 163

06   The ADI Check Test 174

The appointment 175
Your pupil 176
The car 176
Presenting the lesson 176
Instructor grading 179
At the end of the test 182

07   The Driver 183

Driver licensing 184
Driving abroad 192
Visitors and new residents 192
Road traffic law 194
Motor vehicle insurance 205
Legal obligations of a supervising driver 208
Advanced driving tests 210
Eco-driving 217

08   The Car 218

Mechanical principles 218
Vehicle safety checks 235
Vehicle controls and operation 238
Vehicle regulations 245
Documents 252

09   Driver Training 256

Methods of learning 256
Teaching and learning 263
The learner's needs 264
Skill training 266
Structuring the learning 275
Driver training syllabus 279
Route planning 283
Instructions and terminology 287
Corrections on the move 295
Intervention and dual controls 295
Assessments and standards 301
Driver's record 305
Pass Plus syllabus 306
'L' driver errors 309
Assessing progress 311

10   Disabilities and Impairments 317

Assessing the needs 318
Notes on disabilities 319
Vehicle adaptations 321
Impaired vision 325
Impaired hearing 326
Other impairments and distractions 327
Methods of teaching 332
Applying for the driving test 334
Instructor courses 336

11   The Driving Test 337

Theory and hazard perception test 337
Practical test 344
Marking system 355
Driving test faults 362
Car and trailer test 367
Extended driving test 370
DSA service standards 370

12 Driving Large Vehicles 372

LGV driving licences 373
Health and eyesight 374
Applying for a licence 374
LGV theory test 375
LGV practical test 380
Driver CPC 385

13 LGV Instruction and Fleet Driver Training 390

Instructor qualifications 390
Register of LGV instructors 390
Fleet Driver Training Register 397

Appendices
I Useful Addresses 409
II Driving Standards Agency – Contacts 417
III Reference Books 419
IV The Official Register of Driving Instructor Training (ORDIT)
– Terms and Conditions of Membership 420

Index 424
Index of Advertisers 435

ABOUT THE AUTHOR

John Miller has been involved in the driver training industry for over 35 years and was an ADI for more than 30 years. For most of that time he ran his own driving school for both car and lorry drivers as well as an instructor training facility in Chichester. He is now a training consultant to the industry.

As well as *The Driving Instructor's Handbook*, John's other books include *Practical Business Skills for Driving Instructors* (published in 2010 by Kogan Page) and *Practical Teaching Skills for Driving Instructors* (also published by Kogan Page and co-authored with the late Margaret Stacey).

Practical Teaching Skills for Driving Instructors is a useful resource book, not only for new instructors who are training for the ADI exams, but also for experienced instructors in their everyday work in driver training at all levels. It is particularly helpful for anyone wanting to improve and extend their teaching and coaching skills and for enhancing their 'continuing professional development'.

Practical Business Skills for Driving Instructors focuses more on the business of setting up and running your own driving school from home or operating within a franchise. It includes information about business administration, the benefits and legal requirements of working for yourself, using your home as an office and advice on sales, marketing and promotion.

Both *The Driving Instructor's Handbook* and *Practical Teaching Skills for Driving Instructors* are listed by the Driving Standards Agency as essential material for the ADI examinations.

John Miller can be contacted at Johnmiller07@btinternet.com.

Note: While every effort has been made to ensure that the book is as up to date as possible, continual changes take place in the driver training industry and with legislation. This means that some changes may have occurred since going to print. To keep yourself completely up to date, we recommend that you regularly refer to *Despatch* (the Driving Standard Agency's own periodic e-magazine for instructors) and the DSA's websites at www.dft.gov.uk/dsa and www.direct.gov.uk/en/motoring. You will also benefit from joining one or more of the national associations as well as your local group.

Give Yourself the Advantages of MSA Membership

Are you aware of the advantages that can be gained by joining the MSA? Here we answer some often asked questions, and outline the advantages of membership which is open to qualified ADIs and those becoming ADIs, at any stage of their qualifying process.

The Motor Schools Association of Great Britain is the senior national association for ADIs, first established in 1935. Full membership is reserved for Approved Driving Instructors, however, trainees, potential driving instructors, driving school proprietors and other interested parties may also join but are not allowed to vote at AGMs. Potential Driving Instructors (PDIs) are welcomed into MSA membership and on qualification are converted to full membership at no extra charge.

Who owns the MSA?

The MSA is a non-profit making association, without shareholders, owned by and run for the benefit of its membership. With regional centres of activity throughout the country, it is perfectly placed to give you real support and superb value for a modest annual subscription. All these benefits are available to members.

How much does it cost?

For around £1 per week you will be kept fully informed on all the very latest developments within your industry, belong to the senior association for ADIs and make your opinion count.

What does the MSA do for me?

Most of what the Motor Schools Association does can be divided up into the three headings listed below:

Information

Information is provided to all MSA members every month through the association's own newspaper, Newslink. This contains up-to-the-minute news, views and gossip about the training industry. Each year, every member is sent the association's Annual Report and Handbook, which lists local contacts for both the MSA and the DSA. The MSA also provides inexpensive guides exclusively to members, the Driving Test Guide, the ADI Check Test Guide, the PDI Guide and the ADI Part 2 Guide.

Representation

Numerous government departments, national and international bodies, consult the MSA including the Driving Standards Agency (DSA), Department for Transport (DfT), the Driver and Vehicle Licensing Agency, the Parliamentary Advisory Council on Transport Safety (PACTS), and the European Secure Vehicle Alliance (ESVA). In Europe, the MSA represents members through the European Driving Schools Association (EFA).

Services

Free legal advice. Free technical advice. MSA Insurance Services. Personal taxation service. Free public liability insurance for £5million. Free professional indemnity cover for £3million. MSA Supplies by RCM Marketing Ltd, everything from roof signs to dual controls and appointment cards to theory test books. Local seminars and meetings with DSA examiners and other officials in attendance and many more...

INTRODUCTION

The Driving Instructor's Handbook was first published by Kogan Page in 1982 and since 1989 it has been listed by the Driving Standards Agency (DSA) as recommended reading for the ADI exams and the Check Test. This, the 17th edition, contains all the latest information on driving licences, driving tests, teaching and coaching skills, the ADI Register Exams, the ADI Check Test and driving large vehicles. It includes detailed information on driver training, structuring the lesson, dealing with disabilities and impairments and Continuing Professional Development (CPD).

Over the years the *Handbook* has been regularly updated by John Miller and continues to be recommended by the DSA both for new entrants and for qualified instructors. To quote a previous DSA ADI Registrar: 'With the many changes taking place over the whole range of activities in the driver training industry, those involved at all levels of training are strongly recommended to use *The Driving Instructor's Handbook* as resource material.'

The Check Test for qualified instructors is becoming much more demanding in its assessment of the ADI's skills in identifying, analysing and remedying the pupil's faults. In many ways it can be more like the ADI Part 3 exam. Many instructors with years of experience struggle to retain their ADI grading, with an increasing number now being graded as substandard. Those ADIs who have not kept themselves up to date with modern teaching and coaching skills should appreciate that new entrants to the Register are much better placed to compete for customers who are nowadays much more discerning in their expectations. Rather than finding themselves in a situation where they are downgraded, they might find it well worth their while to consider taking some form of refresher training prior to their Check Test. Coaching and teaching skills are dealt with in more detail in *Practical Teaching Skills for Driving Instructors*.

Drivers of most vehicles now have to pass a theory and hazard perception test for each group of licence acquisition. Additionally, anyone passing the test for car drivers is restricted to driving vehicles of up to 3,500 kilograms or with a maximum of eight seats. Anyone wanting to drive larger vehicles has to take an additional test, as does someone wanting to tow a large trailer behind a car or commercial vehicle.

Under the New Driver Act, newly qualified drivers who accumulate more than six penalty points on their licence within two years of passing the test lose their licence. The offender then has to reapply for a provisional licence and retake both the theory and the practical test. Recent figures show that about 14,000 drivers each year have their licences revoked, but that only about 8,000 retake and pass the practical test.

All of these requirements mean that, as well as preparing drivers for the ordinary 'L' test, ADIs need to be able to deal with drivers at all levels of ability and experience. To do this they need to be effective teachers who will be able to develop safe attitudes in their pupils.

Teaching people to change attitudes and to fully understand the requirements for driving a car in today's road and traffic conditions is far more complex than simply teaching practical vehicle control skills. This is why there is now a move to encourage instructors to use more up-to-date methods of coaching, rather than just 'instructing'. These skills are outlined in Chapter 9 and in more detail in *Practical Teaching Skills for Driving Instructors*.

Training to become a driving instructor is neither cheap nor easy; in fact, it can be relatively costly and certainly time-consuming. However, the time, effort and expense involved in preparing for all three parts of the ADI exam should be considered as an investment in your future. Latest figures show that between 18,000 and 20,000 people start the application process each year, but only about 4–5,000 candidates actually complete the programme and qualify as ADIs.

A wide variety of training courses is available to the prospective instructor. Before you make your choice or pay out any large sums of money in advance, study carefully Chapter 2 of this book. It explains the structure of the examination and how long it may take you to qualify. Chapters 3, 4 and 5 go on to explain, in more detail, the training you will require and the different types of course available.

It's important that you select a tutor who is completely up to date with the examination syllabus and who is a qualified and experienced trainer of ADIs. The ORDIT register of trainers is a useful guide to available trainers in your area. For details of ORDIT, see pages 10–12. Bear in mind that, although a local driving instructor may be extremely good at teaching new drivers, there is a vast difference between 'teaching to drive' and 'teaching to teach'.

As there is a limit of three attempts on the Part 2 Test of Driving Ability and the Part 3 Test of Ability to Instruct, you should make sure you are well prepared before you attempt these elements of the examination. The pass rate for the Part 3 is now running at less than 30 per cent, so it pays to make sure that you receive a realistic amount of quality training from a qualified and experienced ADI tutor. Listen carefully to the advice given by your tutor. There are no short cuts! Remember, if you fail, there will be more pressure on you at the next attempt.

When you have qualified, you should bear in mind that you are now a professional. You are your best advertisement! Make sure you set a good example by driving correctly at all times. Dress smartly and keep your car in a clean and roadworthy condition. Treat all of your clients with respect and put in your best effort with all of them. If you follow these basic rules, and so long as your instruction is to a high standard, you will get a lot of personal recommendations and your business will flourish.

The number of qualified instructors has steadily increased over the past few years, with more than 44,000 currently on the ADI Register. This figure increases steadily each year and in the current climate of redundancies it is expected to continue to do so. Therefore, with a changing market and the sustained level of competition in the industry, you cannot afford to sit back and wait for the telephone to ring. You must be proactive and prepared to seek out new markets and prospective customers for yourself. Chapter 1 gives a few ideas and suggestions for maintaining an adequate level of business and keeping ahead of the competition.

When you pass the exams and qualify as an ADI all that is tested by the DSA is your ability to give instruction. To become a successful self-employed or franchised instructor and to run a small business you need much than this. For this reason, business skills and customer care are dealt with in detail in *Practical Business Skills for Driving Instructors* (published by Kogan Page in 2010).

This publication includes how to set up and run your own business, the responsibilities and obligations of being self-employed and how to market yourself and your business.

As a practising ADI, are you happy with the grading you achieved in your last Check Test? Even though you may have a reasonable pass rate, your teaching style may be a little out of date – especially if you qualified some years ago. Although the Check Test is covered in Chapter 6, you will find it helpful to update your knowledge and teaching style so that your methods are comparable to those of your newly qualified competitors, who may well have had more rigorous and thorough training. In this respect, listen to any advice given to you by the DSA Examiner at the time of your regular Check Test. Make sure that you are completely up to date with modern driving and teaching techniques and that you are working with the latest editions of *The Official Highway Code*, *The Official DSA Guide to Driving – The essential skills* and *The Official Guide to Learning to Drive*. These publications should also form the basis of preparing your pupils for the theory test.

Looking to the future the Driving Standards Agency has recruited a trial group of 48 ADIs who have been trained to deliver a proposed new syllabus for learner drivers. The syllabus is based on the new 'National Driving Standards' (available from the DSA's website) and covers the whole range of knowledge, skills and attitudes needed for safe and responsible driving. This approach to driver training aims to encourage pupils to take more responsibility for their own training, rather than relying purely on instruction from the instructor. The trial will measure the effectiveness of the new syllabus and teaching methods, with results probably being available early in 2012.

The Driving Instructor

01

This chapter gives an outline of the driving instruction industry and includes information on:

- the instructor's role;
- the qualities of an instructor;
- the ADI qualification;
- how to select your trainer;
- ORDIT – the Official Register of Driving Instructor Training;
- further qualifications;
- driving instruction opportunities;
- ADI associations and organizations;
- the instructor's code of conduct.

The instructor's role

In today's fast-moving and complex road and traffic systems, the driving instructor's role is now much more challenging than when the driving test was first introduced in 1935. The scope of work within the driving instruction industry has also become much more diverse. Although most qualified ADIs focus their businesses on teaching new drivers, there are now far more opportunities to add interest and variety to the job. These include:

- theory books and courses;
- pre-driver training;
- teaching people who have disabilities;
- 'Pass Plus' training;

- defensive and advanced driver training;
- company and fleet driver training;
- minibus driver training;
- training in the towing of trailers and caravans;
- corrective driver training for traffic offenders;
- assessments for older drivers;
- driver training schemes run by local authorities and police.

More details of these opportunities are included later in this chapter.

Qualities of the effective driving instructor

To become an effective driver trainer you need to be much more than a good driver who enjoys motoring. The speed and density of today's traffic, together with increasingly complex driving situations, make the ADI's job an extremely demanding one. The aim of the truly professional instructor should be to improve the standards of new and experienced drivers in order to reduce the numbers of accidents, deaths and casualties suffered on our roads.
    You will need to:

- have a thorough understanding of the rules and principles involved in safe driving;
- be able to put these principles into practice by driving thoughtfully and efficiently;
- be able to patiently teach your pupils how to apply those principles, while other drivers around you are trying to get from A to B as quickly as possible;
- instil safe attitudes into clients at all levels of driving.

One of your main aims should be to produce drivers who will help make our roads safer, but at the same time to ensure that they will enjoy their lessons and future motoring.
    The number of drivers killed in road accidents is far too high, particularly among newly qualified, young drivers. You will need to work hard to encourage pupils to develop safe attitudes towards themselves, their vehicle and, last but by no means least, all other road users. Drivers who are taught to accept and compensate for the mistakes of others are far less likely to become involved in 'road rage'.
    If you think you have a future in improving driver standards, and that you will be able to carry out all these objectives, to qualify as a Driving Standards Agency (DSA) ADI, you must be prepared to:

- study hard for the theory and hazard perception test, the ADI Part 1;
- work at enhancing your personal driving skills for the driving test, the ADI Part 2;

- be prepared to invest in sufficient, good-quality training to stand a reasonable chance of passing the instructional test, the ADI Part 3.

The ADI qualification

If you wish to teach driving for reward, to either complete beginners or experienced drivers, the only official qualification is that of Driving Standards Agency (DSA) Approved Driving Instructor (ADI) (car). In Northern Ireland the official title is Department of the Environment Approved Driving Instructor (DOE ADI). You must have had a minimum of four years' experience as a driver and meet all of the other requirements laid down in the Road Traffic Act. A full explanation of the qualifications for registration is given in Chapter 2.

For an application form and full details of what is involved in the qualification, you should apply for the DSA's information pack *Your Road to Becoming an Approved Driving Instructor* (ADI 14). You can download a copy from the DSA website. The pack includes the application forms you will need to get started on the process of taking the exams and qualifying to become an ADI.

For contact details, see page 409.

Applicants in Northern Ireland should apply for an ADI 1 to The Registrar of Approved Driving Instructors, DVA Testing, 66 Balmoral Road, Belfast BT12 6QL (tel: 0289 054 7933). The ADI1 can also be downloaded from www.dvta.gov.uk.

To qualify as an ADI, you have to pass an examination that is conducted in three separate tests:

- Part 1: Theory and Hazard Perception Test;
- Part 2: Eyesight and Driving Ability Test;
- Part 3: Test of Ability to Instruct.

You must take and pass all three tests within a two-year period. The format of the exam and how to apply is explained in Chapter 2.

Selecting a course

One of the most important decisions to be made is on the method of training that can best be fitted in around your other commitments, particularly if you are currently in full-time employment. You also need to bear in mind that, although appointments for theory and hazard perception tests are available virtually 'on demand', the waiting time for practical test appointments is sometimes as long as three months.

Learning to become a driving instructor needs a huge commitment in terms of the time needed to:

- **Study in depth all of the recommended books and other materials.** Not only do you need to prepare yourself for the theory and hazard perception tests, but if you are to become an effective instructor you will need a thorough understanding of all of the principles covered in the full syllabus. This means that learning the question bank by rote will not be sufficient!
- **Enhance your personal driving skills.** This is not only so that you are properly prepared for the ADI Part 2 exam, but also so that your driving will be to a consistently high standard.
- **Invest in sufficient good-quality training.** This is necessary so that you are prepared for the instructional test, and also that your teaching techniques will assist you in the future to produce better drivers to share the roads with us.

Your tutor

The tutor's role includes:

- preparing candidates for all elements of the ADI test;
- retraining/updating experienced instructors;
- preparing qualified ADIs for the Check Test.

Statistics show that less than a quarter of those beginning the process of training will eventually qualify as ADIs. Before you commit yourself to paying out large sums of money on training, it is sensible to arrange for an assessment with an experienced tutor. Obtaining an honest opinion of your potential can avoid lots of heartache and bitterness later on.

Teaching someone to teach driving is totally different from teaching someone to drive. It doesn't follow that good drivers will always make good instructors. Similarly, it is also very true that not all ADIs, though very good at teaching people to drive, will have the complex skills required to train new instructors. A local ADI may have an extremely good reputation for getting learners through the 'L' test, but because of the higher level of skills and knowledge involved, you may have to look further afield for a qualified and experienced tutor who:

- is fully up to date with the requirements of the exams;
- trains instructors on a regular basis;
- has undergone a DSA inspection and is listed in the Official Register for Driving Instructor Training (ORDIT).

With the current pass rate for the instructional test being below 30 per cent, most failures occur at this stage. It's vital therefore that your training is effective and is conducted by someone experienced in the coaching of new instructors.

It is a well-known fact that everyone has a different rate of learning. The good tutor will be able to structure the training programme to suit your particular needs.

The types of course available

The structure of the examination means that you will have to apply for, and pass, each test in sequence and there is often a long waiting list for the practical tests – sometimes as long as three months. You should also bear in mind that, should you fail Part 2 three times, you will not be eligible to take the third part of the exam. Make sure that you will not be paying for what you can't have.

Courses vary a great deal in content, duration and cost. Before deciding on the one that most suits your needs, you should make every effort to find out what you will be getting for your money. Ask for a full description of the syllabus and the format of the training in relation to each element of the exam.

Remember, everyone has a different rate of learning. The training you receive to develop your driving and teaching skills should, therefore, be adapted to suit your particular needs. Examples of the types of training available are:

- distance learning programmes for studying at home for the theory test, with practical training for the driving and instructional tests;
- intensive courses to prepare candidates for all three tests;
- courses preparing candidates for obtaining a trainee licence and working for a driving school while preparing for the instructional test.

Before committing yourself, you should ask for information on the following points:

- What proportion of the training for the practical elements will be conducted in the car?
- How much individual training will you be getting and how much will be on a shared basis?
- If the practical training is shared, how many trainees will be in the car at the same time?
- Does the course allow for training to be structured to suit your particular learning abilities?
- If you opt for working under the Trainee Licence Scheme, will you be receiving proper training and support – particularly prior to being sent out with learners?
- What are your tutor's special qualifications and experience?

Course syllabus

As well as considering these six main points, you should compare the syllabus of the courses on offer with that of the examination. A good training establishment should prepare you properly for each of the three tests. The course should include:

- up-to-date books and materials with questions and answers for the theory test;
- computer-based practice at the hazard perception element;
- sufficient training for Part 2, Eyesight and Driving Ability Test;
- plenty of training, preferably on an individual basis (certainly no more than a ratio of two trainees to one tutor) for the instructional ability test.

(If you opt to take up a trainee licence certain criteria must be met. For example, you must be prepared to have additional training and/or be properly supervised during the licence period. The trainee licence scheme is dealt with in more detail in Chapter 2.)

Course material

To prepare yourself properly for the examination, you will need the following materials, all of which are recommended by the DSA:

- *The Official DSA Guide to Driving – The essential skills.*
- *The Highway Code.*
- *The Official Guide to Learning to Drive.*
- DL25 Driving Test Report form – see page 354.
- *Practical Teaching Skills for Driving Instructors* by John Miller and Margaret Stacey.

Other useful DSA material includes:

- *Helping Learners to Practice – The Official DSA Guide.*
- *The Official DSA Guide to Hazard Perception* DVD.

How long it will take you to qualify

To be realistic, the qualifying procedure is likely to take around 10 months – that is, if you pass each element at the first attempt and there is no waiting for test appointments. It can take considerably longer than this if:

- there is a long waiting time for appointments;
- tests are postponed;
- you fail any of the tests.

This exam structure and time span should be taken into consideration if you are thinking of taking an intensive course. It is highly likely that you will have to return for 'top-up' training nearer the date of your Part 3 test appointment – and this will probably involve additional fees.

Making the decision

Make sure that you are fully aware of the degree of difficulty of the ADI exams.

Out of 18–20,000 candidates applying for a theory test in any one year, just over 4,000 actually qualify as an ADI.

Part 3 has the lowest pass rate at below 30 per cent, so this is the test for which you will need plenty of expert training and preparation.

This change of career will involve a great deal of input in terms of time, commitment and cost. Before committing yourself and enrolling on a course, you should seriously consider the following aspects:

- Do I have the potential to become an effective ADI?
- Can I really afford the expense, given that there are no guarantees of qualifying?
- Does the course allow for training to be tailored to the structure of the exam?
- Will I be getting sufficient individual training in preparation for Parts 2 and 3?
- Will the course be structured to suit my own needs?
- Does my tutor have plenty of experience in the training of new instructors?

ORDIT – the Official Register of Driving Instructor Training

ORDIT is a voluntary registration scheme administered by the DSA, using criteria that were set originally by representatives of the driver training industry. In Northern Ireland the Register is operated by the DVTA (NI).

The Register consists of a list of training establishments that, following inspection by the DSA, have satisfied the criteria of minimum standards.

What is ORDIT?

Members of ORDIT offer professional training to a minimum and consistent standard. They are subject to biannual inspections to ensure minimum standards are maintained.

ORDIT members offer professional facilities and training courses that are designed to:

- develop the skills of those wishing to become driving instructors;
- further develop the skills of existing driving instructors.

All training courses are structured to ensure clients are fully prepared to teach driving as a life skill.

Training programmes

Any type of training programme relating to driver training is acceptable, bearing in mind that quality, and not quantity, is important in all training programmes.

Individual trainers are registered for inclusion on the ORDIT Register when they have demonstrated to the inspector that they can deliver a satisfactory standard of training in one or all parts of the ADI qualifying examinations, ie Part 1 (Theory); Part 2 (Driving Ability); and Part 3 (Instructional Ability). For example, a trainer can be registered to give only ADI Part 2 training. A trainer who is assessed as giving satisfactory ADI Part 3 training will also be registered to give ADI Part 2 training.

The time allocated for inspections enables training establishments adequate opportunity to plan a structured programme, which should allow the tutor to demonstrate the quality of the training being given. The inspector's report relates only to the training being seen – training offered by the establishment but not seen by the inspector cannot be assessed.

It is important that inspection programmes are properly planned to show the inspector the range and quality of the training being offered.

What the inspector looks for

The DSA inspector observes and assesses:

- any course material;
- the application and validity of training aids;
- the practical application of the training programme.

The final assessment is based on: 'Did the training programme meet the needs of the student(s) in relation to DSA criteria?'

The inspector also observes and assesses:

- training and interpersonal skills;
- ability to 'teach how to teach';
- subject knowledge;
- role-play and fault simulation;
- fault identification, analysis and remedial action;
- use of routes, timing directions, etc.

It is at the discretion of the DSA to decide whether or not they wish to call for written materials to be presented to assist in the evaluation before placing the establishment on the Register. At the end of an inspection the inspector will offer a debrief and report. The assessment is made on the quality of the training seen in each session and whether it has been matched with the student's needs and his or her level of ability.

Inspection criteria

The criteria used for the assessment of teaching skills are based on:

- the level of teaching;
- the trainer's level, type and style of instruction;
- whether the training meets the needs of the pupil in all situations;
- whether the training is of a consistent standard.

The core competencies must be sound and consistent. The training course should follow a planned structure. Training records must be kept and must be available for inspection.

Lesson plans suitable to the needs of the student should be used. The trainer should be flexible and able to change the original plan in relation to the student's needs. Trainers should show confidence and demonstrate good interpersonal skills. Sound subject knowledge must be evident.

Training aids should be used where appropriate, whether in the classroom or in the car. They should be suitable and capable of showing the key points being covered.

Weaknesses in student skills should be recognized and dealt with constructively at the appropriate time.

During Part 3 training, role-play should be correct and consistent in relation to the character being portrayed. Simulated faults should be realistic in all aspects of training. They should be pitched at the correct level. The student should be clear in his or her own mind when the tutor is in or out of role. 'Question and answer' should be used when appropriate and should be effective.

Future development

The DSA is taking a positive role and is working with the industry to develop and improve the quality of training offered to members of the public. The ORDIT Register is currently under review, and the DSA is committed to keeping the industry fully informed about future developments that might affect training establishments and tutors.

For full details of ORDIT terms and conditions of membership, see page 420.

Associations for driving instructors

When you have qualified you should make an effort to keep yourself up to date, as this will benefit both you and your pupils. Although you will receive the DSA's *Despatch* magazine, it only contains a limited amount of information. To be kept more informed with all of the trends, and also to be able to take advantage of some of the professional and commercial services you will require, you should join at least one of the major national associations.

Three main organizations are open to individual membership:

- Approved Driving Instructors National Joint Council (ADINJC);
- Driving Instructors Association (DIA);
- Motor Schools Association of Great Britain (MSAGB);

as well as DISC (The Driving Instructors Scottish Council) in Scotland and NIADIA (Northern Ireland Driving Instructors Association) in Northern Ireland.

The ADINJC – Approved Driving Instructors National Joint Council

The ADINJC is a national organization set up and operated by working driving instructors for the benefit of driving instructors. Its slogan says, 'ADIs working together for ADIs'. It is a non-profit organization and none of its officers are paid any salary.

History

Soon after its formation in 1973, the ADINJC was granted consultative status by the then Ministry of Transport. It still holds this privilege today with the Driving Standards Agency. The organization was originally set up to bring unity to the driving instruction industry by amalgamating all major organizations into one body. Since then it has always been at the heart of decision-making and change in the industry. It convened the first meetings that lead to the setting up of ORDIT; it played an important role in the development of an NVQ in Driving Instruction and was integral in the introduction of the ADI green badge. The ADINJC remains at the forefront of action to protect the ADI and his or her livelihood. It aims to further the professional and financial interests of ADIs and to keep members informed of matters of interest.

Membership

Membership is made up of many local driving instructor associations, each of which sends representatives to ADINJC meetings. It is the association that joins the ADINJC and then circulates the information to its members. However, every member of the local group is a full member of the ADINJC once the group has joined. Each member organization has one vote at meetings. Any representative may present motions for debate, voting and action by the organization.

The ADINJC makes representation at national level. It ensures members are aware of any DSA or government proposal that may affect them. It provides discussion documents and circulates information provided by the DSA.

Individual ADIs can also take part in the ADINJC by joining its Driving Instructor Group (DIG). This section was formed in 2001 in response to requests from ADIs to be able to join without necessarily belonging to a local association. This group has a separate secretary who looks after DIG members and votes for them at meetings after consultation with them.

Benefits

Primarily the ADINJC helps its members with any problems or concerns. News is sent out immediately to members so they can be kept at the forefront of what is happening in the industry.

The ADINJC holds a popular national conference each year, usually in September or October. The conference is open to any ADI and other interested parties, whether or not they are members.

It also provides other seminars and workshops for the benefit of members and non-members to help in their 'continuing professional development' and a monthly newsletter is issued to all members.

Contact

Learn more about the ADINJC at www.adinjc.org.uk or by speaking to the liaison officer, Clive Snook, who is available to take calls in person each weekday afternoon and early evening. The number to call is 01747 855091 or email adinjc_liaisonofficer@hotmail.co.uk. ADINJC's postal address is: 47 Sweetmans Road, Shaftesbury, Dorset SP7 8EH.

For matters of policy you may also contact the General Secretary, Lynne Barry, at lynne@lbsom.co.uk.

The Motor Schools Association of Great Britain (MSAGB)

History

MSAGB was formed in March 1935, just before the driving test was introduced. The association's main aims, then as now, are to keep members informed of all matters of interest to them; to represent the views of members to government, its departments and various agencies; to provide services which will be of benefit to members; and to set standards of professional and ethical behaviour for driver trainers.

Membership

Full membership of MSAGB is only available to DSA ADIs. However, those training to become ADIs may join as probationary members and when qualified will be converted at no extra charge to full membership of the association. Membership is also available for LGV instructors and motorcycle instructors. All benefits of membership are available to all categories of members but only full members can vote at AGMs.

How it is run

MSAGB is a company limited by the guarantee of its members and is run on behalf of members by the Board of Management. Board members, who are all working driving instructors, are elected at local elections held in each of the MSA regions and nations. They are not paid a salary for their work on behalf of the association.

Information

MSAGB prides itself on the information available to its members. Most of the information passed on to members is contained in MSAGB's national publication, *Newslink*. Published monthly, it is sent to every member every month. MSAGB members also receive a copy of the association's handbook and annual report, which contains details of local committee members. Information is also passed to members via www.msagb.com and members can follow the association at www.twitter.com/MSAGB.

Representation

MSAGB represents driver training interests to all relevant government departments and agencies. The association is also a member of the Parliamentary Advisory Council for Transport Safety (PACTS), the European Secure Vehicle Alliance (ESVA) and the Royal Society for the Prevention of Accidents (RoSPA). European involvement is as the UK representative to the European Driving Schools Association (EFA).

Services

MSAGB offers members a wide range of services. Some, such as the £3 million professional indemnity and the £5 million third party liability insurance cover, are included in the membership fee (these start the day your membership is accepted). Other services such as MSAGB branded roof signs, various insurances including car, health and the special one-day cover for ADI Part 3 tests, are arranged to make sure members get great value for money when they buy driver trainer-linked products or services.

Assistance

Also included in the membership fee is a free advice service. Whether your problem is of a technical, legal or contractual nature MSAGB will try to help. With over 75 years' experience in the business, if MSAGB doesn't know the answer to your problem they will know someone who does.

Joining

Driver trainers can join online, over the phone, at local meetings or by post. MSAGB is a forward-looking organization always open to new ideas and improved methods.

For further information, check out the website www.msagb.com.

Further information

MSAGB can be contacted by letter, phone, fax or e-mail: MSAGB, 101 Wellington Road North, Stockport SK4 2LP (tel: 0161 429 9669; fax: 0161 429 9779; e-mail: mail@msagb.co.uk).

The Driving Instructors Association (DIA)

The DIA was founded in 1978 to represent the interests of the professional driving instructor and is the largest trade association in the UK for ADIs and road safety specialists. It is regularly consulted by all the relevant government bodies, has representation in parliament and enjoys influence in Europe and throughout the world.

Membership is open to anyone working in the driver and rider training industry and provides a voice for the future. It provides valuable membership advantages, access to information and further training opportunities via the continuing professional development programme.

The DIA has founded the Driving Instructors' Accident and Disability Fund, a registered charity set up to provide benefits for driving instructors and their families in need. In 1995, the Driving Instructors Association also became a registered charity.

Structure

The DIA remains a proprietary association, the proprietors being DIA (Int) Limited, a trading company and publishers. Individual members are therefore fully protected from any financial liability to the DIA. The DIA is guided by a General Purposes Committee that is elected from the membership at its annual general meeting. It is committed to improving standards of driver education and promoting road safety, while working to promote the welfare and business interests of professional driving instructors.

Consultation

The DIA has consultative status with the Department for Transport (DfT), the Driver and Vehicle Licensing Agency (DVLA), the Driver and Vehicle Agency (DVA) and the Driving Standards Agency (DSA) and its theory-training organization on the Pass Plus Board and the Modernising Driver Training

Strategic Board. It is represented on the Parliamentary Advisory Council for Transport Safety (PACTS) and other government committees in the UK. The DIA maintains extensive links with similar trade associations internationally and has consultative status with the European Parliament and United Nations through its Chief Executive, who is president of the International Association for Driver Education (IVV).

Membership

The work of the DIA is comprehensive on behalf of its membership and is carried out by a small team of dedicated staff. Each member receives regular copies of *Driving* magazine and *Driving Instructor*, leading high-quality publications for advanced drivers, road safety specialists and driving instructors. Members also receive public liability and professional indemnity insurance as part of their membership fee. Services provided for members vary from DIA mail order at preferential rates, training courses, conferences, exhibitions, DIA recovery service, medical and hospital plans, discounted car rental and branded advertising schemes to professional accounting services and legal advice. The DIA promotes the DIA Motor Insurance Scheme (formerly DIA Direct Insurance), a service set up to provide the very best training car insurance service to the industry.

Diplomas

The DIA has instituted a higher education programme including the Diploma in Driving Instruction and DIAmond Advanced Instructor qualifications and degree courses at Middlesex University. It promotes the DIAmond Advanced Motorist Test scheme to improve driving skills, and also consults with the DSA on large goods vehicle (LGV), passenger carrying vehicle (PCV), motorcycle, advanced and fleet driver training issues.

Information

A free membership information pack and complimentary copy of *Driving* magazine and *Driving Instructor* can be obtained by telephoning, faxing or writing to: The DIA, Safety House, Beddington Farm Road, Croydon CR0 4XZ (tel: 020 8665 5151; local rate: 0845 345 5151; fax: 020 8665 5565; e-mail: dia@driving.org; website: www.driving.org).

Driving Instructors Scottish Council (DISC)

DISC was originally formed in 1955 and has grown in membership over recent years and has now reached a position where it represents more Scottish ADIs than any other organization.

DISC has adopted the slogan – 'Together we can make a difference'.

The full Council membership is made up of two representatives from each of the various local associations that are spread throughout Scotland.

Council meetings are held on four occasions each year where the council members have the opportunity to discuss issues that are relevant to their individual members.

DISC holds an annual conference where members' collective views can be expressed and at consultative meetings with the DSA.

Membership

Membership of DISC is currently made up by local associations from most of the counties in Scotland, including Angus, Argyll, Aberdeen, Clackmannan, Fife, Lanark, East Lothian, Midlothian, West Lothian, Moray and Stirling. Individual ADIs can also ask to be represented by DISC.

Consultation

DISC has full consultation status with the Driving Standards Agency. It is also represented on both the DSA's Modernising Driver Training Working and Steering Groups as well as representation on the Go Skills Transport Committee.

Continuing Professional Development (CPD)

DISC is working in partnership with the Motor Schools Association GB, Go Skills and Cardonald College to present CPD courses in Glasgow and Edinburgh with the intention of expanding courses to other locations around Scotland.

Contact

Further information about DISC can be obtained from: Aeneas MacRitchie, DISC Secretary and CPD trainer (tel: 01506 855455; e-mail: aeneas.disc@ tiscali.co.uk; website: www.d-i-s-c.org.uk).

Northern Ireland Approved Driving Instructor Association (NIADIA)

Purpose

NIADIA's purpose is to be the collective voice of Approved Driving Instructors in Northern Ireland; professionally representing their views to all concerned in driver education and road safety, to maintain and enhance the unique and important role of ADIs who impart driving skills for life.

Aims

To be recognized by the Driver and Vehicle Agency (DVA) as the primary voice of ADIs in Northern Ireland.

To ensure that driving instruction is accredited with the image and respect it merits as a profession.

To actively contribute to a reduction in road accidents in Northern Ireland.

Contact

NIADIA, PO Box 528, Craigavon BT62 3YB; e-mail: info@niadia.org; tel: 07801 644719.

SmartDriving

Although SmartDriving is not an association in the same way as the other organizations, it is a very useful facility for practising ADIs.

SmartDriving is an independent organization that was founded in 1999 by John Farlam. John, a regular contributor to industry periodicals, started the SmartDriving web project (www.smartdriving.co.uk) to offer practical support and advice to driving instructors in response to the increasing requests for assistance he received each time he published an article. The SmartDriving website includes information on all aspects of teaching new drivers ranging from basic teaching skills to more advanced coaching skills and business development.

SmartDriving brings both commercial and personal benefits to members – commercial benefits with an increasing range of services and affiliate programmes with other companies and personal benefits with a strong emphasis on career development. There are currently two levels of membership, Standard and Gold Circle. Standard members get full access to online information and resources plus a weekly newsletter with training and business tips. In addition to the benefits enjoyed by Standard members, Gold Circle members get regular audio updates and access to supporting materials.

In addition to providing information for driving instructors, SmartDriving also provides resources for learner drivers via the DriverActive website (www.driveractive.co.uk) and extensive advice for drivers in the open area of the SmartDrive website.

SmartDriving is a member organization of the ADINJC with all SmartDriving members automatically qualifying for ADINJC membership.

The driver training industry

The 'L' driver market

Nearly 2 million 'L' tests are conducted every year by the DSA, and over 90 per cent of candidates have tuition with an ADI. This is therefore the main source of business for most ADIs. The biggest market for 'L' driver training is in the 17–20 age range and, in order to establish the viability of starting up a driving school in your area, there are various ways of finding out about population trends. These include consulting the local electoral register and contacting local sixth form schools and colleges.

The number of lessons learners need

Teaching driving as a 'skill for life' is much more difficult now than when the driving test was first introduced. However, too many learners seem to think that a driving licence is a right and not a privilege. They want to pass the test as quickly and as cheaply as possible and, even though road systems and the volume of traffic are changing all the time, some parents still compare learning today with 20 years ago. All too common is the statement 'Well, I only had 10 lessons!'

Although you will want your pupils to achieve good test results, your decisions will sometimes need a delicate balance between conscience and reality. You obviously want to keep your clients, and therefore will sometimes have to come to a compromise between your ideal standard and what they will accept. Your main consideration when reaching this compromise is whether the pupil will be at the very least safe on the road.

Putting theory into practice

Driving instruction involves a combination of theory and practice. By encouraging your pupils to study for the Theory Test, you can teach them how to put the principles into practice during their practical lessons. This, in turn, should result in a better understanding of why the rules and regulations are in place.

To teach 'safe driving for life', in addition to the books that are needed to study for the ADI theory test, you will need to have a thorough understanding of the DSA's recommended syllabus for learners. You will find this in the DSA book *The Official Guide to Learning to Drive*.

Theory and hazard perception test training

It will be your responsibility to ensure that new drivers are made aware of the importance of understanding the principles and rules for driving safely. Candidates have to study a number of books for the Theory Test. You can increase your profitability by buying these in bulk (usually at discounted rates) and selling them on at the full price.

Try to encourage pupils to study by emphasizing that the more time they spend studying for the Theory Test, the better they will understand the rules and be able to apply them. This in turn should result in their needing fewer practical lessons.

There are various CD-ROMs and DVDs available for the hazard perception test. Have some of these available for your pupils to practise with.

Preparing pupils for the Theory Test does not necessarily mean investing in classroom facilities. There are different ways of organizing training while at the same time increasing your earning potential. These include:

- taking some time out of on-road lessons to cover elements of the theory syllabus;

- teaching small groups of clients in your office;
- hiring a room once a week to run a modular course so that clients can attend at their own convenience and still cover the entire syllabus;
- giving talks at youth clubs and schools;
- setting up a classroom and offering theory training for pupils of other ADIs who do not wish to become involved with theory training.

The personal contact you will build up as a result of running theory courses, particularly for those who are not yet your clients, could result in an expansion of the practical training element of your business.

Information technology

Theory tests are all computer-based and most pupils have access to computers – whether this is at home, or in school or college. It's therefore important for you to be able to offer your pupils the appropriate CD-ROMs for effective learning. Interactive programmes can be particularly helpful for pupils who have learning difficulties such as dyslexia. The appropriate computer programs will also enable you to prepare personalized business stationery, handouts and other training aids; and you should be able to reduce the cost of professional fees by 'balancing your books' with an appropriate accounting package.

The 'Pass Plus' scheme

The 'Pass Plus' scheme was set up by the DSA in an effort to encourage newly qualified drivers to undergo further training with an ADI in a wider variety of road and traffic conditions than is required for the 'L' test. You can encourage your pupils to take the extra training by emphasizing that many insurance companies offer substantial discounts to successful participants, usually equivalent to one-year's no-claims bonus.

Pass Plus is designed to 'make newly qualified drivers better drivers'. For details of the Pass Plus syllabus, see pages 306–09. Training can be taken up to a year after passing the Practical 'L' Test. The insurance discount can be deferred for a further two years if the participant is driving on someone else's insurance.

Although the number of drivers taking Pass Plus is slowly increasing, this is still a vastly untapped market with very few instructors taking advantage of its potential. When ADIs were asked by the DSA for the secret behind successful promotion of Pass Plus, some of the tips given were to:

- mention the scheme when pupils first contact you for information;
- try to involve parents, getting them to recognize the added reassurance Pass Plus gives;
- give a reminder about the scheme before and after pupils take the Practical Test;

- inform pupils and parents of the statistics of newly qualified drivers being involved in accidents.

Since the major part of an ADI's work is teaching new drivers, the Pass Plus scheme adds a little more variety to the job.

To register, contact the DSA for your instructor's starter pack. These packs include all the necessary course material and are available from the DSA in Nottingham for £37 (at January 2011); refill packs cost £29. For contact details see page 409.

Pre-driver training

Driving is now accepted as a life skill. With this in mind, you might consider getting yourself known to those in the pre-driver age group. Setting up courses will not only give young adults some background knowledge before they take to the roads, but it will also ensure that your name will come to mind when they reach driving age. To highlight the benefits of these courses, you should contact:

- the local education authority;
- schools or colleges with sixth forms;
- youth organizations/groups;
- the local road safety officer.

Defensive driver training

There are now more than 30 million full-licence holders in the UK, and a significant number of these would benefit from some form of 'defensive' driver education.

Company drivers

Many companies and organizations now take more seriously the health and safety aspects of operating motor vehicles. More and more of them are beginning to look for professional expertise to conduct assessments and provide remedial training for their employees. These may include current staff members with records of accidents, or potential new employees.

In order to demonstrate a professional approach, you will need to have a properly structured system for making your assessments and presenting reports. Your possible customers might include:

- local companies;
- voluntary groups;
- education departments;
- health authorities.

All of the above are employers of groups of full- and part-time, as well as voluntary drivers.

Traffic offenders

Some traffic offences now attract a compulsory or discretionary order for disqualification and/or a requirement to take a further driving test. Your local solicitors would be interested in a professional assessment and reporting service that could benefit their clients in preparation for court hearings.

Drivers who require their skills to be updated

There are large numbers of drivers who have held a licence for many years but have either not driven for a while, or simply lost their confidence. You could advertise retraining or refresher courses to bring drivers up to date with the latest rules and regulations, to modernize their skills and rebuild their confidence. You could also give short talks about defensive driving to groups such as:

● Young Wives and Women's Institutes;
● Round Table and Ladies' Circle;
● Rotary and Inner Wheel Clubs;
● Lions and Probus clubs.

All you have to do to increase your business and add variety to your work is to carry out a little research and gather information on the above types of company or organization in your area.

Vocational training

With the many changes taking place to driving licence categories and testing procedures for drivers and riders, there is a vast market which is still largely untapped by the ADI. If you have the appropriate licences, you should consider training in the following areas, particularly with the recent introduction of compulsory training and refresher training for all LGV.

Fleet driver training

This is now an ever-increasing market, with several national companies offering training to corporate customers. There are special qualifications for this type of training and a separate register of instructors. For instructors wanting to expand their training facilities by moving into this interesting and rewarding type of training see details of the Fleet Driver Training Register on page 397.

Motorcycling

This is an increasing market involving motorcyclists and moped riders at various levels:

- compulsory basic training (CBT);
- pre-test instruction;
- 'Direct Access'.

Special instructional qualifications are needed for the different elements of training. Courses for CBT and Direct Access instructors are conducted at the DSA Training Centre at Cardington. For contact details see page 30.

Minibuses

Drivers with a full licence issued after January 1997 are only allowed to drive vehicles with up to eight seats. A separate test is required to drive vehicles with more than eight seats. Many colleges, schools and other organizations have staff and volunteer drivers who would probably require training or assessments for driving this type of vehicle.

Lorries

With staged testing starting at vehicles of 3.5 tonnes, and the voluntary register of LGV instructors, there is a growing market for training in medium-sized goods vehicles. Although there is, under the voluntary register scheme, a test for LGV instructors, there is no specific instructional qualification as long as you hold the appropriate driving entitlement.

More information on LGV training is included in Chapter 12.

LGV instruction

Training lorry drivers is another area where specialized qualifications are required. Although there is no statutory or compulsory registration at the present time, the Voluntary Register of LGV Instructors will become the official qualification when the Road Safety Act 2006 is implemented. With the introduction of driver CPC and the compulsory re-training of all professional LGV drivers on a regular basis over the next few years, there will be an increased demand for LGV instructors in the future. To find out more about Driver CPC and LGV driver training see Chapters 12–13.

Qualities of the driver and instructor

To be able to enhance your personal driving skills and ensure that you are driving in line with modern techniques, you need to be aware of the qualities required by the good driver as described by the Driving Standards Agency in its book, *The Official DSA Guide to Driving – The essential skills*. Additionally, you will need similar attributes to become an effective instructor.

Responsibility

As a driver: you should always show proper concern for the safety of yourself, your passengers and all other road users. You should also be aware of the need to drive economically and in an environmentally friendly manner.

As an instructor: always have the safety and well-being of your pupils at heart, particularly those in the early stages of their driving careers. Avoid taking them into situations they are unable to cope with. Remember: you are responsible for their safety.

Concentration

As a driver: you must concentrate at all times. Just a moment's distraction from the driving task can have disastrous effects in today's heavily congested and fast-moving traffic. *As an instructor:* sitting next to inexperienced drivers, your concentration is even more vital. You have to read the road much further ahead than they will, taking into account any developing situations so that you can keep your pupils safe, relaxed and eager to learn.

Anticipation

As a driver: the ability to predict what might happen is an important part of the skills needed to avoid danger. You need to be aware of any possible hazards in time to safely deal with them.

As an instructor: anticipation is even more important. You will be sitting in the passenger seat beside someone much less able at the controls of your car. You will have to learn to recognize the needs of each individual and anticipate how different pupils may or may not respond to changing situations.

You have to plan as far ahead as possible and anticipate any potential hazards. This will allow time for you to give either positive instructions or prompts, so that your pupil will be able to take any action necessary to avoid problems.

Patience

As a driver: always show patience and restraint with other drivers when they make mistakes. Not everyone is as thoughtful as you!

As an instructor: displaying a positive attitude to your pupils will not only set a good example to them but, if you have your name on your car, it will also be good advertising.

Remember, we all had to learn to drive, and some find it more difficult than others! If you lose patience with a pupil it will only make matters worse. Most people are aware when they have made a mistake anyway, so be patient and always willing to give more help – even when you have explained things several times before.

Demonstrating tolerance will also go a long way in building up your pupils' confidence and also their belief in you. Hopefully your tolerant attitude will rub off on them!

Confidence

As a driver: the conscientious and efficient driver displays confidence at all times. This confidence results from being totally 'at one' with the vehicle. You should always be travelling at a speed to suit the road, weather and traffic conditions, with an appropriate gear engaged and in the correct position on the road. Planning well ahead and anticipating hazards, the confident driver can avoid the need to make any last-minute, rushed, and usually unsafe, decisions.

As an instructor: not only do you need to be confident yourself, but you will also need the skills required to help develop your pupils' confidence. To do this, you will need to ensure that the routes you select for teaching each aspect of the syllabus are matched to each individual's ability. Avoiding those situations a pupil is not ready for will help you gradually build up his or her skills and confidence.

Knowledge

As a driver: not only do you need a sound knowledge of the rules and regulations contained in *The Highway Code* and *The Official DSA Guide to Driving – The essential skills*, but you also need to be able to apply them in all situations.

As an instructor: you will need to pass on this knowledge so that the drivers you teach will also be able to apply the same principles for driving safely. Remember – they will eventually be sharing the roads with us!

Be prepared to make the effort to keep yourself up to date with the changes taking place so that you are able to:

● handle your vehicle sympathetically and economically;

● apply modern teaching techniques;

● maintain a safe teaching environment;

● recognize the need for keeping your vehicle roadworthy;

● offer advice to pupils on driver licensing requirements, basic mechanical principles, and the rules and regulations for safe driving on all types of road;

● answer pupils' queries confidently.

As well as enhancing your driving skills, having a sound knowledge and understanding will help in your preparations to become an effective instructor. Remember:

● your knowledge will be tested in the theory element of the ADI examination;

- how you apply this knowledge will be assessed in the driving ability test;
- how you pass the information on to pupils will be assessed in the instructional ability test.

Communication

As a driver: you have to continually communicate your intentions to other road users. Methods of signalling these intentions include:

- using the indicators and arm signals;
- brake lights;
- early positioning on the road;
- reversing lights;
- horn and flashing headlights;
- hazard warning flashers;
- eye contact.

As an instructor: you will need to develop ways of communicating effectively with the wide variety of pupils you will be dealing with. You may sometimes have to adapt the terminology you use so that all of your pupils understand exactly what you mean.

Not only will you need to be able to teach your pupils how to apply the relevant procedures and driving techniques, you also need to be able to explain why these procedures need to be followed. This 'why' reasoning should lead to a better understanding that will result in safer drivers sharing the road with us.

There are numerous ways in which you can communicate with your pupils, including:

- establishing the level of understanding of the individual pupil;
- finding the most appropriate method and style of communication;
- explaining new principles in a clear and straightforward way;
- using visual aids so that the pupil can 'see' what you mean;
- giving practical demonstrations of any complicated procedures;
- developing confidence and success by talking the pupil through any new procedures;
- giving your directional instructions clearly and in good time so that the pupil has time to respond safely;
- giving encouragement through positive feedback and praise where deserved;
- finding out whether the pupil has fully understood your instructions by asking appropriate questions;
- encouraging the pupil to ask questions if you feel that he or she does not understand.

Awareness

Modern driving techniques are becoming relatively easier through advances in technology and design, making cars much more efficient and safe. However, road and traffic conditions are becoming more and more complex and congested, and in order to keep your clients safe, you need to be aware of the major causes of road accidents. These include:

- other drivers' ignorance of, or total disregard for, the rules of the road;
- lack of concentration and response to developing situations;
- carelessness;
- driving while under the influence of drink or drugs;
- driving when feeling unwell;
- driving with deficient eyesight;
- some drivers' willingness to take risks;
- using vehicles that are not roadworthy;
- driving while under the stress of modern needs to rush everywhere;
- using mobile phones or other in-car equipment.

All of these elements mean that new drivers have to be taught to a far higher standard than ever, with hazard awareness playing a major role in their development. It will be up to you to ensure that you teach drivers at all levels to:

- handle their vehicle sympathetically and economically;
- drive with courtesy and consideration;
- look and plan well ahead, anticipating what may happen;
- take early action to avoid problems;
- compensate for the mistakes of others;
- understand what they are doing and why they are doing it.

To be able to do all of these things, you, as an ADI, must be prepared to keep yourself up to date with the changes taking place relevant to driving and the teaching of it. We all need to update and adapt our driving procedures and habits from time to time and adjust them to meet current rules and regulations, as well as to deal with ever-changing road and traffic conditions.

The DSA sends an online copy of its magazine *Despatch* to all ADIs who register for it. This contains some of the latest information. Sign up at www.dsa.gov.uk/despatch to make sure that you receive regular copies. However, most instructors tend to work in isolation and it is very easy to become complacent and just 'plod along' without giving any thought to either updating themselves or improving their skills.

Continuing professional development (CPD)

Teaching learners is very rewarding, but when you have been working as an ADI for a while, you should consider taking more training and other qualifications. The DSA recommends that we should all be seeking to remain updated through continuing professional development.

The level of competence you attain to pass the ADI examination is the minimum standard required to enable you to teach driving professionally. However, road and traffic conditions, the driver training industry and also the law are in a continual state of change. You should strive to keep your knowledge up to date and also improve your personal driving skills and teaching techniques. This will help to equip you for driver training at all levels.

The most obvious first step is to consider the various advanced driving tests. The Institute of Advanced Motorists (IAM) and RoSPA are probably the most well known. Their tests are outlined in Chapter 7. The Cardington Special Driving Test and the DIAmond Advanced Test are industry-based.

The Cardington Special Driving Test

This test is available to all ADIs, and the standard required is much higher than that needed to pass the ADI Part 2, Eyesight and Driving Ability Test. Tests are conducted by permanent staff instructors at the DSA Training Centre at Cardington, near Bedford. You have to demonstrate that you can handle your car efficiently and accurately on all types of road including a motorway and while carrying out a variety of manoeuvre exercises.

For the test, the car you use must have:

- manual transmission;
- an interior instructor mirror;
- integral head restraints for both driver and assessor.

To achieve the grade A assessment you need to show that you have the ability to control the speed and position of the car safely, systematically and smoothly. Your driving will need to be at a consistently high standard, based on concentration, effective observations, anticipation and planning.

During the test you are required to carry out several manoeuvres. These include:

- moving away smoothly from rest to include, where possible, moving off on reasonably steep uphill and downhill gradients;
- moving away at an angle from behind a stationary vehicle;
- overtaking, meeting and crossing the path of other vehicles;
- turning right and left corners;
- stopping as in an emergency;

- driving the vehicle backwards and entering limited openings to the left and right;
- reverse parking (in a car park and on the road);
- turning the car round in the road by using forward and reverse gears.

At the end of the test your assessor will give you the result and a briefing on any faults that were recorded. At a later date you will receive written confirmation of the report. If you attain a grade A, you will be eligible to receive the Special Test Certificate.

The fee for this test at January 2011 was £144 but this is under review. For further information write to: Special Test Booking Section, The DSA Training Centre, Cardington, Bedford MK42 0TJ (or tel: 01234 744011).

The DIAmond Advanced Motorist Test

Originally introduced in 1992, the DIAmond Advanced Driving Test was made available for ADIs to offer their customers an advanced test based on the DSA's Cardington system of marking, as an alternative to the police 'system of driving' advanced tests.

Today it is internationally acclaimed as the benchmark of driving excellence, conducted by a network of professionally qualified trainers and examiners. Both the Advanced and Special tests are accredited by the International Association for Driver Education (IVV) and the Driving Standards Agency (DSA). Both tests meet the stringent requirements of the Register of Fleet Trainers' test of driving ability (Part 2). It was the first advanced driving test to be ISA 9001:2000 accredited.

DIAmond tests are offered in a variety of vehicle, including car, motorcycle, taxi, mini-bus, PCV and LGV. DIAmond also offers a desert test in Dubai under licence with Belhasa Driving Center.

DIAmond works with many individuals, organizations and governments on a local, national and international level to improve driving and training standards.

Passing either of the DIAmond tests can help to reduce your insurance premiums by up to 30 per cent. For details, see www.driving.org.

The Diploma in Driving Instruction

This qualification is awarded by the DIA. The qualification is not restricted to ADIs, and anyone involved in driving instruction, road safety or other occupations related to driving may apply. The overall aims of the diploma are to improve standards of driver training and to provide wider public recognition of the services offered by those who hold it.

The examination consists of five modules, each tested in a two-hour examination. These are:

1 legal obligations and regulations;
2 management practices and procedures;

3 vehicle maintenance and mechanical principles;

4 driving theory – skills and procedures;

5 instructing – practices and procedures.

A certificate is issued for each module, and the Diploma is awarded when all five have been passed. Examinations are conducted in April/May of each year at any DIA-approved examination centre. Further information about this qualification is available by phoning the DIA on 0845 3455151.

City & Guilds Further Education Teacher's Certificate

The qualification is relevant for anyone teaching in adult education – no matter what their specialist subject may be. You may find it particularly helpful for getting into the theory training market. The course will help to build up the confidence needed to adapt your teaching from the normal one-to-one in-car situation, to standing in front of a class. It will also give you a greater understanding of different teaching techniques, and you will discover how and why people learn at different rates.

One of the main advantages of achieving this certificate is that it is a recognized teaching qualification that is accepted by most educational establishments. You will therefore have an advantage over your competitors when you apply to run courses through schools and colleges.

Courses are held at colleges of further education throughout the country and are normally run on a part-time basis. For full details, contact your local college or education authority.

Certificate in Education (CertEd)

This is aimed at those who would like to develop more as professional teachers. It is normally a continuation of initial teacher training (such as the FE Teacher's Certificate) and is designed to build on current teaching experience. The scheme is modular, being broken down into four parts. Continuous assessments are made throughout and there is no examination involved. Depending on current qualifications, this part-time course can be taken over a one- or two-year period.

The CertEd fits into the Credit Accumulation and Transfer Scheme (CATS) that, by accumulation of credit points, can open up a wide range of further training and development opportunities. For information on the availability of courses contact your local education authority.

NVQ in driving instruction

The driving instructor's biggest potential market is the new driver. Most young people now leaving schools and colleges are aware of the NVQ system. They recognize the qualification as a guarantee of a minimum standard of achievement. To gain an NVQ, all you have to do is collect evidence of your everyday work. The evidence has to show that your work is conducted in line with the DSA syllabus. Your portfolio of evidence then has to be verified by assessors who have been qualified by the awarding body.

Although the DSA's ADI qualification is the only official requirement before you can give driving instruction for payment, there is no obvious way for would-be learners to differentiate between the quality of instruction different ADIs give. Sometimes selecting a name from Yellow Pages can be a hit-and-miss affair, but if you have an NVQ, this will immediately be recognized.

BTEC qualifications

Other courses and qualifications for ADIs include the BTEC in Driving Science run by A2OM (website: www.a2om.com/btec; tel: 0 7000 123 400) and the BTEC in Coaching for Driver Education offered by the Tri-Coaching Partnership (website: www.tri-coachingpartnership.co.uk; tel: 0800 048 1808).

Code of practice for approved driving instructors

The Code of Practice has been agreed between the Driving Standards Agency (DSA) and the main bodies representing Approved Driving Instructors (ADIs); it is a framework within which all instructors should operate.

Personal conduct

The instructor will at all times behave in a professional manner towards clients.

Clients will be treated with respect and consideration. The instructor will try to avoid physical contact with a client except in an emergency or in the normal course of greeting.

While reserving the right to decide against giving tuition, the instructor will not act in any way that contravenes legislation.

Business dealings

The instructor will safeguard and account for any monies paid in advance by the client in respect of driving lessons, test fees or for any other purpose and will make the details available to the client on request.

The instructor, on or before the first lesson, should provide clients with a written copy of his/her terms of business to include:

- legal identity of the school/instructor, with full address and telephone number at which the instructor or his/her representative can be contacted;

- the price and duration of lessons;
- the price and conditions for use of a driving school car for the practical driving test;
- the terms under which cancellation by either party may take place;
- procedure for complaints.

The instructor should check a client's entitlement to drive the vehicle and his/her ability to read a number plate at the statutory distance on the first lesson. When presenting a client for the practical driving test the instructor should ensure that the client has all the necessary documentation to enable the client to take the test and that the vehicle is roadworthy.

Instructors will advise clients when to apply for their theory and practical tests, taking into account local waiting times and forecast of clients' potential for achieving the driving test pass standard. The instructor will not cancel or re-arrange a driving test without the client's agreement. In the event of the instructor's decision to withhold the use of the school car for the test, sufficient notice should be given to the client to avoid loss of the DSA test fee.

The instructor should at all times, to the best of his or her ability, endeavour to teach the client correct driving skills according to DSA's recommended syllabus.

Advertising

The advertising of driving tuition shall be honest; claims made shall be capable of verification and comply with codes of practice set down by the Advertising Standards Authority.

Advertising that refers to clients' pass rates should not be open to misinterpretation and the basis on which the calculation is made should be made clear.

Conciliation

Complaints by clients should be made in the first instance to the driving instructor/driving school/contractor following the complaints procedure issued.

Failing agreement or settlement of a dispute, reference may be made to the DSA's Registrar of Approved Driving Instructors who will consider the matter and advise accordingly.

Should the Registrar not be able to settle the dispute he or she may set up a panel, with representatives from the ADI industry, to consider the matter further or advise that the matter should be referred to the courts or other statutory body to be determined.

The ADI Register

02

To comply with the requirements of the Road Traffic Act anyone giving driving instruction for money or money's worth must either be registered with the Driving Standards Agency as an Approved Driving Instructor (ADI) or hold a current 'licence to give instruction'.

The Register of ADIs, which is operated in England, Scotland and Wales by the DSA, has now been in existence for more than 40 years and in that time there have been considerable changes to the structure of the exams and the standards required for entry to the Register. This means that candidates now have to demonstrate a much higher standard of knowledge, driving and instructional skills in order to qualify and to remain on the Register.

In Northern Ireland the Register is administered by the Driver Vehicle Agency. For details about how Registration varies in Northern Ireland see page 47.

Qualifications

To become an ADI you must:

- Hold a full UK or European Union (EU)/European Economic Area (EAA) unrestricted car driving licence; any EU/EAA licence must be exchanged for either a GB licence or a Community Licence.
- Have held the licence for a total of at least four out of the six years prior to entering the Register after qualifying. A foreign driving licence, an automatic car driving licence or a provisional licence held after passing the driving test all count towards the four years.
- Not have been disqualified from driving at any time in the four years prior to being entered in the Register.

- Be a 'fit and proper' person to have your name entered on the Register. All spent and unspent convictions, both motoring and non-motoring, are taken into account when your application is assessed by the DSA. This includes fixed penalty offences such as speeding. The decision in this respect rests with the Registrar, who will take into account any motoring convictions acquired in the last six years as well as your criminal record, if any. Any motoring offences that result in current endorsements totalling five penalty points or more will be looked at closely and could result in the application being refused.

- Pass the two qualifying practical exams within two years of passing the theory and hazard perception tests.

- Apply for registration within 12 months of passing the final part of the exam.

To accompany a learner drive you must be 21 or over and have held a full UK or EU/EAA driving licence for at least three years. A foreign licence counts towards this three-year period as long as it is a licence that is exchangeable for a full UK licence.

Criminal history checks are now made on all applicants for the Register and on existing ADIs when they re-register. For details, see page 37.

Full details about the qualifying process, pre-entry qualifications and registration are in the DSA booklet *Your Road to Becoming an Approved Driving Instructor (ADI 14)*, which can be obtained from the DSA at: The Axis Building, Upper Parliament Street, Nottingham NG1 6LP (tel: 0300 200 1122; website: www.dft.gov.uk/dsa/instructors). In Northern Ireland the booklet is *Your Guide to Becoming an Approved Driving Instructor*, published by: DVA (testing), Driver Policy and Standards, Balmoral Road, Belfast BT12 6QL (tel: 02890 547 933; website: www.nidirect.gov.uk/motoring).

Candidates with disabilities

New arrangements were introduced in 1996 that created a new category of ADI who can be registered to teach only in automatic transmission cars. The qualification is available for candidates whose driving licence restricts them to driving cars with automatic transmission because of a disability. The ADI exam is exactly the same as for other people except that the candidate takes the practical parts of the test in a car with automatic transmission.

To be considered for this category you need to have an assessment of your ability to take control of the car in an emergency. The DSA will advise of where the assessment is to be carried out. If this assessment is satisfactory you will be issued with a certificate as a pre-condition of qualifying.

Once you have qualified your ADI certificate will show that you are restricted to giving instruction in a car with automatic transmission and which has the appropriate additional controls fitted.

The car that you use on the qualifying test of instructional ability must allow the examiner to drive it.

An existing ADI who becomes restricted to driving a car with automatic transmission because of a disability is allowed to transfer to this category of ADI qualification without having to re-qualify, provided they have been issued with the appropriate control certificate.

Application for registration

The initial application to have your name entered into the ADI Register is made at the same time as applying for the Part 1 Theory and Hazard Perception Test. Application forms are included with the ADI 14 booklet, which is available online from the DSA. You can apply by using the application form in the ADI 14 or online at www.dft.gov.uk/dsa. Your name will only be entered into the Register when you have passed the final part of the exam and have sent off your pass certificate with the registration fee, which is currently £300. Examination and registration fees are reviewed from time to time. For details of the current fees you should ask your tutor, enquire with the DSA when you apply for the ADI 14, or check the DSA website.

To apply for registration as an ADI you need to provide details of two people – not relatives – who have known you for at least two years and who would be prepared to give a character reference for you if required. If possible one of these people should be a present or previous employer or at least someone who has known you in a professional, rather than personal, capacity.

To provide driving tuition for money or the equivalent, you must:

- have passed all three parts of the qualifying examination and be a DSA ADI (Car). The examination consists of:
  - Part 1, Theory and Hazard Perception Test
  - Part 2, Test of Driving Ability
  - Part 3, Test of Ability to Instruct.
- have paid the current registration fee;
- agree to take a test of 'continued ability and fitness to give instruction' (Check Test) when required to do so by the Registrar.

Alternatively you must have passed Parts 1 and 2 and hold a Trainee Licence. This allows you to gain experience before taking the Part 3 instructional ability test. For details of the three parts of the exam, see Chapters 3, 4 and 5. Full details of the requirements for a trainee licence are on pages 37–38.

Practising with friends or relatives before your test

To supplement your training, you may wish to practise without giving up your current job to work for a driving school. It is permissible to teach friends or relatives during your period of training, as long as you do not make any charge or receive payment of any kind, for example in petrol or goods. Alternatively, you may opt to work for another instructor under the Trainee Licence Scheme.

Criminal history checks

If you are a new entrant to the Register the procedure involves obtaining a criminal record disclosure before submitting your initial application to the DSA. The disclosure has to be issued to you before the application can be processed by the DSA.

Existing ADIs whose registration is due for renewal will receive a reminder, including the disclosure notice, a few months ahead of the renewal date. In this case you would then obtain a disclosure notice from the appropriate disclosure agency and send it to the DSA as soon as possible.

Having a criminal record does not necessarily mean that you would be barred from becoming an ADI or that an existing ADI would be removed from the Register. In general terms the DSA would look at various factors when assessing the suitability of an applicant. These factors include:

- the seriousness of the offence and its relevance to the safety of customers;
- the length of time since the offence;
- whether the offence was part of a history of offending, or just a one-off;
- whether the applicant's circumstances have changed since the offence was committed, making re-offending less likely;
- the degree of remorse, or otherwise, expressed by the applicant.

Full details about the suitability of ex-offenders are available from the DSA and through its website.

If you are in doubt, or have any queries about criminal record disclosure you can contact the criminal record information line: 0115 936 6506.

Trainee licence

With a trainee licence you are allowed to work for payment for a driving school or an ADI while preparing for the instructional test. Under the provisions of the Road Traffic Act, a six-month licence to give instruction can be issued to suitable applicants (the fee at January 2011 is £140). If you wish to take up this option, you can apply for a licence after you have passed Part 2 of the ADI exam, have completed the required amount of specified training and you have a sponsoring ADI. Only one licence will normally be granted and a second licence may only be issued in exceptional circumstances.

To qualify for a licence to instruct you must:

- have passed Parts 1 and 2 of the qualifying examination;
- have undergone 40 hours of training with a qualified ADI;
- be sponsored by an ADI.

Trainee licences are granted under the following conditions:

- The trainee instructor is only authorized to give instruction for the school whose address is shown on the licence.
- For every trainee licence holder there must be at least one ADI working from the sponsor's address.
- The trainee must receive 40 hours' practical training from an ADI. This period of training must start no earlier than six months before, and be completed by, the date of issue of the licence.
- You must not advertise yourself as a fully qualified instructor.
- You must receive a further period of 20 hours training or be supervised on 20 per cent of your lessons for the first three months of the licence. In Northern Ireland there is no requirement for specified training, but the 20 per cent supervision still applies.
- Whenever a trainee is giving driving lessons under this scheme, the licence must be displayed in the left-hand side of the car's windscreen. If requested by a police officer or any person authorized by the Secretary of State the licence must be produced. Failure to do this is an offence. For display details in Northern Ireland, see page 92.

For more detail about the training and supervision requirements for the trainee licence see Chapter 4, pages 91–93.

Northern Ireland trainee licence

The rules for a trainee licence are slightly different: two licences, each of six months, are allowed, but the application for the second licence must be made before the expiry of the first one.

Exemptions to the ADI regulations

The ADI regulations apply to instruction in the driving of cars. They do not apply to instruction in:

- riding motorcycles;
- driving large goods vehicles (although there is a separate voluntary register for LGV instructors);
- driving large passenger-carrying vehicles.

Police officers are exempt from the ADI regulations when giving instruction as part of their official duties, provided this is with the authority of the Chief Constable. Road safety officers are also exempt while carrying out their official duties. The exemptions for police and road safety officers do not apply when officers are giving instruction outside their official duties.

Examination structure

You must take and pass all three parts of the examination in the following sequence:

- Part 1: theory and hazard perception test.
- Part 2: eyesight test and a practical test of your driving.
- Part 3: a test of your ability to give driving instruction.

From the date of passing the theory and hazard perception test, you have two years in which to pass the two practical tests. You may take the theory and hazard perception tests as many times as it takes you to pass both on the same occasion. However, there is a limit of three attempts on the driving and instructional tests.

Note that in Northern Ireland you are limited to a maximum of three attempts at each part of the exam in a two-year period.

Part 1: theory and hazard perception

The application for this part of the exam is included with the ADI 14 starter pack, *Your Road to Becoming an Approved Driving Instructor*. The test covers a wide range of subject knowledge, including:

- the rules and regulations for driving on our roads;
- mechanical principles;
- teaching techniques;
- dealing with disabilities.

Tests are conducted, in English only, at 'L' test theory centres throughout the UK. If you are dyslexic it may be possible for special arrangements to be made. However, you must state this condition on your application form and you will need to supply some proof of it. Applications can be made online, by phone or by post. For details see page 52.

The test is 'touch screen' based, but don't worry if you are not familiar with interactive computer programs. You will be allowed to work through a practice session before starting. There will also be staff on hand to help if you experience any difficulty.

You have to answer 100 multiple-choice questions by selecting one answer from a choice of four and you have 90 minutes to complete the test. The screens are easy to read with only one question at a time being shown. The programme allows you to move backwards and forwards through the questions to check on any you may not be sure about, or to change an answer should you wish. The system will also alert you if there are questions you have not answered.

The banding system

The questions are banded into four subject groups. These are:

- road procedure;
- traffic signs and signals; car control; pedestrians; mechanical knowledge;
- driving test; disabilities; law;
- publications; instructional techniques.

There are 12 different set tests, and the questions are set randomly for each candidate. This allows for an equal degree of difficulty for all candidates. For details of the subjects in each band, see pages 52–55.

The pass mark

To pass you need to score an overall mark of 85 per cent. However, the DSA need to ensure that prospective ADIs have an adequate knowledge in all of the subject areas. You must therefore score a mark of 80 per cent in each of the four bands. So, for example, if you get a maximum score of 100 per cent in three of the bands but only 79 per cent in the fourth, you will fail.

Following completion of the theory test, you will be given a short break before taking the hazard perception test.

The hazard perception test

This test consists of watching 14 video clips each lasting about one minute. As with the multiple-choice element of the exam, you will be allowed a short practice session before starting the test. Each hazard is allotted a maximum score of five points, and the earlier you spot it the more points you will achieve. However, you have to be careful not to click too many times as this will result in a negative score.

The pass mark

To pass you must score 57 out of a possible 75 marks. If you fail this part of the test you will have to take both parts again. (Fee: £90 at January 2011.)

Results

You will receive the results for both parts within a few minutes of completing the hazard perception test. If you pass, you will be given information about applying for the Part 2, Eyesight and Driving Ability Test.

Should you fail, you may apply for a re-test as soon as you wish. You are allowed to take this test as many times as it takes to pass both elements within the same session. (For more information on the syllabus, sample theory questions and how best to prepare for these two tests, see Chapter 3 of this book and Chapter 5 of *Practical Teaching Skills for Driving Instructors*.)

Part 2: driving ability

You may apply as soon as you have passed the theory and hazard perception tests. You are allowed to take it at any centre of your choice – you will find a list of these on the application form. Send your application with the current fee (£111 at January 2011) to the DSA in Nottingham. You will be sent a letter confirming your appointment. When you attend for the test, take this and your driving licence and, if necessary, some photographic identification (such as your passport) with you.

The format of the test

The test lasts for about an hour and, if you wish, your trainer may accompany you. Sometimes senior DSA staff may accompany examiners on tests. This is to ensure uniformity so don't worry – they're not there to test you.

Eyesight

You will first of all be asked to read a number plate from a distance of 27.5 metres, with glasses or contact lenses if you normally wear them. If you cannot read the plate the rest of the test will not be conducted.

Vehicle safety questions

At the start of the test the examiner will ask several questions about vehicle safety. As with the 'L' test, these questions are on a 'show me'/'tell me' basis. Three questions require you to describe how to check on the condition and operation of various components ('tell me'), and with two questions you need to demonstrate an actual check ('show me').

The syllabus for this part of the test includes:

- tyres and brakes;
- steering;
- lights and reflectors;
- direction indicators;
- audible warning devices;
- fluids used in the engine, braking or steering system;
- coolants and lubrication;
- wipers, demisters, brake lights, fog lights, head restraints, ABS warning lights, correct operation of all relevant controls and switches.

Sample questions:

- 'Identify where you would check the engine oil level and *tell me* how you would check that the engine has sufficient oil.'
- '*Tell me* how you would check that the brakes are working before starting a journey.'
- '*Show me* how you would check that the power-assisted steering is working before starting a journey.'
- '*Show me* how you would check that the headlights and tail lights are working.'

Each incorrect answer is recorded as a *driving fault* up to a maximum of four faults. If all five questions are answered incorrectly a *serious fault* is recorded, meaning that you would fail.

Driving technique

This test is of an advanced nature and a very high standard of competence is expected. You must drive in a brisk and 'business-like' manner, demonstrating that you have a thorough knowledge of the principles of good driving and road safety; and that you put them into practice at all times. Routes used include:

- heavy and fast-moving traffic, for example motorways and dual carriageways;
- rural sections;
- urban areas.

You must satisfy the examiner on your:

- expert handling of the controls;
- application of correct road procedure;
- anticipation of the actions of other road users and taking the appropriate action;
- sound judgement of speed, distance and timing;
- consideration for the convenience and safety of other road users.

The result

During the test the examiner will be making an assessment of your personal driving skills and will mark any relevant faults on the Driving Test Report Form – DL25. You will be given the result as soon as the test is completed.

When you pass

To achieve a pass you need to score six or fewer *driving faults*. Your examiner will give you an oral debrief and explain any driver faults that have been recorded. You will also be given an application form for the Part 3 instructional test.

If you fail

All faults are recorded throughout the test and *driving faults* (those of a minor nature) will accumulate. You will fail if you commit more than six of these driver faults, or one serious or dangerous fault. Your examiner will give you a brief explanation of the faults recorded. You will also be given an application form for a further test. *If you fail this test three times, you will not be allowed to apply for Part 3.*

After failing a third attempt, should you wish to continue the process of qualifying, you will have to wait until a two-year period has expired from the date you passed the theory test. You will then have to start the whole process again, by taking the theory and hazard perception tests. It therefore makes sense to have sufficient good-quality training to ensure that your personal driving skills are up to the standard required.

For more information on preparing for the ADI Part 2 driving test see Chapter 4.

Part 3: instructional ability

You can apply for this test as soon as you have passed the Part 2 driving test. Tests are conducted at the centres listed on the application form and, as with the driving test, you can take it at the one of your choice. Send your application to the DSA with the current fee (£111 at January 2011). The appointment will be confirmed by letter and, when you attend for the test, take this with you along with your driving licence and some photographic identification such as your passport.

The test

The test lasts for about an hour and is conducted by a specially qualified senior DSA examiner. It is designed to test whether you can pass on your knowledge to pupils with different levels of ability through your practical teaching skills. The test is conducted in two parts. In Phase 1, you have to teach a beginner or a learner with limited driving skills; and in Phase 2 you have to make an assessment and give remedial instruction to either a learner who is about at test standard or a qualified driver who is undergoing driver development training.

The role play situation

Your examiner will describe each pupil to you, and a different type of pupil will be portrayed for each phase. You will need to adapt your instruction to suit the personality and level of ability of each. *It is extremely important, at this stage, that you listen very carefully to the description of each pupil and to the level of experience being described by the examiner.* For example, you may be asked to teach a beginner how to move off and stop. Even this basic subject will require setting the base line at varying levels depending on whether this is the pupil's first attempt to move the car, or the pupil has moved off and stopped before.

As soon as the examiner 'goes into role', you must try to behave as you would with a 'real life' pupil by confirming prior knowledge with a few simple questions. The information given should then allow you to decide on the start point for the lesson. (You will find more information on 'setting the base line' in Chapter 5.) Examiners are trained to play the role of pupils with a variety of personalities and abilities. Part of this test is to assess whether or not you have the ability to adapt your methods and level of instruction appropriately to suit different pupils so that maximum learning can take place.

The marking sheet

During the test you will be assessed under the following headings:

- Core competencies.
- Instructional techniques.
- Instructor characteristics.

These are sub-divided into the following categories:

1 Core competencies:
  (a) Identification of faults
  (b) Fault analysis
  (c) Remedial action.
2 Instructional techniques:
  (a) Level of instruction
  (b) Planning
  (c) Control of the lesson
  (d) Communication
  (e) Question and answer techniques
  (f) Feedback/encouragement
  (g) Instructor's use of controls.

3 Instructor characteristics:

  (a) Attitude

  (b) Approach to pupil.

As shown in the marking sheets on pages 164–73, each element of instruction is marked on a scale of 1 to 6, with a maximum grade of 6. To pass you need to attain a minimum grade of 4 in each. By taking into consideration the markings in columns A and B of the ADI 26 marking form, an overall assessment will be made and a corresponding grading awarded. For example, if you identify a serious error, because of this failure, nothing will have been done to correct the problem. The examiner would therefore mark the appropriate box in column A under 'not covered' or 'unsatisfactory'. This would then be transferred to column B under the heading 'identification of faults'. (You will find a breakdown of how these different elements are assessed in Chapter 5.)

At the end of the test

So that your examiner can make a fair assessment of your overall performance, you will be asked to wait for about 30 minutes while all elements of your performance are considered. You will then be given an oral debriefing together with the relevant ADI 26 form. If you do not wish to wait, the form will be posted to you.

In Northern Ireland, the procedure is slightly different in that the result is posted on to the candidate within a few days of the exam. The instructor can then arrange a debriefing with the SE by contacting DVA HQ and making an appointment.

As well as studying Chapter 5 of this book, you should find *Practical Teaching Skills for Driving Instructors* particularly helpful for this part of the examination. For details of all reference books see page 419.

When you pass

You will be given a letter confirming the result and you may apply for entry onto the Register of Approved Driving Instructors (Car) as soon as you wish. Complete the application form on the reverse of the letter and send it with the current fee to the DSA in Nottingham. This must be done within 12 months of the date you pass.

Registration declaration

When you apply for registration, you must sign a declaration to the effect that you will:

● notify the Registrar of any change of name, address or place of employment;

- notify the Registrar if convicted of any offence;
- return the certificate if your registration lapses or is revoked;
- agree to undergo, when requested by the Registrar, a Check Test conducted by DSA staff.

The ADI Certificate

You should receive your official green ADI Certificate of Registration within a week. This will remain valid for four years. You will then have to renew your registration. The certificate incorporates:

- your name;
- your photograph;
- your ADI number;
- the date of issue;
- the date of expiry of the certificate.

Displaying your ADI Certificate

As a qualified instructor, whenever you are giving tuition for money or the equivalent, you must display the official green certificate on the left-hand side of the car's windscreen, and produce your certificate if requested by a police officer or any person authorized by the Secretary of State. Failure to do so constitutes an offence. If you can satisfy the Registrar that your certificate has been lost, damaged or destroyed, a duplicate can be issued on payment of the current fee.

In Northern Ireland the requirement is for you to display the certificate either on the car windscreen or worn on a lanyard.

If you fail

Using the application form on the reverse of the letter, you may apply for a further test if you are still within the two-year qualifying period and the failed test was your first or second attempt. Otherwise, if you wish to continue, you will have to wait until a two-year period from passing the theory test has elapsed before you can apply for Part 1 again. It therefore makes sense to have sufficient good-quality training to ensure that your instructional skills are up to the standard required to become an effective driving instructor!

Requesting more information

Whether you pass or fail, if you would like a more detailed explanation of your test result, you may ask for an appointment to see your examiner. Examiners are normally available on Friday mornings.

For details of the Check Test see Chapter 6.

Northern Ireland – a summary

ADI certificates and licences are issued by the Driver Vehicle Agency (DVA), 66 Balmoral Road, Belfast BT12 6QL (tel: 02890 547 933).

For detailed information, you should make sure you have an up-to-date copy of the ADI 1 *Your Guide to Becoming an Approved Driving Instructor*, which is available from the DVA at 66 Balmoral Road, Belfast BT12 6QL (tel: 02890 547 933; website www.nidirect.gov.uk/motoring).

As indicated previously in the chapter, the processes and procedures for ADI registration in Northern Ireland are very similar to the rest of the UK, but with a few significant differences, including:

- *Trainee licence.*
  - Two licences can normally be issued, but an application for the second licence must be made before the expiry of the first one.
- *Supervision.*
  - A trainee instructor must be supervised for 20 per cent of the instruction time during the licence, but there is no requirement for specific training.
- *Part 3 exam (Instructional Ability).*
  - The pre-set Tests relate to learner drivers only. There is no provision for instructing a full licence holder.
  - The result of the Part 3 is posted out to the candidate within a few days of the exam. A debrief, if required, can be arranged by contacting the DVA and making an appointment with the SE.
- *Check test.*
  - There is no provision for a 'role play' check test. A pupil must be provided.
- *ADI certificate.*
  - An ADI certificate issued in England, Scotland or Wales can be exchanged for a Northern Ireland certificate, but a registration fee is payable.
- *Fees:*
  (at January 2011)
  ADI Part 1 (theory): £72
  ADI Part 2 (driving): £130
  ADI Part 3 (instruction): £138
  Registration/renewal: £240
  Trainee licence: £120.

DSA service standards

Information on the DSA's service standards for all matters relating to driving instructors and the Register is available in leaflet form from the DSA. The leaflet can be obtained by contacting the DSA by phone on 0115 936 6666 or at www.dsa.gov.uk. It includes information on:

- The DSA's role.
- Its customers.
- Its aims.
- Service standards, for:
  - its customers;
  - those taking theory tests;
  - those taking practical tests;
  - ADIs.
- More information on:
  - keeping customers informed;
  - listening to customers;
  - how customers can help the DSA;
  - equal opportunities;
  - if things go wrong;
  - compensation code;
  - complaints procedure.

The leaflet also lists the various phone numbers for enquiries relating to all subjects listed.

Keeping up to date

Many instructors who have been on the Register for a number of years are now finding it a struggle to retain their grading. In recent years, a higher proportion than ever before are being graded as 'substandard' and subsequently removed from the Register. Even if you have only been on the Register for a short time it may be beneficial to seek some refresher training.

You will find more information on preparing for your Check Test in *Practical Teaching Skills for Driving Instructors*. Detailed advice on preparing for all parts of the qualifying examination and the Check Test is given in Chapters 3 to 6; for full details of the ADI exams, see Chapters 3, 4 and 5.

Further information about the exams can be found in the DSA starter pack *Your Road to Becoming an Approved Driving Instructor (ADI 14)* and in *Practical Teaching Skills for Driving Instructors*. Details of all recommended books and publications are on page 419.

ADI Part 1: Theory and Hazard Perception

To be a safe driver and an effective instructor, you need a thorough understanding of the principles, rules and regulations included in all of the reading materials recommended by the Driving Standards Agency (DSA). As a professional driver trainer, you should be able to:

- apply these principles, rules and regulations whenever you are driving;
- pass on all of this information to your pupils to help them acquire the skills needed to put them into practice effectively;
- give accurate answers to any questions your pupils may ask.

Theory test

To be able to carry out your work as a responsible ADI, you need a wide range of subject knowledge and skills. For this reason, the theory test syllabus includes:

- The principles of road safety in general and their application in specified circumstances.
- Correct and courteous driving techniques:
  - car control;
  - road procedure;
  - hazard recognition and proper response;

- dealing safely with other road users and pedestrians;
- the use of safety equipment.
- The theory and practice of learning, teaching and assessment.
- The tuition required to instruct a pupil in driving a car, and:
  - the identification, analysis and correction of errors;
  - your manner and the relationship between instructor and pupil.
- Simple vehicle adaptations for drivers with disabilities.
- A knowledge of *The Highway Code*.
- A knowledge of the DSA book for 'L' test candidates, *The Official Guide to Learning to Drive*.
- How to interpret the 'Driving Test Report', Form DL25.
- A knowledge of basic mechanics and the design of cars adequate for the needs of driving instruction.

Resource materials

To ensure that you cover all the elements included in this syllabus, the DSA recommends that you study the following materials:

- *The Official DSA Guide to Driving – The essential skills.*
- *The Official Highway Code.*
- *The Official Guide to Learning to Drive.*
- *Prepare for your practical driving tes*t – DSA.
- *The official DSA Guide to Hazard Perception* DVD.
- *Helping Learners Practice – the Official DSA Guide.*
- *Instructional Techniques and Practices* by Les Walklin.
- *Know Your Traffic Signs*, published by The Stationery Office.
- The Motor Vehicles (Driving Licences) Regulations 1999, available from The Stationery Office.
- *Practical Teaching Skills for Driving Instructors.*
- D100 leaflet *What You Need to Know about Driving Licences – DVLA*.

The multiple-choice theory test questions are based on information in these books. Make sure that you have the latest editions of these publications.

For details of all books and resource materials, see page 419.

Studying the syllabus

Don't be misled into thinking that it will be enough to just learn a set of questions and answers by rote! Learning something 'by rote' means *memorizing through repetition*. This way of learning, although useful for remembering such things as multiplication tables and other basic facts, will not give you the understanding you need to be properly prepared to:

- be able to discriminate between the correct and incorrect answers given in the theory test;
- gain the maximum benefit from your practical training;
- pass the practical tests within the limited number of attempts allowed;
- effectively carry out your role as an ADI.

You should also consider that, if you are not properly prepared, there is the additional expense of failing two or three tests.

You need to prepare yourself properly for the exam for all of the reasons indicated above, especially as it is highly unlikely that you will be able to memorize the answers to specific questions. One hundred questions are set randomly in 12 different papers to allow an equal degree of difficulty for all candidates, and the questions will not appear in 'banded' order. To make things more difficult, some questions are negatively worded and others require you to know exact quotes from the official publications.

Even if you enrol on an intensive classroom course, you will still have a lot of studying to do in your own time. There are no short cuts to gaining all of this knowledge and understanding. Be prepared to exercise a good deal of self-discipline and set enough time aside for your studies.

Organizing your studies

Because of the wide range of topics involved, picking up a book and reading it from cover to cover will be of little benefit – unless, of course, you have a photographic memory! You need to develop your study skills by:

- making time available;
- finding the best place to carry out your studies;
- formulating a study plan.

You need to make the best use of your time by:

- organizing study periods to fit in with your existing commitments;
- setting yourself achievable objectives;
- not overloading yourself by trying to learn too much at once;
- following a properly structured study programme;
- dividing the materials into related topics;
- monitoring your progress throughout your course;
- seeking the advice of your tutor if there are any points you don't understand.

You will find more information on how to develop your study skills in Chapter 5 of *Practical Teaching Skills for Driving Instructors*.

Booking the ADI theory test

You can book the theory test if:

- your application for registration has been processed by the DSA;
- the 'fit and proper' tests on you have been completed; and
- you have received written confirmation from the DSA.

The most convenient way to book is online at www.businesslink.gov.uk/
transport. To do this you will need:

- a valid UK or EU driving licence;
- your ADI reference number;
- debit or credit card details.

To book by phone, you will need to contact the booking office on 0300 200
1122. The office is open from Monday to Friday between 8 am and 6 pm. With
both online and phone bookings, you will be allocated a booking confirmation
number and will receive an appointment letter within a few days. For bookings
by post, send your completed application form to: Driving Standards Agency,
Booking Department, PO Box 381, Manchester M50 3UW.

The cost of the ADI theory test (at January 2011) is £90, but up-to-date
fees are shown on www.businesslink.gov.uk/dsafees. To cancel or postpone,
you need to contact the DSA online or by phone at least three clear working
days before the test otherwise you are likely to lose the fee.

In Northern Ireland the fee is currently £72.

Special needs

Facilities are available for candidates who have special needs.

If you have reading difficulties, including dyslexia, you can request a
voiceover. You may also be allowed extra time to complete the multiple-
choice part of the exam. To be allowed these facilities you will need to
produce evidence of your particular reading difficulty and you must make
the request for facilities at the time of your application.

If you have another type of special need you can contact customer services
at the DSA to discuss your particular requirement and the facilities that
might be available.

The theory test banding system

The questions are banded into four subject groups:

1 road procedure;
2 traffic signs and signals; car control; pedestrians; mechanical knowledge;
3 driving test; disabilities; law;
4 publications; instructional techniques.

Example questions

Band 1 – road procedure

Q. You should not attempt to overtake a cyclist:
   a. on a dual carriageway;
   b. on a left hand bend;
   c. just before turning left;
   d. on a one-way street.

Q. You are moving off from behind a parked car. You should:
   a. look round as you move off;
   b. always give a signal;
   c. look round before starting to move;
   d. use all three mirrors as you pull out.

Q. You are driving at night and are dazzled by the headlights of an oncoming vehicle. You should:
   a. use full beam headlights;
   b. switch on your front fog lights;
   c. slow down and stop if necessary;
   d. flash your headlights to warn the other driver.

Q. You are about to turn left into a side road where pedestrians are crossing. You should:
   a. wait for them to cross;
   b. move out round them;
   c. sound the horn to warn the pedestrians;
   d. flash your headlights.

Band 2 – traffic signs and signals; car control; pedestrians; mechanical knowledge

Q. If you can see regular street lighting, but no speed limit signs, the limit is usually:
   a. 20 mph;
   b. 30 mph;
   c. 40 mph;
   d. 50 mph.

Q. Flashing amber lights at a pelican crossing mean that you should:
   a. give way to pedestrians who are waiting;
   b. proceed, but carefully;
   c. give way to any pedestrians who are on the crossing;
   d. stop.

Q. A bus lane showing no indication of times of operation means:
   a. there is no restriction on entering it;
   b. it operates 24 hours a day;
   c. it only operates during peak hours;
   d. you can enter it if there are no buses.

Q. On a wet road the back of your car is sliding to the right. You should:
    a. steer to the left;
    b. steer to the right;
    c. brake firmly in a straight line;
    d. accelerate gently.

Band 3 – the driving test; disabilities; the law
Q. A person who is profoundly deaf would be allowed to drive:
    a. any category B motor vehicle ;
    b. specified vehicles only;
    c. with a special note on the licence;
    d. no motor vehicles.

Q. After passing the driving test, you develop a health problem that could affect your driving. You need to:
    a. inform the police;
    b. not do anything;
    c. inform DVLA;
    d. notify DSA.

Q. During a lesson, your pupil is involved in an accident where no one is injured, but there is damage to someone else's property. The property owner is not about. You are required to:
    a. report the accident to your insurance company;
    b. report the accident to the police as soon as possible;
    c. try to contact the property owner;
    d. tell someone who lives nearby.

Q. A driving test pass certificate is valid for:
    a. 1 year;
    b. 2 years;
    c. 3 years;
    d. an unlimited amount of time.

Band 4 – publications; instructional techniques
Q. When teaching a pupil to stop they should be taught:
    a. to select a lower gear;
    b. to change down through the gears;
    c. that a gear change is not always necessary;
    d. to use 1st gear.

Q. You are approaching a set of traffic lights that are out of action. You should teach the pupil to:
    a. stop and look each way;
    b. be prepared to stop for traffic from any direction;
    c. stop; unless someone is close behind you;
    d. only stop if there are any large vehicles about.

Q. In order to start learning effectively, the pupil should:
  a. want to learn;
  b. understand some basic car mechanics;
  c. have good hand/eye coordination;
  d. be technically minded.

Q. If a pupil gives only a part answer to a question you should:
  a. give praise, but ask a supplementary question;
  b. offer a full explanation;
  c. tell the pupil to study the subject in more detail;
  d. repeat the question.

Taking the theory test

You must take with you the necessary documents: your photo-card driving licence and the paper counterpart, or your signed driving licence and current passport or other form of visual identity. Make sure you arrive in good time. If you are late you may not be allowed to take the test.

You are allowed plenty of time for this test – don't rush yourself. As you can see, the questions are very wide-ranging and some will need careful consideration. Don't worry if you see people leaving their computer after only half an hour. Learners use the same centres and their test only takes about 35 minutes compared with the 90 minutes allowed for the ADI exam.

If you have been thorough with your studies, you should have no problems, but make sure you:

- take your time;
- read each question carefully and at least twice;
- carefully consider the choice of answers;
- eliminate the obviously wrong answers quite quickly, where possible, but take time to consider the options when faced with negatively worded questions;
- leave questions you're not sure about and go back to them when you've answered those you find easier;
- check that you've answered all of the questions.

Multiple-choice pass mark

The overall pass mark is 85 per cent. However, the DSA needs to ensure that you have an adequate knowledge in all of the subject areas and you need a score of 80 per cent in each band to pass. This means that, even if you score 99 per cent in three of the bands and 79 per cent in the fourth, you will fail. This should emphasize to you the need for a thorough understanding of the principles covered in all of the recommended materials.

Following completion of the theory test, you will be given a short break before taking the hazard perception test.

Hazard perception test

Before you start this, as with the theory element, you will be allowed a short practice session.

The test consists of 14 video clips. You must watch carefully and respond to the hazards by clicking on the mouse. As each hazard develops, you need to keep registering a response to the changing situation – just as you would be assessing and reassessing developing situations when driving.

Each hazard is allotted a maximum score of five points, and the earlier you spot the hazard, the more points you will achieve. Provided your responses are made to correspond with the potential hazards or changing situations, you should be able to achieve a maximum score.

A skilled driver could be expected to click, on average, 10 or 12 times in one clip. However, you have to be careful not to click too early, or at random, as this will result in a negative score.

Resource materials

It's sensible to practise your skills at responding to 'on-screen' hazards. Your trainer should be able to supply you with one or more of the wide variety of CD-ROMs and DVDs that are now available.

The DSA produces a very effective interactive DVD on hazard perception. As well as preparing you for the ADI theory exam, it is useful material for your pupils. For more information, contact the DSA on 0300 200 1122 or at www.direct.gov.uk/motoringpublications. Other suppliers of theory test materials are shown on pages 411–12.

Hazard perception test pass mark

To pass you must score 57 out of a possible 75 marks. If you fail this part of the test you will have to take both parts again.

After the test

The result of both parts are given to you within a few minutes of completing the test.

When you pass you will be given a confirmation letter showing the marks for each part of the exam. If you fail, you can apply again straightaway.

Note that in Northern Ireland you are allowed only three attempts at the Theory Test.

Although this chapter is mainly concerned with the theory and hazard perception tests, try to remember that you are preparing for a job that has serious responsibilities attached to it.

As an ADI you will be preparing new drivers to share the roads with all of us, or assisting more experienced motorists to improve their driving skills. You should always be prepared to consistently apply the rules and regulations whenever you are driving, and keep up to date by maintaining a library of the latest publications.

ADI Part 2: Driving Ability

T his part of the ADI exam lasts about one hour and consists of three elements:

1 an eyesight test;

2 vehicle safety questions;

3 a practical driving test.

You must pass all three parts on the same occasion.

The 'Driving Ability' Test is not simply a longer version of the 'L' test – it is a very demanding advanced driving test, with a pass rate currently running at less than 50 per cent. To quote the Driving Standards Agency:

> This test is far more difficult than the learner test. It is of an advanced nature; a very high standard of competence is required. You must show that you have a thorough knowledge of the principles of good driving and road safety and that you can apply them in practice. (*Your Road to Becoming an Approved Driving Instructor*, DSA booklet ADI 14)

Application

When you passed the theory and hazard perception test you will have been given an application form for this part of the exam. You may then apply as soon as you wish and can take the test at any centre of your choice, although if you offer an alternative centre you may find that you can get an appointment at an earlier date.

Send the form, together with the appropriate fee (£111 at January 2011 and £130 in Northern Ireland), to the DSA at Nottingham. You will receive a letter confirming your appointment. When attending for the test, take the letter with you. You will also need to take both parts of your photo-card licence. If you still have an old-style paper licence you should take your passport (or some other form of visual identity) with you as photographic proof of your identity. The test will not be conducted if you do not produce the correct documentation.

The car

You must provide a suitable vehicle that:

- is properly taxed and insured;
- has a valid MOT certificate if required;
- is a saloon or estate car in proper working condition with front and rear seatbelts in working order;
- is capable of the normal performance of vehicles of its type;
- has manual transmission (except for applicants with a disability);
- is right-hand drive;
- has a readily adjustable seat, with head restraint, for a forward-facing front-seat passenger;
- is not displaying 'L' plates;
- has an additional, adjustable interior mirror for use by the examiner;
- does not have a 'space saver' tyre fitted.

If the car does not meet these requirements it will not be possible for the test to be conducted and you will lose the fee.

From time to time a member of the DSA staff may accompany your examiner to ensure the uniformity of the tests. All seatbelts front and rear must therefore be in working order, otherwise the test might be cancelled. Anyone who accompanies you on the test would also be expected to wear a seatbelt.

Eyesight

You will be asked to read a vehicle number plate from a distance of 26.5 metres for new-style registration plates, or 27.5 metres if it is an old-style number plate with the larger digits. If you need to wear spectacles or contact lenses to do this, you must wear them for the driving part of the test.

If you are unable to complete the eyesight test satisfactorily, you will not be allowed to continue with the driving test and it will be counted as a failure.

Vehicle safety questions

As outlined in Chapter 2, the examiner will choose three of your car's components and ask you to explain ('tell me') how to carry out checks on their condition and safety. You will be asked to demonstrate ('show me') how to make checks on the condition and operation of two other items. Incorrect answers are marked as 'driving faults', but if all five questions are answered incorrectly this will be marked as a 'serious fault'.

For details of the syllabus for this part of the test and for typical questions, see pages 41–42.

The driving test

During the test you will be assessed on your driving in a variety of situations, including:

- urban areas;
- rural roads;
- motorway or dual carriageways;
- roads that carry heavy and/or fast-moving traffic.

The syllabus

During the test you will be assessed on your:

- handling of the controls;
- application of correct road procedure;
- anticipation of the actions of other road users and taking appropriate action;
- judgement of distance, speed and timing;
- consideration for the convenience and safety of other road users.

The examiner will also be assessing whether you drive in an environmentally friendly manner.

Specific exercises include:

- moving away – straight ahead and at an angle;
- dealing with other vehicles when:
  - overtaking;
  - meeting;
  - crossing their path.
- turning left- and right-hand corners correctly and without undue hesitancy;

- controlled stop;
- reversing into openings to the left and right;
- reverse parking into a space behind another parked vehicle;
- turning the car around in the road using forward and reverse gears;
- reversing into a parking bay.

Normally during the test you will be following the specific direction instructions of the examiner, but for a period of about 10 minutes you will be asked to drive 'independently'. You will be asked to follow road signs to a particular location, or a series of verbal directions, or a combination of both.

You will also be required to give a commentary for a few minutes on what you see and how you intend to deal with particular hazards.

To pass this part of the ADI Exam you must show a high standard of competence, demonstrating the principles of eco-friendly driving. Your driving should be well-planned, positive and progressive, keeping to speed limits but attaining national speed limits when it is safe to do so.

Resource material

To be able to drive skilfully and safely, you need a thorough understanding and working knowledge of the rules and regulations. You should have done most of your studying when preparing for the theory test; now you must demonstrate that you can apply the rules sensibly and correctly. To help with your application of the correct routines and procedures you should continually refer to *The Official DSA Guide to Driving – The essential skills*, *The Official Highway Code* and *Know Your Traffic Signs*.

For details of reference books and resource materials, see page 419.

Preparation

Even if you have already passed an advanced driving test, the syllabus and style of driving of the other motoring organizations may differ from those of the DSA. It is therefore advisable to have an assessment with an experienced ADI tutor. Although instructors at a local driving school may be extremely good at preparing candidates for the 'L' test, they may not be fully conversant with the higher level of assessment required for this test.

Tutors registered under the ORDIT scheme know what the DSA's requirements are and are skilled at assessments at this level. They will be able to advise you on any adjustments needed to enhance your driving style and efficiency.

Even if you have been driving for many years, you may need to modify some aspects of your driving to streamline your performance in line with modern driving techniques. It is often said that 'unlearning' something you've been doing for years is far more difficult than learning something from scratch, so be aware that some experienced drivers find it difficult to adapt to a new style of driving.

Effective training

Training with a qualified, experienced tutor is essential for several reasons:

- If you are still driving in the style you have been using for many years, you may be applying inefficient or out-dated methods.
- Although you will have passed the theory test at this stage, there may still be some deficiencies in areas of your knowledge that could result in failure. A trained tutor will be able to identify these and teach you how to apply the rules and procedures correctly.
- The standard of driving required by the DSA is higher than that of some other advanced driving organizations.
- You may have some false assumptions about the test and its content – a good tutor will be able to advise you correctly.
- An assessment given under test conditions will be invaluable experience.
- The training you receive from your tutor will provide you with a demonstration of the teaching techniques you will need to acquire to become an effective instructor.

Failure is expensive, and it increases the pressure when attending for retests. In addition, if you do not take training with a specialist, you may well be at a disadvantage when it comes to taking your instructional ability test, as you will not have seen demonstrated the teaching skills you need to acquire. A good tutor will make an objective assessment of the current level of your personal driving skills and be able to guide you along the route to improvement and to explain why you might need to make changes to your style or methods.

> **You are allowed a maximum of three attempts at this test so be prepared to invest in sufficient training.**

It is sensible to have a couple of 'mock test' sessions with your tutor prior to taking the test just in case you have any last-minute doubts or queries, and need any advice or reassurance.

Remember – your examiner will be expecting to see you drive with skill and confidence. You are an experienced driver – it will therefore be obvious to the examiner's trained eye if you are trying to put on a show of being 'extra careful'. If you do this, there is the likelihood that it will cause you to make incorrect decisions and to fail to make proper progress.

To prepare for the test, you should:

- take advice from your tutor on the aspects of your driving that need improvement;
- continue to refer to the recommended books;

- get as much practice as possible on different types of road and in differing conditions;
- apply the correct procedures whenever you are driving so that they become natural;
- try to maintain progress in relation to the conditions, the law and your car;
- practise giving yourself commentaries as you are driving along.

As well as making progress, you should also take into consideration vehicle sympathy, economy and the comfort of your passengers. To maximize progress, you should:

- make sure you can reach all of the controls properly;
- use the controls smoothly and progressively;
- hold, turn and straighten the steering wheel properly;
- demonstrate vehicle sympathy by selecting gears at the correct time and in accordance with speed and power requirements;
- plan well ahead so that you can use 'accelerator sense' to avoid unnecessary stops, excessive use of the brakes and engine braking;
- maximize fuel economy by keeping the engine revs at the correct level.

To maintain progress and demonstrate your personal driving skills, you should:

- look and plan well ahead, anticipating and preparing for hazards before you reach them;
- adjust your speed to avoid any unnecessary stops;
- start looking early at junctions so that you can take opportunities to proceed as soon as you are sure it's safe;
- always be aware of the speed limit and make progress by driving up to it in relation to the road, weather and traffic conditions.

To protect yourself, your passengers and road users all around, you should:

- be aware of what is happening all around your car at all times by using all of the mirrors on a regular basis;
- respond properly to what you see in the mirrors;
- anticipate and make allowances for the mistakes of other road users;
- exercise self-discipline when threatened by others;
- show courtesy and consideration to anyone else using the road;
- always be prepared to give way, even if you have priority.

Show that you can handle your car efficiently in all of the manoeuvre exercises by:

- maintaining absolute control on all gradients, using the handbrake when necessary;

- making effective observations throughout, and responding correctly to the presence of any other road users – which means giving them priority when appropriate;
- demonstrating accurate steering skills to complete each exercise effectively;
- stopping the car in a controlled manner, avoiding skidding; but if you do skid, you must demonstrate that you can correct it properly.

If you put all of these principles into practice, passing the Test of Driving Ability at your first attempt should not be a problem.

During the test

Try not to let the examiner's presence put you off or influence your decision-making. If you are putting into practice the principles of safe driving from the recommended books and as taught by your tutor, you should base your decisions solely on what is happening all around you.

Remember, your decisions to act should be based only on what you know is safe for the particular circumstances. Examiners, who are specially trained, will recognize from the all-round situation what you are basing the decisions on.

Your examiner will assess your driving skills under some of the headings listed on the DL25, Driving Test Report form reproduced on page 354. (Any numbers not listed relate to tests on other categories of vehicle.) You will be assessed on:

1 (a) *Eyesight* – you must be able to read a number plate from the prescribed distance.
(b) *Vehicle safety* – you must be able to describe and demonstrate how to check the condition and safety of a number of the car's components.
(c) *Highway Code* – you must demonstrate that you can apply the rules.

2 *Controlled stop* – you must be able to stop your vehicle safely, promptly and under full control. Firm, progressive braking should result in a prompt and safe stop. Avoid braking so harshly that your car skids, or if your car has an anti-lock braking system, that it is activated. Remember you are supposed to be stopping under control.

3 4 and 5 *Reverse exercises*

Reverse left into a limited opening:

- *Under control:* taking account of any gradients; full control should be maintained throughout.

- *With proper observation:* all-round checks should be made throughout and you should respond to the presence of other road users. This means giving priority when appropriate or proceeding if you are sure the other driver is waiting.

- *Reasonably accurately:* you are an experienced driver; you should be able to maintain a reasonable degree of accuracy throughout the manoeuvre and finish in a safe position.

Reverse right into a limited opening:

- *Under control:* as for the left reverse you should take account of any gradients, and maintain full control throughout.

- *With proper observation:* as you will be manoeuvring on the wrong side of the road you will need to pay particular attention to the front, responding to the presence of other road users. This means giving them priority when appropriate.

- *Reasonably accurately:* as an experienced driver, you may switch the focus of your observations from offside to rear to nearside in order to maintain a reasonable degree of accuracy. This will also help keep you up to date on the presence of others.

Reverse parking – either on the road or into a parking bay:

- *Under control:* take account of any gradients, and maintain full control throughout.

- *With proper observation:* as you may be manoeuvring into a more confined space from the middle of the road, you will need to pay particular attention to the presence of other road users. This means giving them priority when appropriate.

- *Reasonably accurately:* whether reversing on the road or into a parking bay, you need to steer into the space accurately and finish up with your vehicle straight.

6 *Turn in the road:*

- *Under control:* take account of any gradients, and maintain full control throughout, using the handbrake where necessary.

- *With proper observation:* keep checking in all directions and give other road users priority when appropriate.

- *Reasonably accurately:* you should be able to complete this manoeuvre in three movements. However, if the road is particularly narrow, you may need to take an extra movement.

11 *Take proper precautions before starting the engine:* make a habit of checking that the parking brake is secure and the gear lever is in neutral before starting the engine. However, if you happen to stall in an awkward situation and wish to get moving quickly, it is more efficient to keep your footbrake on, clutch down and switch on. You must, however, retain full control of your vehicle at all times.

12 *Control – you should make proper use of:*

- *Accelerator:* progressive, gentle use and good accelerator sense should result in full control, a smooth ride and economical use of fuel.

- *Clutch:* use good clutch control without excessive wear and tear, as for example happens when it is used for very short stops. Avoid coasting over prolonged distances.

- *Gears:* use selective changing up and down the box to suit the circumstances and to achieve optimum fuel economy.
- *Footbrake:* progressive use of the brakes should result in smooth stopping.
- *Parking brake:* used for stops that are likely to last for more than a few seconds and where other traffic and pedestrians are present and, of course, to avoid rolling backwards or forwards on gradients.
- *Steering:* an efficient method should be used to give maximum efficiency, leverage and control.

13 *Move off:*
- *Safely:* make full all-round observations to ensure that no other road users will be affected when you move off.
- *Under control:* maintain full control when moving away in all situations – level, uphill, downhill and at an angle.

14 *Use of the mirrors well before:*
- *Signalling:* check mirrors well before making any decision to signal so that discrimination is effective and signals are timed correctly.
- *Changing direction:* no action to change direction should be taken unless you are sure that you will not be affecting another road user.
- *Changing speed:* always be sure of the all-round situation before changing your speed, whether you are speeding up or slowing down.
- Use the mirrors–signal–manoeuvre (M–S–M) routine effectively.

15 *Give signals by direction indicators/arm:*
- *Where necessary:* if any other road user (including pedestrians) would benefit from a signal, use one. If appropriate – that is, if you have time and your window is open – consider giving an arm signal for stopping at a zebra crossing if you think an oncoming driver or pedestrian might benefit. The horn should be used as a warning of your presence and can be helpful when you are approaching a blind bend or summit.
- *Correctly:* use only signals that clearly show your intentions to move off, stop or change direction.
- *Properly timed:* time your signals so as not to confuse other road users. For example, if you are waiting to move away from the kerb and vehicles are approaching from the rear, too early a signal may make the other drivers think that you are likely to pull out in front of them. If you are taking a second road on the left, make sure you time your signal so as not to encourage a driver waiting in the first one to emerge in front of you. You should also remember that early positioning helps confirm your intentions, for example when passing parked vehicles where you could consider that a signal is not needed.

16 *Clearance/obstructions:* where there are parked vehicles, work out whose priority it should be, but also anticipate what the oncoming driver is likely to do. Priorities do not really matter if the other driver is determined to take the road space. Sometimes it is courteous to make a positive decision to give way, for example if you are travelling downhill and there is a larger vehicle coming up the hill towards you.

17 *Response to signs and signals – take appropriate action on all:*

- *Traffic signs:* road signs are there for your information and guidance. Respond to them early by checking your mirrors and taking the appropriate action. Check for signs whenever you are approaching a different type of road, and make sure you are always aware of the speed limit for the road you are using.

- *Road markings:* are also for your guidance. Look and plan well ahead, and respond to hazard warning lines by checking your mirrors and looking for any possible dangers. Plan early for any lane changes so that you do not have to take any late action that might affect others. Be aware of any stop lines and make sure you bring your vehicle to a complete stop.

- *Traffic lights:* plan your approach according to the colour already showing – remember they could change at any moment. If the lights are on green, check your mirrors, adjust your speed and be prepared to stop until you reach that point of no return when it would be unsafe to stop. Demonstrate that you know the meaning of amber. If, when it shows, you are so close to the line that you would need to brake sharply to stop, you should continue – particularly if someone is close behind you. If red is showing, check your mirrors, adjust your speed and be prepared to stop if it remains on red, or to change to an appropriate gear and proceed if it changes to green.

- *Signals given by traffic controllers:* obey any signals given by authorized persons such as police officers or school patrol wardens.

- *Other road users:* although most drivers use signals correctly, some do not! If an approaching driver is signalling to turn into your road, make sure that he or she is actually going to turn. Similarly, if other drivers flash their headlights at you to proceed, do not just go without checking all-round safety for yourself.

18 *Use of speed:* speed limits are maximum speeds. Although you should make proper progress, your speed should be dictated not only by the limit for the road you are on, but also by the weather, the condition of the road surface, the traffic volume and any pedestrian activity.

19 *Following distance:* always keep a safe distance between yourself and other vehicles. If the vehicle in front of you stops, you should have time to take action without getting too close to it. Leave a gap of at least a metre for every mph of your speed – or use the two-second rule. In very wet conditions, you will need at least twice this distance. If

someone is following you too closely, drop back even further. This will allow you to give the following driver more time to stop, because you will be allowing for their stopping distance as well as your own.

20 *Maintain progress:* drive at a realistic speed appropriate to the road and traffic conditions. Approach all hazards at a safe and controlled speed, without being over-cautious or interfering with the progress of other traffic. Be ready to move away promptly from junctions. When you have to stop, keep looking in all directions for a suitable gap in the traffic and have your car ready to move smoothly into it, building up your speed and changing up efficiently so as not to affect any other road user.

21 *Junctions (including roundabouts):*

- *Speed on approach:* try to time your arrival at junctions in accordance with the sightlines. That is, if the junction is opening up, without slowing down excessively, give yourself time to start making early observations. If your sightlines are very restricted, do not waste too much time on the approach if you will not be able to see until you get there!

- *Observations:* you cannot make any safe decision to proceed until you have looked properly in all directions. On the approach to T-junctions, as soon as sightlines begin to open up (no matter in which direction), start looking and keep looking in both directions until you are absolutely sure you will not affect another road user. At crossroads, keep looking in all directions – even when you have priority. Remember, even a green light does not give you 100 per cent safety – check there's no one proceeding through on the wrong colour.

- *Approaching traffic:* your actions should never make another driver slow down or change direction. Before you make any decision to cross another driver's path, make sure you have enough time and, just as importantly, make sure you know what is happening in the new road.

- *Turning right:* when turning from main roads into a side road, position your car close to the centre of the road to avoid holding up the following traffic. Make sure you know what is happening in the new road before you commit yourself to turning in. When emerging from wide roads, position yourself just to the left of the centre line so as not to impede the flow of left-turning traffic. However, if the road is narrow, keep farther to the left to allow more room for vehicles turning in.

- *Turning left:* whether turning in or emerging, maintain your normal driving position, about a metre from the kerb, to allow plenty of room for the rear wheels to clear the kerb.

- *Cutting corners:* make sure you position correctly, according to the width of the road, and if you have to wait for oncoming traffic, that you wait just short of the point of turn. This should ensure that you turn in on your own side of the road, avoiding cutting corners. However, if there are parked vehicles near the end of the road making an ideal turn impossible, move a little further forward before turning, to give you a better view.

22 *Judgement:*

- *Allow adequate clearance to stationary vehicles and obstructions.* Allow sufficient room for doors opening, drivers moving off without signalling or people walking between vehicles. This means you should, in ideal circumstances, be allowing about a metre's clearance.

- *Meeting other traffic:* when the width of the road is restricted, be prepared to give way, no matter whose priority it may be. Remember, the oncoming driver may not be as courteous as you are! If there are vehicles parked on both sides, but there is room to proceed through, then allow an equal amount of clearance to both sides – in other words, drive down the centre of the road. On roads where there is a need to maintain the traffic flow but you cannot give the ideal clearance, then slow down and drive through cautiously, allowing time to respond if the situation changes.

- *Overtaking:* this is potentially *the* most dangerous manoeuvre! Before you decide to overtake you should ask yourself, *is it safe, legal and necessary?* Make sure you know what's happening behind you and that you can see far enough ahead so you know you'll have sufficient time to execute the manoeuvre quickly and efficiently without affecting any other road user. Allow plenty of room when overtaking cyclists and motorcyclists.

- *Crossing the path of other traffic:* never rush to beat an oncoming vehicle when turning right. If you have to rush, there is a risk involved, and you should never put yourself into a situation your eyes have not visited first.

23 *Positioning:* normally position your vehicle well to the left. On a road of reasonable width, your normal driving position should be about a metre from the kerb – or even a little farther out if there are large puddles and pedestrians around. Give cycle lanes the same distance. On narrower roads, in rural areas for example, you may have to drive a little nearer the edge of the road, in which case you will need to adjust your speed according to the situation and the presence of any other road users. On left bends, keep to the centre of your lane to maintain safety from oncoming vehicles. On right bends, keep to the left to improve your view.

- *Driving in lanes:* exercise lane discipline and drive in the centre of your lane, avoiding straddling the lines. Look and plan ahead and select your lane early. When a lane change is necessary, apply the M–S–M routine early, carrying out the manoeuvre safely and gradually.

24 *Pedestrian crossings:* dealing with the light-controlled crossings is relatively straightforward, as you have to obey the light sequences. Anticipate when they are likely to change and apply the M–S–M routine in good time. Stop at the stop line and secure your car with the parking brake.

At *zebra crossings*, it can be slightly more complicated. You need to be on the lookout for pedestrians likely to step out at any moment. Look and plan well ahead, apply the M–S–M routine and always be travelling at a speed at which you can stop within the distance you can see is clear. Be patient and only proceed when you know it is safe. Pedestrians have priority anywhere in the road – be ready to anticipate their actions and, if possible, give them time to get onto the pavement.

At *toucan crossings*, be prepared to give way to cyclists as well as pedestrians.

25 *Position/normal stops:* drivers who are under test conditions sometimes feel they must stop as soon as they are asked to do so! However, you must make sure that you only stop where it is safe, legal and convenient. Remember, you should be demonstrating that you know and understand the rules by applying them correctly.

26 *Awareness and planning:*

- *Pedestrians:* people do not always do as they should, and pedestrians do not normally read *The Highway Code*. Always expect the unexpected and, in any area where there is pedestrian activity, try to anticipate what might happen. Check your mirrors and be ready to slow down or stop.

- *Cyclists:* give as much clearance as you can to cyclists. They are unpredictable and could wobble into your path at any time, particularly in windy conditions. Expect them to ride off pavements without warning and to cycle in between lanes. Always check to your sides before moving off in queues of traffic.

- *Drivers:* these are pedestrians on wheels – they do not always act as they should. That they know the rules does not mean they will always apply them. Look and plan all around, watching out and allowing for drivers moving off, changing lanes or stopping suddenly; cutting corners; turning across your path; taking priority when it should be yours; not using signals correctly; following you too closely; not obeying traffic signs and signals.

27 *Ancillary controls:* you should maintain constant all-round visibility in your car. Without needing to look down at the controls, use the washer/wipers, demisters and fan as necessary. If you use the air conditioning, make sure you switch it off if you open your window – this includes during any of the manoeuvre exercises. For normal driving, having the windows open in hot weather causes drag and will use more fuel than the air-conditioning unit does.

Eco-safe driving

In the Part 2 ADI exam you are expected to be an experienced driver and will need to show that you are aware of the need for fuel efficiency and an environmentally friendly approach in all aspects of your driving. As an ADI you will need to be able to encourage your new drivers in the use of all these various techniques. Fuel-efficient driving is now part of the ADI Part 2 exam as well as the 'L' driver test.

Eco-friendly driving can make a significant impact on the global use of conventional fuels and make a positive contribution to the reduction of carbon emissions. This process starts with an awareness of the availability of vehicles with alternative fuels such as electric and 'dual fuel' power.

To make an improvement in fuel efficiency, you can consider several areas of your own style of driving, including:

- *Acceleration.* Your use of acceleration should be steady, smooth and progressive whenever possible, avoiding unnecessary speed peaks. A smooth driving style can save up to 10 per cent of fuel used. Where appropriate, use the cruise control, as this can be more efficient on fuel usage.

- *Braking.* Any use of the footbrake should be smooth and positive, with a certain amount of tapering on and off. Avoid any harsh use of the brakes by easing off the accelerator earlier where possible.

- *Gear changes.* Make gear changes effectively, with block changes up and down where appropriate. Move into the higher gears reasonably quickly. Cars with manual gear change are more fuel-efficient than automatics.

- *Hazard awareness* and forward-planning techniques should be used effectively to minimize any unnecessary or harsh changes of speed or direction.

- *Vehicle sympathy.* Keep engine speeds relatively low whenever possible. Generally, keeping the engine speed to about 3,000 rpm can save a considerable amount of fuel. Use all vehicle controls smoothly to avoid any unnecessary sharp fluctuations in speed.

- *Manoeuvring.* Reversing into a parking space and then driving out forwards is generally regarded as more fuel-efficient than reversing out when the engine is cold.

- *Speed.* Keep to all legal speed limits and plan well ahead for any changes. Some experts reckon that reducing your top speed by 10 mph can save a considerable amount of fuel.

- *Air conditioning.* Avoid using air con or climate control unless it is necessary, as this can be detrimental to fuel consumption. Avoid driving with the car windows or sunroof open, as this can create 'drag' and an increase in fuel consumed.

Individually, these savings may not seem much, but collectively they can make substantial reductions, not only on your own costs but also on the global use of carbon fuels.

Marking

Eco-safe driving faults are marked on the DL25 as a 'driving fault' by the examiner, using one of the spare boxes on the form. The DL25 form is illustrated on page 354.

The main areas that the examiner will be looking for include:

- *Hazard awareness and planning:* hazards are identified at an early stage, giving adequate time to respond and to decelerate as appropriate.
- *Speed limits:* complied with all legal speed limits. Speed is appropriate to all road, traffic and weather conditions.
- *Starting up and moving off:* avoids excessive use of the accelerator. Moves off promptly and smoothly.
- *Accelerator:* used smoothly. Accelerator was properly coordinated with the other controls.
- *Gears:* used efficiently and effectively, with the appropriate gear engaged at all times.
- *Engine braking:* used effectively to take advantage of engine braking power where appropriate.
- *Engine power and torque:* utilized higher gears at lower engine speed where appropriate without causing the engine to labour.
- *Cruise control:* used in appropriate situations, but without compromising road safety.

Remember – this is not just about saving fuel in your vehicle; it is also to do with releasing less polluting chemicals into the atmosphere and conserving fuels globally.

Marking system

This test demands a high level of driving skill and, as a result, the marking system is more critical than on other tests. Faults are assessed under three categories:

1 *Driving faults* – errors that detract from the 'perfect' drive.
2 *Serious or potentially dangerous faults* – faults that cause potential danger or damage, and in different circumstances could lead to a serious situation arising.
3. *Dangerous faults* – faults that cause actual danger.

To pass this part of the exam you must have no serious or dangerous faults and a maximum of six driving faults.

Examples of different types of fault:

Driving faults:

- ineffective use of the mirrors and lack of response;
- making too many unnecessary gear changes;
- signalling incorrectly; lack of observations during manoeuvre exercises.

Serious or potentially dangerous faults:

- failure to respond to the presence of other road users during a manoeuvre exercise;
- cutting a right corner with no other road user present.

Dangerous faults:

- turning right across the path of an oncoming vehicle;
- emerging from a junction and slowing down another driver;
- driving too slowly for the conditions and missing opportunities to proceed in busy situations.

The examiner will offer a debrief on any of your driving faults and you will be given the top copy of the DL25 form. At this stage your trainer may be present, but will not be allowed to take part in the discussion.

When you pass, an application form for the test of instructional ability will be given to you. If you fail, you will be given an application form for a further attempt at the driving test.

Remember, you may only have three attempts at this test. If you fail on the third, and still wish to continue with the qualifying process, you will have to wait until the two-year period elapses from passing the theory/ hazard perception test. You would then have to start the whole process again by taking Part 1.

Your driving skills

In preparation for your ADI driving test and for a future of effective, economical and safe driving, you need to know something about the theory behind good driving principles. As driving is mainly a practical skill it can be developed only through effective practice and experience. It involves a complex mixture that combines:

- knowledge;
- understanding;
- awareness; and
- attitude.

In order to practise 'safe driving for life' in your own driving you need to identify all these elements. To become an effective trainer of new drivers there are other aspects of driver behaviour that you need to understand.

It is extremely unlikely that 'the perfect driver' exists. However, perfection is something that we should all try to achieve. As instructors, we should take a pride in our driving and be able not only to analyse and improve our own performance, but also to offer constructive criticism to our pupils. In striving for perfection, we need to recognize some of the main ingredients and characteristics of 'the perfect driver', which include skill, knowledge and attitude elements.

Profile of 'the perfect driver'

Skill

To the perfect driver, 'vehicle sympathy' means being 'at one' with, and in total control of, the car at all times. All actions should be smooth, positive and precise. The vehicle should:

- be in the correct position on the road;
- be travelling at a safe speed for the road and traffic conditions;
- have an appropriate gear engaged to suit the speed and power requirements.

Observation, anticipation and forward planning – all of which require total concentration – are essential at all times. Too often, a driver's ability is judged only on manipulative and control skills. Perfection in these practical skills alone, however, will not compensate for a lack of knowledge or a defective attitude. Optimum performance requires not only the ability to think for oneself, but also the skill to read the road and traffic conditions effectively and to take account of what other road users may do.

Knowledge

The good driver will know and understand the laws, rules and regulations relating to road procedure. Without this knowledge, even the most skilfully adept person cannot become a complete driver. It is generally accepted that knowledge generates positive attitudes. In driving instruction, as in general education, the more the knowledge and understanding are developed, the better and safer the outcomes will be.

Attitude

Knowledge of the subject and skill in handling the car are not sufficient qualities in themselves. They need to be applied in a safe, sensible manner.

This means taking into account mistakes other drivers make and being prepared to make allowances for them.

Attitudes have a profound effect on the quality of driving, and although relatively easy to define in general terms, they are more difficult to assess in the individual driver. The perfect driver never drives in a spirit of competition or takes revenge on another road user and is always considerate, courteous and tolerant.

For the instructor, these qualities are even more important. The attitude you display during lessons or on a demonstration drive will be transmitted to your pupils.

Attitude affects the behaviour of drivers, with reckless or unsafe actions being attributed to a negative one. Opinions are not always objective when judgements are made about a traffic situation or another driver. Judgement in any situation may be influenced by attitudes assumed previously in a similar event. An incorrect attitude can sometimes make drivers see things not as they actually are, but as they imagine them to be. One of your most important jobs as an instructor will be to develop favourable attitudes in your pupils and change any negative ones they may have.

Motivation describes the personal needs and drives of the individual. It ranges from the need to survive to a feeling of well-being and achievement of desires. Motivation can be used in a positive way to improve driver behaviour. However, it may sometimes cause illogical and potentially unsafe driving. For example, drivers may take uncharacteristic risks if they:

- are late for work or an important appointment;
- want to get the better of another driver;
- wish to demonstrate a superiority of skill;
- are trying to gain the admiration of friends.

Emotion is the general term used to describe feelings such as love, hate or fear. Intense emotions such as anger, frustration and grief tend to turn the focus of the mind in on itself. This in turn lowers the attention being paid to the driving task and limits perceptive abilities.

Anger may result from an argument. Frustration may result from being held up behind a slow-moving vehicle. Anxiety may be the result of worries about work or other personal problems.

Inexperienced drivers who lack self-confidence may suffer from ill-founded fears that they cannot cope. Driving is in itself a stressful activity, and deficient knowledge or skill can result in frustration and may generate destructive emotions.

Personality is described as 'distinctive personal qualities'. However, what we may think of ourselves may be completely different from the way in which others see us. Personality tends to be inconsistent and, faced with varying circumstances, drivers may display different sides of their personality.

There is some evidence to suggest that extrovert drivers are more likely to be involved in accidents than someone who is more introverted. This may be partly explained by the extrovert driver's inability to concentrate on the driving task for longer periods.

Perception is the brain's interpretation of information it receives from the eyes, ears and other senses. The perception of a particular traffic hazard is carried out by the primary information-processing functions of the brain. This involves a need to compare the current situation with existing knowledge and previous experience.

Hazard recognition requires an active and rapid assessment of the potential risks involved in a particular situation, and the driver must anticipate events before they occur. This anticipation relies heavily on stored memories of similar experiences.

Perception is the driver's visual and mental awareness, and it provides information on:

- speed;
- position;
- timing.

Drivers may have limited perceptual capacity and are often faced with an overload of information from the environment. In order to maintain safety when this happens, it becomes necessary to prioritize. This means that the important pieces of information will need to be attended to while other aspects will have to be ignored.

A more detailed explanation and analysis of driver behaviour is in Chapter 9, Driver Training.

On the road

Road sense

Driving is a continuous process of observing, responding and attending to constantly changing needs involving the vehicle, the road layout and traffic conditions. You need to continually recognize, assess and reassess hazards and respond correctly in good time. These responses involve the M–S–M and P–S–L (position–speed–look) routines.

Within the individual elements of these routines, you should:

- look, assess and decide what action can safely be taken in relation to the information received from the all-round situation;
- look, assess and decide whether a signal is required;
- assess whether the signal is having the required effect on others;
- look, assess and decide what effect any changes in position and speed are likely to have on others;
- decide what further looks may be required.

To be a good driver you need to assess the part you are taking in the changing road and traffic environment. For example, you should not only respond to developing situations, but you should also see yourself as an active part of those situations – often contributing to them. Assessing risks, and deciding on the appropriate response to a hazard, involves a continuous process of assessing and reassessing the constantly changing traffic situation. This means:

- assessing the degree of risk;
- deciding on the priorities;
- focusing attention on the most important aspect;
- deciding on a specific course of action;
- responding in good time;
- reassessing.

Anticipation is having the ability to predict the actions of other road users and is part of the visual search skills. As a good driver, you need to know:

- why, where and when you must look;
- the kind of things to look for;
- what to expect;
- how to see effectively as opposed to just 'looking'.

Risk assessment is influenced by knowledge and previous experience. It can be learnt on a trial-and-error basis or through controlled exercises. Most drivers will recognize that there is a bend in the road; however, they might not all think of the possibility of there being an obstruction hidden from view.

Most collision accidents result from deficiencies in a driver's information-processing skills and not from deficient car control. A large proportion of accidents could be avoided if drivers were more aware of the risks involved, knew what to look for and what to expect, and were prepared to drive defensively by taking avoiding action.

Visual awareness

The good driver is constantly gathering information from the all-round traffic scene. An active visual scan not only provides more information at an earlier stage, but also gives more time to respond. The eye movements of experienced drivers need to be very rapid, moving quickly from one point of interest to another, checking and rechecking areas of risk. Drivers should practise an effective visual search system that involves:

- looking well ahead – allowing you to steer a safe and smooth line;
- keeping the eyes moving – to help you build up a more complete picture and improve awareness;

- getting the big picture – looking all around assists with the judgement of speed and position;
- allowing others to see you – positioning your car so that you can see and be seen;
- looking for alternatives – working out an action plan that may be required if events change.

Hazard recognition

The natural inclination of many drivers is to keep going, unless it is obviously unsafe, for example by steering away from a moving hazard rather than slowing down to avoid it. You need to:

- actively search the road ahead;
- assess the safety of proceeding;
- recognize the consequences of your actions.

When reading the road ahead, rather than waiting for something to happen, you need to anticipate it and respond in good time so that you attempt to avoid any potential problems. To do this you need to obtain as much relevant information about the road and traffic situation as you can. For example:

- To *steer accurately and adjust to safe speeds before reaching a hazard*, look well ahead for bends, gradients, road signs, junctions and obstructions such as parked cars, road works and traffic hold-ups.
- To *maintain tyre and road surface adhesion*, drive smoothly and approach hazards at a suitable speed, taking into account weather conditions, road surface and any camber on bends.
- To *anticipate and act on the actions of other road users*, scan the road for anything with a potential for moving into or across your path.
- To *be able to stop well within the distance you can see to be clear*, you need to identify any blind areas and adjust your speed accordingly.
- To *avoid problems with road users to your sides and rear*, make full use of all of the mirrors and use your peripheral vision. You also need a good understanding of the principles of communicating with other road users. You also need to exercise good lane discipline.

Making decisions

Some drivers' decisions often polarize between 'stop' and 'go' where neither is necessarily the correct decision. Inadequate information and hurried assessments are often major causes of incorrect decisions. Try to make decisions early enough to create extra time and leave you with alternatives. For example, when you are approaching a parked vehicle where there is a line of slow-moving traffic approaching from the opposite direction, there could be three choices:

1 It is safe to proceed.

2 It is unsafe to go now.

3 We need more information to reassess the situation before a decision can be made.

Any decision – whether it is to proceed, hold back, give way, or stop – must be continually reassessed. Make your assessments in advance and keep all options open. For example, when approaching a green traffic light you should be anticipating the possibility of it changing and be ready with the decision to stop. At some point on the approach, however, you will be too close to pull up safely, and the only safe decision is to continue. When approaching any traffic lights, no matter what colour is showing, you need to continually reassess what to do if they change.

Response and control skills

Communication

Methods of communication between road users are complex, and involve much more than merely using the commonly recognized means of signalling by using:

- indicators;
- brake lights;
- arm signals;
- horn;
- flashing headlights;
- hazard warning flashers.

An effective communication system involves:

- the position of the vehicle on the road;
- the speed of the vehicle;
- implied signals of intent;
- eye contact;
- courtesy signals and acknowledgements.

Signalling by position

In general, the driver who maintains a correct course, speed and position on the road should not need to signal. Although this is not completely valid for all circumstances, there is an element of truth to it, and you can often anticipate an intended act from another vehicle's position.

Taking up the correct position will help to confirm your signals. Where the position does not appear to confirm a signal, other drivers may become confused. For example, a vehicle may be signalling left, but if the car's position is more towards the centre of the road, other drivers may understandably become confused as they are receiving conflicting information.

Signalling by speed

Changes in speed can also be used as an indication of a driver's intended action. For example, in a situation where a vehicle is signalling to turn left, is positioned correctly and is obviously slowing down, there is a combination of evidence to suggest a left turn will be made, and other road users do not have to rely on one single factor.

Other examples of where speed clearly signals another driver's intentions are when a car is approaching a junction far too quickly for it to give way, and when a driver is accelerating rather than slowing down near a zebra crossing. By slowing down well before crossings, you can clearly signal your intentions to the pedestrians waiting to cross as well as letting any other drivers know what you are doing.

Defensive signals

These are the signals you might use to warn other road users of your presence. They include the use of flashing headlights, the horn and hazard warning lights. The use of the horn would normally be considered in relatively slow-moving traffic conditions. Use it when you think another road user might not be aware of your presence, for example when approaching blind summits, sharp bends on narrow roads, or when you see vehicles reversing from driveways. On higher speed roads, such as motorways, because the noise of traffic would drown the sound of the horn, flashing the headlights would be more effective.

Use the hazard warning lights only when stationary or in an emergency, unless you are coming to a stop for a traffic hold-up on a motorway.

Implied signals, eye contact and courtesy

Not only do you need to recognize and interpret the speed and movement of other traffic, but you must also be alert to implied or potential movement, for example the pedestrians standing at the edge of the pavement near a zebra crossing.

A vehicle waiting at a give-way line always has the potential to move into your path. Treat the implications with respect and be ready to slow down.

Eye contact is another valid form of communication. For example, when you are slowing down on the approach, or waiting at a pedestrian crossing, it helps to reassure pedestrians they have been seen; or when you are waiting to pull into a line of slow-moving traffic it may persuade others to hang back and allow you to move out into the traffic stream.

Speed adjustment

The senses used in the judgement of speed are sight, hearing, balance and touch.

The interpretation of speed can be very difficult at times, particularly in a modern car with a sound-insulated interior. In the absence of vibration and noise on a smooth road that has no nearby side features such as buildings, speed can seem deceptively slow.

Speed is usually assessed through a combination of factors that involve an established speed 'norm' learnt from previous experiences. It can be judged from:

- the rate at which visual images disappear to the sides;
- road, wind and engine noise;
- the sense of balance when changing speeds and direction;
- the general 'feel' of the vehicle on the road;
- comparisons with established 'speed norms'.

These speed norms can sometimes be misleading, for example when approaching the intersection at the end of the slip road after leaving a motorway.

Speed adjustments are required to maintain sufficient safety margins so that you can stop well within the distance you can see to be clear and in accordance with the traffic conditions, visibility and regulations. These adjustments must take into account the critical perceptual and attention overload limitations of any driver.

As your speed increases your focus point needs to be farther ahead, while there will be a corresponding reduction in your peripheral vision. Where you need to attend to foreground detail, you must reduce your speed. Peripheral vision will assist in the judgement of your speed and position. If you do not reduce your speed you may well miss important risk factors, and your awareness of lateral position and safety margin will be limited.

To attain maximum awareness you need to apply an active visual scanning process for observing the road and traffic environment in its entirety, including signs, markings and traffic flow. By using this scanning process, and by maintaining proper control of your speed, you should be able to maintain a safe course while at the same time watching for the potential movement of other road users and compensating for them in good time.

You should always be travelling at a speed at which you can stop safely within the distance you can see to be clear. This means also taking into consideration how closely you are being followed. If a driver is far too close for comfort, you will need to take responsibility for his or her safety as well as your own. To do this you should:

- ease off the gas gradually;
- drop back from the vehicle ahead;

- look and plan as far ahead as possible;
- slow down early, braking gently when you see a hazard.

By allowing more space between you and the vehicle ahead, and braking early and gently, you will be creating more time for the following driver to respond.

Position

As well as being in the correct position in relation to the type of road and any change in direction you may be considering, you also need to consider your distance from the vehicle ahead. Positioning properly, safely and with consideration involves:

- your driving position in the road;
- driving in the centre of your lane;
- changing lanes early and gradually;
- allowing sufficient safety cushion between you and the vehicle ahead;
- allowing sufficient safety margins when passing parked vehicles or other obstructions;
- maintaining safety margins that will allow for the unexpected movement of others;
- selecting safe parking positions;
- taking up suitable positions on the approach to junctions so that you can take effective observations;
- positioning correctly when turning so that minimum disruption is caused to the traffic flow.

To position yourself correctly in order to maintain good sightlines and visibility of the road ahead, you need to position out towards the centre of the road when approaching parked vehicles, and be prepared, when giving way to oncoming traffic, to wait well back from the obstruction.

Other considerations when waiting in traffic include not obstructing crossings or access to side roads and entrances, and not stopping so close to the vehicle ahead as to be unable to pull out around it should the need arise.

Gathering information

Failing to take precautionary measures in doubtful situations can often result in the situation becoming critical and making extreme measures necessary. Before making any commitment to act, you need to gather relevant information so that you can deal with any situation safely and effectively.

Driving is not just a series of decisions to stop or go. In many situations you will need to put into effect an information-gathering exercise. For this, you will need to slow down to create time for the situation to develop, and keep your options open before making a definite commitment to keep moving or stop. Take precautionary measures when your vision is restricted or where there may be an unseen hazard, for example over the brow of a hill or around a bend.

Hold-back procedure

There are various ways of holding back from problems, including momentarily easing off the accelerator to maintain a safe gap. Maintaining safety where there are hazards normally means:

- looking and planning well ahead;
- anticipating any changing circumstances and potential hazards;
- maintaining good vehicle control at all times;
- slowing down early enough to hold back from the hazard.

Hold-back procedure involves actively reducing the speed with a view to looking, deciding or waiting, and maintaining safe options in moments of uncertainty to create a safety cushion.

Progress

Whereas the hold-back procedure involves slowing down with a view to looking, waiting and deciding on what action is required, *powered progress* involves proceeding after considering all the available information and deciding it's safe to go. This often includes *creeping and peeping*. Using first-gear clutch control, slowly edge forwards so that you can look round any obstruction, or in all directions at blind junctions, before making any commitment to proceed.

For making powered progress away from hazards, the point at which the decision to go is taken will dictate which gear to select. Remember, *gears are for going – not for slowing!* Select a gear that will be appropriate for the speed and power requirements.

Speed control and steering

The control skills required will depend on the need either to make powered progress or to hold back. *Powered progress* involves holding the car still or moving off under full control on all gradients, then making efficient progress through the gears, taking into account changing conditions and gradients. *Holding back* involves slowing down using either deceleration or controlled rates of braking, depending on gradients, and stopping if the need arises and securing the vehicle. Which procedure is necessary depends on the road and traffic environment.

You need to demonstrate that you have a thorough knowledge of all the different skills involved in proper speed control. You also need to demonstrate that you understand about the safe use of speed in relation to the acceleration, braking and cornering limitations of your vehicle, and the qualities of adhesion between the tyres and road surface. You should be aware of the overall stopping distances in both good and poor driving conditions, and have the ability to apply them.

Pay particular attention to signs and markings so that you are aware of the speed limit for the road you are using. You should be aware of the need to make proper progress according to the road and traffic conditions. Demonstrate that you are a confident driver – if you put on a show of being over-cautious, you may inconvenience other people or put them in danger. Maintain all-round awareness by keeping a check on what is happening all around your vehicle before you make any changes to your speed or direction.

System of car control

An efficient system of car control should take into account the natural and mechanical forces that affect the stability of a vehicle in motion. Your system of driving must take into consideration other road users' actions by having built-in safety margins that should help to compensate for:

- human error;
- deficient skills;
- minor lapses in concentration;
- mistakes by other road users.

Applying an efficient system should ensure that you will always have time to maintain control of your vehicle in a sympathetic manner. Points to remember are:

- The speed of your vehicle should always be such that you can stop in a controlled manner well within the distance you can see to be clear. To do this you need to look for and respond to:
  - obstructions on your intended course;
  - the potential for other road users to move into your intended course from blind areas;
  - restrictions to your sightlines caused by road features such as bends, hill crests or dips in the road;
  - obstructions that may be hidden by restricted sightlines.

- Control and speed should take into account the natural and mechanical forces that affect the stability of vehicles in motion. You should demonstrate an awareness of the:
  - physical road-holding and handling limitations of your car;
  - tyre and road surface adhesion;

- increased stopping distances in wet and icy conditions;
- effects of camber and gravity;
- aerodynamic forces acting on the vehicle.

- To minimize the effects of the forces that affect the stability of vehicles in motion, you should:
  - use the accelerator, brakes and steering smoothly and progressively;
  - avoid excessive acceleration or braking when negotiating bends and corners;
  - avoid changing gear when your hands would be better engaged on the steering wheel, for example when negotiating sharp bends and turns;
  - avoid unnecessary gear changes when selective changing is more appropriate;
  - keep both hands on the wheel when braking, accelerating and cornering;
  - accelerate progressively when negotiating a curved path.

If you are sympathetic to the needs of your vehicle, you will improve fuel efficiency and prolong the vehicle's working life. Try to:

- avoid unnecessary or fidgety movements on the accelerator;
- use the accelerator and footbrake early and progressively;
- avoid excessive clutch slip, drag and unnecessary coasting;
- avoid excessive tyre wear by cornering at lower speeds;
- avoid using the gears to reduce speed;
- use cruise control if it's available.

Handbrake

Use the handbrake:

- when the vehicle is stationary on up- and downhill slopes;
- if you're going to be stationary for more than a few seconds, that is, for longer than the time it would take to apply and then release it again; and, of course,
- when parked.

However, if you plan ahead properly and anticipate any changing circumstances, you should be able to minimize the number of times you need to come to a complete stop. By planning and creeping slowly forwards, you are creating time for the hazard to clear, making the stop either unnecessary or minimal. For such short stops the use of the handbrake is obviously unnecessary.

Brakes and gears

When slowing down, keep both hands on the wheel and (unless you are on an uphill gradient) use the footbrake to reduce speed. After slowing down, change to a gear that is appropriate for negotiating the hazard. For example, when approaching a left turn in, say, fourth or fifth gear, brake to reduce the speed sufficiently and then change into the gear required to negotiate this particular corner. When approaching a T-junction where your view of the main road is restricted, brake to slow down until the car has almost stopped, push down the clutch and release the pressure from the brake to allow the vehicle to roll slowly. Just before stopping, change into first gear, ready to go again. As well as being a waste of fuel, changing down to reduce the speed is unsympathetic and causes unnecessary wear and tear on the clutch, gearbox and transmission.

However, it is sometimes useful to use a lower gear on downhill gradients to offset the effects of gravity. In these circumstances, use the brakes initially to bring the speed under control before selecting the appropriate gear. This provides increased engine braking and reduces the risk of brake failure from overheating due to continuous use on long downhill stretches of road.

Double-declutch

This technique is not generally necessary. Although still recommended in some advanced driving manuals, it can be inappropriate in a modern vehicle with gears protected by synchromesh and increases unnecessary wear on the transmission system. However, when it is required, the procedure should be:

To change up:
Hand to gear lever and cover the clutch.
Clutch down, off the accelerator.
Move the gear lever to neutral.
Clutch up quickly and then down again.
Engage the higher gear.
Raise the clutch and accelerate.
To change down:
Hand on gear lever and cover the clutch.
Clutch down, off the accelerator.
Move the gear lever to neutral.
Clutch up and depress the accelerator quickly, releasing it immediately.
Clutch down quickly and engage the lower gear.
Raise the clutch; continue braking/accelerating.

Factors influencing stopping distances

The overall stopping distance consists of two separate components: the thinking distance and the braking distance. Thinking distances are based on the average person's reaction time of about two-thirds of a second in normal driving conditions. This reaction time is that between recognizing an emergency and the act of beginning to apply the footbrake. In an artificial 'emergency stop' situation this reaction time may be reduced – but only slightly.

The conversion of speed from miles per hour to metres per second shows that, at a speed of 60 mph with a reaction time of two-thirds of a second, the 'thinking distance' will be about 18 metres (or 60 feet). This distance is proportional to the speed. The exact distance may vary slightly from one driver to another and from one situation to another, depending on the driver's fitness, health, reactions and state of mind.

A combination of factors can affect the braking distance, including the:

- size and weight of the vehicle;
- effectiveness of the vehicle's braking system;
- type of tyres, their pressure and depth of tread;
- condition of the road surface.

Whereas thinking distances increase proportionally with speed, braking distances increase much more rapidly at higher speeds. For example, if you increase your speed from 20 to 40 mph it is going to take four times the distance to stop (24 metres instead of 6 metres). At 60 mph, the braking distance is nine times the distance covered at 20 mph.

With good brakes and tyres on a dry road, the car should normally stop in the distances shown in Table 4.1. On wet or slippery roads, these distances will be much greater, and can be up to 10 times the braking distance in extreme conditions.

TABLE 4.1 Stopping distances

Speed			Thinking distance		Braking distance		Overall stopping distance	
Mph	Metres per sec	Feet per sec	Metres	Feet	Metres	Feet	Metres	Feet
20	9	30	6	20	6	20	12	40
30	14	45	9	30	14	45	23	75
40	18	60	12	40	24	80	36	120
50	23	75	15	50	38	125	53	175
60	27	90	18	60	55	180	73	240
70	32	105	21	70	75	245	96	315

The cause and correction of skidding

Although the vehicle and road surface condition may contribute to a skid, the main cause of most skids is without any doubt the driver. There are three different types of skid and these are usually caused by:

1 excessive speed for the road conditions and/or traffic situation;

2 excessive acceleration, braking and/or cornering forces being applied to the tyres;

3 a combination of both.

The rear-wheel skid occurs when the rear wheels lose their grip. It is usually the result of excessive speed and cornering forces. Sometimes it also occurs in combination with harsh acceleration or, more usually, excessive braking. This type of skid is more easily recognized because the rear of the car slides away from the centre of the corner. If uncorrected it could cause the vehicle to turn completely round.

It is essential to eliminate the cause, for example to release the accelerator and/or footbrake and compensate with the steering.

Because, in this type of skid, the driver will see that the vehicle is pointing in the wrong direction, the natural reaction will be to steer back on course. There is a danger however, particularly with the quick response of radial tyres, for drivers to over-steer, causing the vehicle to spin the other way.

The front-wheel skid occurs when the front wheels lose their grip, leaving the driver with no directional control. It usually occurs because of turning sharply into a corner or bend at excessive speed and/or under hard acceleration or braking. It can be recognized when the vehicle fails to go in the direction in which it is being steered.

To correct the skid, the cause must be eliminated and steering control regained by momentarily straightening the wheels and/or reducing pressure on the accelerator or brake.

The four-wheel skid occurs when all four wheels lose their grip. It is usually caused by excessive speed for the road conditions or traffic situation, resulting in uncontrolled over-braking. On a wet or slippery surface the driver may even feel that the speed is increasing. Steering control is lost and the vehicle may turn broadside. The control can be partially restored by momentarily releasing the brake to allow the wheels to start turning again and then quickly reapplying the brake in a rapid on–off action. Many new cars are fitted with an anti-lock braking system that will work in the same way, allowing the driver to regain control much more easily.

More information on skids is contained in the DSA publication *The Official DSA Guide to Driving*. The prevention of skids is better than the cure! It is important to recognize danger signs early and act on them. For example, slowing down early when you see a group of children playing near the road will mean less braking pressure would be needed if one of them dashes out. Concentration, planning and the early anticipation of the possible actions of others is essential.

In snow and ice, slow down early with light braking pressure. Gentle braking is less likely to cause skidding than changing into a lower gear. Use gradual acceleration and keep in the highest gear possible without distressing the engine. When going uphill in snow, try to maintain a steady momentum by staying well back from the vehicle ahead.

Drive at safe speeds for the road surface conditions. Accelerate, brake and corner gently. Drive more slowly on wet, icy and slippery surfaces. Watch out for loose gravel, fallen leaves and damp patches under trees. Make sure your tyres are correctly inflated and that they have a minimum of 2 mm of tread all around. Never mix cross-ply and radial tyres on the same axle. If you must use a mix of tyres, fit the cross-ply to the front and the radials to the rear axle.

Keep off soft verges! Read the surface conditions and slow down well before reaching any bumpy parts and speed humps. Avoid heavy braking on loose gravel and muddy surfaces and when driving through damp patches under trees.

The combination of oil, rubber dust and water can make the surface very slippery after a light summer shower following a long dry spell. In freezing temperatures, remember that black ice forms on exposed bridges first.

Emergency braking

You need to be realistic about the distance it can take to stop, particularly in wet conditions. When you have to brake quickly:

- Pivot promptly from accelerator to brake.
- Apply the brake progressively and firmly.
- Keep both hands on the wheel to keep the vehicle on a straight course.
- Apply maximum braking force just before the wheels lock up.
- Avoid braking so hard that the wheels lock up, as this will considerably lengthen the stopping distance.

If the wheels lock up, particularly in wet, slippery conditions, the brake should be released momentarily and then quickly reapplied – this is called cadence braking and it will allow the tyres to regain their grip. This method of rapid on–off braking is how an anti-lock braking system (ABS) works – and should not be used if the car is fitted with ABS, when pressure on the pedal should be maintained. Cadence braking and ABS give the driver greater braking efficiency and increased directional control should the wheels lock.

Whenever you drive, you need to:

- exercise self-discipline;
- concentrate all the time and read the road well ahead;
- drive at speeds at which you can stop safely within the distance you can see is clear;

- anticipate actual and potential hazards;
- be courteous, patient and considerate;
- apply the controls gradually and smoothly;
- drive in a safe, sympathetic, effective and economic manner.

Your own driving should be an example to your pupils and to the public in general. Your aim should be to teach them to drive confidently and to a similar style. PRACTISE WHAT YOU PREACH! Try to maintain a good, professional standard in your driving at all times.

Trainee licence – 'licence to instruct'

Once you have passed the Part 2 exam you are eligible to apply for a 'Trainee Licence'.

It is not necessary to use the trainee licence scheme if you want to go straight on to obtaining full qualification, but it does offer you the opportunity to gain valuable work experience with genuine pupils while you are preparing for the Part 3 exam.

Application

To obtain a licence you will need to send the appropriate form (ADI 21T) to the DSA together with the fee and a recent passport-style photo. Make sure that you put your ADI reference number on the back of the photo. The form will need to be signed by the person who will be responsible for your training and/or supervision while you are under licence.

The current fee (January 2011) is £140 and in Northern Ireland it is £120.

Qualification

To qualify for a licence you must have taken at least 40 hours of specified training with a qualified ADI – 25 per cent of which must be practical in-car training with a ratio of not more than two trainees to each ADI tutor. All the training must have been received in the six months preceding the application.

Training in all of the following subjects must be received:

- explaining the controls of the vehicle, including use of the dual controls;
- moving off and making normal stops;
- reversing into openings to the left and the right;
- turning the car around using forward and reverse gears;
- parking close to the kerb, using forward and reverse gears;
- using the mirrors and making emergency stops;

- approaching and turning corners;
- judging speed and making normal progress;
- road positioning;
- dealing with junctions and crossroads;
- dealing with pedestrian crossings;
- meeting, crossing the path of, overtaking and allowing adequate clearance for other vehicles and anticipating other road users;
- giving correct signals;
- understanding traffic signs, including road markings and traffic lights;
- method, clarity, adequacy and correctness of instruction;
- the general manner of the driving instructor;
- manner, patience and tact in dealing with pupils;
- ability to inspire confidence in pupils.

Eligibility

In addition to the training requirement you must be eligible to take the Part 3 test and must not have exceeded the two-year qualifying period. If you are unsuccessful in Part 3 on three attempts the licence would be revoked.

Duration

A trainee licence is valid for six months. A second licence can only be issued under exceptional circumstances.

Northern Ireland trainee licence

The rules for a trainee licence are slightly different: two licences, each of six months, are allowed, but the application for the second licence must be made before the expiry of the first one.

Training

Once the licence has been issued there is a further requirement for on-going training or supervision.

You have two options at this stage:

Supervision. Your sponsoring ADI must supervise 20 per cent of all the lessons you give. A record of all lessons given, along with the supervision received, must be kept on form ADI 21S. Both you and your sponsor must sign this form, which must then be returned to the DSA as soon as the licence expires.

Alternatively, a minimum additional 20 hours' training covering all of the above topics must be undertaken. This extra training must take place within the first three months of the issue of the licence or before taking a first attempt at Part 3, whichever is the sooner. (A record of this training must be kept on form ADI 21AT and must be sent to the DSA before the end of the three-month period, or presented to the examiner who conducts the Part 3 test, whichever is the earlier.)

At least 25 per cent of the period of training has to be practically based and in a car at a maximum instructor-to-trainee ratio of no more than two trainees to one ADI.

If the training option is selected and you subsequently fail either the first or second Part 3 test, a further five hours' training must be taken before you are allowed to take another test. A declaration signed by you and your sponsor has to be provided to the examiner on the day of the test. Failure to do this will result in the test being cancelled.

Displaying the Trainee Licence

Whenever a trainee is giving driving lessons under this scheme, the licence must be displayed in the left-hand side of the car's windscreen. If requested by a police officer or any person authorized by the Secretary of State the licence must be produced. Failure to do this is an offence.

In Northern Ireland there is currently no requirement to display a trainee licence, but it is a good idea to do so to show that you are permitted to instruct for reward.

If you hold a Trainee Licence

If you are working under the Trainee Licence Scheme, have signed for the training option, and are attending for your first attempt at the Part 3 exam within the first three months of the licence, you will have to produce your ADI 21T form. Both you and your trainer should sign this form to confirm you have had a minimum of 20 hours' extra training. This is in addition to the 40 hours' training required to obtain the licence.

If you have to take the test for a second or third time, you will need to provide a declaration, signed by you and your trainer, to confirm that a minimum additional five hours' training has been received. If you fail to produce any of the training declarations your test will be cancelled and you will lose the fee.

ADI Part 3: Instructional Ability

05

In Part 3 of the ADI test, your ability to teach pupils at different stages of learning will be assessed. This chapter discusses and explains the different aspects of your instructional techniques that are tested and also includes:

- application for the test;
- the car you use;
- the format of the test;
- structuring lessons at the correct level;
- subjects tested and their key elements;
- the marking system;
- training and practice for the exam.

Your future role as a professional driver trainer will involve teaching the complete range of driving skills to pupils who have varying degrees of ability and aptitude. This involves teaching pupils 'safe driving for life' and not just preparing pupils for the 'L' test.

Application

When you pass the Part 2 Eyesight and Driving Ability Test, the examiner will give you an application form for Part 3. Tests are conducted at the centres listed on this form and can be taken at whichever one you choose. Send your application to the DSA with the current fee (£111 at January 2011) and you will receive written confirmation of your appointment. Take this confirmation letter with you when you attend for the test, along with both parts of your photo-card licence. If you still have the old-style paper licence you will need to take your passport (or some other form of visual identity) as photographic proof of your identity. A trainee licence is also acceptable.

The application for tests in Northern Ireland is currently £138.

The car

You must provide a suitable vehicle for the test. It must:

- Be properly taxed and insured, including any liability of the examiner as a driver. The insurance should cover any DSA examiner, as the DSA cannot guarantee that a specific person will conduct the test.
- Have a valid MOT certificate if required.
- Be a saloon or estate car in proper condition with front and rear seat belts in working order.
- Have manual transmission and be right-hand drive.
- Have a readily adjustable driving seat and a seat for a forward-facing front passenger, both with head restraints.
- Have an internal rear view mirror for use by the examiner.
- Not be fitted with a 'space-saver' tyre.
- Display the statutory 'L' plates (or 'D' plates in Wales, if you prefer).

As a working instructor, you must be continually aware of the all-round situation. You also need to know how your pupil is responding to the situation behind and to the sides of your car. It is therefore essential that you have at least one extra rear view mirror. Many instructors also fit a supplementary mirror so that they can monitor their pupils' mirror work and their response to the situation to the rear.

From time to time members of the DSA staff accompany examiners on tests to ensure uniformity. All seat belts must therefore be in working order. If they are not, the examiner will cancel the test. Similarly, anyone accompanying you on your test must wear a seat belt. If you want your tutor to accompany you, you will need to inform the examiner before leaving the waiting area.

Test format

The test is conducted by a specially qualified DSA senior examiner and lasts for about one hour. You will have to demonstrate, through your practical teaching skills, that you are able to pass on your knowledge to pupils with different levels of ability.

There are two parts to the test. In the first part (Phase 1), the examiner will play the role of a beginner or a learner with limited driving skills. For the second phase, the examiner will play the role of either a learner who is about at driving test standard or a qualified driver undertaking driver development training.

If a qualified driver is to be portrayed, the examiner will describe one of several situations:

- a driver who is preparing for a job interview that will require a driving assessment;
- someone who has not driven in the UK for a few years;
- someone who has not driven regularly for some time, but who now needs to commute between different urban locations;
- the driver who has difficulty with reverse parking because he or she was not taught this manoeuvre during his or her initial training.

The 'qualified driver' role is selected randomly, with the examiner making an amendment to the marking sheet as appropriate.

(Note: In Northern Ireland the 'qualified driver' role is not used.)

Structuring the lesson at the correct level

At the beginning of each phase, the examiner will give you a brief description of the 'pupil' with an outline of the current standard of his or her driving.

The examiner will normally begin the briefing by saying something like this:

This is the start of your test as an instructor. I shall ask you to give me instruction as if I am a pupil. Please regard me as your pupil and instruct me in the same way as you normally would. Don't alter your instruction in any way. It may be necessary for me to interrupt from time to time. If I do, this will be because we need to move on to the next stage or perhaps time is running short.

You must:

- listen very carefully to this information;
- ask the examiner to repeat anything you have not understood;
- prepare to structure your tuition at an appropriate level to suit the pupil described.

You must make every effort to add realism to the lesson. You can do this by:

- trying to treat the examiner as a real pupil;
- getting into your 'instructor role' by asking questions to establish the pupil's knowledge;
- listening very carefully and giving extra useful information.

If the examiner is to portray a full licence holder (rather than a 'partly trained' learner) in the second part of the test, you should use a slightly different approach. Your technique should take into account the previous experience of the 'pupil', and would particularly apply to:

- the person who is a regular driver, but who is now preparing for a job interview that will involve a driving assessment;
- the driver who has a lot of driving experience abroad, but who is now returning to the UK;
- someone who has not driven for some time, but who will now need to drive for work or business purposes.

In these circumstances, avoid being over-fussy about driving habits that may have built up over a period of years, but at the same time do not expect too much from the person who might not have driven since passing the test.

You will need to be reasonably diplomatic but firm if there are any major problems to rectify but, for example, do not be too pedantic about methods of steering. If the pupil has been using a rotational method for a number of years rather than pull/push, your task will be to make sure that his or her steering is safe and under complete control, rather than introducing a new method.

Similarly, you may well find that the person who has been driving for some time will be in the habit of changing up and down through the gears consecutively and using intermediate gears unnecessarily. You might need to be diplomatic but firm in dealing with this problem and changing a long-standing habit; use your coaching skills by emphasizing modern techniques and the changes in vehicle technology.

With this type of pupil, there will be a tendency to overdo the use of signals – frequently signalling when unnecessary and often with a late or inadequate mirror check. Try to guide the pupil (particularly with the use of questions) into being selective by encouraging him or her to make early and appropriate use of mirrors and all-round observations. By doing this, the pupil should begin to develop a feel for when signals should be given, as well as the importance of correct timing.

Examination topics

The list of topics tested in this part of the exam covers some of the subjects included in the DSA's officially recommended syllabus for learners. You will find full details in *The Official Guide to Learning to Drive*. Your tutor should show you how to teach all of the subjects in the syllabus, as well as teaching you how to:

- structure lessons;
- check pupils' knowledge;
- assess the needs of pupils with differing abilities;

- plan routes suitable for the level of the learner and the subject under instruction;
- teach hazard perception and anticipation.

You will find information on all of these topics in Chapter 9 of this book, and guidance on how to put them into practice in *Practical Teaching Skills for Driving Instructors*.

The examiner will select one topic from each of the following lists.

Subjects specified in Phase 1

- Safety precautions on entering the car and explanation of the controls.
- Moving off and stopping.
- Turn-in-the-road exercise.
- Reversing (to the right or left).
- Emergency stop and use of mirrors.
- Dealing with pedestrian crossings and giving signals by indicators/arm as appropriate.
- Approaching junctions to turn either right or left.
- Dealing with emerging at road junctions.
- Dealing with crossroads.
- Meeting, overtaking and crossing other traffic, allowing adequate clearance for other road users and anticipation.

Subjects specified in Phase 2

- Dealing with crossroads.
- Meeting, overtaking and crossing other traffic, allowing adequate clearance for other road users and anticipation.
- Approaching junctions to turn either right or left.
- Dealing with emerging at road junctions.
- Dealing with pedestrian crossings and giving signals by indicators/arm as appropriate.
- Making progress and general road positioning.
- Reverse parking.

Where a particular exercise includes two or more subjects the examiner will, in the initial briefing, nominate which topics you are to cover. Listen carefully, taking brief notes if you wish, to make sure that you cover the important items and avoid wasting time on irrelevant ones.

Dealing with the key elements

Each subject consists of a number of key elements. On a normal lesson, you may feel that you can cover all of these elements of the subject, but on the ADI exam you will probably only have time to cover some of them during your explanation. To a certain extent the content of your lesson will depend on the briefing from the examiner. However, once on the move, you must ensure that all of the correct procedures and routines are put into practice.

Lesson format

Please note that, throughout this chapter, the word 'pupil' is used to describe either your 'real life' pupil or the examiner playing that role for the test. On the test, once the examiner has described the 'pupil' and that role is assumed, try to treat the examiner as a 'real life' pupil. Remember that a different pupil will be portrayed for each phase, and you will have to adapt your instruction to suit each one.

Try to tailor each 'lesson' to suit the time available and the standard of the pupil described. How much instruction you give while stationary will be governed by the pupil's prior knowledge; and remember that this is a test of your practical teaching ability. Do not 'waffle' – try to focus on the key elements of the subject and ensure that learning then takes place through practice.

During your introduction to the lesson you may refer to brief notes or subject headings if you need to. However, you need to look professional. You will not be able to achieve this if you quote lengthy paragraphs from books. Use training aids where appropriate, particularly if the pupil is unfamiliar with the subject or if you feel that an illustration would be helpful to explain something a little more complex.

Keep the pupil involved by asking the occasional question. This could be to confirm a *Highway Code* rule or a principle outlined in *The Official DSA Guide to Driving – The essential skills,* for example. Make sure that you do not confuse the pupil with complicated questions that are not appropriate to the skill level being portrayed. Remember, you're supposed to be building up your pupil's confidence, not destroying it!

Structure of the test

Phase 1 – key elements

- Establish the base line for the lesson by asking a couple of questions and correcting any misunderstandings.
- Explain the routines and procedures to be learnt.
- Offer a demonstration if it's appropriate.

- Give talk-through instruction until the pupil's skills begin to develop.
- Gradually reduce the amount of instruction and use questions to prompt and to develop independence.
- Do not restrict yourself to the nominated topic, but also react to what is happening around you. When opportunities arise to teach awareness and anticipation, take advantage of them.
- Identify and analyse faults when they arise and give advice on how to improve.
- Give the pupil plenty of encouragement and feedback, quoting *The Highway Code* or other driving principles outlined in *The Official DSA Guide to Driving – The essential skills*.

The examiner will assess your ability to teach a new subject to the pupil, or to reinforce and practise a subject where the pupil has some prior knowledge.

Establishing the base line for the lesson

Setting the base line will often include confirmation of why the topic is necessary in order to build up the skills required to become a 'safe driver for life' and not just to prepare for the 'L' test. Each lesson has to have a start point. To set this base line you will need to listen carefully to the examiner's description of the pupil and what previous experience he or she has. You can do this by asking a few questions relevant to the subject. Asking questions at this point will help you establish whether the pupil is studying for the Theory Test. Depending on the responses, you may have to either go through all the key elements, or reinforce anything the pupil omitted or appears to have misunderstood.

Visual aids

If the pupil appears to be having difficulty in understanding, you should use training aids. Not only do these help pupils to visualize what you mean, but they can also serve as memory joggers for you.

Demonstrations

These may be offered where appropriate: for example if, when you're explaining a difficult principle or manoeuvre to your pupil, there appears to be some confusion or misunderstanding. In the test situation, time is limited and the examiner would normally decline the offer of a demonstration. If, however, your offer of one is accepted it must be accurate. You might even consider combining a 'talk-through' explanation with the demonstration.

There are times when you may need to carry out part of a manoeuvre or procedure, and other times when you should execute the exercise in slow motion. You may also need to replicate the way the pupil is carrying out the procedure and compare this with the correct routine.

Learning through practice

If the subject is relatively new to the pupil, you should be prepared to give full 'talk-through' instruction to build up the pupil's confidence. In the early stages of learning, the pupil will need plenty of help. You have to be prepared, therefore, to repeat procedures and to give as much assistance as is necessary.

Remember that your instruction should not be restricted to the lesson topic. Mention any unusual situations that arise during the drive. For example, if you are dealing with junctions, do not ignore the possibility of meeting oncoming traffic where there are vehicles parked on the road.

Question and answer (Q&A) on the move

Avoid over-instruction and be ready to reduce the amount of instruction when you can see the pupil's skills beginning to develop. Asking a few simple questions at an early stage can encourage a pupil to take a little responsibility for carrying out routine procedures. For example, to encourage effective safety checks before moving off, you could ask, 'Is there anyone to your right?' or, 'Is there anyone in your blind area?' When using Q&A on the move, try to ensure that the pupil does not have to respond with a lengthy answer.

Positive correction

When correcting pupils it is far more effective to make a positive comment. For example if the car is being driven too far from the kerb, you could advise 'Try to drive about a metre from the kerb' rather than 'You're driving too far out.' If while waiting to emerge from a junction, the pupil only looks in one direction, you could encourage better observations by asking, 'Can you see clearly both ways?' or giving a direct instruction to 'Keep looking both ways until you know it's safe to go.'

Maintaining control and safety

As an instructor, you are responsible for the all-round safety of your pupil, other road users and, of course, yourself. Do not allow potentially dangerous situations to arise. You must maintain control of the lesson. For example, if you feel your pupil is going to emerge from a junction and you know that he or she has not looked effectively, or can't see far enough because of restricted sightlines, a positive instruction to 'wait' may be all that is required.

Retrospective correction

Giving a reprimand after allowing a pupil to emerge unsafely could be too late! It will be no consolation after a 'near miss' situation to confirm that 'You shouldn't have pulled out without looking properly.' Learning is more likely to take place if the pupil deals with the situation correctly in the first place. In this example, it would be more effective to ask your pupil, 'Can you see if there's anyone approaching?' However, sometimes things happen quickly before you have time to act. In these cases, you may have to give corrective advice after the event.

Developing the pupil's understanding

Whenever an error is committed and you are giving corrective advice, you must give a valid reason by finishing with the 'because' element. This does not mean saying, 'Because I say so' or, 'If you don't, you'll fail your test'! You should base your reasoning on the correct application of the rules, regulations and procedures for driving safely and considerately – in other words, in order to survive. You could also quote the official publications to add authority.

Giving feedback and encouragement

This is an important aspect of your job as an instructor. No matter what the standard and ability of your pupils let them know what progress they have made during the lesson. Give an indication of where they might need improvement and more practice. Encourage pupils to ask for more information if they don't understand something you've been working on. Confirm that you will record any items necessary for pupils to revise before the next lesson. Encourage them to study for the Theory Test or to revise rules and procedures for topics that you will be covering on the next training session.

Remember to finish on a 'high'. Give praise for those areas where improvement took place.

Phase 2 – key elements

During this part of the exam, the examiner will be checking on your ability to:

- assess what the pupil already knows and can do;
- identify and analyse errors or weaknesses;
- give remedial instruction to achieve improvement.

Establish any underlying problems

Listen very carefully to the examiner's description of the pupil and of previous driving experience. Ask a couple of questions to confirm that the pupil has understood the key elements of the topic. This will also help you to pitch the lesson at the correct level. Again, listen carefully to the answers as they may give an indication of any underlying problems or misunderstandings. If so, confirm the correct routines and procedures.

Assessing ability through practice

You should aim at getting the car moving as soon as possible. Your first priority, with pupils at this level, is to assess their strengths and weaknesses, and then to give the necessary advice to improve understanding and skills.

Over-instruction

Unlike the Phase 1 lesson, which is all about your teaching ability, the second phase of the exam is where your assessment skills are tested. Treat your pupil as a driver and avoid the temptation to carry on where you left off with the first pupil by giving too much instruction and assistance. Allow your pupil to demonstrate the ability to make decisions and to put the correct procedures into practice. If any patterns of error occur, you can then intervene and start working on correcting the faults.

Identifying faults

Never assume that your pupil will carry out all the correct routines and procedures.

Part of your job is to identify, analyse and correct faults. You need to be able to identify those faults that could lead to problems, whether or not they relate directly to the topic under instruction. You then need to give some corrective advice and create opportunities to practise the correct routines.

When identifying or analysing 'faults', make sure you differentiate between a mistake and a fault. The pupil might be fully aware of an individual mistake, whereas a fault can have various causes. Always look for the cause, rather than the effect. For example, if the pupil cuts a right-hand corner, was it because of errors of speed, control or observation? This can then be analysed at another level: was the pupil rushing to avoid oncoming or following traffic? Was the lack of control due to problems of steering or braking? Was the poor observation caused by not looking early enough or by concentrating too much on the following traffic? Was it due to a lack of understanding?

This list of mistakes, errors, faults and causes can be extended and applied to most driving situations.

Dealing with faults on the move

Although you will have been given a specific subject to deal with, you may find that unrelated driving faults are introduced. You should try to deal with them, but without 'nit-picking'. Where minor mistakes occur on a one-off basis, they may not even be worth a mention, but if similar errors keep recurring, or if you are unsure, then query them. You may be able to deal with these minor errors on the move by asking a simple question or making a positive comment. For example, if your pupil forgets a couple of checks of the nearside door mirror prior to turning, you could ask, 'Where should you be checking before you turn left?'

Dealing with more serious faults

You will need to deal with serious errors in more detail – for example, if your pupil turns right across closely approaching traffic before you have time to prevent it. This is a potentially dangerous error and the pupil will need some corrective advice. To discuss the problem safely, and to avoid distracting the pupil's attention from the driving task, you should confirm that you would discuss the point as soon as you can find somewhere safe to stop. Whatever the error, remember to finish with a positive explanation.

Recognizing faults

Watch what the pupil is doing all of the time, as he or she will make mistakes and errors can crop up unexpectedly at any time, for instance:

- doors – not properly closed;
- seat – not adjusted properly;
- seat belt – forgotten or twisted;
- mirrors – not adjusted properly, not checked regularly, incorrect response to what is happening;
- safety checks – handbrake and neutral checks omitted before switching on;
- observations – no shoulder checks prior to moving away;
- control – jerky use of clutch – could be caused by lapse between lessons, practice in a different car or incorrect seat adjustment;
- signals – unnecessary, badly timed, not cancelled or reapplied, or incorrect;
- observations – ineffective looks in all directions at junctions;
- positioning – normal driving, driving in lanes.

Try to make learning a positive experience by watching for these errors and correcting them by asking:

- Are all the doors closed properly?
- Can you reach and operate the controls comfortably?
- What do you need to put on before you drive?
- Can you see to the rear and sides?
- Do you need to check anything before you turn the key?
- What should you be looking for before moving away?
- The clutch may feel strange at first; take your time until you get used to it.
- Who were you signalling to? What does *The Highway Code* say about flashing headlights?
- Where should you be looking before you emerge?
- What is the normal driving position?

Assessment of instructional ability

During the test you will be assessed on each of the following:

1 Core competencies:
   (a) Identification of faults
   (b) Fault analysis
   (c) Remedial action.
2 Instructional techniques:
   (a) Level of instruction
   (b) Planning
   (c) Control of the lesson
   (d) Communication
   (e) Question and answer techniques
   (f) Feedback/encouragement
   (g) Instructor's use of controls.
3 Instructor characteristics:
   (a) Attitude
   (b) Approach to pupil.

1. Core competencies

1 (a) Identification of faults

Having passed Part 2 of the ADI exam you have shown that your own driving is of a very good standard. Your job as an instructor is to prepare your pupils to share the road with you. You should therefore be teaching them to drive to a similar style. Although they will not necessarily achieve the same standard until they have had more experience, they will be learning to apply a sound system of car control that will result in safe driving for life.

When assessing your new drivers you should therefore base your judgement on what you would be doing in similar circumstances. Where anything deviates from your driving norm you need to ask yourself, 'What would I be doing here?' Based on this concept you need to:

● recognize all faults that you consider need correcting;
● identify, and bring to the pupil's attention, any faults that are serious or that are repeated;
● categorize the errors as minor, repeated, serious or dangerous.

You have to identify faults that require correction as part of an effective teaching/learning process. Having identified a fault, ask yourself whether it is a 'one-off' minor error and not really worth mentioning or whether it could lead to future problems and needs to be addressed.

When you have ascertained that a fault is worthy of a mention, you now have to decide when and how to deal with it. With a minor error, it may be appropriate to draw the pupil's attention to it at the time. If the error is of a more serious nature, you may have to delay your explanation until a more appropriate and safer time.

1 (b) Fault analysis

When you have identified an error, analyse the cause of it as accurately as possible. Key elements in the fault analysis process are:

- Accurately analyse faults you have identified.
- The analysis must be complete.
- Follow the analysis with a remedy.

For example, if your pupil swings out to the right after turning left, you need to confirm what caused the problem. Was it because:

- the speed was too high on the approach?
- positioning was incorrect on the approach?
- late gear selection affected the steering?
- the steering technique was inefficient or ineffective?
- the pupil failed to look well down into the new road?
- or a combination of some of these?

1 (c) Remedial action

- You need to be able to offer solutions for all of the identified problems.
- Your corrective advice must be effective; remember to explain the 'why'.
- You must create opportunities to practise the correct procedures to help eradicate the problems and improve the pupil's knowledge, skill and understanding.

When you have identified and analysed an error, give some constructive advice on how to remedy it. Using a visual aid if appropriate, explain to the pupil what he or she should have done. Finish your explanation with an appropriate reason for the action by explaining what might have happened.

With some more complex faults, a demonstration might be appropriate if you have time. Finally, you should create opportunities for the pupil to practice the correct procedure.

(Chapter 4 of *Practical Teaching Skills for Driving Instructors* gives more information on fault identification and analysis.)

2. Instructional techniques

2 (a) Level of instruction

To be an effective instructor, you need to be able to match your instruction to the level of ability of each individual pupil, and then adapt it to suit the driving skills demonstrated. You therefore have to follow these rules during each phase of the ADI test by not under- or over-instructing.

There should be a complete match of your instruction to the stated level of experience, knowledge and needs of the pupil. This helps you set appropriate tasks that are not too difficult for the inexperienced driver and not too easy for the more experienced pupil. Having matched the level of your teaching to the stated experience and ability of the pupil, you must ensure that your instruction remains consistent. This is necessary to avoid confusing the pupil. If the pupil does appear to become confused, then you will need to make further adjustments to the level of your instruction to ensure that some learning or improvement takes place.

As each lesson progresses, make any adjustments so that your instruction matches the pupil's apparent strengths, weaknesses and perceived improvement.

(More information on levels of instruction can be found in Chapter 4 of *Practical Teaching Skills for Driving Instructors*.)

2 (b) Planning

This part of the exam covers how you plan the lesson according to the pupil's needs and in relation to what actually happens. It relates to the sequence of your instruction and the amount of practical activity. The examiner assesses your teaching methods on whether they are appropriate and effective. While assessing your teaching ability, the examiner will also take into consideration the complexity of the lesson topic.

Plan your instruction methodically and deliver it in a clear and logical manner. To do this, work on what the pupil already knows, then lead into the new elements. In other words, you are moving from the 'known' to the 'unknown'.

Key elements involved with lesson planning are:

- Each 'lesson' must be well planned and properly structured.
- Deal with each subject in a logical and methodical way.
- Allocate the time between theory and practice sensibly.
- Your presentation of the subject should be well organized.
- You must demonstrate that you understand the level of complexity of the subject.
- Take all opportunities that arise during each lesson to develop your pupil's skills through practical experience.
- Create opportunities to revisit situations to confirm skill and understanding.

(More information on lesson planning can be found in Chapter 4 of *Practical Teaching Skills for Driving Instructors*.)

2 (c) Control of the lesson

Maintaining safety while at the same time building up pupils' confidence requires good interaction with pupils and the ability to remain in full control in all situations. Under this heading you will be assessed on:

- How you allocate the available time between theory and practice.
- Whether you are capable of changing the plan according to how the pupil responds.
- Your reaction to critical situations.
- Your response to the needs of other road users.

You will need to demonstrate an ability to anticipate what the pupil may do, taking appropriate action on any potential errors or danger in order to maintain a firm degree of control over the pupil.

To maintain safety, and to ensure that positive learning takes place, you need to constantly check on your pupil's reactions to each set of circumstances. To do this, you must:

- allocate a proper balance between theory and practice, to ensure that learning is reinforced;
- be alert and show awareness and perception to changes in the all-round situation;
- judge the pupil's ability to identify and react to the different situations and changing circumstances;
- watch the pupil's actions, observations and reactions at critical times, such as at junctions and other hazards;
- be ready to take control when necessary.

(More information on maintaining control can be found in Chapter 4 of *Practical Teaching Skills for Driving Instructors*.)

2 (d) Communication

It is important that your pupils readily understand your instructions. Under this heading, the examiner assesses your ability to adapt and to use language and terminology that suits each pupil.

Do not restrict yourself to 'technical' or 'authoritative' jargon simply because you have read it in books. You should adopt an easy, descriptive and concise style of instruction and communication that suits your personality.

When you are giving any verbal information, make sure it is fluent and that you avoid repeating yourself. You should be able to adapt and adjust your vocabulary so that the less able can clearly understand you, and the more articulate ones do not feel patronized.

Give your directions clearly and in good time. Use simple and straightforward instructions so that there is no chance of any misunderstanding. Be ready to give more information if, for instance, a junction does not conform to normal rules.

Key elements involved in the communication process include:

- the presentation of new information in an easy-to-understand manner;
- explaining routines and procedures in a logical sequence;

- explaining the meaning of any jargon you use;
- using straightforward terminology;
- the avoidance of repetition;
- adjusting your method of communication to suit the level of understanding of each pupil.

(More information on communication skills can be found in Chapter 4 of *Practical Teaching Skills for Driving Instructors*.)

2 (e) Question and answer (Q&A) technique

Your pupils will eventually be sharing the roads with all of us! Your job as a professional driver trainer will be to teach all your pupils to cope safely and effectively with today's road and traffic conditions. To do this you will have to help pupils to develop a proper understanding of the need to drive defensively and to maintain a safe attitude towards themselves, their vehicle and all other road users. To assist in the development of this level of understanding, you will need to incorporate an effective Q&A technique into your driving instruction.

Depending on the type of pupil you are teaching and the circumstances you are in, you will need to decide on when Q&A is appropriate. Your early-stage pupils should be made to feel comfortable about the Q&A process, so do not bombard them with complicated questions to which they are not likely to know the answers. Ask a simple one when you feel it will help to improve their skills or promote a better understanding of a routine or driving rule. As pupils' skills progress, use questions that are more searching. This should help you establish whether the correct procedures and a safe attitude are understood.

There are times when you will not need to ask any questions at all: for example, when your pupil is driving well and dealing safely with everything that is happening. There are also circumstances when you should not distract a pupil's attention from the driving task: for example, when you are in a busy traffic situation that requires the pupil's full concentration.

Questions that require a simple 'Yes' or 'No' response will not tell you what the pupil thinks or understands. For example, if you ask a pupil, 'Should you look round before moving off?' the answer 'Yes' does not confirm that the pupil understands what he or she is looking for. To be effective you should use more searching questions based on 'what', 'when', 'where', 'why' and 'how'.

The 'why' can be an important type of question. Be careful though in using 'why'. Understandably, some pupils might feel threatened if you ask 'Why did you do that?' As in the example given above, you are looking for feedback on whether or not the pupil understands the reason for a particular action or shows a safe attitude for the particular circumstances. You would therefore get better feedback if you ask, 'Where should you look before moving off, and what are you looking for?'

After asking a question, you can usually tell from body language whether the pupil has fully understood. If you feel that the pupil is unsure try asking the question in a different way or by using a supplementary question.

You can use questions to:

- recap on a previous lesson or topic;
- prompt;
- establish knowledge and understanding;
- encourage pupil participation.

Questions used should:

- be relevant to the pupil's ability and the circumstances;
- be asked at the correct time;
- be worded in such a way as to be thought-provoking;
- not distract the pupil at a crucial moment.

Q&A works both ways.

From the beginning of a course of training and at the start of a lesson, encourage your pupils to ask questions, and allow time for them. Try not to allow irrelevant questions to distract from the topic under instruction. If pupils ask questions that do not relate to the lesson, you can tactfully delay any discussion by confirming that you will be dealing with that particular topic later.

Key elements involved in the successful application of Q&A include:

- Use Q&A only when it will be of obvious benefit to the pupil.
- Use questions that are set at a suitable level for the needs of each pupil.
- Phrase your questions simply so as not to cause confusion.
- Use Q&A only when it is the most appropriate method for dealing with a problem.
- Only use it when there is sufficient time for the pupil to respond.
- Make sure it is not too late for a question to be relevant.
- Do not ask questions when the pupil needs to concentrate on driving.
- Encourage the pupil to ask you questions.
- Do not ignore pupils' questions.
- Answer questions accurately but concisely.
- If your pupil appears to have become demoralized by your over-use of Q&A, or cannot respond correctly, then drop it for a while.
- Ask questions that will encourage pupils to think about their skills and progress and, depending on the responses, adjust the level of your instruction accordingly.

To be able to answer your pupils' questions correctly, you need to keep yourself continually up to date with the official publications.

2 (f) Feedback/encouragement

We all respond to positive feedback and praise! When your pupils achieve success, you need to let them know by giving encouragement and positive feedback. You should be able to:

- give feedback to clearly indicate each pupil's level of achievement at any given point during a lesson;
- respond with the appropriate advice and guidance when you recognize from your pupil's body language that he or she is unsure or uncertain;
- confirm when a pupil has done well by using verbal confirmation, positive eye contact or body language;
- make use of all opportunities to give praise and encouragement where appropriate to develop the pupil's confidence;
- encourage pupils to ask questions so that you can give accurate feedback.

Key elements in giving and gaining feedback include:

- Ensure that your feedback is not ambiguous or confusing.
- Act positively on the feedback you get from the pupil.
- Acknowledge and give praise for good performance.
- Demonstrate your skills as a teacher by prompting questions from your pupil.
- Answer all questions, giving correct and complete information.
- Respond to your pupils' uncertainties by providing positive confirmation on their achievements, confirming which aims and objectives they have achieved.
- Confirm how progress will lead into the next subject to be covered.

2 (g) Your use of controls

As an instructor, an important part of your job is to maintain safety in all situations. This does not just mean being able to use dual controls. During the test the examiner will be assessing how you use any control necessary to maintain safety for you and your pupil and to avoid inconvenience to other road users. You will be assessed on how you:

- use the dual clutch and brake;
- protect the gear lever at appropriate times;
- assist with the handbrake;
- correct steering problems;
- help with, or explain about, the use of other controls such as indicators, lights, horn, demister, visor.

If you have to use the dual controls or any ancillary controls in the car, make sure your pupil knows the reason you did so. For example, after operating the indicators for the pupil when leaving a roundabout, tell the pupil, 'I put the signal on for you there so that the drivers wanting to enter the roundabout won't be waiting unnecessarily for you.'

If condensation develops, show your pupil how the demisters work and explain about the importance of maintaining good all-round vision. Similarly, respond if you can see that your pupil is becoming too warm by explaining about the fan or air conditioning. If pupils are squinting because of bright sunlight, help by lowering the visor – before they remove both hands from the wheel to do it themselves!

It can sometimes be helpful to use the dual controls as a positive supplement to your instruction, for example when giving a demonstration of clutch control during a manoeuvre. Remember however, dual controls arc mainly to prevent damage or danger. If your pupil is not responding to a developing hazard, give a verbal prompt. If this does not work, then give a definite instruction, avoiding the use of the dual controls until it becomes a necessity – that is, when the pupil has not taken the appropriate action.

The usual sequence of actions following this pattern would be:

Do you think you can get through that space safely? (The prompting question.)

Check your mirrors, slow down and give way to that oncoming car! (The instruction to take some action.)

Wait! (The firm request.)

Take some action by either using the dual controls to stop the car or by helping the pupil steer through the space. (The final action that is necessary to maintain safety.)

Following your use of the dual footbrake, you must confirm why you took action. You could explain, 'I had to stop you there because it was the other driver's priority and there wasn't room for us both to get through.'

There may be times when you need to use the dual controls to prevent a stall in heavy traffic, or to stop the car from moving off at an inappropriate time. Keep these to a minimum, as you should always try to prompt the correct action from your pupil. When any form of control has been used, you must explain when and why it was used.

Key elements involved in using the controls include:

- Use them only in a positive manner to:
  - prevent danger or damage;
  - encourage understanding through demonstration;
  - assist with in-car vision and comfort;
  - help other road users.
- Use them only when other methods of prompting a pupil's response to potential hazards have failed.
- Explain why it was necessary for you to take action.
- Avoid using the dual controls as a punitive measure.

3. Instructor characteristics

3 (a) Attitude

The skills needed by instructors to create a relaxed but supportive and learning environment are extremely important. It is vital that you show a positive attitude towards your job, your pupil, and other road users as well as towards road safety in general. The more positive you are in demonstrating a safe and considerate attitude, the more likely your pupils will be to develop these attributes.

3 (b) Approach to pupil

You will need to be able to establish a good rapport with all of your pupils, striking a balance between being friendly, fair and firm so that you create the right learning atmosphere for each individual. At the same time, you will need to show a professionalism that will gain respect and that will encourage the pupil to work with you. You should endeavour to:

- put pupils at ease;
- instil confidence;
- establish an atmosphere that is conducive to a good instructor/pupil relationship and positive learning.

Key elements in the characteristics of a good instructor are:

- Try to be natural, using an approach that suits your personal characteristics.
- Combine friendliness with professionalism.
- Be approachable without being patronizing, so that the pupil remains at ease.
- Show that you are:
  - responsible and considerate;
  - keen for your pupils to learn;
  - interested in your work and also road safety.

(More information on instructor characteristics can be found in *Practical Teaching Skills for Driving Instructors*.)

Preparation

While studying for the ADI theory test you will have gathered a good deal of the background knowledge you will need for teaching new drivers. Similarly, while training you for the ADI driving test, your tutor will be demonstrating the teaching skills that you will have to learn to put into practice as an instructor. A good tutor should teach you how to:

- establish prior knowledge by using Q&A techniques;
- break down subjects into their key elements;
- adopt the teaching principle of explanation–demonstration–practice;
- use Q&A techniques to maximize understanding and obtain feedback during practical sessions;
- give full talk-through instruction;
- give more responsibility to learners by decreasing the level of instruction at the appropriate time;
- improve learners' awareness and understanding by encouraging commentary driving;
- supervise and assess more experienced learners;
- use visual aids to assist learners' understanding;
- identify, analyse and correct errors made by drivers of differing abilities;
- avoid problems on the road by early verbal intervention;
- explain about the use of the dual and ancillary controls.

Training and practice

Although practice with real learners can be beneficial in the later stages of your training, it is not sensible to try it too soon. Therefore, whether you are practising with friends or relatives, or are gaining experience under the Trainee Licence Scheme, it is essential that you get plenty of properly structured training from your tutor before you practise with learners.

To teach you the main elements outlined previously and to give you a feel of the job under controlled conditions, a good trainer will realistically portray drivers with differing abilities and learning aptitudes. Your tutor should be covering:

- setting the base line for lessons by establishing prior knowledge;
- planning the instruction to suit the level of ability of each pupil;
- organizing routes so that pupils can cope;
- how to avoid inconveniencing other road users;
- maintaining safety for your pupils, yourself and others;
- how to transfer responsibility as skill levels increase;
- the avoidance of danger and damage;
- how to give positive feedback and advice;
- how to link forward to the next lesson.

Pass rates

Remember, this is an intense test of your ability to instruct covering a wide range of topics with pupils at different levels of learning and driving ability. As a result, the pass rate is currently running at about 30 per cent. It pays, therefore, to make sure you have a realistic amount of quality training with a qualified and experienced tutor.

Useful tips for the Part 3 examination (from the DSA)

1   During your training make sure that you have plenty of practical experience at giving instruction to pupils at varying levels of ability.

2   Listen carefully to the examiner's description of what you will be asked to instruct on and to the description of the 'pupil' that the examiner intends to portray.

3   In general terms, a beginner or partly trained 'pupil' will need positive instruction and guidance, whereas a trained 'pupil' will benefit much more from thought-provoking questions.

4   The test consists of two separate half-hour phases. Your briefings should be appropriate to the 'pupil's' knowledge and must be geared to the available time.

5   Remember that you are in charge of the lesson; check to see how the 'pupil' is responding and adjust your instruction to meet the needs of the 'pupil'.

6   It is important that you respond to the 'pupil's' performance. You will be expected to correct other driving faults in addition to those included in the specific exercises.

7   It is not always necessary to stop to deal with some driving faults. Some faults can be corrected more effectively on the move.

8   Pupils will benefit from praise and encouragement where appropriate.

9   There are no tricks or traps in the exam. The examiner's job is to test your instructional ability. Listen carefully to questions and comments from the 'pupil'.

10 The test of instructional ability is recognized as the most difficult of the three parts of the ADI qualifying process. It is important that you do not attempt this part of the examination until you are confident that you can give instruction on all of the preset tests to a satisfactory standard.

The test

The Part 3 exam is not a test of your knowledge – that is assessed in the theory test. Neither is it a test of your driving skills – those are assessed in the Part 2. It is purely a test of your ability to give practical driving instruction. You need to be able to demonstrate that you can pass on your knowledge and skills in a way that results in your pupils understanding and acquiring good driving practices.

In the test the examiner plays the role of a beginner or partly trained pupil in phase 1, and that of a learner at about driving test standard or a full licence holder in phase 2.

The examiner will describe the type of pupil to be portrayed and will nominate the particular subject or topic to be covered at the start of each phase. This is done by the examiner giving a briefing such as:

> I would like you to regard me as a pupil who has had six or seven lessons with another instructor using a car that is similar to this one and he indicated that today we would be dealing with turning in the road (or some other topic). Also, please correct any faults in my general driving.

Note that there is a requirement to correct any general driving faults as well as teaching the particular topic that is nominated. For detailed examples of briefings for each driving topic, see 'The Preset Tests' on pages 117–61.

You will be asked if you wish anything to be clarified, and once this has been done, the role of the pupil will be taken on.

During the test you should demonstrate your ability to:

- Explain clearly the key elements of the topic.
- Give the necessary help and talk-through instruction to develop and improve the pupil's skill.
- Use Q&A to help the pupil understand why certain rules and procedures must be followed. For example, to encourage effective observations at junctions, you could ask the following questions:
  - 'Keep looking each way – can you see in each direction?'
  - 'How far can you see?'
  - 'Is it clear all around?'
- Develop the pupil's confidence by transferring responsibility when skills improve.
- Identify, analyse and correct errors by explaining how you would have dealt with situations.
- Create opportunities to practise the correct procedures.
- Give feedback and encouragement when improvement takes place.

Because of the time constraints of this test, you may not be able to cover every essential detail of the topics that you would cover in a normal lesson. However, you must ensure that all the key elements are included, whether this is during the explanation at the beginning of each 'lesson' or while the pupil is driving.

Fault assessment

An important part of your job is fault identification and assessment. Although you do not need to pick on every minor error, you should deal with any mistakes that could develop into bad habits and, of course, any that are potentially serious or could result in danger. The easiest way to recognize and deal with faults is to ask yourself, 'Would I be doing this if I were driving?' You can then transfer your thoughts by asking the pupil for a reason and explanation as to why he or she did it. The response will dictate how you need to deal with the problem.

During the Part 3 test, any major faults will normally be associated with the lesson topic. However, the examiner, in the role of the pupil, may introduce other faults and you should deal with them effectively. When you recognize that something has deviated from a normal driving pattern, you should:

- query the fault;
- ask the pupil if he or she understands the correct procedure for dealing with such a situation;
- explain how you would have dealt with it;
- give the reason;
- practise the correct procedure to reinforce the point.

Subjects tested

Your tutor should give you guidance on how to teach the officially recommended syllabus as outlined in the DSA book *The Official Guide to Learning to Drive*. The instructional test does not encompass all these subjects, but you will need to be able to teach them to your pupils. For this reason, the next section includes guidance on how to deal with the more complex subjects of dual carriageways and roundabouts.

Key learning points

The topics for instruction are itemized along with a list of their key learning points. It is important that you cover these key elements, in either the explanation or the practical part of the lesson. There are 10 preset tests, and the DSA's marking sheets for these are shown on pages 164–172. You will also find more information on them in Chapter 7 of *Practical Teaching Skills for Driving Instructors*.

The subjects are dealt with in a logical (staged) sequence, rather than listed in the preset test numerical sequence. The test topics are mixed so that your teaching and coaching skills can be tested during Phase 1 and your assessment and correction skills can be tested during Phase 2.

Learning to teach

Teaching driving can involve a complex set of tasks. It is not always possible to work through each topic individually in a set sequence – there will often be an overlap. To help with your training, the subjects are covered in the next section in a logical sequence, as if you were working through the syllabus with a genuine learner. You will need to adapt your instruction and terminology for each pupil to suit the varying road and traffic situations. You cannot hope to teach different subjects to people of varying abilities by learning set scripts.

You should refer to the books *The Official DSA Guide to Driving – The essential skills* and *The Official Guide to Learning to Drive* for more information on the subjects covered in the official syllabus for learners. Use this syllabus to help formulate some lesson plans. If you do this, it will help to reinforce the key elements in your memory.

The DSA officially recommend the following books to help you in your preparations for the Part 3 exam: *Practical Teaching Skills for Driving Instructors*, by John Miller and Margaret Stacey, and *Instructional Techniques and Practice for Driving Instructors*, by Les Walklin. For details of all books and resource materials see page 419.

The preset tests

At the start of each phase the examiner will give a briefing on the subject matter to be covered during the lesson, the type of pupil to be portrayed and details of the pupil's previous driving experience. Examples of typical briefings are given on the following pages at the start of each section. Remember that, as well as dealing with the appropriate subject matter, you are also expected to pick up on any general driving faults.

Controls lesson

Preset Test 01 – Phase 1

I would like you to regard me as a beginner and instruct me on the safety aspects on entering the vehicle for the first time and on the main controls of the car. If time permits, also instruct me on moving off and making normal stops. This is my first driving lesson and I have never driven before.

The main objectives of a first driving lesson are to:

- allow you and your pupil to get to know each other;
- reassure the pupil and gain his or her confidence;
- explain the use and functions of the main driving controls;
- give the pupil experience in moving off and stopping if time allows.

Lesson structure

The pupil's first lesson is normally booked either on the phone or in the office. When you meet the pupil for the first time, therefore, you need to establish how you will address each other. This usually depends on the pupil's age, sex and background. For example, if your pupil is a teenager you will probably be on first-name terms. However, if you are teaching a more mature person, it may be appropriate to take a more formal approach. In the test your examiner will describe the 'pupil' and give you an outline of his or her background, and you will then need to establish how you will be addressing each other.

You now have to set the base line for the lesson. This means establishing whether or not the pupil knows anything about the controls of the car, and if he or she has any previous driving experience. For example, if the pupil is an 18-year-old garage mechanic, you should not have to go into quite as much detail as you would need to with a middle-aged learner who has absolutely no knowledge of cars. Ask a couple of questions to find out what is known, then decide on the level of instruction needed to cover the key elements.

For the purposes of your training, we are covering this subject in detail so that you will be able to deal with someone with no knowledge. Your tutor should explain how to adapt your instruction so that you can also deal with the same subject with someone who has more experience. However, do not be patronizing. Most people have been passengers in cars and consequently will have picked up some knowledge.

Confirm that your pupil has a valid driving licence and can read a number plate from the prescribed distance. On your test, you may be asked to conduct the lesson at the test centre. However, it's normal, with pupils who have no experience, to drive them to a quiet training area with a stretch of reasonably straight road and very few hazards. During this drive, find out a little about the pupil and his or her reasons for learning to drive. You can ask if another pupil recommended you.

Ask whether the pupil has taken, or applied for, the theory test. While driving, you can briefly explain some of the routines you are putting into practice.

Lesson content

Remember that this is not a test of your knowledge! Consider how much information the pupil is likely to absorb. Avoid overloading your explanations with irrelevancies. For example, at 9 am on a sunny morning, do you really need to include information about all the lights, gauges, dials and other equipment? You can confirm that this information will be covered in a future lesson when the need arises; for example, how to use the wipers, lights and other ancillary equipment.

Timing your explanation

The time you spend on each of the key points should depend on whether the pupil has any prior knowledge or understanding. Most people have been passengers and will probably know about seat belts; and a trained mechanic will probably be able to tell you a thing or two about, for example, how the clutch works and the relationship between power requirements and gears. Many new pupils will also have ridden a bicycle or motorbike. This means that they will have an understanding of the use of gears and some road sense. Remember to ask questions at intervals to confirm what the pupil may already know. Learning a script for the lesson is a total waste of time – you must adapt your instruction to take prior knowledge into consideration and in line with how your pupil responds.

Driver checks

Doors If you have driven the pupil to the training area, explain the need for safety checks before opening any door, looking either for pedestrians on the pavement side or traffic in the road. It is sensible to wait by the driver's door while the pupil gets into the driving seat. You can then make sure that the door is secured. Using your own door, explain about the safety catch by opening it and demonstrating the light click when the door is not properly closed. Do this by getting the pupil to check in the door mirror for body alignment. Get him or her to listen to the firmer sound when you close the door properly. Confirm the dangers of driving along with doors not properly closed. Also, explain how to open the doors safely in windy conditions.

Handbrake and neutral Explain how the extra weight of people getting into a car can affect it; and of the need to check the handbrake and neutral for security.

Seat adjustment Explain how to adjust the seat and back rake to ensure that all the controls can be reached comfortably and controlled properly. The driver's left knee should be slightly bent when the clutch is fully depressed, and there should be a slight bend at the elbows when the hands are placed on the steering wheel in the 'ten to two' or 'quarter to three' positions.

Remember that everyone is different. You have to be flexible with what you want your pupils to do. For example, for most people, keeping the left heel down on the floor when using the clutch will result in good control as well as taking the pressure off the calf muscle. However, if you have a very tall or short pupil this position may not be possible or comfortable.

If your car has steering height adjustment, explain how it works if appropriate.

Head restraints Show the pupil how to adjust the head restraints and explain their purpose: that is, to prevent neck and spinal injuries. You could demonstrate what happens to the body if the car has to be stopped suddenly.

Mirrors Teach the pupil to adjust the interior and two door-mounted mirrors to give maximum vision to the rear and sides. Explain why they are made of different types of glass, confirming that all decisions must be made from the true image seen in the interior mirror. You could get the pupil to compare the size of objects in the three mirrors to confirm what you are saying.

Even with three mirrors, explain that there are still areas around the car that can hide things. These are known as 'blind areas'. You can confirm that they will be covered in more detail prior to moving off.

Seat belts Explain how to put on and release the seat belt safely by keeping hold of the buckle. Watch for any twists across the lap or chest. Remember, your pupil will have been a passenger and will therefore have some experience in using these; do not be patronizing. It may be more appropriate to ask one or two relevant questions on *Highway Code* rules to confirm the pupil's knowledge about drivers' responsibilities. If this is lacking, then ask the pupil to study the relevant rules, as you will be asking more questions in the next lesson.

Switching on the engine At this point you may wish to complete the 'cockpit drill' by getting the pupil to check the handbrake is on and neutral selected prior to switching on the engine. However, you may prefer to leave this until later, when you have explained about the main controls.

The main controls

The steering Explain how to position the hands between 'ten to two' and 'a quarter to three' and the importance of not holding the steering wheel too tightly. Describe how the hands will naturally follow the eyes, and emphasize the importance of looking well ahead up the road to help maintain a straight course. Emphasize the importance of maintaining full control by using the methods described in *The Official DSA Guide to Driving – The essential skills*, and by trying to keep each hand on its own side of the wheel.

Indicators Remember not to be patronizing – most people know something about cars. Ask the pupil to work out which stalk is the indicator, and also which way it's operated for signalling left and right. Relate this to the direction in which the wheel will be turned. You could ask, 'Which way will you turn the wheel for going to the right? So, which way do you think the indicator will need to go?'

Let the pupil practise a couple of times by keeping the hand on the wheel and extending the fingers to switch the indicators on and off for left and right.

Horn Show the pupil where the horn is, confirming that it should not normally be used while stationary. Refer to *The Highway Code* and ask a couple of questions about when not to use it. Confirm that you will be asking more questions on the next lesson.

The need for explaining other ancillary controls will be dependent on the light and weather conditions. Remember not to overload the pupil with too much information that is not directly relevant to the lesson.

Handbrake Explain how this normally operates on the rear wheels. Explain its purpose:

- It holds the car securely when stationary.
- It acts as a back-up system for securing the car.
- It allows the driver to hold the car on a slope when both feet are occupied with accelerator and clutch.

Give one or two examples of where to use the handbrake: pedestrian crossings and traffic lights or when stationary for more than a few seconds. Let the pupil practise releasing and applying the handbrake. Before doing this, it is a good idea to tell the pupil where the footbrake is and ask him or her to apply it. This should help the pupil develop an understanding of the relationship between these two controls. (Explain that you will be giving more information about the footbrake later in the lesson.)

Gear lever While the car is stationary, give a simple explanation on gears and their use. Remember, a visual aid might help the pupil as well as serve as a memory jogger for you. Explain about the power and speed requirements – for example, first gear would normally be used for moving off because it is the most powerful and has to get the weight of the car moving – and the spring-loaded mechanism on most new cars that allows the lever to come back to its natural position between third and fourth gear.

In order for the pupil to develop a feel for smooth and accurate gear selection, allow for plenty of practice. You might demonstrate with your right hand, showing how to 'cup' the lever in the direction it has to go. Explain the 'palming' method, relating the position of the first four forward gears to that of the road wheels on the car. (This may help those will less natural aptitude for driving.) Allow practice at changing up and down in sequence, and then show the pupil how to use the 'block-changing' method. Finally, ensure the pupil looks ahead through the windscreen while moving the gear lever.

Encourage the pupil to ask questions, so that anything that he or she has not understood can be repeated.

Accelerator, footbrake and clutch Emphasize that it is more important to be able to stop the car than to make it go faster. Ask the pupil to position the right foot squarely over the brake pedal, with the heel acting as a pivot between it and the accelerator. Remember – be flexible. Although it is preferable to keep the heel on the floor, if it is not comfortable or possible (because of the pupil's height, for example) don't insist on it. Discomfort can be a distraction from the driving task.

Explain in simple terms what each of these controls does. The accelerator works like a tap: the more the pedal is pushed down, the more fuel will flow into the engine to make it go faster. Releasing the pressure will slow down the flow of fuel, therefore slowing the car. It should be used gently and progressively. The brake works on all four wheels to slow the car down and eventually to stop it. Initial pressure should be light, gradually becoming firmer and then eased just prior to stopping in order to bring the car to a smooth stop. The mirrors should be used prior to use; the initial pressure on the brake will activate the brake lights to warn following drivers.

Outline some of the terminology you will be using, for example:

- 'gas' relating to the accelerator;
- set the gas;
- cover the brake;
- more gas/less gas;
- brake gently/brake firmly.

The clutch Keep your explanation simple – use an illustration if you think it will help. The main purpose of the clutch is to connect and disconnect the power from the engine to the road wheels so that it is possible to make smooth gear changes.

When you have explained about the main controls, encourage questions from the pupil. Stationary practice will help to build the pupil's confidence and assist in developing vehicle sympathy.

Before turning on the engine, allow the pupil to cover and feel for the pedals without looking down. Explain how to use the ignition key and, to encourage good habits from the outset, remind the pupil to check the handbrake is on and the gear lever is in neutral before switching on. Allow some practice in:

- pivoting the right foot between the brake and gas pedals;
- setting the gas;
- checking the mirror before braking, explaining about the brake lights;
- listening and feeling for the range of the clutch.

On a normal driving lesson, you would go on to explain how to move off and stop. However, in the test situation, time is limited and you may not get this far. We are therefore covering the subject briefly. A full explanation is given in Preset Test 2.

Moving off and stopping

- Explain how to put the mirrors–signal–manoeuvre (M–S–M) routine into practice for moving off and stopping.
- Confirm the need to make safety checks of the blind areas before moving. It is important at this stage to confirm what the driver is looking for.
- Ensure that you time your instructions correctly for moving off to ensure initial success.

- Give full talk-through for moving off, changing gear, steering and stopping, including the selection of safe places, referring the pupil to rules in *The Highway Code*.

Building up confidence

Try to ensure early success by giving your instructions in the correct sequence and properly timed. By doing this you can assure the pupil that driving is not as difficult as he or she might previously have thought. These first attempts at moving and stopping the car will show the pupil what effect the main controls have on it. Plenty of practice at this, and in gear changing, will also help build that all-important self-confidence of the more anxious pupil, or help to satisfy the expectations of the more able.

Summary of the key points

- Entering and leaving the car safely (safety in opening and closing doors).
- Carrying out the driver checks (doors, handbrake, neutral, seat, head restraint, mirrors, seat belt and switching on engine).
- Assuming a correct seating position for reaching the foot controls and steering wheel.
- Use, adjustment and purpose of seat belts and head restraints.
- Checking the handbrake and neutral and starting the engine.
- Identifying the function of the main driving controls: steering/indicators/handbrake/gear lever/accelerator/footbrake/clutch.
- Stationary practice with gears and foot controls to build up pupil confidence.
- Explaining the M–S–M routine and giving 'talk-through' instruction for moving off, changing gear, steering, and stopping in a safe position.

Moving off and stopping

Preset Test 02 – Phase 1

I would like you to regard me as a beginner and instruct me on moving off and making normal stops. Give me instruction on the use of mirrors and also precautions before moving off. I have had one lesson before in a car similar to this. The instructor explained getting into the car and the controls but we did not get around to moving off.

The main purposes of this lesson are for you to help the pupil to understand the principles behind the M–S–M routine and develop basic car control skills in order to:

- move off safely and under control;
- stop smoothly and parallel with the kerb;
- understand why we need to stop in safe places.

Lesson structure

Following the initial introductions, you need to establish the base line for the lesson. Use Q&A to establish what was covered on the previous session. For example:

> On your last lesson, were the main controls explained?
> Did you move off and stop at all?
> Was the M–S–M routine explained? Could you tell me what it means?

The point at which you start the lesson will depend on the answers given. With a real pupil you would normally drive to a reasonably quiet training area and use the time to establish any prior knowledge. However, because of the time constraints of the test, you may have to begin the lesson at the test centre.

If the pupil has moved off before

If the pupil has moved off and stopped before, you will need to confirm what he or she understands and can do. To do this, ask a few questions such as:

> Are you familiar with this type of car?
> Can you reach all the controls comfortably?
> Have you made all your driver checks?
> What can you see in the mirrors?
> What can you tell me about the blind areas?
> Do you know what 'set the gas' and 'find the biting point' mean?
> Have you moved off and stopped before?
> Are you studying for the theory test?
> Do you understand the M–S–M routine? Can you explain it to me?

You will need to reinforce what the pupil has already learnt and then work on improving car control skills for moving off and stopping in different circumstances.

If the pupil has not yet moved a car

If the pupil has no previous experience, the objective will be: 'By the end of today's lesson, you should be able to move off and stop safely and under control.' You will need to:

- explain about the M–S–M routine;
- allow the pupil to practise using the foot controls and selecting gears as necessary while stationary;
- give a full talk-through of, and practice in:
  - moving off and stopping (level, uphill and downhill, if circumstances allow);
  - moving off, building up speed and changing gear;
  - driving along and checking the mirrors;

- slowing down and changing down;
- stopping smoothly in safe places;
● give feedback and encouragement.

Explanation of the M–S–M routine

Mirrors Decisions should be taken on what is seen in all mirrors. To confirm why this is so, ask the pupil to compare the images between the three mirrors. Confirm what the blind areas consist of and the importance of checking there are no road users in them prior to moving off.

Explain that the M–S–M routine should be applied when any change in speed or direction is intended. That is, the routine needs to be used for:

● signalling;
● moving off;
● changing direction (passing parked vehicles, overtaking, turning corners);
● slowing down and stopping.

Confirm that no decisions should be taken before assessing what effect any actions may have on other road users.

Signals Explain the purpose and use of signals and relate them to *The Highway Code*. Introduce discrimination at this stage in order to develop the pupil's 'look, assess and decide' processes. Before moving away you could ask, 'Is there anyone around who would benefit from a signal?'

M–S–M routine Explain how and why this sequence should be followed for every change of speed or direction, including moving off, overtaking and stopping.

Precautions before moving off

Explain about the blind areas. If parked at the side of the road, pick out an object on the offside pavement that will be in the pupil's blind area. Ask if he or she can see it without turning round to check. Confirm what could happen if he or she moved off when a cyclist was emerging from a driveway in that blind area.

Another way of emphasizing the need to look round is to get the pupil to watch in the mirror for a vehicle approaching from behind. Then get him or her to follow it into the offside mirror and keep watching until it disappears into the blind area. It is important that the pupil develops an understanding of what might happen if blind areas are not checked.

Coordination of the controls

By giving full and properly timed 'talk-through' instruction you can usually ensure that the pupil achieves success first time. This will build up the pupil's own confidence and his or her faith in you as a teacher. Remember that your learner may be feeling a little anxious during the first few tries. Do not attempt too much too soon. Talk the pupil through moving off and stopping over quite short distances until you can see skill and confidence are improving. You can then lead gently into building up a little more speed and progressing through the gears.

Recognizing and avoiding problems

In the early stages, pupils will often do only what they are told to do – no more and no less. You must ensure that you tell them everything in the correct sequence to enable them to control the car smoothly and build up their confidence.

During initial practice at moving off, and so that problems can be avoided, make sure that you respond immediately should things start to go wrong. For example, if the pupil eases pressure from the accelerator, you could say, 'Keep the gas set.' If the clutch is allowed to come up too far, say, 'Clutch down a little.' Try to imagine how your pupil will feel if, when moving off for the first time, the engine stalls – hardly the best way to build up confidence!

Be ready to correct any steering errors. If the pupil is steering towards the kerb or out towards the centre of the road, ask where he or she is looking and explain how 'The hands follow the eyes. Look well ahead at where you want to go.'

Normal stop control

Before moving off, explain how the M–S–M routine will be applied when stopping. After moving off for the first time and driving for a short distance, prepare the pupil for stopping. To encourage early development of mirror use, ask if there is anyone behind. Give the instruction to apply the left signal if needed. Be ready to help with this if necessary.

Give full talk-through instruction to ensure a smooth and safe stop. That is, say, 'Cover the brake and the clutch. Brake gently. Clutch down, brake gently to a stop.' Give the instruction, 'Keep both feet still. Put the handbrake on and the gear lever into neutral. Now, rest your feet.' This will ensure that the engine keeps running and will assist in building the pupil's confidence in his or her ability. (Sometimes a feeling of relief at stopping can cause pupils to release the foot controls before the car has been properly secured. The resultant stall can lead to a sense of inability and disappointment.)

Carry out the moving off and stopping exercise a couple of times, and if the pupil begins to respond favourably, encourage him or her to try the procedure without your assistance. You should, however, be ready to give more help if needed.

Normal stop position

Introduce *The Highway Code* rules relating to stopping. Ask the pupil for a couple of examples of where and why it would not be safe or legal to stop. For example:

Give me three examples of where you shouldn't stop or park your car.
Why should you not stop near a bend or the brow of a hill?
What problems could you cause if you stopped too near or opposite a bus stop?

Try to time your initial instructions to coincide with safe stopping places. If, however, the pupil stops somewhere unsafe or inconvenient, ask, 'Why do you think this is not a good place for stopping?'

Making progress by building up speed and using the gears

Practice should now be given at:

- moving off;
- building up speed;
- changing through the gears to make progress;
- stopping.

It is vital that your pupil's confidence is built up through the car's response. Remember to time your instruction so that it sounds and feels smooth. For example, after moving off and building up a little speed you will need to ensure the change to second gear is smooth. Your instructions should allow for the pupil being a little slow and the car losing some momentum. You can compensate for this by allowing a little more speed to be built up than is necessary, particularly if driving uphill, and preparing the pupil for the change by saying, 'Can you hear the engine getting louder? We're going to change to the next gear.'

Next get the pupil to put his or her left hand on to the gear lever, palm towards you, before adding the instructions:

Off the gas and clutch down.
Gear lever straight back to second.
Ease up the clutch and back to the gas.
Hand back on the wheel, check the mirrors and gently accelerate.

Encourage the pupil to build up speed and progress through the gears following the above instructions, changing the wording to suit whichever gear is being selected. Encourage use of the mirror while driving along. This will help pupils develop the habit of regularly checking on the situation to the rear. This, in turn, should result in a more natural application of the M–S–M routine for dealing with hazards.

Teach the differences between moving off on the level, uphill and downhill. To develop vehicle sympathy explain about the effects of different gradients on the power requirements (uphill) or the use of the footbrake (downhill).

Summary of the key points

- Setting the base line for the lesson (the briefing): confirm what the pupil knows; explain the objectives of the lesson, that is, to further improve or to learn how to move off, change through the gears and stop the car, applying the M–S–M routine.

- Mirrors: explain the need to use them well before changing speed or direction, and stopping.
- M–S–M: explain the system of car control as defined in *The Highway Code*, *The Official Guide to Learning to Drive* and *The Official DSA Guide to Driving – The essential skills*.
- Precautions before moving off – confirming problems associated with blind areas.
- Coordination of the controls – explain and practise using the controls smoothly.
- Normal stop: explain and practise how to stop smoothly.
- Normal stop position: explain about the importance of selecting safe places for stopping.

The emergency stop and using the mirrors

Preset Test 05 – Phase 1

I would like you to regard me as a partly trained pupil. Instruct me in how to make an emergency stop and also instruct me in the correct use of the rear view mirrors. I have had five lessons previously. Also, please correct any faults in my general driving.

Teaching pupils about using the mirrors effectively should be part of an ongoing programme from their first driving lesson. During the early stages of the pupil's learning you should be introducing an element of hazard perception and anticipation by pointing out possible problems and explaining how to respond.

By definition, the word 'emergency' means 'a situation of a serious and often dangerous nature, developing suddenly and unexpectedly, and demanding immediate action'. Emergencies cannot therefore be planned for, so one could happen at any time during a pupil's career as a learner. You need to know that your pupil will be able to cope. Introducing this exercise during the early stages, as an extension of braking and stopping exercises, will help develop the pupil's control skills and confidence.

The main purposes of the lesson are to:

- confirm what the pupil knows about the adjustment and use of mirrors;
- improve the pupil's general driving skills and all-round awareness;
- teach the pupil how to stop promptly and under control;
- give basic advice on how to correct a skid.

Lesson structure

As there are two topics to be dealt with, this Phase 1 exercise can be split into two sections. The first covers how to adjust and use the mirrors. You can then check, during the drive to the training area, whether the pupil has understood all the correct routines and procedures and is putting them into practice. Give feedback confirming the importance of using the mirrors correctly and being aware of the all-round situation. The second phase involves explaining how to stop in an emergency and what to do in the case of a skid.

Introduce yourself in the usual manner and establish the base line for the lesson by confirming the pupil's previous knowledge. This means that you should:

- check that the pupil is in the correct seating position and has adjusted all the mirrors so that they can be checked without an exaggerated head movement;
- confirm the reason for checking blind areas and make sure that these checks are made properly;
- ask a few questions about when mirrors should be checked in relation to moving off/speeding up and slowing down/changing direction/passing parked cars/overtaking/M–S–M routine.

Fault analysis

During the drive to the training area, watch closely to make sure that the pupil is making regular checks of the appropriate mirrors. Assess the pupil's understanding through his or her actions: that is, checking the mirrors regularly before moving off, changing speed or direction, signalling or stopping; and reacting properly to what is seen in the mirrors, putting into practice the M–S–M routine by:

- deciding whether or not a signal is required;
- deciding how actions may affect any following driver;
- delaying signals if necessary;
- signalling earlier and braking more gently if appropriate before turning and when stopping;
- keeping a safe distance from the vehicle ahead if someone is following too closely.

Avoiding conflict No matter how good an instructor you may be, it is not possible to check every time a driver uses a mirror. In order to avoid arguments, if you are not quite sure whether a mirror check was carried out, simply ask, 'Did you check the mirrors before signalling?' Then follow this up with, 'Why is it important to check the mirrors before you do anything else?' The responses given will confirm whether or not the pupil understands the principles behind the M–S–M routine, and whether you will need to give more information when you reach the training area for carrying out the emergency stop.

You can now link the two subjects by confirming that:

- A good driver uses all of the mirrors regularly and is aware of the all-round traffic situation.

- Emergencies can arise at any time.

- If an emergency arises, there may be no time for another mirror check, but you should be aware of the situation behind.

How to avoid emergencies

Emphasis should be placed on the fact that good drivers plan well ahead, taking into consideration what is happening. They also anticipate what might happen where they can see a possible hazard developing, or where they cannot see at all. For example, no one can see around a bend, so how can a driver know what may be there? What you cannot see, you don't know.

Quick reactions

In an emergency, the priority is to react promptly and stop the car quickly and safely. Referring to the stopping distances in *The Highway Code*, relate these to the road and weather conditions, and explain how these will dictate the safe amount of pressure to apply to the brakes. Explain that progressive, firm pressure is required as harsh braking may result in a skid and this will only create further risk. Allow the pupil to practise the pivot between the accelerator and footbrake.

Ask your pupil where the driver's hands should be when braking. Confirm that a firmer hold than usual is necessary since more than normal braking pressure is being applied. This should also help to keep the car travelling in a straight line. Remind the pupil that engine braking can help to slow down the car more quickly. Confirm what the clutch is used for when stopping the car, and ask the pupil whether it will be different in an emergency situation.

Stopping the car is the priority, not necessarily keeping the engine running. Reassure the pupil that stalling is not a serious error as long as the necessary precautions are taken before restarting the engine. Explain about securing the car after stopping and confirm that this is even more important in an emergency, as the all-round situation needs to be checked before moving off again. Also confirm that, because the car was stopped in an unusual (a driving) position, checks of blind areas all around the car sides will need to be made prior to moving off again.

Skidding

What is required here is to provide information on what can cause the most common types of skid, and to reassure the pupil of what to do if he or she brakes too harshly and the car skids. Ask the pupil about the causes of skidding, and confirm that these normally only occur when a driver is not responding properly to the road and weather conditions. Harsh braking can cause a skid, and the most common type is the rear-wheel skid.

Explain that if a skid occurs the driver needs to remove the cause, in this case by releasing the brake pedal, and apply and release the brakes until they take effect again. Explain that this is how ABS works and confirm whether your car has one. If the car has ABS, explain how this should be used. Then explain how to steer into the skid by straightening up the front of the car. Use a model car, or show an illustration to clarify what you mean by 'steering into the skid'.

Maintaining safety

Explain the signal you will be giving when you want the pupil to stop. Once on the move, sit still and try not to make any movements that may distract the pupil into stopping prematurely. Remember, as an ADI, you will be responsible for the safety of yourself, your passenger, your vehicle and other road users. Make sure that you carry out this exercise in complete safety. Ideally this should be:

- not too near to any parked vehicles;
- where there are no nearby pedestrians;
- clear of junctions.

Check properly to the rear, and only give your stopping signal when there is no one close behind. After stopping, make sure that the car is secured. Get your pupil to check on the position in the road, and ask what blind areas will need to be checked before moving away. Practise the exercise two or three times, giving any necessary remedial advice on the pupil's reactions and use of the controls.

Summary of the key points

- Establish what the pupil knows about mirror adjustment and use.
- Identify and analyse faults, giving remedial advice as necessary.
- Explain how to avoid emergencies by planning ahead.
- Describe how to react quickly and use the controls to stop promptly and under control.
- Explain about skids and how to correct them.
- Practise the emergency stop and give feedback and advice.

Approaching junctions to turn left and right

Preset Test 07 – Phase 1

I would like you to regard me as a partly trained pupil. Please instruct me on approaching junctions to turn left from a major into a minor road. I have had four lessons previously. Also correct any faults in my general driving.

Preset Test 03 – Phase 2

I would like you to treat me as a pupil who will be taking a test next week. Please give corrective instruction on approaching junctions to turn right. I have had a total of 30 lessons so far. Also correct any faults in my general driving.

It is important to gradually build up pupils' skills and confidence by introducing topics in a logical manner. When the pupil has attained a reasonable level of skill in moving off and stopping, introduce basic junction routines. Beginning with simple left turns, it is normal to teach pupils how to turn into a side road and continue to the next left turn, which might be another side road on the left, or involve emerging onto a main road. Practise until a sound routine is established, then transfer this knowledge into dealing with right turns, following a similar pattern and introducing the differing elements.

The objectives of the lesson are to:

- establish what the pupil already knows about the M–S–M routine and how this system is applied at junctions;
- teach the inexperienced how to deal safely with junctions;
- assess how the more experienced learner deals with junctions;
- identify and analyse faults;
- give remedial advice and create opportunities to practise the correct routines.

Unless the examiner says that the pupil's previous lessons were with you, you will need to introduce yourself. Establish the base line for the lesson by asking a few questions and assessing what the pupil already knows and can do.

The main element of the lesson is the correct application of the M–S–M routine, breaking this down as follows:

- Mirrors:
  - checking early to see what is happening;
  - working out how any other road user may be affected by the manoeuvre;
  - deciding if and when to signal.

- Signal:
  - to warn or inform other road users at the correct time, and so as not to confuse.
- Manoeuvre:
  - position: early to confirm the signal; appropriately for the direction, the width of the road, any obstructions, vision;
  - speed: appropriate for vision, the required gear, obstructions, oncoming traffic, pedestrians;
  - look: all around prior to turning for obstructions, other road users, pedestrians.

Phase 1 – Dealing with a pupil who has very little or no experience

Where you set the base line will depend on whether the pupil has any previous knowledge or experience at dealing with turning left and right. Remember pupils should be studying for the theory test and therefore should be able to answer simple questions on the M–S–M routine. However, assume nothing! Their answers will give you feedback on their level of knowledge and understanding – or lack of it.

If the pupil has not yet dealt with any turns, you will need to give a more detailed explanation of the routines. Use a visual aid if you think it will help. Here are a few examples of questions that you can use, either during your explanation or during the practical part of the lesson:

What routine do you use when you are moving off and stopping?
Why is it important to check the mirrors, and what are you looking for?
When does *The Highway Code* tell you to use signals?
If a pedestrian is crossing the road you are turning into, who has priority?
Whose priority is it when you're turning right, yours or the oncoming driver's?
How will you be able to work out whether it's safe to turn right when there's an oncoming car?
Why would it be dangerous to cut the corner?

To begin with, you will need to give full talk-through instruction to confirm the correct routines, reducing the level of help as the pupil's skill and understanding improves. However, be ready to give more help when necessary.

If the pupil has some previous experience Use a Q&A session to confirm whether the pupil has some previous experience. Find out what is known about the routines and then get on the move so that you can make an assessment. You should soon be able to tell how much or how little help is needed, and adapt the level of your instruction to:

- give full talk-through instruction;

- help only when things are forgotten or routines carried out in incorrect sequences;
- assist when more difficult circumstances arise;
- intervene to ensure safety is maintained.

Encouraging hazard awareness Whenever your car is moving, take advantage of every available opportunity to develop hazard awareness. Do not restrict your teaching to the topic in hand, but be ready to deal with other problems as they arise. For example, if there are parked vehicles or obstructions, encourage the pupil to think about the possibility of oncoming traffic and give a full talk-through to maintain confidence and safety.

Phase 2 – Dealing with the more experienced pupil

Ask a few questions to confirm knowledge and understanding. Listen carefully – something may be quoted out of sequence or omitted altogether. Reaffirm any points you think are necessary, and get on the move so that you can make a practical assessment. If your pupil appears to be experiencing difficulty, or shows a lack of understanding, give as much help as is necessary until there is an improvement in his or her understanding and skills.

Not all errors committed will relate directly to the subject in hand. Deal with any potentially serious problem. The degree of the error will dictate whether you can deal with it on the move, or whether you will need to find somewhere safe to stop for a more detailed discussion.

Fault assessment Whatever the standard of the pupil, positive correction is better than negative or retrospective correction. If you can see a problem developing ahead and the pupil appears not to be responding, give some positive prompt to encourage some action. This is far safer, and more effective, than allowing a potentially dangerous situation to arise, particularly where other road users are involved.

During any drive assess whether your pupil is putting all of the established routines into practice. Identify and analyse any problems. Give advice on how to improve, and give your reasons.

Common faults

- A lack of understanding of the M–S–M routine.
- Not checking the mirrors effectively.
- Signalling at the same time as checking the mirror.
- Signalling too early or too late.
- Not positioning correctly according to the circumstances.
- Not using the brakes effectively to slow down in good time.
- Making unnecessary gear changes or changing down too early or late.

- Coasting around corners.
- Approaching too fast and swinging out on left turns.
- Lack of awareness of pedestrians and the need to give priority.
- Crossing approaching traffic.
- Not looking effectively into the new road.
- Cutting corners.

Summary of the key points

- Confirm the correct application of the M–S–M/position–speed–look (P–S–L) routine for turning left and right.
- Assess the pupil's ability and adapt the level of your instruction to suit.
- Identify, analyse and give remedial advice on weaknesses, and allow practice to improve.
- Give more help/tuition when required.
- Give feedback on where improvement has taken place and where more work is needed.

T-junctions – emerging

Preset Test 8 – Phase 1

I would like you to regard me as a partly trained pupil. Please instruct me on approaching and emerging from side roads onto a main road. I have had six lessons. Also correct any faults in my general driving.

Preset Test 4 – Phase 2

I would like you to regard me as a pupil who has recently failed my driving test on 'emerging at junctions'. I had 30 lessons prior to my test. Please give corrective instruction and also deal with any general driving faults.

It is clear that you cannot keep turning into roads without eventually coming to the end of one. Most instructors therefore initially deal with 'emerging' in conjunction with turning into side roads. The main objectives are to:

- establish what the pupil already knows about the M–S–M routine and its application at T-junctions;
- teach inexperienced pupils how to approach and emerge safely;
- assess how the more experienced learner deals with T-junctions;
- identify and analyse faults;
- give remedial advice and create opportunities to practise the correct routines.

Introduce yourself and establish the base line for the lesson by finding out what the pupil already knows and understands about junctions. The main elements of the lesson are to:

- confirm the application of the M–S–M routine;
- explain about 'Give Way' and 'Stop' junctions;
- emphasize the importance of taking effective observations;
- encourage safe decisions to proceed or hold back according to sightlines;
- outline correct position according to circumstances:
- turning left or right;
- wide or narrow roads;
- obstructions;
- one-way streets;
- pedestrian activity.

Phase 1 – Dealing with a pupil with very little or no experience

Set the base line for the lesson. Confirm previous experience by asking a few questions on the M–S–M routine and its application when turning left and right into side roads. Ask what the pupil knows about 'emerging' from junctions.

Although 'emerging' may be a new topic, the pupil should already have turned left and right into side roads. You now need to build on this knowledge and transfer it to the new circumstances. You should explain about:

- the different types of junction, 'Give Way' or 'Stop' – ask the pupil to describe the signs and markings and to tell you their different meanings;
- positioning on the approach, depending on:
  - the direction to be taken,
  - the width of the road;
- vision:
  - restricted sightlines in one or both directions,
  - good vision in one direction only,
  - good vision all around,
  - emerging safely without affecting others, including pedestrians.

Practice You will need to give full talk-through instruction until the pupil's understanding and control skills begin to develop. Gradually reduce the amount of instruction as the pupil's skills develop. However, be ready to give more help when necessary, and to intervene to prevent a pupil from emerging unsafely.

Phase 2 – Dealing with the more experienced pupil

The more experienced pupil will have had plenty of practice at emerging but may have weaknesses. Try to establish what these are as quickly as you can so that you can create maximum time for practising the correct routines. If the weaknesses do not become obvious in your short Q&A discovery session, you will need to get on the move and watch carefully to see what problems develop. You must ensure that the correct routines and procedures are being put into practice.

Pay attention to the all-round traffic situation and assess how your pupil is responding to it. Do not allow a potentially unsafe situation to arise. For example, if you feel the pupil is about to emerge unsafely before being able to see properly in all directions, you should give some positive command, such as 'Wait!' Follow this up with, 'Have you checked both ways?', 'How far can you see?' or, 'What if something is approaching out of the blind area at 40 mph?'

It may be appropriate, when convenient, to pull in and give more information on sightlines and the importance of being able to see properly before emerging.

Fault assessment

As previously indicated, positive correction is better than negative or retrospective correction. Preventing a potentially dangerous situation, such as emerging unsafely, should result in a greater degree of safety for everyone, and more positive learning and understanding taking place.

Common faults are:

- A lack of understanding of the M–S–M routine.
- Ineffective application of the M–S–M routine.
- A failure to identify or respond to the type of junction, 'Give Way' or 'Stop'.
- Not taking into consideration restrictions to sightlines.
- Not looking early enough at 'open' junctions.
- Stopping unnecessarily when safe to proceed.
- Not looking effectively in all directions.
- Not responding to pedestrians.
- Emerging unsafely.

Summary of the key points

- Establish prior knowledge and understanding of the M–S–M/P–S–L routines.
- Confirm the correct application of the routines.
- Ensure that the pupil has a good understanding of sightlines and vision.
- Identify and analyse faults.
- Give remedial advice with reasons.

- Create opportunities to practise the correct routines.
- Give feedback where improvement has been made.

The reverse and turn in the road manoeuvres

Preset Tests 3 and 4 – both Phase 1

> I would like you to regard me as a partly trained pupil and instruct me in turning the car around in the road using forward and reverse gears/reversing into a side road. I have had six lessons before in a car similar to this. My last instructor said that during this lesson he would be teaching me how to turn the car around in the road/reverse. Also correct any faults in my general driving.

Because of their similarity, and to avoid a great deal of repetition in this book, we are combining the explanation for these two manoeuvres. You will find detailed information on each exercise in the DSA publications, *The Official DSA Guide to Driving – The essential skills* and *The Official Guide to Learning to Drive*. Use the information in these books to build up your lesson plans.

The main purposes of the manoeuvre exercises are to:

- develop the pupil's car control skills;
- improve car control skills and confidence;
- develop an awareness of the importance of observations;
- teach the pupil how to respond to other road users.

Lesson structure

Introduce yourself and establish the base line by asking a few questions about what the pupil has learnt previously and understands about clutch control. All of the manoeuvring exercises are based on coordination between:

- clutch;
- accelerator;
- footbrake;
- steering;
- observations.

Safe and smooth control can be affected by something as basic as sitting too close or too far from the pedals. You should therefore confirm, at the beginning of the lesson, that the correct 'cockpit drill' is carried out and the controls can be reached comfortably.

Confirm prior understanding by asking how to control the car at low speed. For example:

> How do you hold the car steady when moving off up a hill?
> How do you creep slowly forwards to get a better view at junctions?
> Which pedals would you use to control the car on a downhill slope?

Confirm that you will be assessing these control skills during the drive to the practice area. This may be some distance away, so to give a detailed explanation of the exercise at this point will be of little use. The pupil will have other things to concentrate on and may have forgotten all you said, resulting in your wasting valuable practice time having to repeat what you said before.

Use this opportunity to check on the pupil's application of the M–S–M routine and particularly watch out for any problems with car control skills. As you drive along, use simple questions for confirming understanding of any relevant points.

When you arrive at the training area, give positive feedback on progress, adding any necessary remedial advice where improvement is needed.

Lesson content

Put into practice the general teaching principle of 'explanation/ demonstration/practice'. Confirm that it is a safe, legal and convenient place to carry out the exercise. Relate this to the rules in *The Highway Code* and ask a few questions, for example:

Are there any signs or road markings that would make the manoeuvre illegal?
Do you think we will be inconveniencing other road users?
Are there any parked vehicles or obstructions nearby that could affect us?

Transferring previously learnt skills

If the pupil has previous experience, ask him or her to explain the procedures. Listen carefully, and add any information or clarification you feel is necessary. Allow the pupil to practise the exercise so that you can make your assessment. Be ready to give help if the pupil is experiencing difficulty.

With the turn in the road manoeuvre, bear in mind that this involves various sub-skills that the pupil will have acquired on previous lessons, including clutch control, the angled start, an uphill start, observations and judgement of other traffic, reversing and turning/steering. The turn in the road is not the time or place to start learning these skills.

Dealing with the subject for the first time

If the pupil has not carried out the manoeuvre previously, give some reassurance by confirming that it only involves coordinating all of the skills previously learnt: that is, combining the use of the foot controls to keep the speed low, which in turn will give more time to work on the steering and make the observations.

Explanation

Use a visual aid if you think it will help the pupil understand the main principles. Your explanation should include:

- The importance of good all-round vision. For reversing to the left this will involve turning round in the seat, removing the seat belt where necessary.
- Confirming the position of reverse gear and letting the pupil practise selecting it while stationary.
- Describing each element of the exercise, including:
  - the control of speed with either the clutch and gas, or the footbrake if downhill;
  - steering;
  - observations: that is, where to look and how to respond;
  - checking into the new road for safety and convenience prior to the exercise.
- Confirm that control is of major importance and accuracy will come with practice.

Demonstration

Offer a demonstration if you think the pupil will benefit. Remember, however, you will have more time to do this on a real lesson than during the Part 3 test. You might consider combining a demonstration with your explanation. Do this by changing seats and talking yourself through the exercise. This could benefit you in two ways: the more anxious pupil will see the exercise is easier than it sounds, and it will take less time than giving the explanation and demonstration separately.

Practice

One of your main aims when teaching a new topic should be for the pupil to achieve a reasonable degree of success. To build up the pupil's confidence, therefore, you should ensure that your talk-through is effective and that you respond promptly if the pupil is having difficulty.

Try to imagine how your pupil might be feeling. All of the control skills learnt in previous situations now need to be combined, and the pupil has the extra task of checking around for other road users. Expect a little loss of memory, and give as much help as possible to encourage success and confidence. If after a couple of attempts you can see the pupil's skill developing, ease off on the level of instruction. Be ready, however, to give more help if necessary.

Observations and safety

As discussed several times previously, you are responsible for the safety of yourself, your pupil and other road users! Because at this stage pupils' observations are likely to be very superficial, you must remain fully aware of what is happening all around you, all of the time. If you see other vehicles approaching, draw the pupil's attention to their presence by telling him or her to pause, then ask: 'Have you seen that other car? Let's wait and let it pass.'

At this early stage, the pupil does not need the extra pressure of knowing that another driver is being held up. As long as it is safe – and you have checked all around – avoid this pressure by encouraging the other driver to proceed. Confirm that other road users should be given priority. As your pupil's confidence increases you will be able to encourage him or her to respond to others according to the circumstances – for example, if it's obvious that another driver is being considerate and has decided to wait. On these occasions, you must emphasize that observations should also be made in the other directions to check that it's safe before proceeding.

A topic that crops up regularly is whether the pupil is expected to wave other drivers past during the turn in the road manoeuvre. To decide on the appropriate answer, ask yourself whether you would advise pupils to use a similar signal in other situations:

- beckoning pedestrians across at a crossing;
- waving other drivers out at junctions;
- flashing headlights to give way.

Giving feedback

Praise goes a long way in building confidence. Confirm where progress and improvement have taken place. Explain any weaknesses; confirm that more practice will be given. Encourage revision of the main points before the next lesson.

Summary of the key points

- Set the base line by confirming previous knowledge.
- Assess the pupil's control skills and general driving, giving remedial advice as necessary.
- Explain the manoeuvre, including observations and how to respond to others.
- Give full talk-through and decrease the help as skill improves.
- Ensure the pupil is given feedback on progress.

Meeting, crossing the path of, and overtaking other traffic. Allowing adequate clearance to other road users and anticipation

Preset Test 2 – Phase 2; Preset Test 8 – Phase 2;
Preset Test 10 – Phase 1

I would like you to regard me as a trained pupil and instruct me on how to meet/cross the path of and overtake other vehicles/allow adequate clearance/anticipate the actions of other road users. Treat me as a pupil who is having difficulty with one of the above (for example, allowing adequate clearance to other vehicles). I have had a total of 30 lessons. Also correct any faults in my general driving.

Note: Only three out of the five topics are used on this subject. For example – 'meet, cross, and anticipate' or 'overtake, allowing adequate clearance and anticipation'.

If you are to develop safe attitudes in your pupils, anticipation is something that you should introduce during the early stages of learning. There are so many vehicles parked on our roads that it is almost impossible for a new driver not to encounter some of them. It is important, therefore, that you take advantage of situations that arise to teach your pupils how to:

- read the road ahead and to the sides;
- consider the all-round situation;
- think about priorities;
- anticipate what others might do;
- work out the safest way to respond.

The main objectives are to:

- establish how much experience the pupil has in dealing with other traffic;
- teach the partly trained driver about priorities when:
  - dealing with parked vehicles,
  - turning right,
  - dealing with pedestrians and cyclists;
- assess the trained pupil on all of the above aspects of driving;
- explain how to overtake safely;
- identify and analyse faults;
- give remedial advice and create opportunities to practise the correct routines.

As there are a number of different elements involved in the preset tests covering them, your examiner will identify those topics on which you must concentrate. Listen very carefully so that you can plan the lesson around the selected topics, and do not necessarily try to cover everything.

Introduce yourself and establish the base line for the lesson by finding out what the pupil already knows about the topics. Confirm the M–S–M routine for approaching all hazards and then focus on those subjects that need either teaching or reinforcing.

Meeting other traffic, allowing adequate clearances

The key elements are:

- looking and planning ahead for parked vehicles;

- deciding on priorities by acting on available information:
  - obstruction on the left side of the road,
  - obstruction on the right side of the road,
  - speed, position and size of oncoming traffic,
  - uphill or downhill situation;
- applying the M–S–M routine and waiting in the hold-back position, to:
  - maintain a view of the road ahead,
  - be able to steer through in a straight line when safe;
- allowing clearances for parked vehicles relative to:
  - the volume of traffic,
  - pedestrian activity;
- adjusting the speed to suit the available space: the narrower the gap, the lower the speed to give more time to respond;
- clearances for cyclists.

Crossing other traffic

The key elements are:

- Priorities when turning right:
  - speed and distance of oncoming traffic;
  - if there's time to walk across, there should be time to turn safely;
  - is it safe to turn? What is happening in the new road?
  - is there time to turn without cutting the corner?
- Selecting lanes in good time to avoid cutting across the path of others.

Overtaking

The key elements are:

- Safe. Is there an adequate view of the road ahead? Consider vision:
  - bends/brows of hills/dead ground;
  - any junctions ahead.
- Legal (refer to *The Highway Code*):
  - Are there any pedestrian crossings ahead?
  - What road markings are there?
  - Are there any signs that would make overtaking illegal or dangerous?
  - What is the speed limit and will it have to be exceeded to complete the manoeuvre?
- Necessary:
  - At what speed is the vehicle ahead travelling in relation to the speed limit?

- Will we be turning off soon?
- Do we need to get by to make progress?

Following at a safe distance

Explain that this is not only to allow sufficient braking distance, but also to give a better view of the road ahead.

Mirrors–position–speed–look (MSPL), M–S–M:

- Mirrors.
- Position – by moving out or in to obtain a better view.
- Mirrors.
- Speed – select a lower gear if appropriate.
- Look – check all around again.
- Mirrors – check that it is safe to carry out the manoeuvre.
- Signal – if appropriate – to let other drivers know of your intended manoeuvre.
- Manoeuvre – quickly and efficiently.
- Mirrors – check before returning to the left without cutting in.
- Accelerate away.

Anticipation

Teaching anticipation is an ongoing process that should start from day one of a pupil's driving career.

The key elements are:

- looking for other vehicles whose drivers may:
  - emerge from junctions,
  - open doors or move off without warning,
  - take priority when they should be giving way;
- looking and planning ahead for any pedestrian activity:
  - expecting them to walk into the road,
  - at junctions between parked cars/behind buses/at crossings – in fact, anywhere;
- looking and planning ahead for cyclists, expecting them to:
  - ride into the road without warning,
  - change position or turn at junctions without signals,
  - cycle around obstructions without checking,
  - ride alongside near crossings, at junctions and in traffic lanes.

Dealing with pupils who have very little experience

Establish prior knowledge and driving experience. Using a visual aid if appropriate, explain how to approach and deal with the different types of hazard. If the pupil has very little experience of driving in busier areas, give sufficient talk-through to ensure both safety and confidence. Look and plan well ahead and describe what you can see happening, and encourage the pupil to respond early enough to avoid problems.

Even where the pupil has previously driven in busier areas, be ready to assist when necessary to avoid uncomfortable or unsafe situations developing. Identify any weaknesses in the pupil's general driving and explain how improvements can be made. Remember, when you suggest alternative action, you need to give a valid reason for it. Give encouragement where the pupil carries out the routines correctly and safely.

Dealing with more experienced pupils

At this stage, the pupil will be experienced at driving in traffic. You may only need to confirm prior knowledge by asking a few questions on how to approach and deal with the different types of hazard. If overtaking is to be covered, you will need to know whether the pupil is familiar with the difference from the normal M–S–M routine. If not, you may need to give an explanation. Should an opportunity to overtake arise during the drive, talk the pupil through the procedure.

At this stage, you should be constantly monitoring the pupil's performance in relation to correct driving procedures and hazard recognition. Anything that deviates from the driving 'norm' needs to be addressed, either briefly if the error is minor, or by stopping somewhere safe if it is a more serious error.

Common faults

- Failing to anticipate hazards or potential risk situations.
- Taking priority when it should have been given.
- Not applying the M–S–M routine when approaching hazards.
- Shaving parked vehicles on the left.
- Shaving parked vehicles on the right on narrow roads.
- Moving out too far and meeting oncoming traffic dangerously.
- Not allowing for the actions of pedestrians, cyclists or other drivers.
- Turning right across the path of approaching traffic.
- Showing an unsafe attitude and general lack of consideration.

Summary of the key points

- Establish prior knowledge and experience.
- Give adequate information on any new subject, particularly when meeting other traffic/passing parked vehicles/driving in busy areas/overtaking.

- Ensure that all the correct routines are put into practice.
- Identify and analyse weaknesses.
- Give remedial advice and create opportunities to practise the correct routines.
- Give feedback where improvement has taken place and confirm where more practice is needed.

Crossroads and roundabouts

Preset Test 1 – Phase 2

I would like you to regard me as a trained pupil and give corrective instruction on approaching and turning right at crossroads. I failed my test last week and don't know why. I previously had more than 30 lessons. Also correct any faults in my general driving.

Preset Test 9 – Phase 1

I would like you to regard me as a partly trained pupil who has had five lessons and instruct me on approaching and turning at crossroads. Also correct any faults in my general driving.

Having taught your pupils how to turn into and out of T-junctions, you can then transfer this knowledge and develop their skills at dealing with the differences that apply at crossroads. The main objectives are to:

- establish what the pupil knows about the M–S–M routine and the different types of junction;
- teach a partly trained pupil how to adapt the procedures to deal safely with crossroads;
- assess how the trained pupil deals with crossroads;
- identify and analyse faults;
- give remedial advice and create opportunities to practise the correct routines.

Establish the base line for the lesson by finding out what the pupil already knows and understands about different types of junction. Confirm that the M–S–M routine also applies at crossroads, emphasizing that more observations are needed in all directions.

The main elements of the lesson are to explain or confirm:

- the application of the M–S–M routine at crossroads;
- priorities at junctions with different markings;
- the requirement for extra all-round observations, regardless of the direction being taken;
- positioning for turning right, offside and nearside;
- observations and priorities when turning right.

Dealing with the less experienced pupil

Confirm the pupil's knowledge of the M–S–M routine by asking a few questions on it. Check whether crossroads have been dealt with in previous lessons and, if so, what the pupil knows about them. If the pupil has no experience and there are quiet crossroads nearby, this will give you the opportunity of establishing the different aspects to be introduced without the hassle of too much traffic.

Use a visual aid if you think it will help to explain the need for the extra all-round observations at crossroads, no matter who has priority. Explain how to respond to other road users and be willing to give way if unsure, particularly when turning right.

While allowing the pupil to drive and put into practice what he or she already knows about junctions, be ready to help with talk-through instruction at the crossroads. This applies particularly to the observations. Make sure that the correct routines are applied as opportunities arise when:

- driving through crossroads with the priority;
- approaching uncontrolled crossroads;
- emerging from 'Give Way' or 'Stop' lines;
- dealing with traffic lights.

Watch carefully to ensure that the pupil is making effective observations in all directions at crossroads, no matter who has priority. Confirm that the pupil should be looking for anyone who may be emerging or crossing.

If the local road layout dictates that you have to deal with traffic-light controlled or busier junctions, you may need to explain how to turn nearside-to-nearside and offside-to-offside. Remember the level of ability of your pupil – you will probably have to give some verbal assistance to build up confidence.

Dealing with more experienced pupils

By this stage, the pupil should have had experience in driving on most types of urban road. The procedures for dealing with crossroads should, therefore, merely need confirming with a few relevant questions. Listen carefully for any weaknesses in knowledge or understanding. Confirm what the main dangers are when turning right at crossroads, and what the pupil should be looking for.

Once on the move, assess how the pupil is responding in all situations. Look and plan well ahead. If you feel that the pupil is not reacting early enough to any situation, try to instigate the correct action by prompting with a question or suggestion, particularly where lane changes are necessary. Be careful, however, not to over-instruct. Avoid giving definite instructions unless you can see a potentially serious situation developing.

You will usually be able to deal with minor or one-off errors 'on the move', as long as this will not distract the pupil. However, if more serious faults or repeated errors occur it may be necessary to stop to discuss them.

Fault assessment and feedback

Whatever the level of the pupil, you must be constantly looking for:

- weaknesses in his or her knowledge;
- correct application of the rules;
- effective, all-round observations – including at traffic lights;
- response to the all-round traffic situation.

Let the pupil know when improvement has taken place and confirm where more work needs to be done.

Common faults at crossroads

When driving along main roads:

- proceeding through without adjusting speed or checking the side roads;
- turning left and/or right without checking in all directions;
- turning left and/or right without applying the correct M–S–M routine;
- cutting corners.

Approaching 'Give Way' or 'Stop'-controlled crossroads:

- failure to apply the correct routine on the approach;
- lack of awareness of the type of junction being approached;
- lack of effective all-round observations before emerging;
- incorrect response to other road users;
- failing to stop at 'Stop' signs.

Traffic-light controlled junctions:

- lack of forward planning and anticipation;
- incorrect application of the M–S–M routine on the approach;
- incorrect positioning for:
  - the type of junction,
  - road markings,
  - presence of other drivers;
- proceeding before it's safe;
- crossing closely approaching traffic;
- failing to look in all directions before turning.

Roundabouts

Roundabouts are junctions designed to improve traffic flow. Although they are not dealt with as a separate item in the Part 3 exam, you will find them in most urban areas, including the test routes! You will need to teach your pupils how to deal effectively with the different types of roundabout.

To avoid too much repetition here, refer to the section dealing with approaching junctions and, structuring the lesson as described to suit each individual pupil, ensure that you include information and practice on:

● Forward planning and anticipation.

● Reading signs and markings.

● Application of the M–S–M routine.

● Emphasizing the use of all mirrors on multi-lane roads.

● Lane selection and discipline.

● The 'give way' rule.

● Looking in all directions to anticipate gaps in the traffic and maintain road position.

● Making progress by taking opportunities to proceed.

● Mirrors and signal before leaving.

● Position in the new road.

Encourage your pupils to learn the relevant *Highway Code* rules and the procedures described in *The Official DSA Guide to Driving – The essential skills* and *The Official Guide to Learning to Drive*.

Dealing with a pupil with no experience

Introduce this subject by including 'basic rule' roundabouts, progressing to more complex ones as the pupil's skills increase. If possible, and of course depending on local road layouts, begin with left turns, progressing to following the road ahead, then introduce taking roads to the right.

To build up skills and confidence, as with any new subject, you will need to give full talk-through instruction until the pupil can cope. Give as much help as you can to assist with this building of confidence.

Entering a large roundabout for the first time can be very confusing to the pupil and all of the exits may look similar. You will need to identify the exit road quite clearly. For example, if you want your pupil to take the road to the right, which is the third exit, you can identify this by similar wording to this:

> At the roundabout, I'd like you to take the road to the right – it's the third exit.
> It's the one where (for example) there's a pelican crossing.
> I'd like you to take the road ahead – signposted Brighton.

The pupil should be encouraged to use the directional signs on the approach to visualize the correct exits. You can then give further assistance as you proceed through the roundabout by adding as you pass the first two exits:

> This is the first exit.
> This is the second.
> We're taking the next exit so check your mirror and signal left for leaving.

Dealing with more experienced pupils

As with all of the previous subjects, you will need to find out what your pupil knows and what sort of roundabouts have been dealt with on a previous lesson. You can then assess the skills and continue the pupil's development.

During the later stages of training, try to create opportunities for practice on as many different types of roundabouts as your area will allow. If necessary, plan for longer lessons to drive to different areas for this purpose. If this is not possible, then encourage pupils to sign up for further training under the Pass Plus scheme.

Common faults at roundabouts

- Lack of planning and anticipation.
- Failure to read signs and markings.
- Incorrect application of the M–S–M routine.
- Late mirror use resulting in unsafe lane changes.
- Failure to look in all directions resulting in:
  - missing gaps in the traffic;
  - an incorrect course being followed through the junction.
- Lack of anticipation of other vehicles taking an incorrect course.
- Driving in the blind areas of larger vehicles.
- Lack of mirror use before changing lanes, resulting in:
  - a lack of awareness of drivers to the rear and sides;
  - leaving in the wrong lane for the circumstances.

Summary of the key points

- Establish prior knowledge and understanding for dealing with crossroads and roundabouts.
- Confirm extra observations required.
- Ensure that all the correct routines are being put into practice.
- Identify, analyse and give remedial advice on any weaknesses.
- Give feedback on where the pupil has made improvement and where more practice is needed.

Pedestrian crossings and the use of signals

Preset Test 06 – Phase 1; Preset Test 07 – Phase 2; Preset Test 09 – Phase 2

I would like you to regard me as a partly trained pupil (or trained pupil) and instruct me on how to deal with pedestrian crossings and also give me instruction on the use of signals by arm and by indicators. I have had eight lessons previously (or 30 lessons if Phase 2). Also correct any faults in my general driving.

The main objectives involved with teaching these subjects are:

- establishing what pupils know about the use of different methods of signalling;
- assessing whether the pupil understands and can correctly apply the M–S–M routine;
- teaching the pupil how to approach and deal safely with pedestrian crossings;
- identifying and analysing faults;
- giving remedial advice;
- creating opportunities to practise the correct routines.

Lesson structure

Establish the base line for the lesson by finding out what your pupil already knows. At this stage of his or her training the pupil should have a reasonable level of car control skills and an understanding of the basic driving routines. These skills include knowledge of the M–S–M routine, and the use of signals. Remember that, as pedestrians, your pupils will probably already have an understanding of crossings and their use.

Using signals

Whether you are dealing with a partly trained or a more experienced pupil, he or she should have previously learnt how to:

- check the mirrors regularly;
- be aware of the all-round situation;
- decide whether or not a signal is required;
- use the signals:
  - correctly,
  - when necessary,
  - at the appropriate time;
- respond safely to signals given by others.

Confirm the M–S–M routine by asking a few relevant questions. Ask for examples of the different methods of signalling. These should include:

- using the brake lights;
- indicators;
- reversing lights;
- early road positioning;
- the appropriate use of arm signals.

Arm signals

Although seldom used, in the appropriate conditions arm signals can be helpful when approaching zebra crossings. Ask your pupil if he or she has ever been waiting at a crossing when a driver from one direction has stopped but the one approaching from the opposite way has not. An arm signal would have alerted that driver to the fact that the other was stopping.

Allow some stationary practice in the use of this signal; and advise study of the others contained in *The Highway Code*. Draw pupils' attention to the fact that, should the indicators fail on their car, they may need to be able to let others know of their intentions.

Dealing with pedestrian crossings

Your pupils will all have used pedestrian crossings – do not be patronizing. Most of them will also be studying for the theory test. By asking a few relevant questions, you should be able to confirm whether they understand the basic rules relating to the different types of crossing. Ask how many types of crossing they can think of. The list should include:

- zebra;
- pelican;
- puffin;
- toucan;
- pegasus (equestrian);
- school crossings.

Sample questions

What sort of sign might you see on the approach to a pedestrian crossing?
What markings would you see on the road?
What do the zigzag lines mean?
How would a pedestrian claim priority at a zebra crossing?
What is the sequence of the lights at a pelican crossing?
What is the difference at a puffin crossing?
Who is a toucan crossing for?
How is the pegasus (equestrian) crossing different?

Because of the number of different types of crossing, and the limited time available, you will probably only be able to deal with the main types, zebra and pelican. However, if the lesson is taking place at the relevant time and there are children making their way to or from school, it may be appropriate to mention school crossings and the patrol staff. If you are asked questions relating to a specific crossing, or there are any other types peculiar to the local area (for example toucan, pelican, puffin or equestrian), then obviously you will need to include these.

The key elements to be emphasized are:

- looking ahead for signs and markings;
- anticipating and planning for pedestrian activity;
- the effective application of the M–S–M routine;
- approaching at the correct speed to allow a safe stop if necessary;
- planning for the lights to change at controlled crossings;
- using all signals safely and correctly.

Dealing with the less experienced driver

If the pupil has never dealt with crossings, you will need to give some talk-through instruction to encourage forward planning, the correct application of the M–S–M routine, and to build up confidence. As skill improves, gradually reduce the level of tuition and transfer the responsibility by asking the pupil to tell you how far ahead he or she is looking and what he or she is planning to do. Remember – always be ready to give further assistance if required, particularly if safety is at risk.

Dealing with the more experienced driver

Allow the pupil to drive for a few minutes so that you can assess the level of his or her skill and understanding. If any problems arise, identify and analyse them. Whether you can do this on the move, or whether you will need to stop will depend on:

- the degree of the error;
- how much detail you need to go into;
- the situation you are in;
- whether there is anywhere convenient to stop.

Fault assessment

Where fault assessment is concerned, no matter what the standard of the pupil is, positive correction is better than negative or retrospective correction. If your pupil is not responding to a developing hazard, give a positive prompt to encourage the pupil to take some form of action. This is far safer and more effective than allowing a potentially dangerous situation to arise, particularly where pedestrians are involved.

For example, you are approaching a pelican crossing and have noticed the 'Wait' sign lit up and pedestrians waiting to cross. Your pupil appears not to be anticipating any change in the situation. Which of the following options do you think will result in more positive learning:

- trying to get the pupil to react by asking, 'What do you think is going to happen at that crossing?', or
- waiting to see if action is going to be taken and then, when nothing happens, using the dual controls to stop the car at the latest possible moment?

Practice

Plan the lesson to include as many crossings as possible. During the drive, assess whether the pupil is putting all the established routines into practice. Identify and analyse problems. Give advice on how to improve, and when you make a correction, remember to give a good reason for it. On the Part 3 test, of course, the examiner does the route planning for you.

Common faults

- Lack of planning and anticipation.
- Incorrect application of the M–S–M routine.
- Signals:
  - given incorrectly;
  - unnecessarily;
  - badly timed.
- Not reinstating signals that have cancelled themselves.
- Not cancelling signals after use.
- Misuse of the horn and/or flashing headlights.
- Inviting pedestrians or other road users to move forward.
- Approaching crossings too fast.
- Failure to respond to traffic lights.
- Failure to stop when necessary.
- Blocking crossings in traffic queues.
- Not securing the car when necessary.
- Moving off from crossings prematurely.
- Not responding safely to others' signals.

Summary of the key points

- Establish what the pupil knows about the different methods of signalling.
- Confirm use of the M–S–M routine in all situations.
- Outline the rules relating to the different types of crossing.
- Emphasize the importance of approaching at the correct speed and stopping when necessary.
- Identify and analyse weaknesses.
- Give remedial advice with valid reasons.
- Create opportunities to practise the correct routines.
- Give feedback on where learning or improvement has taken place and link forward to the next lesson.

Reverse parking

Preset Test 6 – Phase 2

> I would like you to regard me as a pupil who has had about 30 lessons. I failed my test on reverse parking and don't understand why. Please apply corrective instruction on this subject and also correct any general driving faults.

This exercise is important in developing the pupil's control skills and teaching the pupil to park in smaller spaces. By the time you introduce this manoeuvre, the pupil should have developed his or her vehicle control skills reasonably well. These skills learnt previously will transfer into dealing with parking in more challenging conditions.

The main elements of the lesson are to:

- assess the pupil's general driving;
- confirm the site for parking: safe – legal – convenient;
- teach the manoeuvre if it has not been done before, with coordination of controls, accuracy and observations;
- reinforce each element of the exercise as above if it has been practised before;
- confirm how gradients and cambers will affect control;
- identify and analyse any problems.

Lesson content

Confirm what the pupil already knows about manoeuvring and the control skills involved. Confirming that you will be driving to a suitable site, ask the pupil to drive on, putting all previously learnt routines and procedures into practice.

During this drive, make an assessment, identifying strengths and weaknesses. Analyse these and give remedial advice if necessary. You should be able to deal with most of the minor errors on the move, but if any serious ones occur, comment on them and, if necessary, deal with them in more detail when you stop.

Confirm that the site is safe, legal and convenient. Explain that the exercise sometimes has to be carried out where there are other road users and that traffic flow must be maintained. Consideration needs to be exercised if too much delay will be caused to others.

Pupils who have previous experience

If the pupil has practised the exercise before, ask a few questions on the different elements and then assess the level of knowledge, understanding and skill. Should problems arise, be ready to help in order to encourage improvement.

The pupil with no previous experience

Prior to starting the exercise, get the pupil to work out what effect any up- or downhill gradient may have on control of the car. Encourage an initial look around for pedestrians and other road users. A full talk-through for the first attempt should encourage success and build confidence. Depending on progress, you can then either give more help or encourage the pupil to try the exercise unaided.

The most common problems are caused by:

- the pupil not taking the gradient into consideration;
- the amount of movement of the wheel required for cars with and without power-assisted steering;
- lack of observations, or response to the presence of others.

With a pupil who has been driving regularly but who has not previously been taught this manoeuvre, try to build on what he or she already knows and can do. For example, the pupil will probably have a lot of experience in reversing generally and may have tried reverse parking on his or her own, but without much success. You can use your question and answer skills to determine where and how to start the lesson and should employ your coaching skills, rather than simply 'instructing', as the lesson progresses.

The manoeuvre

Confirm the application of the M–S–M routine to get into position alongside the other vehicle. The signal element will depend on the presence of other road users – indicator, confirming arm signal, brake lights and/or reversing lights. Assess the gradient and confirm how the speed will need to be controlled.

Building on the pupil's current knowledge of reversing round a corner to the left, confirm the point at which the wheel will need to be turned, and explain that it will need to be straightened earlier than when driving around a corner, and then turned to the right and straightened again. Explain that less effort is required if the car has power-assisted steering.

Emphasize the need for regular observations and of responding to other road users' actions. Ensure the pupil checks the front of the car is clearing the other vehicle. Confirm that, once the other car is cleared, looking through the rear window well down the road will give a better perspective for keeping the car straight. Complete the manoeuvre with the wheels straight.

Practising the reverse park

Plenty of practice may be required to ensure consistency. However, from the point of view of good public relations you should not reverse around the same vehicle more than twice. It will be of greater benefit to drive somewhere else so that the exercise can be carried out under different circumstances – for example, on a different gradient or a narrower road.

Use simple terms for reference. For example, a 90-degree angle would be used for reversing around a right-angled corner before straightening, while a 45-degree angle would be needed for reverse parking.

Common faults

- Not putting into practice the M–S–M routine prior to the exercise.
- Lack of consideration of the gradient or camber, resulting in incorrect use of the controls.
- Lack of coordination of the controls.
- Not looking in the direction of travel.
- Under- or over-steering.
- Not keeping a check on the all-round traffic situation.
- Not responding to other road users.
- Finishing in an unsafe position.

Summary of the key points

- Confirm the pupil's previous experience.
- Assess driving and give remedial advice where necessary.
- Confirm the elements involved – control/accuracy/observations and response.
- Practise the exercise and encourage confidence.
- Give feedback of improvement and confirm where more practice is needed.

Making progress; hesitancy and road positioning

Preset Test 05 – Phase 2; Preset Test 10 – Phase 2

I would like you to treat me as a pupil who has had 30 lessons with another instructor. My previous instructor said that I am weak on my road positioning and on making progress. Please give corrective instruction on these points and also correct any general driving faults.

To deal with today's congested conditions and complex road systems, drivers need to be skilful, confident and considerate. As an ADI, it will be your job to teach your pupils to become safe and effective, and to develop in them positive attitudes towards themselves, their vehicle and other road users. Therefore, even though they probably will not achieve the same standard, you should be teaching your pupils to drive in a similar style to the one you use in your own driving.

Your main objectives will be to teach new drivers to be aware of the need to make progress when it is safe, according to the type of road, and the road, weather and traffic conditions; to have the confidence to take all safe opportunities to proceed at junctions; and to drive positively on roads with higher speed limits.

Make sure that pupils are aware of the need to:

- be travelling at a safe speed for the conditions;
- have the correct gear engaged for the speed, power and economy requirements;
- be in the correct position in relation to:
  - the type of road,
  - width of the road,
  - vision and safety margin,
  - other road users.

By the time your pupils are approaching test standard, their personal driving skills should be well developed. They should be applying all of the correct routines and procedures for driving in different road and traffic situations. Your main objectives are to confirm knowledge of:

- the speed limits for different types of road;
- braking, following and stopping distances and the 'two-second rule';
- the factors that should influence the speed – for example the type of road/surface/weather conditions/volume of traffic/pedestrian activity;
- the need to make progress when safe;
- what effect driving too slowly for the conditions may have on other drivers.

At junctions, check that your pupils look for gaps in the traffic and that they have the car ready for moving off efficiently. When moving into a gap in traffic make sure that the speed is built up positively. Check that they position correctly for the type of road, direction to be taken, speed and position of other vehicles, and volume of pedestrian activity.

Explain what the objectives are and establish the pupil's previous knowledge and understanding by asking a few questions. For example:

What's the speed limit in a built up area?
What's the speed limit on a two-way road with a national speed limit sign?
What's the stopping distance at 30 mph?
Explain the 'two-second' rule to me.
Would you drive at 30 mph past a school at 3.30 in the afternoon?
What happens to your stopping distance on wet roads?

Driving on dual carriageways

An important part of your job is to prepare your pupils for driving on all types of road. Dual carriageways are normally safer than single-carriageway roads, as the traffic on each carriageway is all travelling in the same direction. There are also fewer problems caused by traffic having to cross the path of other drivers. Teach your pupils to:

- look and plan well ahead for obstructions or junctions;
- use all of the mirrors even more frequently;
- maintain lane discipline;
- read the signs and markings;
- anticipate early changes in direction;
- apply the M–S–M routine in good time to allow for safe lane changes;
- keep up to date with traffic to the rear and sides;
- avoid driving in other drivers' blind areas for prolonged distances;
- drive positively to suit the conditions.

Fault assessment

You will need to assess how your pupils are driving in relation to the conditions. Remember to query anything that deviates from normal standards.

Failure to make progress If pupils are missing too many gaps at junctions, encourage them to:

- start making their observations earlier;
- work out when their gap is going to arrive;
- have the car ready to move promptly into the space;
- build up the speed and change up through the gears efficiently.

When pupils drive too slowly for the conditions, or miss opportunities to proceed, encourage them to make progress by talking through a few situations to demonstrate what you mean. This should not be classed as over-instruction because, after all, if they cannot drive appropriately to suit the conditions, then you have to teach them how to do so.

Driving too fast for the conditions When pupils drive too fast, without considering the possible dangers, you must be firm and get their speed under control. When this becomes necessary, you must give valid reasons. For example, if you are on a road where there is a lot of pedestrian activity, you will need to confirm what speed you would be driving at and explain what you would be looking for.

Positioning Encourage correct positioning at all times. Ensure that your pupils:

- maintain the normal road position when driving along;
- position correctly at junctions, according to the type and width of the road;
- plan well ahead and select the correct lane in good time;
- maintain lane discipline.

Common faults

- Moving off slowly and not changing up through the gears efficiently.
- Driving too slowly on roads with higher speed limits.
- Breaking the speed limit.
- Driving too fast in unsafe conditions.
- Missing opportunities to proceed at junctions.
- Not looking in all directions at junctions.
- Looking only to the right at roundabouts and getting out of position.
- Not using the mirrors regularly.
- Being unaware of drivers to the rear and sides.
- Lack of planning on dual carriageways resulting in becoming 'boxed in'.
- Positioning incorrectly on narrow roads or one-way streets.
- Driving too close to the kerb, or too far out.
- Incorrect positioning on bends.
- Not maintaining lane discipline.

Summary of the key points

- Establish prior experience.
- Confirm the importance of planning ahead and making progress where safe.
- Ensure that safety margins are maintained according to the conditions.
- Confirm the importance of being in the correct place on the road at all times.
- Identify and analyse faults and give remedial advice with reasons.
- Give feedback on improvement and emphasize where more practice is needed.

The preset tests

To ensure that all candidates have a test of equal difficulty, and that there is a balance between the two phases, the exercises are arranged as 'preset tests' (PST). Some subjects – for example, pedestrian crossings and signals – are used more often than others. Where a test exercise involves several subjects, for example 'meet, cross and overtake other traffic', your examiner will give a clear indication of those subjects you are to include. Make sure that you listen carefully and structure your lesson accordingly.

Interpreting the marking sheet

The marking sheets for the PST are reproduced on pages 164–73.

Using the markings in columns A and B on the marking sheets, your overall performance on both phases is assessed. In particular, the examiner will assess your ability under the three main headings of core competencies, instructional techniques and instructor characteristics. The maximum grade attainable in each phase is 6. The minimum level for a pass is grade 4 in each phase. However, the examiner makes an overall assessment by taking into consideration the markings of both columns A and B.

For example, if a candidate fails to identify a serious error and does nothing to correct the problem, the examiner would mark the appropriate box in column A under 'not covered' or 'unsatisfactory'. This would then be transferred to column B under the heading 'identification of faults'.

Criteria for grading

6: Overall performance to a very high standard with no significant instructional weaknesses.

5: A good overall standard of instruction with some minor weakness in instructional technique.

4: A competent overall performance with some minor deficiencies in instructional technique.

3: An inadequate overall performance with some deficiencies in instructional techniques.

2: A poor overall performance with numerous deficiencies in instructional techniques.

1: Overall standard of instruction extremely poor or dangerous with incorrect or even dangerous instruction.

You must remember that because of this overall assessment of what actually happens on the day, no two tests can ever be the same. Even the manoeuvre exercises cannot be rehearsed, and you will need to be able to adapt to what is happening in different circumstances. This is all part of the test of your potential to become an effective teacher of driving.

When you pass

You will be given a letter confirming the result, and you may apply for entry on to the Register of Approved Driving Instructors (Car). Complete the application form on the reverse of the letter and send it with the current fee (£300 at January 2011). This must be done within 12 months of the date you pass. Registration then becomes renewable every four years.

With your application for registration you will need to enclose the appropriate payment and a recent passport-style photo.

Registration declaration

When you apply for registration, you must sign a declaration to the effect that you will:

- notify the Registrar of any change of name, address or place of employment;
- notify the Registrar if convicted of any offence;
- return the certificate if your registration lapses or is revoked;
- agree to undergo, when requested by the Registrar, a Check Test conducted by DSA staff.

If you fail

Using the application form on the reverse of the letter, you may apply for a further test if you are still within the two-year qualifying period, and if the test was your first or second attempt. Otherwise, if you wish to continue, you will have to wait until the two-year period has elapsed before you can apply for Part 1 again. It is therefore sensible to be prepared to invest in sufficient training with an experienced tutor before taking your Part 3.

Regardless of whether you pass or fail, you can obtain more details about your test by contacting the DSA. You can do this by telephoning the examiner on a Friday, when he or she will be able to give advice to help with your instructional techniques.

Common problems

The most common contributory factors for failing the examination are:

- Briefing which is too long, muddled or repetitive.
- Expecting too high a standard from the 'pupil' in the beginner or part-trained stage.
- Not instructing at a level appropriate to the pupil's needs, eg over-instruction or under-instruction.
- Inability to recommence instruction at a different point or to go back and explain again.
- Weaknesses in one or more of the core competencies – fault identification, fault analysis or remedial action.
- Treating the 'pupil' as a beginner in the trained/full licence holder stage.

DSA – ADI 14 –*Your Road to Becoming an Approved Driving Instructor.*

The ADI certificate

After passing the instructional test, you should receive your official green ADI Certificate of Registration within a week. This will incorporate your name, photograph, ADI number and the date of issue and expiry of the certificate, which will be four years from the date of its issue. As a qualified instructor, whenever you are giving tuition, you must display the official green certificate on the left-hand side of the car's windscreen, and produce your certificate if requested by a police officer or any person authorized by the Secretary of State. (Failure to do so constitutes an offence.) If you can satisfy the Registrar that your certificate has been lost, damaged or destroyed, the DSA will issue a duplicate on payment of the current fee.

DRIVING STANDARDS AGENCY
SAFE DRIVING FOR LIFE

Instructional Test - Part III

The Examiner has marked each aspect of your performance in
columns A and B below. Please see overleaf for explanatory notes.

Register of
Approved Driving
Instruction
(Car)

Candidate's Declaration

I certify that
- the vehicle I have provided for the test is properly
  insured under the Road Traffic Act 1988 and
- I do/do not have to wear seat belts under the Motor
  Vehicles (Wearing of Seat Belts) Regulations 1982.

Signed

Date

Centre

Date

Make & model

Reg Mark

Dual Controls   Fitted   Not Fitted

Candidate's Name

Ref. No

Column A

PST No.1 Exercises 1B and 10T

Phase 1-1B Beginner-Controls

	Not Covered	Unsatisfactory	Satisfactory
Doors			
Seat/Head Restraint			
Seat Belt			
Mirrors			
Accelerator			
Footbrake			
Clutch			
Handbrake			
Gears			
Steering			
Indicators			
Starting			
Precautions before moving off			
Normal stop position			
Normal stop use of MSM			
Normal stop control			

Phase 2-10T Trained / FLH* - Crossroads

Mirror-Signal-Manoeuvre			
Speed			
Gears			
Coasting			
Observation			
Emerging			
Position right			
Position left			
Pedestrians			
Cross approaching traffic			
Right corner cut			

The results of your test are:

Phase I Grade   Phase II Grade

Examiner's name

Examiner's
Signature

Column B

In this column the top line of boxes to Phase I and the
bottom line of boxes refer to Phase II

1/2/3 = Unsatisfactory   4/5/6 = Satisfactory

Core Competencies

	1 2 3	4 5 6
Identification of faults		
Fault analysis		
Remedial action		

Instructional Techniques

	1 2 3	4 5 6
Level of instruction		
Planning		
Control of lesson		
Communication		
Q/A Techniques		
Feedback/Encouragement		
Instructor use of controls		

Instructor Characteristics

	1 2 3	4 5 6
Attitude and Approach to Pupil		

* delete as applicable   ADI 26/PST/01 Rev 10/06

Instructional Test - Part III
The Examiner has marked each aspect of your performance in
columns A and B below. Please see overleaf for explanatory notes.

Candidate's Declaration

I certify that
- the vehicle I have provided for the test is properly insured under the Road Traffic Act 1988 and
- I do/do not have to wear seat belts under the Motor Vehicles (Wearing of Seat Belts) Regulations 1982.

Signed

Date

Centre

Date

Make & model

Reg Mark

Dual Controls   Fitted [ ]   Not Fitted [ ]

Candidate's Name

Ref. No

Column A

PST No.2 Exercises 2B and 11T

Phase 1-2B Beginner-Moving off / stopping

	Not Covered	Unsatisfactory	Satisfactory
Briefing on moving off/stopping			
Mirrors vision and use			
Mirrors, direction, overtaking and stopping			
Mirror signal manoeuvre			
Precautions before moving off			
Co-ordination of controls			
Normal stop position			
Normal stop control			

Phase 2-11T Trained/FLH*-Meet, cross and overtake other traffic allowing adequate clearance for other road users and anticipation

Mirror-Signal-Manoeuvre			
Meet approaching traffic			
Cross approaching traffic			
Overtake other traffic			
Keep a safe distance			
Shaving other vehicles			
Anticipation of pedestrians			
Anticipation of cyclists			
Anticipation of drivers			

The results of your test are:

Phase I Grade [ ]   Phase II Grade [ ]

Examiner's name

Examiner's Signature

Column B

In this column the top line of boxes to Phase I and the bottom line of boxes refer to Phase II

1/2/3 = Unsatisfactory   4/5/6 = Satisfactory

Core Competencies

	1 2 3	4 5 6
Identification of faults		
Fault analysis		
Remedial action		

Instructional Techniques

	1 2 3	4 5 6
Level of instruction		
Planning		
Control of lesson		
Communication		
Q/A Techniques		
Feedback/Encouragement		
Instructor use of controls		

Instructor Characteristics

	1 2 3	4 5 6
Attitude and Approach to Pupil		

*Delete as applicable   ADI 26/PST/02 Rev 06/08

Instructional Test - Part III

The Examiner has marked each aspect of your performance in
columns A and B below. Please see overleaf for explanatory notes.

Candidate's Declaration

I certify that
- the vehicle I have provided for the test is properly insured under the Road Traffic Act 1988 and
- I do/do not have to wear seat belts under the Motor Vehicles (Wearing of Seat Belts) Regulations 1982.

Signed

Date

Centre

Date

Make & model

Reg Mark

Dual Controls   Fitted   Not Fitted

Candidate's Name

Ref. No

Column A

PST No.3 Exercises 4P and 7T

Phase 1-4P Partly trained-Turn in the road

	Not Covered	Unsatisfactory	Satisfactory
Briefing on turn in the road			
Co-ordination of controls			
Observation			
Accuracy			

Phase 2-7T Trained-Approaching junctions to turn either right or left

	Not Covered	Unsatisfactory	Satisfactory
Mirrors			
Signal			
Brakes			
Gears			
Coasting			
Too fast on approach			
Too slow on approach			
Position			
Pedestrians			
Cross approaching traffic			
Right corner cut			

The results of your test are:

Phase I Grade   Phase II Grade

Examiner's name

Examiner's Signature

Column B

In this column the top line of boxes to Phase I and the
bottom line of boxes refer to Phase II

1/2/3 = Unsatisfactory   4/5/6 = Satisfactory

Core Competencies

	1 2 3	4 5 6
Identification of faults		
Fault analysis		
Remedial action		

Instructional Techniques

	1 2 3	4 5 6
Level of instruction		
Planning		
Control of lesson		
Communication		
Q/A Techniques		
Feedback/Encouragement		
Instructor use of controls		

Instructor Characteristics

	1 2 3	4 5 6
Attitude and Approach to Pupil		

ADI 26/PST/03 Rev 06/06

Instructional Test - Part III

The Examiner has marked each aspect of your performance in columns A and B below. Please see overleaf for explanatory notes.

Candidate's Declaration

I certify that
- the vehicle I have provided for the test is properly insured under the Road Traffic Act 1988 and
- I do/do not have to wear seat belts under the Motor Vehicles (Wearing of Seat Belts) Regulations 1982.

Signed

Date

Centre

Date

Make & model

Reg Mark

Dual Controls   Fitted   Not Fitted

Candidate's Name

Ref. No

Column A

PST No.4 Exercises 3P and 9T

Phase 1-3P Partly trained-Reversing

Left Reverse   Right Reverse

	Not Covered	Unsatisfactory	Satisfactory
Briefing on reversing			
Co-ordination of controls			
Observation			
Accuracy			

Phase 2-9T Trained-T Junctions-Emerging

	Not Covered	Unsatisfactory	Satisfactory
Mirror-Signal-Manoeuvre			
Speed			
Gears			
Coasting			
Observation			
Emerging			
Position right			
Position left			
Pedestrians			

The results of your test are:

Phase I Grade   Phase II Grade

Examiner's name

Examiner's Signature

Column B

In this column the top line of boxes to Phase I and the bottom line of boxes refer to Phase II

1/2/3 = Unsatisfactory   4/5/6 = Satisfactory

Core Competencies

	1 2 3	4 5 6
Identification of faults		
Fault analysis		
Remedial action		

Instructional Techniques

	1 2 3	4 5 6
Level of instruction		
Planning		
Control of lesson		
Communication		
Q/A Techniques		
Feedback/Encouragement		
Instructor use of controls		

Instructor Characteristics

	1 2 3	4 5 6
Attitude and Approach to Pupil		

ADI 26/PST/04 Rev 06/06

Instructional Test - Part III

The Examiner has marked each aspect of your performance in
columns A and B below. Please see overleaf for explanatory notes.

Candidate's Declaration

I certify that
- the vehicle I have provided for the test is properly insured under the Road Traffic Act 1988 and
- I do/do not have to wear seat belts under the Motor Vehicles (Wearing of Seat Belts) Regulations 1982.

Signed

Date

Centre

Date

Make & model

Reg Mark

Dual Controls   Fitted   Not Fitted

Candidate's Name

Ref. No

Column A

PST No.5 Exercises 6P and 8T

Phase 1-6P Partly trained-Emergency stop/Mirrors

	Not Covered	Unsatisfactory	Satisfactory
Briefing on emergency stop/mirrors			
Quick reaction			
Use of footbrake/clutch			
Skidding			
Mirrors vision and use			
Mirrors, direction, overtaking and stopping			
Mirror-signal-manoeuvre			

Phase 2-8T Trained / FLH* - Progress / Hesitancy - Normal position

	Not Covered	Unsatisfactory	Satisfactory
Progress too fast			
Progress too slow			
Hesitancy			
Normal position too wide from the left			
Normal position too close to the left			

The results of your test are:

Phase I Grade   **Phase II Grade**

Examiner's name

Examiner's Signature

Column B

In this column the top line of boxes to Phase I and the bottom line of boxes refer to Phase II

1/2/3 = Unsatisfactory   4/5/6 = Satisfactory

Core Competencies

	1 2 3	4 5 6
Identification of faults		
Fault analysis		
Remedial action		

Instructional Techniques

	1 2 3	4 5 6
Level of instruction		
Planning		
Control of lesson		
Communication		
Q/A Techniques		
Feedback/Encouragement		
Instructor use of controls		

Instructor Characteristics

	1 2 3	4 5 6
Attitude and Approach to Pupil		

* delete as applicable   ADI 26/PST/05 Rev 06/06

Instructional Test - Part III

The Examiner has marked each aspect of your performance in columns A and B below. Please see overleaf for explanatory notes.

Candidate's Declaration

I certify that
- the vehicle I have provided for the test is properly insured under the Road Traffic Act 1988 and
- I do/do not have to wear seat belts under the Motor Vehicles (Wearing of Seat Belts) Regulations 1982.

Signed

Date

Centre

Date

Make & model

Reg Mark

Dual Controls   Fitted [ ]   Not Fitted [ ]

Candidate's Name

Ref. No

Column A
PST No.6 Exercises 12P and 5T

Phase 1-12P Partly trained Pedestrian crossings and the use of signals

	Not Covered	Unsatisfactory	Satisfactory
Briefing on pedestrian crossings/signals	[ ]	[ ]	[ ]
Mirror-signal-manoeuvre	[ ]	[ ]	[ ]
Speed on approach	[ ]	[ ]	[ ]
Stop when necessary	[ ]	[ ]	[ ]
Overtaking on approach	[ ]	[ ]	[ ]
Inviting pedestrains to cross	[ ]	[ ]	[ ]
Signals by indicator	[ ]	[ ]	[ ]
Signals by arm	[ ]	[ ]	[ ]
Signals - timing	[ ]	[ ]	[ ]
Unneccessary signals	[ ]	[ ]	[ ]

Phase 2-5T Trained/FLH*-Reverse parking

	Not Covered	Unsatisfactory	Satisfactory
Briefing on reverse parking	[ ]	[ ]	[ ]
Co-ordination of controls	[ ]	[ ]	[ ]
Observation	[ ]	[ ]	[ ]
Accuracy	[ ]	[ ]	[ ]

The results of your test are:

Phase I Grade [ ]   Phase II Grade [ ]

Examiner's name

Examiner's Signature

Column B

In this column the top line of boxes to Phase I and the bottom line of boxes refer to Phase II

1/2/3 = Unsatisfactory   4/5/6 = Satisfactory

Core Competencies

	1 2 3	4 5 6
Identification of faults		
Fault analysis		
Remedial action		

Instructional Techniques

	1 2 3	4 5 6
Level of instruction		
Planning		
Control of lesson		
Communication		
Q/A Techniques		
Feedback/Encouragement		
Instructor use of controls		

Instructor Characteristics

	1 2 3	4 5 6
Attitude and Approach to Pupil		

*Delete as applicable   ADI 26/PST/06 Rev 06/08

Instructional Test - Part III

The Examiner has marked each aspect of your performance in columns A and B below. Please see overleaf for explanatory notes.

Candidate's Declaration

I certify that
- the vehicle I have provided for the test is properly insured under the Road Traffic Act 1988 and
- I do/do not have to wear seat belts under the Motor Vehicles (Wearing of Seat Belts) Regulations 1982.

Signed

Date

Centre

Date

Make & model

Reg Mark

Dual Controls   Fitted   Not Fitted

Candidate's Name

Ref. No

Column A

PST No.7 Exercises 7P and 12T

Phase 1-7P Partly trained-Approaching junctions to turn either right or left

	Not Covered	Unsatisfactory	Satisfactory
Briefing on approaching junctions	☐	☐	☐
Mirrors	☐	☐	☐
Signal	☐	☐	☐
Brakes	☐	☐	☐
Gears	☐	☐	☐
Coasting	☐	☐	☐
Too fast on approach	☐	☐	☐
Too slow on approach	☐	☐	☐
Position	☐	☐	☐
Pedestrians	☐	☐	☐
Cross approaching traffic	☐	☐	☐
Right corner cut	☐	☐	☐

Phase 2-12T Trained / FLH* - Pedestrians crossings and the use of signals

	Not Covered	Unsatisfactory	Satisfactory
Mirror-Signal-Manoeuvre	☐	☐	☐
Speed on approach	☐	☐	☐
Stop when necessary	☐	☐	☐
Overtaking on approach	☐	☐	☐
Inviting pedestrians to cross	☐	☐	☐
Signals by indicator	☐	☐	☐
Signals by arm	☐	☐	☐
Signals timing	☐	☐	☐
Unnecessary signals	☐	☐	☐

The results of your test are:

Phase I Grade   **Phase II Grade**

Examiner's name

Examiner's Signature

Column B

In this column the top line of boxes to Phase I and the bottom line of boxes refer to Phase II

1/2/3 = Unsatisfactory   4/5/6 = Satisfactory

Core Competencies

	1 2 3	4 5 6
Identification of faults	☐☐☐ / ☐☐☐	☐☐☐ / ☐☐☐
Fault analysis	☐☐☐ / ☐☐☐	☐☐☐ / ☐☐☐
Remedial action	☐☐☐ / ☐☐☐	☐☐☐ / ☐☐☐

Instructional Techniques

	1 2 3	4 5 6
Level of instruction	☐☐☐ / ☐☐☐	☐☐☐ / ☐☐☐
Planning	☐☐☐ / ☐☐☐	☐☐☐ / ☐☐☐
Control of lesson	☐☐☐ / ☐☐☐	☐☐☐ / ☐☐☐
Communication	☐☐☐ / ☐☐☐	☐☐☐ / ☐☐☐
Q/A Techniques	☐☐☐ / ☐☐☐	☐☐☐ / ☐☐☐
Feedback/Encouragement	☐☐☐ / ☐☐☐	☐☐☐ / ☐☐☐
Instructor use of controls	☐☐☐ / ☐☐☐	☐☐☐ / ☐☐☐

Instructor Characteristics

	1 2 3	4 5 6
Attitude and Approach to Pupil	☐☐☐	☐☐☐

* delete as applicable   ADI 26/PST/07 Rev 10/06

Instructional Test - Part III

The Examiner has marked each aspect of your performance in columns A and B below. Please see overleaf for explanatory notes.

Candidate's Declaration

I certify that

the vehicle I have provided for the test is properly insured under the Road Traffic Act 1988 and

I do/do not have to wear seat belts under the Motor Vehicles (Wearing of Seat Belts) Regulations 1982.

Signed

Date

Centre

Date

Make & model

Reg Mark

Dual Controls   Fitted ☐   Not Fitted ☐

Candidate's Name

Ref. No

Column A

PST No.8 Exercises 9P and 11T

Phase 1-9P Partly trained-T Junctions-Emerging

	Not Covered	Unsatisfactory	Satisfactory
Briefing on T junctions	☐	☐	☐
Mirror-signal-manoeuvre	☐	☐	☐
Speed	☐	☐	☐
Gears	☐	☐	☐
Coasting	☐	☐	☐
Observation	☐	☐	☐
Emerging	☐	☐	☐
Position right	☐	☐	☐
Position left	☐	☐	☐
Pedestrians	☐	☐	☐

Phase 2-11T Trained / FLH* - Meet, cross and overtake other traffic allowing adequate clearance for other road users and anticipation

	Not Covered	Unsatisfactory	Satisfactory
Mirror-Signal-Manoeuvre	☐	☐	☐
Meet approaching traffic	☐	☐	☐
Cross approaching traffic	☐	☐	☐
Overtake other traffic	☐	☐	☐
Keep a safe distance	☐	☐	☐
Shaving other vehicles	☐	☐	☐
Anticipation of pedestrians	☐	☐	☐
Anticipation of cyclists	☐	☐	☐
Anticipation of drivers	☐	☐	☐

The results of your test are:

Phase I Grade ____   **Phase II Grade** ____

Examiner's name

Examiner's Signature

Column B

In this column the top line of boxes to Phase I and the bottom line of boxes refer to Phase II

1/2/3 = Unsatisfactory   4/5/6 = Satisfactory

Core Competencies

	1 2 3	4 5 6
Identification of faults		
Fault analysis		
Remedial action		

Instructional Techniques

	1 2 3	4 5 6
Level of instruction		
Planning		
Control of lesson		
Communication		
Q/A Techniques		
Feedback/Encouragement		
Instructor use of controls		

Instructor Characteristics

	1 2 3	4 5 6
Attitude and Approach to Pupil		

* delete as applicable   ADI 26/PST/08 Rev 07/06

Instructional Test - Part III

The Examiner has marked each aspect of your performance in
columns A and B below. Please see overleaf for explanatory notes.

Candidate's Declaration

I certify that

- the vehicle I have provided for the test is properly insured under the Road Traffic Act 1988 and

- I do/do not have to wear seat belts under the Motor Vehicles (Wearing of Seat Belts) Regulations 1982.

Signed

Date

Centre

Date

Make & model

Reg Mark

Dual Controls   Fitted   Not Fitted

Candidate's Name

Ref. No

Column A

PST No.9 Exercises 10P and 12T

Phase 1-10P Partly trained-Crossroads

	Not Covered	Unsatisfactory	Satisfactory
Briefing on crossroads	☐	☐	☐
Mirror-signal-manoeuvre	☐	☐	☐
Speed	☐	☐	☐
Gears	☐	☐	☐
Coasting	☐	☐	☐
Observation	☐	☐	☐
Emerging	☐	☐	☐
Position right	☐	☐	☐
Position left	☐	☐	☐
Pedestrians	☐	☐	☐
Cross approaching traffic	☐	☐	☐
Right corner cut	☐	☐	☐

Phase 2-12T Trained/ FLH*- Pedestrian crossings and signals

	Not Covered	Unsatisfactory	Satisfactory
Mirror-Signal-Manoeuvre	☐	☐	☐
Speed on approach	☐	☐	☐
Stop when necessary	☐	☐	☐
Overtaking on approach	☐	☐	☐
Inviting pedestrians to cross	☐	☐	☐
Signals by indicator	☐	☐	☐
Signals by arm	☐	☐	☐
Signals timing	☐	☐	☐
Unnecessary signals	☐	☐	☐

The results of your test are:

Phase I Grade   **Phase II Grade**

Examiner's name

Examiner's Signature

Column B

In this column the top line of boxes to Phase I and the bottom line of boxes refer to Phase II

1/2/3 = **Unsatisfactory**   4/5/6 = **Satisfactory**

Core Competencies

	1	2	3	4	5	6
Identification of faults						
Fault analysis						
Remedial action						

Instructional Techniques

	1	2	3	4	5	6
Level of instruction						
Planning						
Control of lesson						
Communication						
Q/A Techniques						
Feedback/Encouragement						
Instructor use of controls						

Instructor Characteristics

	1	2	3	4	5	6
Attitude and Approach to Pupil						

* delete as applicable   ADI 26/PST/09 Rev 06/06

Instructional Test - Part III

The Examiner has marked each aspect of your performance in columns A and B below. Please see overleaf for explanatory notes.

Candidate's Declaration

I certify that
- the vehicle I have provided for the test is properly insured under the Road Traffic Act 1988 and
- I do/do not have to wear seat belts under the Motor Vehicles (Wearing of Seat Belts) Regulations 1982.

Signed

Date

Centre

Date

Make & model

Reg Mark

Dual Controls   Fitted ☐   Not Fitted ☐

Candidate's Name

Ref. No

Column A

PST No.10 Exercises 11P and 8T

Phase 1-11P Partly trained-Meet, cross and overtake other traffic allowing adequate clearance for other road users and anticipation

	Not Covered/ Incorrect	Unsatisfactory	Satisfactory
Briefing	☐	☐	☐
Mirror-signal-manoeuvre	☐	☐	☐
Meet approaching traffic	☐	☐	☐
Cross other traffic	☐	☐	☐
Overtaking other traffic	☐	☐	☐
Keep a safe distance	☐	☐	☐
Shaving other vehicles	☐	☐	☐
Anticipation of pedestrians	☐	☐	☐
Anticipation of cyclists	☐	☐	☐
Anticipation of drivers	☐	☐	☐

Phase 2-8T Trained/FLH*-Progress / hesitancy - normal position

Progress too fast	☐	☐	☐
Progress too slow	☐	☐	☐
Hesitancy	☐	☐	☐
Normal position too wide from the left	☐	☐	☐
Normal position too close to the left	☐	☐	☐

The results of your test are:

Phase I Grade [   ]   Phase II Grade [   ]

Examiner's name

Examiner's Signature

Column B

In this column the top line of boxes to Phase I and the bottom line of boxes refer to Phase II

1/2/3 = Unsatisfactory   4/5/6 = Satisfactory

Core Competencies

	1	2	3		4	5	6
Identification of faults	☐	☐	☐		☐	☐	☐
Fault analysis	☐	☐	☐		☐	☐	☐
Remedial action	☐	☐	☐		☐	☐	☐

Instructional Techniques

	1	2	3		4	5	6
Level of instruction	☐	☐	☐		☐	☐	☐
Planning	☐	☐	☐		☐	☐	☐
Control of lesson	☐	☐	☐		☐	☐	☐
Communication	☐	☐	☐		☐	☐	☐
Q/A Techniques	☐	☐	☐		☐	☐	☐
Feedback/Encouragement	☐	☐	☐		☐	☐	☐
Instructor use of controls	☐	☐	☐		☐	☐	☐

Instructor Characteristics

	1	2	3		4	5	6
Attitude and Approach to Pupil	☐	☐	☐		☐	☐	☐

*Delete as applicable   ADI 26/PST/10 Rev 06/08

The ADI Check Test

06

I f you are a newly qualified ADI, you will be invited to attend for a Check Test within a year of passing your instructional test. You will be given a grading of 4, 5 or 6 depending on the examiner's assessment of your lesson. If the examiner feels you are lacking in experience, an 'E' (educational) grading will be given. In this case, you will be invited to attend for a further test within a few months.

Once you have been graded, the frequency of subsequent tests will be dependent on the grade you achieve. It is normally:

- grade 5 and 6 instructors – within four years;
- grade 4 instructors – within two years.

Any test resulting in a grade 3, 2 or 1 will require a retest to be taken fairly quickly. For grade 3 this will normally be within three months, grade 2 within two months, and a grade 1 indicates that the instruction seen was dangerous and this will result in the scheduling of an urgent retest. If you are not able to show an acceptable standard of instruction on three consecutive Check Tests you could be removed from the Register.

For details of the procedures for arranging check tests see www.businesslink.gov.uk and follow the links to 'transport and logistics/driving and motorcycle instructors/manage your ADI registration'.

In Northern Ireland the procedures are slightly different. For details see the ADI 1 (*Your Guide to becoming an Approved Driving Instructor*). This document is available from: The Register of Approved Driving Instructors, DVA Testing, 66 Balmoral Road, Belfast BT12 6QL; tel: 028 9054 7933; website: www.nidirect.gov.uk.

The appointment

Tests are conducted during the examiner's normal working hours and the invitation to attend will specify the date and time, and the place – normally local to the area you work in, and often the local driving test centre. You must acknowledge receipt of the invitation.

You do not necessarily need to accept the date given in the invitation letter. It is quite acceptable to change the date if it is inconvenient – for example, a pre-arranged holiday or other important commitments. However, you must contact the DSA promptly either by using the reply slip or contacting them by phone.

If you do not attend at the agreed time, you will be asked to attend at a time and place nominated by the DSA. It is important that you attend the Check Test – not having a pupil, not having a car or not working as an ADI are not regarded by the DSA as acceptable reasons for non-attendance.

DSA
DRIVING STANDARDS AGENCY
SAFE DRIVING FOR LIFE

ADI 40 (Rev 12/99)

Register of Approved Driving Instructors (Cars)

Date _____

Dear Instructor

Test of continued ability and fitness to give instruction (check test)

Please complete the appointment section below and return the top copy of this letter, by return post in the S.A.E. provided. The second copy is for your records.

As you know it is a condition of your continued registration as an Approved Driving Instructor that you will undergo a check test when required to do so. I have therefore arranged to conduct your check test as detailed below:-

* I will attend for a check test on: Date _____   Time _____

Place _____

Name of Driving School _____   ADI number _____

Vehicle to be used _____   Contact telephone number _____

Signed _____   Date _____

* I have decided not to attend for a check test and return my Certificate of Registration.

* Exceptional circumstances prevent me from attending for the check test appointment (evidence to support my claim e.g. medical certificate/Hospital appointment card is enclosed). I will be able to attend for a check test (give details)

*delete as applicable

Please arrange a normal lesson of approximately one hour to begin at the time shown and attend with a car and pupil. You should allow up to 15 minutes for discussion at the end of this lesson (This should not be a lesson that is immediately followed by a driving test). Attached are 'Notes for guidance', which I hope you will find useful.

If you do not return the appointment letter or cannot attend without good reason then the Registrar will require you to attend at a specified time and date. If you think that you may have difficulty attending please read the attached notes particularly the paragraph headed "The Invitation" and contact me as soon as possible so that an alternative appointment can be made.

If, due to unforeseen circumstances, I am prevented from attending the appointment, you should proceed with the lesson in the usual way. If this happens I will contact you and make fresh arrangements. Should you be unable to keep this appointment at the last moment, please telephone me as soon as possible so that alternative arrangements can be made. If I am not available please leave a message on my answerphone, Tel:_____ Please speak slowly and clearly giving your name, ADI number, appointment date and time.

Failure to attend for your check test without good reason, could lead to your name being removed from the Register.

Yours sincerely

Supervising Examiner ADI

Your pupil

If your pupil is a full licence holder rather than a learner, he or she must not be another ADI. The most important thing to remember is that the examiner is assessing your ability to teach and not the pupil's ability to drive. You must therefore ensure that your instruction is pitched at the correct level, whatever standard the driver has attained.

Some instructors make the mistake of selecting their 'favourite' pupil, or one whose driving is at a high standard. It is more important for you to use a pupil whose driving can be improved and worked on during the lesson.

If you do not have any pupils available at the appropriate time and date, you may opt for a 'role play' Check Test. This is very similar to the way in which Part 3 is conducted, except that the examiner will only portray one pupil for the duration of the test. In the role-play type of Check Test the examiner will select the subjects to be covered and the level at which they are to be taught. Whether you provide a pupil or opt for a role-play test, the important thing to remember is that you are in control of the entire lesson.

In Northern Ireland this 'role play' situation is not applicable – a pupil must be provided.

The car

The car you use for the Check Test must be roadworthy, safe and reliable. A soft-top convertible is not acceptable, nor is a car with limited rear seating for the examiner.

A driving-school car should always be kept in a roadworthy condition and display 'L' plates if the driver is a provisional licence holder. It should go without saying that a clean and tidy car (both inside and outside) will create a professional image. If you normally use the back seat of the car as your 'office' with an accumulation of diaries, reference books, teaching aids and so on, make sure that it is reasonable tidy and that the examiner has sufficient room.

If the lesson is to be conducted in a pupil's car, it is sensible for you to check on its condition beforehand and to make sure that it conforms to the test requirements. Your ADI Certificate must be displayed if you are charging for the lesson.

You must make sure that all seatbelts (both front and rear) are in good working order.

Presenting the lesson

When you pick up the pupil from the normal starting point for lessons, allow plenty of time to drive to the test centre or other meeting point for the

Check Test. It is important that you do the driving at this stage so that you start the lesson without a warm up for the pupil and that there is a clear distinction between the previous lesson and this one.

The examiner will want to know something about the pupil before the start, so you could provide a brief written indication of previous lessons and standards achieved to avoid a lengthy verbal explanation.

The format of the lesson should follow the same pattern as on a normal lesson. The fact that it is a Check Test should make very little difference. Following the initial introductions of pupil to examiner and explaining to the pupil the purpose of the Check Test, follow the basic routine:

- Recap on the previous session. At the beginning of the lesson, go over the main points from the previous lesson to establish a base line. This should be a two-way discussion, taking into account the pupil's comments and responses.

- Use questions and answers (Q&A) to establish what has been remembered (or forgotten) from previous lessons.

- Agree the objectives for the lesson by discussing what subjects are going to be covered and what is likely to be achieved by the end of the lesson.

- Keep the instruction at a level that is consistent with the pupil's ability and experience. Give as much help through guided instruction as is necessary, but adjust the amount of prompting depending on the stage of learning of the pupil.

- Identify, analyse and correct errors, giving valid reasons. This is one of the most important skills. Make sure you include an explanation of why the fault occurred as well as offering an explanation of how to correct it.

- End with a summary and a recap on what has been covered during the lesson. You should assess and discuss the level of achievement of the pupil (including any faults).

- The lesson should finish with a discussion on what will be covered on the next lesson.

During the Check Test you will be assessed on:

- Your flexibility to deviate from objectives if necessary. For example, if the objective was given as a manoeuvre exercise, and the pupil made some serious mistakes at junctions, it may be sensible to attend to these and defer the manoeuvring. You should remember to state why you have deviated from the original plan.

- The level of your instruction. This must be suitable for the ability and experience of your pupil.

- The teaching methods used and the clarity, adequacy and correctness of your instruction.

- The effectiveness of your Q&A technique. Use questions at appropriate times during the lesson. Questions should always be well-defined, simply worded and properly timed. They should be thought-provoking and challenging rather than simply testing the pupil's memory. Encourage the pupil to ask questions and allow time where appropriate.

- Your manner, patience, tact and, very importantly, your ability to inspire confidence. You should be self-confident and capable of passing on confidence to the pupil.

- The recap at the end of the lesson and whether feedback on progress is adequate.

The examiner will want to see that learning has taken place during the lesson and that the pupil is able to do something that they were not capable of at the start.

DSA
DRIVING STANDARDS AGENCY
SAFE DRIVING FOR LIFE

WORKING SHEET

| Cert. Expiry Date | | SOM | | Vehicle | |

Dual Controls: Yes ☐   No ☐   Pupil: Male ☐   Female ☐   Practising Privately: Yes ☐   No ☐

Hours of tuition with this ADI ☐   Hours of tuition with another ADI ☐

Please circle main content of lesson: 1 2 3 4 5 6 7 8 9 10 11 12 13 14 15 16 17 18 19

- -

DSA
DRIVING STANDARDS AGENCY
SAFE DRIVING FOR LIFE

Test of continued ability and fitness to give instruction (Check Test)
The examiner has marked each aspect of your performance in columns A & B below. See overleaf for explanatory notes.

Instructor's Name ☐

P.Ref No. ☐   *Grade* ☐

Examiner's Name ☐   Date ☐

Examiner's Signature ☐

	Column A				Column B					
---	1	2	3	*Core Competencies*	1	2	3	4	5	6
1. Controls				*Fault identification*						
2. Move away/stopping				*Fault analysis*						
3. Emergency stop				*Remedial action*						
4. Reverse left/right										
5. Turn in the road				*Instructional techniques*						
6. Reverse park				Recap at start						
7. Mirrors				Aims/Objectives						
8. Signals				Level of instruction						
9. Planning				Planning of lesson						
10. Use of speed				Control of lesson						
11. Junctions				Communication						
12. Roundabouts				Q & A Technique						
13. Meet/Cross/Overtake				Feedback/Encouragement						
14. Positioning				Instructor's use of controls						
15. Adequate clearance				Recap at end						
16. Pedestrian crossings										
17. Anticipation/Awareness										
18. Dual C'way/Motorway				*Instructor characteristics*						
19. Pass Plus Module				Attitude & approach to pupil						

ADI 26CT (A) (Rev 04/06)

Instructor grading

The examiner will be marking your instruction on the working sheet ADI 26. The lowest grade attained in any of the foregoing aspects of your work will normally be the final grade given. The following is an outline of the DSA's description of the six grades.

Grade 6

The instructor's overall performance is to a very high standard with no significant instructional weaknesses.

A concise and accurate recap on the previous lesson was given with realistic, attainable objectives set for the current lesson. There was dialogue, with pupil involvement.

The ADI consistently demonstrated the ability to vary/select the most appropriate instructional techniques to suit the needs, aptitude and ability of the pupil.

The instructor was quick to recognize and address all relevant driving faults and provided thoroughly sound analysis. Prompt and appropriate remedial action took place.

An appropriate route was chosen for the pupil's ability and experience and the instructor took every opportunity to develop the pupil's driving skills and awareness using the problems presented en route.

An appropriate learning environment was created to positively encourage the further development of the pupil's skills and good driving practice.

The lesson concluded with a concise recap, which was an accurate overview of the lesson.

The strengths and weaknesses in the pupil's performance were identified and discussed constructively.

Realistic and appropriate objectives were set for the next lesson.

A professional attitude and approach to the pupil was shown throughout the lesson.

Grade 5

A good overall standard of instruction was demonstrated with some minor weakness in instructional technique.

A recap on the previous lesson was given and the pupil was involved. Objectives were set.

The ADI demonstrated, with only minor weaknesses, the ability to vary/ select the most appropriate instructional techniques as necessary to suit the needs, aptitude and ability of the pupil.

All important driving faults were recognized and addressed with a sound analysis and appropriate remedial action being explained and practised.

An appropriate route was chosen for the pupil's ability and experience, and most opportunities were taken to develop the pupil's driving skills and awareness.

The ADI structured an appropriate learning environment in which the pupil could readily further develop his or her skills and good driving practice.

The lesson concluded with a concise recap, which was an accurate overview of the lesson.

The strengths and weaknesses in the pupil's performance were identified and discussed and the objectives for the next lesson were stated.

The instructor's attitude and approach to the pupil was good throughout the lesson.

Grade 4

The ADI demonstrated a competent overall performance with some minor deficiencies in instructional technique.

The recap was acceptable but with limited pupil involvement and objectives for the current lesson being outlined.

The instructor demonstrated an ability to select and/or vary the most appropriate instructional techniques as necessary to suit most of the needs, aptitude and ability of the pupil.

The ADI recognized and addressed the important driving faults, providing generally sound analysis and remedial action.

An acceptable route was chosen for the pupil's ability and experience, and advantage was taken of most of the opportunities to develop the pupil's driving skills and awareness using the problems presented en route.

The ADI structured a generally appropriate learning environment that provided opportunities for the pupil to develop his or her skills and good driving practice.

The lesson concluded with a general summary, giving an accurate overview of the lesson and the main strengths and weaknesses in the pupil's performance identified.

The ADI's attitude and approach to the pupil was acceptable throughout the lesson.

Grade 3

The ADI demonstrated an inadequate overall performance with some deficiencies in instructional technique.

The recap of the previous lesson was inadequate or sketchy.

The instructor did not properly set out or explain the objectives for the current lesson – nor was the pupil involved.

The instructor demonstrated only a limited ability to vary and/or select different instructional techniques as necessary to suit the needs, aptitude and ability of the pupil.

There was inconsistent identification, analysis and remedy of driving faults.

Some unnecessary retrospective instruction took place.

The route chosen was unsuitable for the pupil's ability and experience.

Opportunities were missed to develop the pupil's driving skills and awareness using the problems that presented themselves en route.

The ADI failed to structure a learning environment to enable the pupil to develop skills and good driving practice.

The summary at the end of the lesson was inaccurate or incomplete.

Many of the strengths and weaknesses in the pupil's performance were not identified, or were treated superficially.

There were shortcomings in the ADI's attitude and approach to the pupil.

Grade 2

The ADI demonstrated an overall poor performance with numerous deficiencies in instructional technique.

There was little or no recap given on the previous lesson and a failure to set objectives for the current lesson.

The instructor was unable to vary/select instructional techniques as necessary to suit the needs, aptitude and ability of the pupil.

Many problems occurred with the correct identification of driving faults and their analysis, and remedial action was very late.

The route chosen was unsuitable for the pupil's ability and experience and numerous opportunities were missed to develop the pupil's driving skills and awareness.

It was a poor learning environment in which the pupil would be unable to develop skills and good driving practice.

A superficial summary was given at the end of the lesson, with the main strengths and weaknesses in the pupil's performance not being mentioned.

The ADI demonstrated serious shortcomings in attitude and approach to the pupil.

Grade 1

The ADI's overall standard of instruction was extremely poor or dangerous with incorrect or even unsafe instruction.

No recap was given on the previous lesson and no objectives set for the current one.

The instructor was unable even to recognize the need to vary/select the most appropriate instructional techniques as necessary to suit the needs, aptitude and ability of the pupil.

Driving faults were not identified, analysed or corrected. Many of these were of a serious or dangerous nature.

A totally unsuitable route was chosen for the pupil's ability and experience.

The ADI failed to use the opportunities that presented themselves en route to develop the pupil's driving skills and awareness.

There was no attempt to structure any kind of learning environment.

No summary was given at the end of the lesson.

The ADI demonstrated very serious shortcomings in attitude and approach to the pupil.

At the end of the test

You will be given a verbal debriefing and handed an ADI 26 form showing the markings under the various headings. A copy of the 'Working Sheet' marked by the examiner during the test is available from the DSA.

Instructor's test results

Your driving school/instructor code is recorded at the beginning of all of your pupils' tests. The DSA collate the information from all tests and you will be provided with a breakdown of your pupils' results. By highlighting those items where there are consistent failures, the analysis should show where there might be shortcomings in your instructional techniques that need to be attended to.

All instructors, whether newly qualified or with years of experience, should use the Check Test as an opportunity to discuss with their SEADI any queries they may have relating to these statistics, or any other matters relating to driving tuition. This applies particularly if:

- a lower grading is achieved than was expected;
- you would like to attain a higher grade;
- pupils are consistently failing for similar errors.

If it's a while since your last Check Test, and there are some areas of instructional techniques you think you may not be up to date with, it may be sensible to have an assessment with a tutor prior to taking your next one!

The Driver

07

A s a professional driving instructor you need to have a thorough working knowledge of the regulations and procedures relating to driving licences. Just as importantly, you need to know where to obtain up-to-date, detailed official information about the law and current procedures. Your pupils will frequently need your advice and assistance with their licence applications and with the various licence entitlements.

This chapter deals mainly with a summary of the legal responsibilities of the driver and instructor in relation to:

- driving licence regulations;
- licence categories and minimum driving ages;
- health and eyesight requirements;
- vocational driving licences;
- photo card licences;
- driving on a foreign licence.

Also included are a summary of road traffic law; driver improvement and driver rectification schemes; the 'New Driver' Act, and advanced driving tests.

To make sure that you are completely up to date with your information you should regularly check some of the following useful points of contact:

- The DSA publication *Despatch*. This magazine is published online at regular intervals and is available to anyone involved in the driver training industry. To receive copies and to obtain previous editions, register at www.dft.gov.uk/dsa.
- The DSA and DVLA websites at www.dft.gov.uk/dsa, www.direct.gov. uk/motoring and www.businesslink.gov.uk/transport.
- The trade magazines published by the main national ADI organizations such as the Motor Schools Association of Great Britain (MSAGB) and the Driving Instructors Association (DIA).
- A subscription-based online service such as Smart Driving – www. smartdriving.co.uk.

Driver licensing

The DVLA at Swansea issues licences for all categories. The licence shows details of all categories for which the driver has entitlement, including lorries and buses. Any provisional entitlement is shown, together with any relevant restrictions such as maximum trailer weight or 'not for hire or reward'. Driving without the appropriate driving licence entitlement usually invalidates the insurance cover.

Only photo-card licences are now issued by DVLA, with the old-style paper licences being phased out. To apply for a photo licence you need to send off the form D750 as well as the licence application form D1, together with your original licence and an identifying document (your passport or birth certificate). To voluntarily exchange an old-style 'paper' licence for a photo licence the fee is £20.00. Details of other licence fees are shown on page 187.

Whereas a paper licence normally has an extended expiry date (usually to age 70), the photo licence has to be renewed after 10 years to keep the photographic likeness up to date. To avoid the necessity of sending off an important document such as your passport or birth certificate, an additional service is available at most main post offices whereby your details and documents can be checked and verified at the time. For this service there is an additional fee as well as the cost of the licence. To take advantage of this service you need to attend in person at a participating post office. Some form of personal identity such as a current UK passport must support your application.

A fact sheet on photo licences (INF61) is available from DVLA (tel: 0300 790 6801; website: www.dft.gov.uk/dvla). Fact sheets are also available from DVLA Customer Services for:

Driving a Minibus	INF28
Minimum Test Vehicles	INF29
Towing Trailers	INF30
Motorcycles	INF31
Driving in GB as a Visitor or a New Resident	INF38
Renewing Your Car Driving Licence	INF40
Drivers of Large Vehicles	INF52

Provisional driving licences

In order to learn to drive and to take the official driving test, a provisional driving licence must be obtained before a vehicle can be taken out on the public roads. The holder of a provisional licence may drive a vehicle only when accompanied by, and under the supervision of, a driver who holds a full licence for that type of vehicle. The supervising driver must be over 21 years of age and have held a full driving licence for the type of vehicle being driven for at least three years. This rule, however, does not apply under certain circumstances and when driving certain vehicles, for example when taking a driving test or when riding a motorcycle. More information on the supervision of learner drivers is provided on page 208.

To validate a provisional motorcycle licence the rider must also hold a valid certificate of basic training (CBT). Note that a provisional motorcycle licence holder must not carry any pillion passenger, even if that passenger is a qualified rider or driver.

In Northern Ireland, a vehicle displaying 'L' plates is restricted to a maximum speed of 45 mph.

Licence categories

The whole subject of driving licence entitlement is now extremely complex. There are so many variables, including different types of vehicle; when the original licence was first issued; and the age of the driver. The DVLA has a 16-page document on the subject, *What You Need to Know about Driving Licences* (D100). As the title suggests, this publication includes full details of licence entitlements for cars, motorcycles, lorries and buses, as well as the different eyesight and medical requirements for each type of licence.

The main categories of licence and the minimum driving ages are shown in Table 7.1, but for full details you need to refer to the D100, or visit the DVLA website.

Your entitlement to drive a particular type of vehicle (or vehicle/trailer combination) depends on several factors including your age, the date your first full licence was issued and the weight of the vehicle. The minimum age for certain types of vehicle is sometimes governed by other factors, particularly in relation to larger and specialized vehicles. The normal minimum age for driving is varied in the case of:

- drivers who receive Disability Living Allowance;
- members of the armed forces;
- trainees in the Young Driver scheme;
- drivers of minibuses and PCVs in limited circumstances.

Passing a driving test for a particular category may entitle you to drive vehicles of some other categories, and may also entitle you to use the licence as a provisional licence for other vehicles. There are also certain restrictions. For example:

- If you pass the test in a car with automatic transmission you are not entitled to drive a car with manual gears.
- Passing the test on a moped does not give you motorcycle entitlement.
- When you pass a test on a category C (rigid) vehicle, this automatically gives to you a provisional licence category CE (articulated or drawbar).

TABLE 7.1 Driving licence categories for tests passed on or after 1 January 1997

Category	Type of vehicle	Min. age
A	Motorcycle	17
A1	Light motorcycle	17
B1	3 or 4 wheel light vehicle	17
B	Motor car	17
B+E	Car with trailer	17
C1	Medium goods vehicle	18
C1+E	Medium goods vehicle with trailer	18/21
C	Large goods vehicle (LGV)	21
C+E	LGV with trailer	21
D1	Minibus	21
D1+E	Minibus with trailer	21
D	Bus or coach	21
D+E	Bus or coach with trailer	21
f	Agricultural tractor	17
g	Road roller	21
h	Tracked vehicle	21
k	Mowing machine/pedestrian controlled vehicle	16
l	Electric vehicle	17
p	Moped	16

Driving licence application

You may apply for a full licence if you have:

- passed the driving test and you exchange the pass certificate for a full licence within two years of the date of the test;
- held a full licence issued in the Channel Islands or the Isle of Man, valid within the last 10 years; or
- held a full British licence or a full licence issued in Northern Ireland granted on or after 1 January 1976.

You may also apply for a full licence if you have been resident in Great Britain for less than one year and you surrender a valid full licence issued in the EC or some other countries (see pages 192–94). Application may be made at any time up to two months prior to the date from which the licence is required, and should be made at least three weeks before the date of commencement of the licence. The appropriate forms are normally available from post offices and local vehicle licensing offices. The completed form should be sent to the Driver and Vehicle Licensing Agency, Swansea SA99 1AB. If you need to make an enquiry about your licence, you are advised to contact the Driver Enquiry Unit, DVLA, Swansea SA6 7JL (tel: 0300 790 6801) quoting your driver number. It is worth making a note of this number in case your licence is mislaid.

If you are disqualified from driving, you will normally have to pay £65 for a new licence (or £90 for some drink/drive offences). Licences are normally valid until the applicant's 70th birthday, at which time a new licence may be issued for one, two or three years at a time, depending on health and other factors. Renewal in these circumstances is free of charge.

TABLE 7.2 Driving licence fees

Licence type	Fee
First provisional licence	
– car, motorcycle, moped	£50
– bus or lorry	Free
Changing provisional for full licence	Free
Duplicate licence	
– licence lost, stolen, destroyed or defaced	£17.50
Replacement	
– change of name and/or address	Free
Exchange	
– Removing expired endorsements (photo-card to photo-card)	£17.50
– Paper licence to photo-card	£17.50
Adding replacement photo	£17.50
Adding a test pass to a full licence	Free
New licence after revocation under the New Drivers Act	£50
Renewing a licence	
– car licence at age 70 or over	Free
– full licence for medium/large goods vehicles, minibus/bus	Free
– provisional for medium/large vehicles, minibus/bus	Free
– for medical reasons	Free
Exchanging a licence from other countries:	
– full Northern Ireland licences	Free
– full EC/EEA or other foreign licence (including Channel Islands and Isle of Man)	£50
New licence after disqualification	
– car, motorcycle	£65
– if disqualified for some drink/drive offences	£90

NOTE: All vocational licences for buses and lorries are now free of charge.

A duplicate or exchange licence is valid for the period of the original licence. A replacement licence that is issued after a period of disqualification is charged at the same rate as a duplicate licence. A driver who is adding an extra category to an existing licence may require an exchange licence, which is also issued where motorcycle entitlement is required, or when a licence contains out-of-date endorsements. A Northern Ireland full licence may be exchanged for a GB licence for the appropriate fee.

A duplicate licence is needed to replace a licence which has been lost, mislaid or defaced. Replacement of a licence following a change of address is made free of charge.

Driving licence information codes

When checking a pupil's licence details you will often find certain information codes adjacent to the entitlement section. These codes specify any particular restrictions that might apply to the individual driver for a variety of reasons (see Table 7.3).

Health and eyesight

When applying for a licence the driver has to make various declarations regarding health and eyesight. You must declare, for example, any disability and any illness that might affect your driving. The law also requires the driver to notify the licensing authority if there is likely to be any worsening of any condition, and if there has been a change in any disability since the issue of the licence. Examples of the kind of health conditions in question are listed in the leaflet D100, but if there is any doubt about whether or not the condition should be reported, drivers are advised to consult their doctor. It is not necessary to report any medical conditions that are not likely to last more than three months.

Epilepsy: under certain circumstances a licence may be issued to someone who has been free of attacks for one year.

Pacemakers: people who are subject to sudden fainting or giddiness have, in the past, not been issued with a licence. The law, however, has been changed, and a licence may now be granted if this disability is corrected by the fitting of a cardiac pacemaker and if other medical conditions are satisfied.

Disabilities: drivers who are physically and mentally capable of driving but are otherwise disabled may be issued with a licence which restricts them to driving a vehicle of special design or construction. This type of licence does not entitle the driver to use it as a provisional licence for other groups of vehicles. If the driver then wishes to learn to drive a vehicle of a different type, he or she must first apply for the appropriate provisional entitlement to be added to the original licence.

TABLE 7.3 Driving licence information codes

Code	Description
01	eyesight correction
02	hearing or communication aid
10	modified transmission
15	modified clutch
20	modified braking systems
25	modified accelerator systems
30	combined braking and accelerator systems
35	modified controls layouts
40	modified steering
42	modified rear view mirror(s)
43	modified driving seat
44	modifications to motorcycle
45	motorcycle only with sidecar
70	exchange of licence
71	duplicate of licence
78	restricted to vehicles with automatic transmission
79	restricted vehicles (details in brackets)
101	not for hire or reward
102	drawbar trailers only
103	subject to certificate of competence
105	not more than 5.5 metres long
106	restricted to vehicles with automatic transmission
107	not more than 8250 kg
108	subject to minimum age limit
110	limited to invalid carriages
111	limited to 16 passenger seats
113	limited to 16 passenger seats except for automatics
114	with special controls required for safe driving
115	organ donor
118	start date is for earliest entitlement
119	weight limit does not apply
120	complies with health standards for category D1

Eyesight: in order to conform to the law there is a minimum standard of eyesight which must be reached (with glasses or contact lenses if necessary). The requirement is to read a motor vehicle number plate in good daylight at a distance of 20 metres (65 ft) or 20.5 metres for the old-style plates with seven digits. In the case of the driver of a mowing machine or pedestrian-controlled vehicle the relevant distances are 45 feet and 40 feet.

If you need glasses or contact lenses in order to attain these standards, you must wear them every time you drive. It is an offence to drive if your eyesight does not meet the required standard.

An applicant who declares a disability to the DVLA may be asked for permission to obtain a report from the applicant's doctor. A licence may be issued for a limited period so that the condition can be reviewed or the licence may be restricted to certain types of vehicles.

When checking a pupil's licence details you will often find certain information codes adjacent to the entitlement section. These codes specify any particular restrictions that might apply to the individual driver for a variety of reasons (see Table 7.3).

The exception to this rule is code 121 – restricted to conditions specified in the Secretary of State's notice. This designates the licence as a 'Provisional Disability Assessment Licence'. This type of provisional licence can be issued by DVLA at their discretion as part of an investigation into an individual's medical fitness to drive. The licence will show a one-year validity on the front. However, the licence may not be valid for driving lessons. There is always an accompanying letter and it is important that you check the details. If it states that the provisional licence is valid for assessment purposes only then you cannot take that person for driving tuition. An assessment can only be carried out at an approved assessment centre.

Procedure for medical assessment

When information about a disability is received, the applicant may be required to authorize his or her doctor to give information about the disability to the Medical Adviser at the DVLA. If the applicant or licence holder fails to do so, or if the information available from the doctor is not conclusive in relation to fitness to drive, the applicant may be required to have a medical examination by a nominated doctor.

Motorcycle licences

A full car licence usually acts as a provisional licence for motorcycles and as a full licence for mopeds. A new provisional motorcycle licence is issued for a maximum of two years. If a full licence is not obtained in this time it is not possible to renew the licence for a period of one year. The provisional licence entitles the rider to use a solo motorcycle with an engine capacity of up to 125 cc. Pillion passengers are not allowed to accompany a learner rider, even if the passenger has a full licence for that type of machine.

A Compulsory Basic Training Certificate (CBT) is required for all riders of mopeds and motorcycles. The learner has to undergo a short course of off- and on-road training before riding unaccompanied on public roads. On successful completion of the course, the learner is issued with a certificate that validates the provisional licence. This applies to anyone riding a motorcycle or moped on 'L' plates, irrespective of when their licence was issued, and includes full Category B (car licence) holders who have not passed the motorcycle test.

After taking CBT the learner may ride on the road, but is limited to machines of up to 125 cc with a maximum power output of 11 kw. 'L' plates must be displayed and pillion passengers are not allowed on a solo motorbike. CBT certificates are valid for two years. To obtain a full licence, both the Theory and Practical Tests have to be passed within a two-year period.

Motorcycle licence categories

Category A1: light motorcycle – not exceeding 125 cc and a maximum power output of 11 kw. This type of licence can be obtained by taking the practical test on a bike between 75 and 120 cc.

Category A: standard motorcycle – any motorcycle. The test must be taken on a bike of more than 120 cc that is capable of at least 100 kph. For the first two years the rider is restricted to a bike of 25 kw unless he or she takes the Direct Access route to obtaining the licence.

Direct Access

Direct Access is a means of achieving an unrestricted licence without waiting for two years. It is available only to those over the age of 21, and must be taken on a motorbike that exceeds 35 kw. Training and practice can only be undertaken under the direct supervision of a specially qualified instructor, with radio communication between instructor and pupil.

Licence application

Provisional licence entitlement for motorcycles is normally granted for a maximum of two years. Learners are not permitted to ride on the roads until they have successfully completed CBT. The only exception to this is when they are under the supervision of an authorized instructor during the training.

Mopeds may be ridden at 16 years, subject to the CBT requirements.

A full car licence normally includes provisional entitlement for motorcycles but a CBT certificate is needed to validate the licence. A full car licence issued before 1 February 2001 includes full entitlement for mopeds, and CBT is not needed in those circumstances.

Vocational licences

The DVLA issues all licences, including those for large goods vehicles (LGVs) and passenger carrying vehicles (PCVs). The entitlement is shown on the photo-card licence, with provisional entitlements indicated on the paper counterpart.

A driver who passes the 'L' test is now issued with a licence for driving vehicles up to 3,500 kg or a maximum of eight passenger seats. For driving anything over these limits, a separate test is needed for each type of vehicle. For example, you need to hold a full licence for cars before obtaining a provisional licence for medium-sized goods vehicles, and a full rigid vehicle licence is required before you can drive an articulated vehicle or draw-bar combinations. There are also restrictions on the type of trailer that can be towed. For example, a separate test and licence entitlement would be needed to tow a large trailer behind a heavy motor car if the combined weight was more than 4,250 kg or if the gross weight of the trailer was more than the unladen weight of the towing vehicle.

The rules relating to vocational licences, medicals and test procedures are dealt with in more detail in Chapter 12, which also deals with training and qualifications for vocational licences.

Driving abroad

Visiting another country

To drive in any country belonging to the European Union or the European Economic Area (EU/EEA) you are allowed to use your GB licence. If you want to drive in a non-EU/EEA country you should check with one of the motoring organizations whether you need an International Driving Permit (IDP). IDPs are issued by the AA, the RAC, RSAC and Green Flag. To qualify for an IDP you must be resident in Great Britain, have passed a driving test and be over 18 years of age.

Moving to another country

If you move abroad you should check with the licensing authority of that country for information about the exchange of licences. If you return to Great Britain from a non-EU/EEA country you may drive for up to 12 months on your foreign licence.

Visitors and new residents

You normally have to be resident in this country to qualify for a full driving licence. There are, however, special rules for the exchange of foreign licences and for driving in this country as a visitor or new resident. These rules vary, depending on the country that issued the licence. There are also some variations for vocational licences – for example for lorries and buses.

European Union and European Economic Area countries

A visitor to Great Britain from these countries can drive using his or her Union licence for as long as the licence remains valid. The licence will show the various types of vehicle that can be driven.

New residents in Great Britain can exchange their EU licence for a GB one at any time. Alternatively, they may drive on their foreign licence up to the age of 70 or for three years, whichever is the longer. Vocational licence holders who do not exchange their licence for a GB one may drive:

- until age 45 or for five years after becoming resident, whichever is the longer;
- if aged over 45 (but under 65), until reaching 66 or for five years, whichever is the longer;
- if aged 65 or over, for 12 months.

Northern Ireland

A licence from Northern Ireland can be used until it runs out. Alternatively, it can be exchanged for a full car, motorcycle or moped licence if the original licence has been valid since 1 January 1976. A lorry or bus licence can be exchanged if it was issued on or after 1 April 1986. A driving test pass certificate is acceptable for exchange.

Gibraltar and designated countries

The 'designated countries', other than Gibraltar, are Australia, Barbados, British Virgin Islands, Canada, Falkland Islands, Hong Kong, Japan, Malta, Monaco, New Zealand, Republic of Cyprus, Republic of Korea, Singapore, South Africa, Switzerland and Zimbabwe. Anyone visiting Great Britain and holding a licence from one of these countries is allowed to drive vehicles up to 7.5 tonnes and with up to 16 passenger seats for up to 12 months, whether or not the vehicle was brought into the country with them. Holders of licences for larger vehicles may only drive vehicles that have been brought into Great Britain from the designated country.

For new residents the rules are slightly different. Small vehicles may be driven for up to 12 months, during which time the foreign licence must be exchanged for a GB one. New residents must not drive medium or large goods vehicles or PCVs until they have passed the relevant GB test.

Vocational licence holders from Gibraltar may drive for 12 months and can exchange the licence within five years of residency.

Jersey, Guernsey and the Isle of Man

Visitors from these islands with ordinary licences can drive any category of vehicle shown on the licence for up to 12 months. Vocational licence holders from Jersey or the Isle of Man can drive large vehicles for up to 12 months. If the vocational licence was issued in Guernsey, only vehicles that have been imported temporarily can be driven.

New residents from Jersey, Guernsey or the Isle of Man may drive for up to 12 months, but should exchange their licence during that period.

All other countries

Visitors from other countries are allowed to drive vehicles up to 7.5 tonnes and with up to 16 passenger seats, provided that the original licence is still valid. With large vehicles, only those that have been registered outside Great Britain and that have been driven into the country may be used.

For new residents, provided that the full licence remains valid, any small vehicle shown on the licence may be driven for up to 12 months. During that time a GB licence must be obtained.

New residents with vocational licences may not drive larger vehicles without passing the GB driving test for that type of vehicle.

Licences from these countries are not exchangeable.

Please note that these are guidelines only. For precise details, refer to the DVLA website at www.dft.gov.uk/dvla, or contact DVLA Customer Services on 0300 790 680.

Road traffic law

Most people are unsure about the law for motorists, although at any time when driving or using a car, they may find themselves faced with some aspect of it. The purpose of this section is to enable you to find out how the law affects you and your pupils.

The motorist is affected by civil as well as criminal law, and an offence in a criminal court may well be followed by another case in a civil court. For example, someone who injures a pedestrian and is found guilty of dangerous driving might later find themself being sued for damages in a civil court.

Most of the relevant motoring law is found in the Road Traffic Act (RTA) 1991. Apart from criminal law, the RTA 1991 gives the Secretary of State for Transport the power to make other regulations regarding various motoring matters. The most important of these are the Motor Vehicles (Construction and Use) Regulations.

Much of the civil law that affects motorists is not contained in special rules relating to the roads. It is a part of the general law of the land. For example, the law of negligence applies to anyone, whether driving or not. Motorists are most likely to encounter the civil law after they have been involved in a road accident in which there has been injury to a person or damage to property. In these cases, the law allows the person injured to claim against the other driver, or the insurance company.

However, a motorist may be guilty of an offence under criminal law even if no accident has taken place. An offence may have been committed even if it was not intended; for example, driving without lights at night is an offence even though the driver checked the operation of the lights before starting his or her journey. There is also a certain amount of confusion regarding *The Highway Code*. Although the *Code* is based on the specific rules of the RTA, a breach of it is not necessarily a punishable offence. However, *The Highway Code* can be used as a reference in a court when assessing the actions of a driver. A breach of a particular part of *The Highway Code* may in some cases amount to a breach of a specific part of the RTA. Nevertheless, the offence will be found to be against a section of the RTA.

Questions of liability may arise when drivers are using vehicles to carry out their normal work or when a vehicle is being used for driving instruction. These questions of liability often arise under the Construction and Use Regulations when the driver, supervising driver and the employer may all be equally guilty of an offence.

Driving offences

Offences that are covered by the 1991 RTA include:

- causing death by dangerous driving;
- dangerous driving;
- causing death by careless driving when under the influence of drink or drugs;
- causing danger to other road users.

These offences are based more firmly than previously on the actual standard of driving. 'Dangerous driving' has to have two main features: the standard of driving falls far below that expected of a competent and careful driver, and the driving must involve actual or potential danger of physical injury or serious damage to property.

The standard of driving is judged in absolute terms and takes no account of factors such as inexperience, age or disability of the driver. It is not intended that the driver who merely makes a careless mistake, of a kind that any driver might make from time to time, should be regarded as falling far below the standard expected of a competent and careful driver.

The danger must be one that a competent and careful driver would have appreciated or observed. It means any danger of injury (however minor) to a person or of serious damage to property.

Careless and inconsiderate driving is defined in relation to 'a person driving a mechanically propelled vehicle on a road or other public place'. This means that non-motorized vehicles and offences on private property to which the public have access may be included. The main constituents in this offence are referred to in terms of 'driving without due care and attention, or without reasonable consideration for other road users'.

Offences of driving without a licence, without 'L' plates, without supervision, or under the age when a licence can be obtained, are now dealt with under the offence of 'driving otherwise than in accordance with a licence'. Penalty points for this offence vary from three to six depending on the circumstances and seriousness of the offence.

Offences incurring disqualification

The following offences carry automatic disqualification:

- manslaughter caused by the driver of a motor vehicle;
- causing death by dangerous driving;
- causing death by careless driving when unfit through drink;
- dangerous driving;
- motor racing on the highway;
- driving, or attempting to drive, when under the influence of drink or drugs, or with more than the permitted blood alcohol level;
- failure to provide a blood or urine sample.

Drink/drive offences

The legal alcohol limits are:

- 35 microgrammes of alcohol per 100 millilitres of breath;
- 80 milligrammes of alcohol per 100 millilitres of blood;
- 107 milligrammes of alcohol per 100 millilitres of urine.

The minimum period of disqualification is 12 months, with a minimum of three years for a second offence within 10 years.

Driver rehabilitation scheme

Drivers who are convicted of a drink/drive offence are normally offered the opportunity to take a voluntary 'driver rehabilitation course'. This enables them to have a reduction of up to one quarter off the period of disqualification. Courses are usually organized at weekends and during the evening, with a total of about 20 hours' instruction. The cost of the course (typically about £150) has to be paid by the offender.

The Extended Driving Test

Courts have the power, for some of the more serious offences, to order disqualification until an 'appropriate' driving test is passed. These offences include motor manslaughter, causing death by dangerous driving and dangerous driving. The test is longer and more rigorous than the normal 'L' test. It therefore provides scope for the driver to be tested in a greater variety of road and traffic conditions.

   In determining whether to make such an order, the court must have regard to the safety of road users. For offences involving obligatory disqualification, the 'appropriate' test is the Extended Driving Test, and this might therefore apply to the driver who has been disqualified under the 'totting up' procedure, and who has been ordered by the court to retake the test. For offences involving obligatory endorsement (as opposed to obligatory disqualification), the appropriate test is the ordinary Test of Competence to Drive.

Penalty points for some offences are graded according to the seriousness of the offence (see Table 7.4). An accumulation of 12 points within three years means that the driver will automatically be disqualified from driving, although the courts are given powers not to disqualify in exceptional circumstances. The three-year period is measured backwards from the date of the latest offence.

The period of disqualification as a result of an accumulation of penalty points is:

- six months, if there has been no disqualification in the past three years;
- one year, if there has been one disqualification in the past three years;
- two years, if there has been more than one disqualification in the past three years.

Disqualification may be imposed for a single offence if the court feels that the offence is serious enough.

TABLE 7.4 Penalty points for driving offences

Offence	Points
Being in charge of a vehicle when unfit to drive	10
Failing to stop after an accident	5–10
Failing to report or to give particulars	5–10
Careless and inconsiderate driving	3–9
Driving while uninsured	6–8
Driving while disqualified by a court	6
Failure to give identity of driver	6
Driving other than in accordance with a licence	3–6
Exceeding a speed limit	
– in court proceedings	3–6
– by fixed penalty	3
Contravention of temporary prohibition or restriction	
– in court proceedings	3–6
– by fixed penalty	3
Contravention of motorway regulations	
– in court proceedings	3–6
– by fixed penalty	3
Unlawful carriage of motorcycle passenger	3
Contravention or failure to comply with C & U Regs.	3
Driving with defective eyesight	3

A penalty points endorsement can be removed after four years from the date of the offence.

An endorsement of disqualification may be removed four years after the date of conviction (11 years for drinking and driving offences).

After a disqualification for a period of more than two years the driver can apply for the disqualification to be lifted after a period of:

- 2 years if the disqualification period is less than 4 years;
- half the period of disqualification if the disqualification period is between 4 and 10 years;
- 5 years if the disqualification was for more than 10 years.

The 'New Driver' Act

This Act affects any newly qualified driver who accumulates six or more penalty points within two years of passing his or her driving test. The accumulation of six or more points (whether arising from court convictions or from fixed penalty offences) means that the licence is automatically revoked by the DVLA and the driver has to revert to a provisional licence. Both the Theory and Practical Tests will need to be retaken before a full licence can be issued. After passing the tests a new full licence will generally include all previous licence entitlements, but the points will carry forward, as these could count towards any future 'totting up'. Recent figures from the Driver and Vehicle Licensing Agency show that about 14,000 new drivers have their licences revoked each year.

Disqualification and the ADI

One of the requirements of ADI qualification is, 'will have held a full driving licence for four years'. An important point to be remembered by professional driving instructors is that any period of disqualification from driving will involve a further period of disqualification from the ADI Register. For example, a one-year disqualification for a driving offence is followed by a four-year disqualification from the official Register. The instructor would, therefore, be unable to work as an ADI for a total period of five years.

Fixed penalties

Traffic wardens and police officers are empowered to enforce the law in connection with various offences by use of the fixed penalty system. The relevant offences include waiting, parking, loading and obstruction as well as offences relating to vehicle tax, lights and reflectors. Driving offences such as making an unauthorized 'U' turn and driving the wrong way in a one-way street are also included.

The ticket is given to the driver or is fixed to the vehicle. Payment must be made within 28 days or alternatively the offender may request a court hearing. If the driver who committed the offence cannot be identified or found, the registered owner of the vehicle is ultimately responsible for payment of the fine. However, in the case of hired vehicles, special rules apply and the person who hires the vehicle will become liable for any fines or excess charges.

The extended fixed penalty scheme covers various moving traffic offences including speeding, failure to comply with traffic directions and vehicle defect offences. The following categories are included in the scheme, and for these offences the issuing of the ticket is normally the responsibility of the police:

- Contravening a traffic regulation order.
- Breach of experimental traffic order.
- Breach of experimental traffic scheme regulation in Greater London.
- Using a vehicle in contravention of a temporary prohibition or restriction of traffic on a road, such as where a road is being repaired.
- Contravening motorway traffic regulations.
- Driving a vehicle in contravention of an order prohibiting or restricting driving vehicles on certain classes of roads.
- Breach of pedestrian crossing regulations.
- Contravention of a street playground order.
- Breach of a parking place order on a road.
- Breach of a provision of a parking place designation order and other offences committed in relation to it, except failing to pay an excess charge.
- Contravening a parking place designation order.
- Breach of a provision of a parking place designation order.
- Contravention of minimum speed limits.
- Speeding.
- Driving or keeping a vehicle without displaying a registration mark or hackney carriage sign.
- Driving or keeping a vehicle with the registration mark or hackney carriage sign obscured.
- Failure to comply with traffic directions or signs.
- Leaving vehicle in a dangerous position.
- Failing to wear a seat belt.
- Breach of restrictions on carrying children in the front of vehicles.
- Driving a vehicle elsewhere than on the road.
- Parking a vehicle on the path or verge.

- Breach of Construction and Use Regulations.
- Contravention of lighting restrictions on vehicles.
- Driving without a licence.
- Breach of provisional licence provisions.
- Failure to stop when required by constable in uniform.
- Obstruction of highway with vehicle.

Penalty tickets for endorsable offences are handed to the driver, as the driving licence will have to be surrendered for possible endorsement with the appropriate penalty points. If the licence shows an accumulation of points which, together with the current offence, would bring the total to 12 points or more, the fixed penalty ticket would not be issued. In those circumstances a prosecution for the offence would follow.

If the licence is not immediately available, it must be produced within seven days at a nominated police station. A receipt for the licence is then issued, and this is an accepted document if for any reason the licence has to be produced at a later date.

The fixed penalty fines of £30, £40 or £60 are payable within 28 days (or as specified in the notice). If payment is not received in time, the charge is increased by 50 per cent. A court hearing may be requested if the driver feels that the ticket was issued incorrectly or unfairly.

National driver improvement scheme

A driver who has been involved in a road traffic incident may be offered an opportunity to attend a driver improvement course as an alternative to prosecution for careless or inconsiderate driving. Attending a course means that you can avoid a fixed penalty fine and the possibility of penalty points on the licence.

Courses usually last about one-and-a-half days and are mainly classroom-based. You can choose to attend at a venue that is convenient to you. There is no examination or end-test – all that is required is your attendance and willingness to take part in the programme.

You are allowed to undertake only one course within a three-year period; if you are involved in another incident that is deemed to be your fault within the three years you will be given a fixed penalty or will have to attend court.

Driver identity

The 1991 Act defines the circumstances in which a person can be required to give information about the identity of a driver who is alleged to be guilty of a road traffic offence. This is particularly important in connection with the identification of drivers involved in speeding or other offences detected by automatic devices, including cameras.

A photograph, showing the registration number, is taken of the offending vehicle. It is not intended that the registered keeper of the vehicle should bear responsibility for the offence detected by the device, if someone else was driving at the time of the offence. It is, therefore, necessary to trace the driver through the registered keeper. The penalty for not providing the information has been increased to three penalty points to provide an incentive to do so.

The existing fixed penalty system requires the vehicle and the person committing the offence to be present at the time the fixed penalty ticket is issued. However, under the provisions of the RTA 1991, a conditional fixed penalty offer is available for all fixed penalty offences, including those detected by automatic cameras and other devices. These provisions allow for the police to issue a notice to the alleged offender by post.

The notice is first issued to the registered keeper of the vehicle, requiring information about the identity of the driver. The conditional offer of a fixed penalty will then be issued to the person identified as the driver of the vehicle when the offence was detected. If the information about the driver is not given, the 'keeper' of the vehicle will have committed an offence, which is now endorsable.

If the driver wishes to take up the offer of the fixed penalty, the driving licence and payment are sent to the Fixed Penalty Office and the payment is accepted, so long as the licence shows that the driver would not be subject to a 'totting up' disqualification. In those circumstances, the payment and licence would be returned and a court summons would then be issued.

Driving licence endorsements

Endorsement offences appear on a driving licence in a coded version which includes details of the court, the offence and of the fine and endorsement (see Table 7.5).

Speed limits

A speed limit of 30 mph normally applies to all vehicles on a road where street lamps are positioned at regular intervals. On occasions a higher speed is allowed on such a road, in which case appropriate signs show the higher limit.

Speed limits apply to roads and vehicles, and where there is a difference the lower limit applies. The maximum speed on motorways and dual carriageways is 70 mph and on single carriageways 60 mph. However, these limits apply to cars, car-derived vans and dual-purpose vehicles adapted to carry not more than eight passengers. A different set of speed limits applies to other types of vehicles (see Table 7.6).

TABLE 7.5 Driving licence endorsement codes

Code	Offence
	Accidents
AC10	Failing to stop and/or give particulars after an accident
AC20	Failing to report an accident within 24 hours
AC30	Undefined accident offence
	Driver banned from driving (disqualified)
BA10	Driving while disqualified
BA20	Driving while disqualified by virtue of age
	Careless driving
CD10	Driving without due care and attention
CD20	Driving without reasonable consideration for other road users
CD30	Driving without due care and attention or without reasonable consideration for other road users
	Construction and use offences
CU10	Using a vehicle with defective brakes
CU20	Causing or likely to cause danger by reason of use of unsuitable vehicle or using a vehicle with parts or accessories (excluding brakes, steering or tyres) in a dangerous condition
CU30	Using a vehicle with defective tyres
CU40	Using a vehicle with defective steering
CU50	Causing or likely to cause danger by reason of load or passengers
CU60	Undefined failure to comply with Construction and Use Regulations
	Dangerous driving
DD10	Driving in a dangerous manner
DD20	Driving at a dangerous speed
DD30	Reckless driving
DD40	Driving in a dangerous or reckless manner, etc
DD50	Causing death by dangerous driving
DD60	Culpable homicide while driving a vehicle
DD70	Causing death by reckless driving
	Drink or drugs
DR10	Driving or attempting to drive with blood alcohol level above limit
DR20	Driving or attempting to drive while unfit through drink or drugs
DR30	Driving or attempting to drive then refusing to supply a specimen of blood or urine for laboratory testing
DR40	In charge of a vehicle while blood alcohol level above limit
DR50	In charge of a vehicle while unfit through drink or drugs
DR60	In charge of a vehicle then refusing to supply a specimen of blood or urine for laboratory testing
	Insurance offences
IN10	Using a vehicle uninsured against third party risks

	Licence offences
LC10	Driving without a licence
LC20	Driving when under age
	Miscellaneous offences
MS10	Leaving a vehicle in a dangerous position
MS20	Unlawful pillion riding
MS30	Playstreet offences
MS40	Driving with uncorrected or defective eyesight or refusing to submit to eyesight test
MS50	Motor racing on the highway
MS60	Offences not covered by other codes
MS70	Driving with uncorrected defective eyesight
MS80	Refusing to submit to an eyesight test
	Motorway offences
MW10	Contravention of Special Roads Regulations (excluding speed limits)
	Pedestrian crossing
PC10	Undefined contravention of Pedestrian Crossing Regulations
PC20	Contravention of Pedestrian Crossing Regulations with moving vehicle
PC30	Contravention of Pedestrian Crossing Regulations with stationary vehicle
	Provisional licence offences
PL10	Driving without 'L' plates
PL20	Driving while not accompanied by a qualified person
PL30	Carrying a person not qualified
PL40	Drawing an unauthorized trailer
PL50	Undefined failure to comply with conditions of a provisional licence
	Speed limits
SP10	Exceeding goods vehicle speed limit
SP20	Exceeding speed limit for type of vehicle (excluding goods or passenger vehicles)
SP30	Exceeding statutory speed limit on a public road
SP40	Exceeding passenger vehicle speed limit
SP50	Exceeding speed limit on a motorway
SP60	Undefined speed limit offence
	Traffic directions and signs
TS10	Failing to comply with traffic light signals
TS20	Failing to comply with double white lines
TS30	Failing to comply with a 'Stop' sign
TS40	Failing to comply with directions of a traffic constable
TS50	Failing to comply with a traffic sign (excluding 'Stop' signs, traffic lights or double white lines)
TS60	Failing to comply with a school crossing patrol sign
TS70	Undefined failure to comply with a traffic direction or sign

	Theft or the unauthorized taking of vehicle
UT10	Taking and driving away a vehicle without consent (or attempting to)
UT20	Stealing or attempting to steal a vehicle
UT30	Going equipped for stealing or taking a vehicle
UT40	Taking or attempting to take a vehicle without consent; driving or attempting to drive a vehicle knowing it to have been taken without consent; allowing oneself to be carried in or on a vehicle knowing it to have been taken without consent
	Special code
XX99	Signifies a disqualification under the 'totting-up' procedure

NOTES:

Aiding and abetting offences are as listed above, but with the 0 changed to 2 (eg UT20 becomes UT22).

Causing or permitting are as listed, but with the 0 changed to 4 (eg PL20 becomes PL24).

Inciting offences are as listed, but with the 0 changed to 6 (eg DD10 becomes DD16).

TABLE 7.6 Statutory speed limits

Vehicle	Single carriageway	Dual carriageway	Motorway
Motorcycles	60	70	70
Cars, including car-derived vans	60	70	70
Cars, towing trailer or caravan	50	60	60
Goods vehicles up to 7.5 tonnes	50	60	70
– towing trailer	50	60	60
Large goods vehicles			
– over 7.5 tonnes	40	50	60
Buses and coaches:			
– up to 12 metres length	50	60	70
– over 12 metres length	50	60	60

Speed awareness course

The national speed awareness scheme is now supported by over 30 police forces since its introduction in 2003. The scheme allows motorists who are caught speeding the opportunity to complete a course rather than face a £60 fine and three penalty points on their licence.

Eligible drivers for the scheme are usually those who have exceeded the speed limit, but not by a large amount. Individual police forces decide what their margins are.

Courses usually last four to five hours at a cost to the individual of about £100, but this varies from one provider to another.

Once you have attended a Speed Awareness Course you are not allowed to do another for at least three years.

Mobile phones

It is illegal to use a hand-held mobile phone while driving. This includes situations such as waiting at traffic lights or level crossings and in queues of stationary traffic. To make a call or to answer the phone you should find a safe and suitable place to park. However, in a lengthy stoppage on a motorway it would be obvious that you were not 'driving' if the engine was switched off.

The only exemption from the regulations is for calls to 999 (or 112) in a genuine emergency where it would be unsafe or impractical to stop.

Using a hand-held phone while driving can incur a fixed penalty fine of £60 with three penalty points. This amount can increase to a maximum of £1,000 if the case goes to court. The regulations also apply to anyone supervising a learner driver. As an instructor you should be concentrating on what your pupil is doing and not be using a phone.

Hands-free equipment is not covered by the regulations, provided that the phone can be used without actually holding it.

Motor vehicle insurance

Compulsory motor vehicle insurance was introduced in 1930. At that time it was decided that insurance was necessary to make sure that people who were injured in a road accident were not left uncompensated. Property damage should be included within the minimum insurance, and this cover is required by the RTA 1988.

Other types of insurance policies have been in operation for many years, as it is recognized that there is a need for more cover than the minimum requirements of the RTA.

Types of insurance

Compulsory insurance

Users of motor vehicles must be insured with an authorized insurer against third party risks. The cover must include compensation in respect of death, injury to another person and also the cost of any emergency medical treatment. All passengers must be covered and no 'own risks' agreements are allowed between passengers and the user of the vehicle. This type of insurance policy (which is very rare) is sometimes known as a 'road traffic only' policy, and leaves the user with a vast amount of risk. As an alternative to insurance, application may be made to the Secretary of State at the

Department for Transport for a warrant to enable a deposit of £500,000 in cash or securities to be made with the Accountant-General.

Third party property damage is a compulsory requirement under the RTA 1988.

Third party insurance only

A 'third party' insurance policy usually requires at least the minimum cover as that described above.

This type of policy would normally cover:

- liability for injuries to other people (including passengers in your car);
- liability in respect of accidents caused by them (for example, causing injury to a passer-by, or damaging his or her property by opening a car door);
- liability for damage to other people's property (for example, damage to another vehicle may be paid in full or in part by your insurance company).

For an additional fee the policy may be extended to include the risks of fire and theft. An additional premium may be required if the car is not kept in a locked garage overnight.

A 'third party, fire and theft' policy offers slightly more than the bare minimum but still leaves a lot of risk with the driver/owner/operator.

Comprehensive insurance

In view of the heavy cost of repairs, two out of three owners these days take out a 'comprehensive' insurance policy. However, the term 'comprehensive insurance' can be misleading, and care should be taken in reading the small print. The term 'comprehensive' as applied to motor insurance means that a variety and a great deal of protection is provided under one policy document, but does not mean that cover is provided against every conceivable contingency of whatever nature.

This type of insurance cover will normally include the risks for third party, fire and theft, together with cover for accidental damage to your own car, medical expenses, and loss or damage to personal effects in the car.

The policy will specify the uses to which the car may be put. For instance, a policy restricting use to social, domestic and pleasure purposes will not provide cover for any business use (including use by a driving school). There may also be a restriction to cover driving by specified drivers only, or the policy may exclude driving by certain persons.

Other restrictions vary from one insurance company to another, but it is normal practice for the company to specify an 'excess' when a young or inexperienced driver is driving the car. The excess is the amount that you would normally have to pay towards the cost of repairing your vehicle in the event of a blameworthy accident. If the accident was the fault of another driver, you might need to recover this amount from that person. In the case of driving school vehicles, the excess can vary and might be up to £250 depending on who was driving the car (or who was in charge of it) at the time of the accident.

Policies are usually invalidated if the vehicle insured is not maintained in a safe and roadworthy condition. Proof that the vehicle is insured in accordance with the RTA is given by insurers in the form of a Certificate of Insurance. The certificate is quite distinct from the policy of insurance itself. It is the certificate that has to be produced when renewing the car licence; it must also be produced to a police officer on request.

Driver's responsibilities

As a driver you must provide details of your insurance to the person who holds you responsible for an accident which results in damage to his or her property. The law also requires you to give insurance details following an injury accident.

For your own convenience you should be prepared to give your insurance details following an accident, or to a police officer, who can ask to see evidence of your insurance at any time.

Therefore it is in your interest, as well as those of accident victims, to keep your insurance details to hand when driving. You are advised, however, not to leave them in the car in case they are stolen.

Even with the new insurance requirements, drivers and other road users can find themselves without a source of compensation. This can happen where the accident is nobody's fault, or where you yourself are in some measure to blame. It is for you, as a driver, to consider whether you take out additional insurance cover against such risks as injury to yourself or damage to your own car in these circumstances.

EC requirements

All UK motor insurance policies must include cover against any third party liabilities that are compulsorily insurable in any other EC member state. The full cover provided under a comprehensive policy can be extended for travel in Europe, if required. A 'green card' is no longer legally necessary but it may be prudent to obtain the card from the insurance company in order to have much wider cover. Possession of the green card can also help to eliminate some of the problems of procedure and language.

Accident procedures

An 'accident' is generally and legally regarded as one that causes injury to another person or animal, or one that causes damage to another person's vehicle or property. If you are involved in an accident you must stop and give your name, address and vehicle registration details. If there is personal injury, your insurance details must be produced to anyone who has reasonable cause to see them. You must also give information about the ownership of the vehicle. If it is not possible to exchange these details at the time, the accident must be reported to the police as soon as possible, and in any case within 24 hours. A police officer may, in certain circumstances, ask for driver and vehicle details if it is thought that the driver may have been involved in an accident.

These responsibilities apply regardless of who is to blame for the accident. Even if you feel that the accident is relatively trivial or that it was not your fault, you still need to follow the procedure outlined in Figure 7.1. The figure and the notes on page 209 give useful guidance for instructional purposes.

With regard to your responsibility as an instructor, it should be noted that the duty to carry out these procedures applies to a person accompanying the holder of a provisional licence and not only to the driver of the vehicle.

Legal obligations of a supervising driver

Anyone supervising a learner driver must have held a full GB licence for at least three years and be over 21 years of age. It is the learner's responsibility to check that anyone supervising his or her practice is covered by these regulations. An offence against the regulations carries a penalty of a fine, discretionary disqualification or two penalty points.

The tuition or practice vehicle must display regulation-size 'L' plates (or 'D' plates in Wales, if preferred) that are clearly visible within a reasonable distance from the front and rear of the vehicle. 'L' plates should be removed from the vehicle when a full licence holder is driving it, except in the case of driving school cars.

As well as all the legal obligations, any driver supervising a learner has certain moral obligations relating to the safety of passengers and other road users. If a driving instructor commits or aids and abets a traffic offence, the subsequent punishment resulting from a successful prosecution is likely to have disastrous effects. Even relatively minor offences will attract a disproportionate amount of bad publicity that not only causes disgrace and inconvenience, as well as possible loss of livelihood, but also stains the character of the driving school industry as a whole.

In addition to the responsibilities as driver, already covered in this chapter, the instructor has further responsibilities. Where a supervisor sees that the 'L' driver is about to commit an unlawful act, whether it is through ignorance or lack of skill, and takes no verbal or physical action to prevent it, a prosecution for aiding and abetting could ensue. For example, if a learner was about to ignore a red traffic light and the instructor allowed the car to be stopped after passing the solid line, an offence would have been committed by both persons – even though it was the instructor who finally brought the car to a stop.

FIGURE 7.1 Accident procedure flowchart

Accident Procedure

Note:
The chart shows the *minimum* legal requirements.

Accident procedure – notes

1 An 'animal' is regarded as horse, cattle, ass, mule, sheep, goat, pig or dog.
2 You must exchange details not only with the other driver, but also with any person who has reasonable grounds for asking for them.
3 'Damage' includes roadside furniture, for example lamp posts and other fixtures.
4 You must report an accident as soon as possible, and at least within 24 hours. Your insurance certificate must be produced at the time of reporting or within seven days.
5 Your details must be given to the owner of the vehicle, property or animal.

Tuition vehicle

You need to pay particular attention to ensure that the tuition vehicle is in a roadworthy condition and that it is taxed and adequately insured for driving instruction and driving test purposes. The vehicle must carry 'L' plates (either 'D' or 'L' plates in Wales) of the prescribed size, showing clearly to the front and rear of the vehicle.

Driving licence and eyesight

Before allowing pupils to drive your vehicle you should make sure that they have a current, valid, signed driving licence and that the eyesight requirements can be met. You must check this even though the pupil may have signed a declaration to this effect on the licence application form. Where glasses are required to meet the minimum standard, they must be worn at all times while driving.

Make sure you are aware of your responsibilities as a driver and an instructor.

Tuition in client's vehicle

On occasions where clients may choose to provide their own car for professional driving lessons, you must give special consideration to all the points previously mentioned, but in particular to the roadworthiness, MOT certificate and insurance cover of the vehicle.

Before agreeing to give tuition in a non-dual-controlled vehicle, you should give serious consideration to the standard, or estimated standard, the client has reached. This is particularly important if you have not had an opportunity to make a valid assessment (for example, a new client booking by telephone).

Due consideration should also be given to the type of vehicle, to see if you can easily reach the handbrake (some cars have the handbrake on the right of the driver or under the dash). Your safety, as well as that of your client and other road users, may be at stake.

Advanced driving tests

The Cardington Special Test

This high-level driving test is open to all Approved Driving Instructors who want to keep their own driving up to standard as part of their continued professional development. One of the strictest tests available, it is conducted by permanent staff instructors operating out of the Driving Standards Agency's Training Centre at Cardington near Bedford.

You have to provide your own car for the test. It must have:

- manual transmission;
- an interior instructor mirror;
- integral head restraints for both the driver and the assessor.

The test normally lasts approximately 90 minutes, and covers a variety of road and traffic conditions, including motorways. The test syllabus includes:

- driving on all types of road;
- a left- and right-hand reverse;
- turning in the road;
- reverse parking;
- hill and angled starts.

Commentary driving is not expected, and there is no element of theory testing.

You will be assessed on your driving technique, and you are expected to demonstrate a systematic and professional approach to all hazards and plan expertly for safe progress at all times. In particular, the assessor will be checking your:

- expert handling of the vehicle controls;
- use of correct road procedures;
- anticipation of the actions of other road users and taking the appropriate action;
- sound judgement of distance, speed and timing;
- consideration for the convenience and safety of other road users.

During the test you will be asked to carry out some or all of the following manoeuvres:

- moving off uphill and downhill on reasonably steep slopes;
- moving off at an angle from behind a parked vehicle;
- overtaking, meeting and crossing the path of other vehicles;
- turning right- and left-hand corners;
- stopping the car as in an emergency;
- reversing into limited openings to the left and right;
- reverse parking (car park and road);
- turning the vehicle round in the road using forward and reverse gears.

The test includes about 10 minutes of independent driving. This element is designed to test your ability to drive safely while making decisions independently. During this phase you will be asked to follow traffic signs or a series of directions or a combination of both.

Each individual fault will be fully assessed in the light of the prevailing conditions. The result is normally confirmed by post within 48 hours and, whether you pass or fail, you will receive a report on those faults observed. If you achieve a grade A, you will also receive the Cardington Certificate.

The fee (at January 2011) is £144, but this is continually under review by the DSA.

To make a booking or to find out more about the test, contact the DSA at The Axis Building, 112 Upper Parliament Street, Nottingham NG1 6LP; tel: 0300 200 1122.

The Institute of Advanced Motorists (IAM)

The IAM was founded in 1956 for the purposes of raising driving standards and to establish an Advanced Driving Test. The Institute believes that a higher standard of behaviour by all road users, and drivers in particular, could reduce road accidents and their grim social consequences more effectively than any other method. The Advanced Driving Test offers to drivers of cars, trucks, and motorcycles an opportunity to check their own abilities under today's road conditions; membership of the Institute for those who achieve the Institute's standards then demands the responsibility that goes with proven skill.

The standard of the test is based on the police system of car control as taught in Home Office Approved Police Driving Schools. The examiners, all of whom are either serving or retired police officers, have to hold an Advanced Driving Certificate. This qualification has never been challenged by the public as it is probably the highest available in the world. The 120 test routes are designed to provide all types of driving conditions and are about 35 miles long. The test takes 90 minutes, which does not include the briefing and debriefing.

There are many books available on the subject of advanced driving, including *Roadcraft: The police driver's handbook* and *How to Be an Advanced Motorist*.

The advantage of taking an advanced test is that IAM members have a 50–75 per cent lower accident rate than the general public. Over 400 commercial concerns put their staff through the test in order to cut costs, as does the British Army. Many insurance companies grant a discount off normal motor insurance premiums of up to 20 per cent. The conviction rate among members appears to be five times lower than the general public. Anyone with a full British driving licence can take the test; it is advisable to receive instruction from an ADI, preferably an IAM member, or contact the local IAM group who will give guidance in preparation for the test.

The IAM is a registered charity and receives full moral support from the Department for Transport, all UK police forces and the Ministry of Defence. The IAM motto is 'Skill with Responsibility'.

Application forms for the test can be obtained from the Institute of Advanced Motorists, IAM House, 510 Chiswick High Road, London W4 5RG (tel: 020 8996 9600; fax: 020 8996 9601; website: www.iam.org.uk).

Candidates will be expected to make reasonable use of the vehicle's performance within the speed limits and normal parameters of safety with regard to the road traffic and weather conditions. Candidates are expected to reverse into a side road and execute a hill start, and will be assessed on their powers of observation.

The test is something that any driver with a reasonable amount of experience and skill should be able to pass without too much difficulty. Candidates do not fail for committing minor faults. Even those who do fail should learn some important lessons from the examiner conducting the test. Successful candidates may:

- display the Institute's badge on their car;
- take advantage of special insurance terms;
- receive *Advanced Driving*, the motoring magazine especially written for those with a keen interest in driving;
- join their local IAM group and participate in the road safety, driving and social events which they organize.

During the test

Examiners look for the following points:

- *Acceleration* should be smooth and progressive. It should be used at the right time and right place. Acceleration should not be excessive or insufficient.
- *Braking* should be smooth and progressive. Brakes should be used in conjunction with the mirror and signals. They should not be used late or fiercely. Candidates will be expected to take account of the road conditions.
- *Clutch control.* The engine and road speeds must be properly coordinated when changing gear. Candidates should not slip or ride the clutch, nor should they coast with the clutch disengaged.
- *Gear changing.* Gears should be selected smoothly and fluently. If automatic transmission is fitted, candidates should make full use of it.
- *Use of gears.* Candidates must make correct use of the gears. The correct gear should be selected before reaching a hazard.
- *Steering.* The wheel should be held correctly with the hands at the quarter-to-three or ten-to-two position. The use of the crossed arm technique, except when manoeuvring in a confined space, is not recommended by the Institute.
- *Seating position.* Candidates should be alert and not slumped at the wheel. They should not rest an arm on the door while driving.
- *Observation.* Candidates should read the road well ahead and anticipate the actions of other road users. They must be able to judge correctly the speeds and distances of other vehicles.
- *Concentration.* Candidates should concentrate on the road and traffic situation and not allow themselves to be easily distracted.

- *Maintaining progress.* With regard to the road, traffic and weather conditions, candidates should make use of their vehicle's performance by driving at a reasonable pace, maintaining good progress throughout.

- *Obstruction.* Candidates should not obstruct other road users by driving too slowly, by positioning incorrectly on the road or by failing to anticipate and react correctly to the traffic situation ahead.

- *Positioning.* Candidates should keep in the correct part of the road, especially when approaching and negotiating hazards.

- *Lane discipline.* Candidates should drive in the appropriate lane and be careful not to straddle white lines.

- *Observation of surfaces.* Candidates should continually assess the road surface, especially in poor weather, and look out for slippery conditions.

- *Traffic signals.* Candidates must observe and respond correctly to signals, signs and road markings, and extend proper courtesies at pedestrian crossings.

- *Speed limits and other legal requirements.* Speed limits and other legal requirements must be observed at all times.

- *Overtaking* should be carried out safely while maintaining a correct distance from other vehicles and using the mirrors, signals and gears correctly.

- *Hazard procedure and cornering.* Candidates must have full control over their vehicle on the approach to a hazard. They must negotiate it in the correct position, driving at an appropriate speed with a suitable gear engaged.

- *Mirrors* should be used frequently, especially before signalling and making changes to speed or course.

- *Signals* given by direction indicator, or arm if required, should be given in the right place and in good time. The horn and headlight flasher should only be used in accordance with *The Highway Code*.

- *Restraint.* Candidates should display reasonable restraint, without being indecisive.

- *Consideration.* Candidates should extend consideration and courtesy to other road users.

- *Car sympathy.* Candidates should not over-stress the vehicle, for example by revving the engine needlessly or by fierce braking.

- *Manoeuvring* should be carried out smoothly and competently.

The RoSPA Advanced Driving Test

RoSPA advanced tests are conducted at locations throughout the UK by Police Advanced drivers. The test normally lasts about 1¼ hours. The cost of the test includes the first year's membership of the RoSPA Advanced Drivers Association.

RoSPA has a unique system of grading successful candidates into gold, silver and bronze grades, which seems to be a fairer way of assessing performance over a wider range of driving ability. It provides incentives for the less experienced seeking to improve on their standard continuously, and at the same time gives a meaningful measure of attainment to the more skilful driver. The highest grade is unlikely to be achieved without a thorough knowledge of *Roadcraft*, the police drivers' manual, and the system of car control it advocates.

Application forms can be obtained from The Administrative Officer, RoSPA Advanced Drivers Association, 28 Calthorpe Road, Edgbaston, Birmingham B15 1RP, tel: 0121 248 2000 or at www.rospa.com.

The test

At the start of the test, examiners try to put candidates at ease. Cars used for the test must be in a roadworthy condition and the candidate's visibility must not be obscured in any way. Examiners will take a serious view of candidates who, for example on a rainy day, attempt to drive while visibility is restricted by condensation on windows and mirrors.

Use of the controls Before starting off, candidates are required to carry out the cockpit drill followed by a brake test shortly after moving.

Candidates are expected to demonstrate their mechanical appreciation by controlling the vehicle smoothly. Examiners will assess the steering method and position of the hands and arms when turning the wheel. The clutch should be used smoothly. Slipping and riding the clutch is frowned upon. Examiners will assess the position of the hand on the gear lever when executing selections, the matching of engine revolutions to road speed and the correct timing of gear changes. The intelligent use of intermediate gears will make a difference to the final grade achieved. The use of the brakes is assessed for smoothness, early braking in correct sequence relating to the 'system', skid avoidance through correct technique and progressive reduction in pedal pressure as the vehicle is brought to a smooth stop. The accelerator should be used firmly when needed, precisely and under control at all times. Acceleration sense in overtaking will be assessed, along with anticipation and the smooth variation of speeds to meet changing road and traffic conditions without braking.

Candidates are expected to use the mirrors in the correct sequence and have an accurate and continuous knowledge of the traffic situation behind. Over-the-shoulder looks are expected at appropriate times. Candidates are also assessed in their use of the horn.

Driving performance Moving off and stopping should be smooth and carried out safely. Examiners will assess the correct application of the system of car control, whether candidates brake before or after changing gear, and whether they signal too late or too early. Particular emphasis is placed on the way the vehicle is positioned at junctions, on the approach to roundabouts, on the open road and in lanes on the approach to hazards.

Candidates will be assessed on their course when cornering and whether the line taken optimizes visibility and safety, and allows for any tendency of the vehicle to over- or understeer to be compensated for. The use of speed and vehicle controls while cornering will be assessed.

Candidates are assessed on whether necessary signals are omitted or wrongly timed, or unnecessary ones are used. The examiner will look for reinforcement of intention by an arm signal where necessary, and assess reactions to traffic signs.

Candidates are required to perform a reversing exercise safely and accurately, and in normal driving to make reasonable use of their vehicle's performance within legal limits and as safety allows, according to the prevailing road and traffic conditions. Examiners will assess whether candidates are asking themselves the appropriate questions before executing an overtaking manoeuvre.

General ability Consideration for others and self-control will be assessed. Temperament while driving should be calm, relaxed and decisive.

Candidates are expected not to abuse their vehicles by 'kerbing' and the like.

Examiners will assess candidates' powers of observation, hazard recognition and planning. Candidates may, if they choose, elect to give a commentary drive or are invited to 'think aloud' for a few minutes by the examiner. Candidates will also be assessed on their ability to judge their own speed and the speeds and distances of other vehicles. This will be linked to candidates' use of braking and acceleration.

The test is concluded with questions on *The Highway Code* and other motoring matters such as those contained in most vehicle handbooks.

After the test

The examiner will discuss any points that have arisen during the test and then allocate a grade according to the performance of the candidate. Candidates are allocated a grade and are expected to take a refresher test within three years. Candidates who are ungraded are permitted to take the test again after three months. All retests are free of charge, as the fees are included in the annual membership subscription.

The DIAmond Advanced Test

The test is administered by the Driving Instructors Association and conducted by specially qualified DIAmond Advanced Examiners. These examiners are ADIs who have qualified for the Diploma in Driving Instruction, have passed the Cardington Special Driving Test and have also passed the DIAmond Advanced Examiners' Course.

The test is based on the DSA method of marking, with no more than six minor faults allowed. During the test a wide variety of road and traffic conditions are covered.

One of the advantages of taking this extra qualification is that you should be able to generate more and different types of business opportunities, such as advanced and defensive driving courses.

More details of the test are available from DIAmond Advanced Motorists Ltd, Safety House, Beddington Farm Road, Croydon CR0 4XZ, tel: 020 8665 5151.

Eco-driving

All advanced driving tests these days – including the ADI Part 2 and the Cardington Special Test – include an element of eco-friendly driving.
Some of the main points that you should bear in mind include:

- Don't leave the car engine to warm up – drive off as soon as practicable after starting the engine.
- Harsh acceleration, sharp braking and generally aggressive driving can all cause an increase in fuel usage.
- Improved engine technology makes it possible to move up through the gears more rapidly – for petrol cars about 2,500 rpm, and for diesel about 2,000 rpm.
- Missing out intermediate gears by 'block changing' up and down through the gears can save fuel.
- Remember that very short journeys of less than two miles produce 60 per cent more pollution than journeys with a warm engine. Catalytic converters can take up to six miles to become really effective.
- Switching off the engine when waiting in queues of traffic uses less energy.
- The optimum speed range for minimum emissions is regarded as being 40–60 mph.
- Make sure that the engine is regularly maintained and properly tuned to keep emissions to a minimum.
- Make sure that tyre pressures are set at the recommended level. If the pressures are low, fuel consumption can be increased by about 2–3 per cent.
- Don't carry unnecessary loads such as roof racks or heavy items in the boot. In these circumstances, fuel consumption can increase by up to 10 per cent. With a heavy trailer – a boat or a caravan, for example – this figure can rise to 30 per cent.

More detail on eco-friendly driving techniques is given in Chapter 4. The latest edition of *The Official DSA Guide to Driving* has a complete chapter on eco-safe driving.

The Car

08

I t is not necessary to know every last detail of the construction of a motor car. However, it is extremely helpful to have a thorough understanding of the basic principles involved, because it will help you to:

- have a better appreciation of your tuition car's workings, resulting in more cost-effective use of it;
- recognize when there is a need to undertake minor repairs and the early diagnosis of potential major faults;
- explain to your pupils in simple terms how the controls work;
- assist your pupils in developing more vehicle sympathy and a keener interest in driving generally.

For these reasons it is important to understand what happens when the driver uses the controls.

This chapter includes a general view of mechanical principles, vehicle control and operation, vehicle safety checks, factors affecting vehicle stability and a summary of the legal requirements of using a motor car. It also gives an outline syllabus for teaching learners the basics of car mechanics and an understanding of how the car works.

Mechanical principles

The motor car is a complex assembly that includes the following main units and systems:

- *Power unit*, including the engine and the systems essential to its operation – for example, cooling, fuel, ignition and lubrication systems.
- *Transmission system* (power train) – this includes a gearbox to match the engine speed to the power required for the road conditions, and a final drive unit that transmits the power to the front and/or rear wheels. The final drive unit incorporates a differential unit to allow for varying wheel speeds when cornering.

- *Braking system* – to slow or stop the motion of the vehicle in either direction.
- *Steering system* – to move the vehicle in the desired direction.
- *Suspension system* – to reduce as far as practicable the shock and vibration from the road wheels to the vehicle body/chassis.
- *Body/chassis* – to act as a mounting for all the other units and assemblies.

The engine

The function of the engine is to convert the heat energy released from the fuel during the combustion process into mechanical energy for powering the vehicle. Most cars are powered by four or six-cylinder engines; each cylinder is a hole bored in a cylinder block. Pistons move up and down inside these cylinders in a sequence called the 'Otto cycle'. The four strokes of this cycle are induction, compression, power (combustion) and exhaust.

The flow of fuel and air mixture into the cylinders and the flow of the burnt exhaust gases out are both controlled by a system of valves incorporated in the cylinder head. The cylinder head bolted to the top of the cylinder block seals off each of the bores, and a gasket is fitted between them to make the joint pressure tight. Combustion of the fuel and air mixture takes place in combustion chambers, which are usually formed in the cylinder head above each of the cylinders but sometimes in the crown (top) of the piston.

FIGURE 8.1 The engine

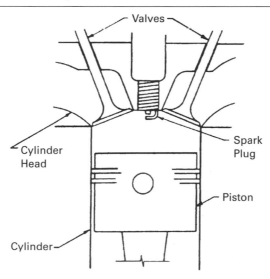

- *Induction* (a in Figure 8.2). During the induction or inlet stroke, the inlet valve is open and the exhaust valve remains closed. The piston moves downward and the suction or vacuum created by this movement causes air and fuel to be drawn into the combustion chamber.
- *Compression* (b). During the compression stroke, both inlet and exhaust valves are closed. The piston moves upwards to compress the air-fuel mixture into a small volume.
- *Power* (c). During the power stroke, both valves remain closed. A spark from the spark plug ignites the air-fuel mixture and the piston is driven downward by the rapidly expanding gas. This stroke delivers the power to propel the vehicle.
- *Exhaust* (d). During the exhaust stroke, the exhaust valve is open and the piston moves upward to push out the burnt gases. On completion of the exhaust stroke, the process begins immediately with another inlet stroke.

Power conversion

The pistons connected by connecting rods to the crankshaft convert the power produced on the power stroke into a rotary motion. A heavy disc called a flywheel is bolted to the crankshaft to make it revolve more evenly and thus ensure a continuous flow of power to the gearbox and driving wheels. One complete Otto cycle rotates the crankshaft twice and carries the engine over the idle (non-power) strokes.

Valve and ignition timing

The arrangement of the valve timing gears and ignition timing sensor ensures perfect coordination with the motion of the pistons; a camshaft controls the opening and closing of the valves. It rotates at precisely half engine speed and in perfect coordination with a sensor, which controls the exact timing of the spark to initiate the ignition stroke.

FIGURE 8.2 The four-stroke cycle (Otto)

FIGURE 8.3 Power conversion

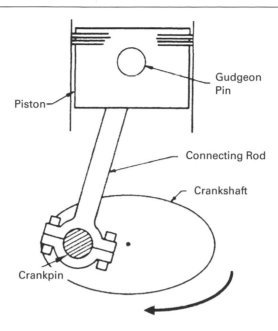

The fuel system (petrol engines)

An engine operates on a mixture of petrol and air.

As the accelerator pedal is depressed, more air is drawn in to the engine through the air filter and through a series of pipes, known as the inlet manifold, which are connected to each cylinder. When starting a cold engine, a much richer mixture is required and this means a higher proportion of petrol to air than for normal running. This is achieved by the injectors delivering more fuel and is controlled by the engine temperature.

With a fuel-injection system, the amount of petrol injected and the timing of its supply is controlled electronically. The accelerator operates a throttle butterfly valve that regulates the amount of air that flows through to the cylinder. At the same time a pump pressurizes the fuel, which is then directed through the injectors into the inlet manifold close to the inlet valves. On some engines the fuel is injected directly into the cylinder.

The ignition system

The combustible mixture of air and petrol is ignited by a spark that occurs between two electrodes (spark plug) in the combustion chamber, at the end of the compression stroke. It is the function of the ignition system to provide a spark of sufficient heat intensity to ignite the charge mixture at the predetermined position in the engine's cycle under all speed and load conditions.

The ignition system converts the low voltage from the battery into a high-tension voltage by means of an ignition coil. High-tension voltage is transmitted through the HT lead from the coil to the spark plug. A coil may be fitted to each spark plug, so eliminating the HT leads.

The timing of the spark is advanced or retarded automatically to ensure that it occurs at the correct moment for the load and engine speed. All modern cars are now equipped with electronic ignition systems that involve less maintenance, longer spark plug life and make starting the car easier.

Engine lubrication

If two surfaces that rub together are examined under a microscope, it will be seen that each surface has a jagged edge (A in Figure 8.4). If these edges touch one another during operation, friction and heat are generated. If they are left without lubrication, these components will either wear excessively or weld themselves together, ultimately resulting in component seizure.

If this situation occurred in the internal combustion engine, it would first lead to audible knocking noises, then to a reduction in power output, and finally to the failure of the component concerned. To overcome these problems, a film of oil (B in Figure 8.4) must separate the two surfaces. It is the function of the 'force-fed' lubrication system to maintain a film of oil between all moving engine components under all operating conditions.

Force-fed lubrication systems are generally of the 'wet sump' type in which the sump acts as both an oil drain return and a storage container. A pump draws oil from the sump and forces it through a filter up into the engine to lubricate all moving parts. Provision of a dipstick enables the level of oil in the sump to be checked. It is vital that the oil level does not drop to near or under the low mark. If this happens, the moving parts of the engine are starved of the lubrication and protection they need.

An oil level that is too high can result in 'foaming' of the oil, so that air enters the lubrication system, causing inconsistent oil pressure. Excess oil splash on to the cylinder bores can also give rise to an increase in oil consumption.

It is essential that the engine oil and oil filter are replaced at the manufacturer's recommended service intervals. Failure to carry out this fairly basic service will cause unnecessary engine wear and tear.

FIGURE 8.4 Engine lubrication

Metals   A   Oil Film   B

An oil pressure gauge or oil pressure warning light indicates a condition of low oil pressure. If this happens, the engine should be switched off straight away.

Oil also acts as a coolant. Some of the engine's excess heat is carried back to the sump, where air flowing over outside carries some heat away.

Potential problems with engine lubrication:

- *Excessive oil consumption*: oil level too high, wrong grade of oil, worn engine components.

- *No oil pressure*: low oil level, worn/faulty oil pump, blocked oil ways and/or filter.

- *Low oil pressure*: low oil level, wrong grade of oil, worn/faulty oil pump, very high oil temperature, worn engine components.

- *High oil pressure*: wrong grade of oil, faulty oil pump, sticking pressure relief valve.

- *Oil leaks*: worn and/or faulty seals and gaskets; oil level too high.

The cooling system

The principle of the petrol engine, which derives its power from the combustion of fuel and air, necessitates the use of some type of cooling system to keep the engine's components at an acceptable working temperature. A typical water-cooled engine comprises a radiator, a water pump driven by a drive belt from the crankshaft, a series of passages running through the engine, and a thermostat. Water is pumped from the radiator, up through the engine past the thermostat and back into the top of the radiator, where it is cooled by the fan and the natural airflow as the car is being driven. Cooled water from the radiator then flows back into the cylinder block.

FIGURE 8.5 The cooling system

Driving school cars in particular do a lot of manoeuvring and slow driving work where there is very little natural movement of air through the radiator to cool the system. Under these circumstances, an electrically operated fan that only functions when a predetermined engine temperature is reached provides additional airflow.

Potential problems with the cooling system:

- *Engine overheating*: water level low, loose or worn drive belt, faulty thermostat, blocked radiator matrix, collapsed radiator hoses, ignition timing incorrect, vehicle overloaded or brakes binding.

- *Overcooling*: thermostat faulty (jammed open), electric cooling fan continuously operating (faulty thermostat switch).

- *Coolant loss*: worn out hoses or loose clips, leaking radiator, water pump or core plugs, failed cylinder head gasket, cracked cylinder head or block.

The transmission system

The transmission of a car (see Figure 8.6) consists of a clutch (B), a gearbox (C) and a final drive unit (F). Their combined purpose is to transmit the drive from the engine (A) through to the road wheels. In the past, cars had an engine and gearbox at the front, with a propeller shaft relaying the drive to the rear wheels via a rear axle unit (D).

FIGURE 8.6 The transmission system

Nowadays, a more common layout is a system in which the engine, clutch and gearbox are in one unit driving the front wheels. This design allows more space for passengers and can give improved handling and control. However, it requires more complicated engineering, including the use of drive shafts fitted with constant velocity (CV) joints (E). These ensure the smooth transmission of power to the drive/steered wheels throughout all wheel movements caused by steering and suspension operations..

The clutch

The clutch enables the engine to be disconnected from the transmission in order to engage or disengage the gears. It provides the means for a smooth engagement of the drive between the engine and the road wheels, and it also allows the car to be controlled at a crawling pace.

The clutch consists of three main parts: a release bearing, a spring-loaded pressure plate and a centre plate. At the back of the engine there is a flat, heavy wheel called the flywheel, which is attached to the crankshaft and revolves at the same speed as the engine. The clutch centre plate comprises a friction material similar to a brake lining. It is connected to the transmission and held firmly against the flywheel by the pressure plate. When the engine is turning, the clutch is also turning.

When the clutch pedal is depressed, the pressure plate is pulled away from the flywheel, thus freeing the centre friction plate and disengaging the drive. When the pedal is released, the centre friction plate is forced against the flywheel by the pressure plate and the drive between the engine and transmission is complete.

Partially engaging (slipping) the clutch allows the car to be controlled at a crawling pace. A release bearing is situated behind the pressure plate and provides the means to allow the pedal linkage to operate the clutch.

FIGURE 8.7 The clutch

Gearbox

The purpose of the gearbox is to enable the car to be driven at varying speeds with the minimum strain on the engine. Lower speeds and harder work will call for lower gears; while for normal cruising a higher gear should be selected.

The modern gearbox usually has four, five or six forward gears and a reverse gear. It also has a neutral position that disengages the engine from the road wheels. All forward gears have a synchromesh mechanism that allows changing from any one gear to another to be accomplished quietly and smoothly. Very simply, it synchronizes the speeds of the gears to be engaged before actually coupling them together.

Lubrication in the gearbox is as essential as it is in the engine. Most gearboxes have a filler/level plug on the side that allows the oil level to be checked at regular intervals. Failure to maintain the correct level of oil could lead to overheating and unnecessary wear and tear.

Note: Do not rest your hand on the gear lever unless snagging or changing gear as this can cause premature wear of the gear selector mechanism.

Potential problems with the gearbox:

- *Noisy or difficult gear selection*: faulty or worn synchromesh units, clutch drag.
- *Jumping out of gear*: worn or faulty synchromesh units, worn out gear selector mechanism.
- *Noisy operation*: worn bearings, damaged or worn gear teeth.
- *Oil loss*: worn gearbox oil seals, damaged or broken gearbox gaskets.

Automatic transmission

Most modern automatic transmission systems use a torque converter, together with an epicyclic gearbox. This enables the system to take up the drive smoothly and for gear changes to be made automatically with the power on. A control system determines when a gear change is needed by a system of sensors, and by comparing the speed of the vehicle with the amount of acceleration. The driver can override the system by, for example, changing to a lower gear by pressing hard on the accelerator (kick down).

The transmission senses when the vehicle speed is increasing or decreasing and whether the accelerator is being used. This means that there will be times when the transmission will change to a higher gear when it is inappropriate, for example going downhill or through a series of bends. To avoid this situation the driver can override the automatic system by manually locking the transmission in a lower gear.

A 'gear selector' replaces the manual transmission gear lever. The usual layout (although this may vary from one type of vehicle to another) is:

P – park. The transmission is locked. 'Park' must only be selected when the vehicle is stationary.

R – reverse.

N – neutral.

D – drive. The transmission will change gear automatically according to the speed of the car and the engine revs.

2 – 2nd gear lock; 1 – 1st gear lock. In both these positions the transmission will not change to a higher gear. On some types of vehicle these selector positions are replaced by a single 'L' position.

Other types of automatic transmission include:

CVT (constantly variable transmission). This system incorporates a centrifugal mechanism allowing the gear ratios to be completely variable.

Semi-automatic. The driver makes the decision about when to select a particular gear, but there is no clutch pedal.

Pre-selector. The required gear is selected by the driver, but the gear change is not made until the gear change pedal (which replaces the clutch pedal) is pressed.

Differential units

The differential is comprised of a small unit that is bolted to the crown wheel and pinion assembly, which contains a number of small gears. Together they form part of the final drive unit. The differential gears enable the inside wheel to turn at a slower rate than the outer wheel when on a curve.

Sometimes a 'limited slip' differential is fitted to cars. It is a device that allows normal differential action of the driving wheels when cornering, but prevents loss of traction in the event of either driving wheel losing adhesion. Its action therefore affords the driver better vehicle control under slippery road conditions.

Exhaust system

An exhaust system is installed for the purpose of collecting burnt gases issued from the engine cylinders and discharging them outside the vehicle. A series of silencers ensure that the gases are exhausted without excessive noise. Exhaust emission consists of a mixture of carbon monoxide (CO), carbon dioxide (CO_2), hydrocarbons (HC) and oxides of nitrogen (NO_2). Some of these emissions are harmful to the environment so modern engine exhaust systems include a catalytic converter to reduce the level of pollutants.

The catalytic converter functions by providing an additional area for continued burning of HC and CO. HC and CO burn completely (or are converted) to water vapour, nitrogen (N) and carbon dioxide (CO_2).

The fuel used in cars equipped with catalytic converters must be lead-free. If lead coats the internal elements of the converter, its effectiveness is greatly reduced.

Precautionary measures for catalytic converters:

- Use only unleaded petrol.

- Do not use fuel additives, unless specifically intended for catalytic systems.

- Excess fuel can damage the catalytic converter. If difficult cold starting is experienced or if the engine misfires, contact the dealer as soon as possible.

FIGURE 8.8 The exhaust system

- Do not use oil additives.
- Allow the engine to return to idle before switching off. This allows the temperature to stabilize in the catalytic converter.
- Keep to the recommended service intervals.
- Never push or tow-start the vehicle.
- Avoid running out of fuel.
- Avoid leaving the engine idling for long periods.
- Do not park or drive over inflammable materials. The high temperatures generated by catalytic converters can ignite dry grass.
- Exhaust gas is very hot; keep away from the tailpipe.

Exhaust turbo charging

A turbocharger is a device that uses the exhaust gases to turn an air pump or compressor that forces an increased amount of air into the engine cylinders. If a corresponding amount of fuel is then added, a large increase in engine power will be obtained. Both petrol and diesel engines can use a turbocharger.

Brakes

Most modern cars use a combination of disc brakes on the front wheels and drum brakes on the rear. Disc brakes are more efficient than drum brakes at higher speeds owing to the improved flow of cooling air over the discs. When the footbrake is applied, a hydraulic system multiplies the pedal pressure. Pistons located inside a calliper squeeze the disc between two friction pads, which then provides the braking force required for slowing the car down.

Drum brakes work on the same friction principle, but wheel cylinders expand the brake shoes outward against a rotating drum to provide the braking force. Because drum brakes are enclosed they are not so easily cooled by an air stream, and generation of excessive heat may result in a condition known as 'brake-fade'.

FIGURE 8.9 Hydraulic braking system

The hydraulic system consists of a master cylinder and a fluid reservoir, connecting pipes, hoses and wheel cylinders. Footbrake pressure is transmitted directly from the master cylinder and applied to the brake shoes and disc pads. This action ensures that the vehicle will pull up smoothly and in a straight line.

All modern brake systems are of the 'dual line' type, where the addition of a second brake line and a special master cylinder (tandem) ensures that in the event of a failure of either line, at least two wheel brakes remain in service.

Brake hydraulic fluid used in most vehicles is 'hygroscopic', which means that it absorbs water from the atmosphere. Water causes corrosion and can boil, so aerating the system. For these reasons, the fluid should be changed at regular intervals, usually two to three years or as specified by the manufacturer.

Handbrake

The parking brake or handbrake is a separate braking system from the footbrake. It is usually mounted on the floor of the car and is connected by cable to the two rear wheels. Care should be taken when applying the brake to squeeze the pawl, thus saving unnecessary wear and tear on the ratchet.

Anti-lock braking system (ABS)

Increasingly being fitted as standard equipment, these systems provide near optimum braking under most prevailing road conditions. When braking on wet or icy roads, the system virtually eliminates the tendency for wheels to lock up. This means that braking efficiency is used to the maximum so that very short braking distances can be achieved (it does not make the brakes more efficient). By preventing the wheels from locking, ABS also assists directional control during braking when cornering.

To prevent the wheel from locking, the system provides pressure modulation in the braking circuits. Sensors fitted to each wheel monitor the rotational speeds of the wheels and are able to detect when there is a risk of wheel locking. Solenoid valves are positioned in the brake circuits to each wheel, and these valves are incorporated in a modulator assembly, which is controlled by an electronic control unit (ECU). The ECU controls modulation of the braking effort applied to each wheel, according to the information supplied by the wheel sensors.

Should a fault develop in the system, a self-diagnostic facility is incorporated in the ECU, which can be used in conjunction with special diagnostic equipment that is available to a dealer, to determine the nature of the fault.

The braking system components used with ABS are similar to those used on models with a conventional braking system. Although ABS provides a major contribution to vehicle safety and driver control, it does not remove the need for responsible driving and for an awareness of road and traffic conditions.

FIGURE 8.10 Anti-lock braking system

Steering

The steering system is used to control the direction of the vehicle. It is designed to control the front wheels over all types of road conditions, through turns and at different speeds. It comprises a linkage system that is attached to the front wheels, the steering wheel and the steering gear. Manual and power steering units are used.

'Rack and pinion' steering is the most popular system used on front-wheel drive cars. The system is used in conjunction with MacPherson strut suspension, which gives more engine compartment room for transverse-mounted engines. Rack and pinion steering consists of a flat gear (the rack) and a mating gear (the pinion). When the steering wheel and shaft turn, the pinion meshes with the teeth on the rack. This causes the rack to move left or right in the housing. This motion moves the remaining steering linkage to turn the front wheels. The system is very practical for small cars that require lighter steering capacity. It is a direct steering unit that is more positive in motion (less lost motion) than steering box/steering linkage systems.

Power-assisted steering

Most cars now have power-assisted steering, which makes steering at low speeds much easier for the driver. The system is operated hydraulically by power steering fluid that is pumped by the engine or an electric pump.

Even though it is physically possible to use the steering while the car is stationary, this should be avoided as it will 'scrub' the tyres as well as putting a strain on the system.

FIGURE 8.11 Rack and pinion steering gear

Suspension

The suspension system of a car is used to support its weight during varying road conditions. The suspension system is made up of several subsystems. These include the front and rear suspension assemblies and the shock absorbers. All these systems must work together to control three different types of body movement – bounce, roll and pitch. Bounce occurs when a car hits a bump or dip in the road. Roll is produced when cornering, particularly at speed, when centrifugal force causes the car to lean away from the centre of the curve – that is, the car leans to the left when you are trying to steer to the right. In extreme cases, a car will roll over. Pitch is the reaction of the rear wheels following the front wheels over a bump. As the front of the car rises, the rear dips; as the rear wheels strike the bump, the front of the car drops, causing a forward and backward movement, similar to a ship pitching in and out of waves.

The suspension assemblies incorporate springs that are interposed between the wheels and the body so that the body is partially isolated from the axles. When a vehicle rides over rough ground, the wheels rise as they roll over the bump and deflect the springs. The energy created as a result of the movement is momentarily stored in the spring and is then released as the spring returns to its original length (rebound). Various types of spring can be utilized – for example, leaf, coil or helical, torsion bar and gas springs.

The suspension design of most modern cars provides for the inclusion of independent front- and rear-wheel suspension systems. These ensure optimum handling and ride comfort.

Several car manufacturers now offer 'active' ride control systems that allow the driver to switch between 'normal' and 'sport' suspension settings. One such system uses a hydro-pneumatic springing medium that is controlled electronically via sensors. The 'normal' setting provides maximum comfort and adapts automatically to driving and road conditions. The 'sport' setting provides a stiffer suspension that is more suited to a sporting driving style.

Shock absorbers

Shock absorbers (dampers) are fitted between the car's body and axle to prevent excessive rolling and bouncing of the body during motion. They also minimize unwanted up and down movement of the wheel and axle when the car negotiates uneven road surfaces.

One shock absorber is used on each wheel. Each shock absorber must control one wheel and axle motion. The springs support the body, but the shock absorbers work with the springs to control movements of the car body. The construction of a basic shock absorber consists of an internal piston contained within an oil-filled cylinder. The piston moves with the axle, and the resistance to movement produced by forcing the oil through small valves in the piston restricts quick action, preventing a continual bouncing movement.

FIGURE 8.12 Shock absorbers

Piston

Oil flow

Tyres

Most modern cars are fitted with radial tyres, with cross-ply tyres only found on much older models.

The construction of the radial-ply tyre reduces cornering wear and considerably increases the overall life of the tyre, but this is usually at the expense of a slightly harder ride at lower speeds. It gives greater high-speed cornering grip than a cross-ply of equivalent size. The cords in the plies run from bead to bead across the crown at right angles, not diagonally as in the cross-ply tyre. This gives great pliability and comfort, but little or no directional stability. Stability comes from the tread-bracing layers, a belt of cords running round the circumference of the tyre beneath the tread. These cords are usually spun from rayon textile or fine steel wire, and are flexible but do not lose their tautness. This firmly restricts any lateral stretching of the tread.

FIGURE 8.13 Radial and cross-ply tyres

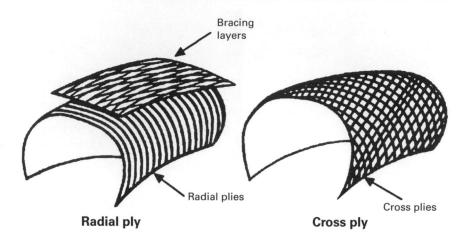

Most cars today are fitted with tubeless tyres; these are basically the same as tyres with an inner but are made airtight by having a soft rubber lining to the casing, thus dispensing with the need for an inner tube. The main advantage of tubeless tyres is that they are less liable to deflate suddenly when punctured, and can be driven without an appreciable loss of air when penetrated by small flints or nails. Statistics show that the risk of tyre failure with a tubed tyre is about three-and-a-half times greater than with a tubeless tyre.

You should ensure that your tyres meet the legal requirements. They should have a tread depth of 1.6 mm throughout the central three-quarters of the breadth of the tyre and around the entire outer circumference.

You should not have a mixture of cross-ply and radial tyres as they each have completely different road-holding characteristics.

Faults:

- *Over-inflation*: causes excessive wear along the centre of the tread.

- *Under-inflation*: causes excessive wear around the outer edges of the tread.

- *Serious structural damage*: a break or cut in the tyre fabric that is deep enough to reach the body cords. Any exposed portion of ply or cord. Any lump or bulge caused by separation of the tyre structure. These faults usually result from heavy contact with the kerb or a foreign body.

- *Incorrect wheel alignment*: causes wear (feathering) on either the inner or outer edge of the tread. Because of the natural self-aligning characteristic of steering system, any mis-alignment of one wheel, for instance 'kerbing', will result in wear being apparent on both tyres. If wear is apparent on one tyre only, it is likely to be caused by some other incorrect angle (for example, camber, caster or swivel axis inclination).

- *Spot wear*: unbalanced tyres will cause a steering wheel shimmy, and rapid and uneven tyre wear. Wear in steering and/or suspension components may also promote excessive tyre wear. Unbalanced wheels will wear a flat at one point only.

Vehicle safety checks

To do the job of driving instruction efficiently, the instructor should not be worrying about the condition of the driving school car. Both instructor and pupil must have confidence in the knowledge that the car is in a sound condition, both mechanically and bodily. Regular servicing and preventive maintenance are both of the utmost importance to an instructor. It is false economy to skimp on car maintenance. Unplanned time off the road causes loss of income as well as the cost of the repair. Cancelling and rebooking lessons causes problems that should not arise if the car is serviced regularly.

Driving test examiners can refuse to conduct a test in a car that their pre-test visual check shows to be in an un-roadworthy condition.

Some of the regular car checks and services that should be carried out include the following.

Daily checks

Windows and mirrors should be kept clean and dangling mascots, badges or self-adhesive 'L' plates should not impair the driver's vision. When cleaning, use a solvent to remove any windscreen smears, but avoid damaging the rear window heating element with any abrasive cleaner. Operation of the lights should be checked each day, with particular attention to the brake lights.

Carry spare bulbs in the car in case of sudden failure. To save time in the event of bulb failure, consult the manufacturer's manual for instructions on bulb replacement.

There should also be a daily visual check of the car tyres for any cuts or bulges, stones in the tread and so on. Checking the operation of the horn, indicator, screen washers and wipers should be part of your daily routine.

Weekly checks

Engine oil level

Make sure that the car is standing on level ground. Remove the dipstick, which is usually situated halfway down one side of the engine, and clean it on a piece of cloth or kitchen paper. Replace it in the dipstick hole, then remove it again and look for the oil mark. The oil level should be between the high (maximum) and the low (minimum) marks. If the oil is near or below the low mark, up to a litre of fresh oil will be needed to top up to the high mark. Care must be taken not to overfill as this could lead to excessive oil pressure in the engine and cause leaks or damage.

Oil leaks

Oil leaks can be detected quite easily by having a quick look round the engine, gearbox, rear axle and the insides of the wheels. Common places for leaks are drain plugs, oil filters, valve cover gasket or any oil or brake pipe. If the car has a regular overnight parking spot, look for drops of oil on the ground. Any leak inside the wheels could mean a faulty brake cylinder, which must receive immediate expert attention.

Cooling system

While the engine is cold, remove the pressure cap from the radiator header/expansion tank. Check the coolant level and top up as necessary with a mixture of water and antifreeze of the appropriate type and strength. If the water level falls regularly, check for leaks or suspect engine overheating, which may require expert attention. Never remove the radiator cap when the engine is hot. High pressure is built up inside the radiator when the engine is running. The steam released when the cap is removed can cause serious scalding.

Brake and clutch fluid levels

Consult the manufacturer's manual for advice on the fluid levels. When topping up brake or clutch reservoirs, always use new fluid. Reusing old brake fluid may damage the brake or clutch systems. Remember that if frequent topping up is required, the fluid must be escaping somewhere. What may be a slight leak one day could be a major loss the next. Never make do with brakes: any suspected fault should receive expert attention without delay.

Windscreen/rear screen washers and fluid levels

It is a legal requirement for screen washers to be in working order and topped up with the appropriate fluid. Add a screen washer solvent to the container, as water alone is insufficient to clear the combinations of road grit and exhaust fumes that congeal on the windscreen. In winter add a proprietary winter screen wash to prevent the system freezing up. Do not add antifreeze as this could damage or discolour the paintwork.

Windscreen wipers

Clean the wiper blade rubbers. Dirt and grit stuck on the rubbers could scratch the glass. Renew blades if there is any sign of perishing or brittleness.

Tyre pressures

Check the tyre pressures, including the spare, at least once a week. Don't forget to replace the valve dust-cap. Remove any flints caught in the tread and inspect the sidewalls for any cuts or bulges. Driving school cars are susceptible to damaged tyre walls as a result of kerbing. Any sign of uneven tread wear should be rectified as soon as possible.

Lights

Check the operation of all lights, including indicator flashers and brake lights. Carry spare bulbs in the vehicle as you might need to replace them at short notice – at the test centre, for example.

Battery

Check the electrolyte level. Top up if necessary, using only distilled water, to about 6 mm above the electrode plates.

Drive belt

Check the tension, looking for cuts and fraying. A loose drive belt can affect the operation of the alternator, which may lead to undercharging of the battery.

Periodic checks

You should be able to carry out your own daily and weekly vehicle checks. Some instructors may have sufficient mechanical knowledge and experience to tackle some of the service items that must be undertaken. It is worth considering further study in this field, for example at evening classes or by home study.

Car manufacturers produce handbooks with service recommendations and do-it-yourself advice. There are many good, clear textbooks on this subject, including *Glove Box Guide: Your Car* (published by Haynes). The oil companies, eg Mobil, Castrol, Shell and BP, produce very good, sound manuals explaining car facts and car care. Vehicle maintenance record sheets are also available and very valuable. The majority of instructors, however, will go to a garage or a professional mechanic. Nevertheless, it is recommended that you should have some knowledge of the work that must be covered by periodic servicing.

Seasonal checks

At the first sign of winter get the strength of the antifreeze checked with a hydrometer at a garage. Top up as necessary. If the radiator requires topping up during the winter, use an antifreeze mixture. In modern cars it is advisable to leave the antifreeze in all year round as it contains an anti-corrosive additive to prevent rusting in the system. A good-quality antifreeze will keep its strength for about two years, after which the cooling system should be drained, flushed and refilled, using the manufacturer's recommended amount of antifreeze.

In the springtime the car should be thoroughly hosed underneath to remove all the corrosive salt and sand that has accumulated from the gritted roads.

Vehicle controls and operation

There are three major operating systems in a motor car:

1 *The main controls*: these enable the driver to start and stop the engine and to control the speed, position and direction of the vehicle.
2 *Driving aids:* these assist the driver to see, to be seen by, and to communicate with other road users.
3 *Instrumentation*: this provides the driver with information about the vehicle, how it is functioning and the speed at which it is travelling.

The main controls

The *steering* provides a means of controlling and changing the direction of the vehicle. To operate the steering, keep both hands on the wheel as much as possible and in particular at high speeds, when braking and also cornering. Position the hands at about the 'ten to two' or 'a quarter to three' position. Try to use the 'pull-push' method of steering outlined in *The Official DSA Guide to Driving – The essential skills*, but directional control and accuracy of the steering is the most important objective. Avoid sudden, jerky movements on the wheel and hold it firmly, but do not grip too tightly. Remember that when cornering, the rear wheels cut into a turn.

The *handbrake* secures the car when it is parked or stationary for more than a short pause, to provide a greater degree of safety and control for some temporary stops. The handbrake should be used only when the car is stationary, except in an emergency, such as failure of the footbrake system. The ratchet release button should be operated before releasing or applying the handbrake. Check that the handbrake is on after entering the vehicle, before starting the engine and particularly before leaving the vehicle.

The *gear lever* provides a permanent means of disconnecting the engine from the driving wheels (neutral). It also provides a selection of different ratios to allow the optimum and most economical engine speeds to be maintained at all road speeds and load requirements. The gears also provide a means of driving the vehicle backwards. Avoid looking at the gear lever when changing. Use a 'cupped' hand on the gear lever and do not use excessive force when moving the gears. Make sure that you do not rest your hand on the gear unnecessarily as this can cause premature wear on the gear selector mechanism.

First gear: the most powerful, but slowest. Used for moving off, low-speed clutch control and for manoeuvring.

Second gear: also powerful, but faster than first gear. Useful for rapid acceleration and for driving at slower speeds through some hazards.

Third gear: a faster gear, used for acceleration from over 15 mph or so. Used for driving through some hazards.

Fourth gear: a more economical gear, with insufficient power for speeds of much lower than 25 mph. Used to provide progressive acceleration from about 25–30 mph and for cruising at constant speeds.

Fifth and sixth gear: used for cruising at sustained higher speeds.

The *clutch* temporarily disconnects the engine from the gearbox/driving wheels to facilitate changing gear and stopping. It provides the means to engage the power source (engine) smoothly and progressively to the load (the road wheels). It is operated by the left foot and is used for moving off, low-speed control, changing gear and stopping. Clutch control involves finding and holding the clutch plates at the first point of contact, the bottom of which is called the 'holding point' and the top the 'driving point'. The full range is called the 'biting range'. Slipping the clutch is an important part of low-speed control. Excessive clutch slip during normal driving, however, causes undue wear and should be avoided. Also, try not to rest your weight on the pedal when driving ('riding the clutch').

The *accelerator* (often called the 'gas') plays a major role in the regulation of vehicle speed. It works by the pedal operating a petrol/air valve, which in turn regulates the power and speed of the engine. The accelerator is operated by the right foot. Any pedal movement and changes in pressure should be progressive. The response to pedal movement is more pronounced in the low gears.

The *footbrake* also plays a major role in the regulation of the vehicle's speed. The footbrake pedal is operated by the right foot. It operates a hydraulic system that presses high friction material against a rotating wheel disc or drum (similar in principle to a bicycle brake). Any changes in pressure should be progressive. The response to pressure changes on the pedal is immediate. Pressure can be varied between the barely perceptible up to the point at which the wheels lock. Braking pressure on bends and corners should be minimized or avoided. Use of the brake should be preceded by mirror checks. When the brake is applied, warning lights on the rear of the vehicle are automatically activated.

The starter controls

Ignition switch key: a safety and anti-theft device. This activates the engine electrical circuits essential to its operation. It includes an engine cut-out system when it is switched off. It also activates a number of warning and other electrical circuits. When the key is removed this usually activates a steering lock.

The *starter* activates the engine via the starter motor. It is usually incorporated into the ignition switch as the final position to which the key is turned. The starter motor should not normally be activated for periods in excess of five to eight seconds. The key should be released as soon as the engine fires. (Some vehicles are fitted with a protection device that will only allow one operation of the starter motor without switching the ignition off.) Before activating the starter circuits, the normal safety checks should be made; that is, handbrake on and gear level in neutral.

Driving aids

Mirrors: interior and exterior mirrors should be clean and adjusted so as to maximize visibility to the rear and minimize unnatural or unnecessary head movements. Even with the most desirable combination of a large interior and two door-mounted exterior mirrors, there will still be areas to the rear and sides of the car not covered by the mirrors' fields of vision. Before making certain types of manoeuvre these 'blind spots' need to be checked; for example, before moving away from the kerb.

The mirrors should be used at frequent intervals on a continuous and systematic basis to take full advantage of the views they afford. They should be used particularly before any manoeuvre involving a change in speed or direction; and well before moving off, signalling, changing lane or direction, stopping and overtaking.

Excessively long or staring looks at the mirror should be avoided, as these are likely to cause problems with both the steering and forward planning. Sensible use of the mirrors involves demonstrating an awareness and sympathy for the speed, distance, actions and movement of other road users.

Direction indicators play an important part in the system of communication between road users. They are operated by the fingertips, but without losing total hand contact with the steering wheel. They are frequently required for moving off, stopping, moving to the left or right, and turning to the left or right at junctions. Generally they should be used in good time, but some traffic situations require special consideration in the timing of them. They must be correct for the situation and cancelled after use. (Automatic self-cancelling mechanisms are not infallible and it is the driver's overall responsibility to reapply prematurely cancelled signals and to ensure that indicators are switched off after a manoeuvre is completed.)

Windscreen, windows, wipers, washers, demisters, defrosters and rear screen heaters all help to maintain good all-round visibility for the driver. The controls vary from car to car (consult the manufacturer's handbook). Avoid using windscreen wipers on dry glass and wiping the insides of windows with bare hands (rings can scratch!). Avoid leaving rear screen heaters on continually when not required. Keep wipers in good condition and the washer bottle topped up with water/solvent. Keep windows clean at all times. Plenty of fresh air inside the car will help to prevent windows misting up. Familiarize yourself with these controls while the vehicle is stationary.

Lights help the driver to see and be seen by other road users. Controls vary considerably from car to car (consult the manufacturer's handbook). Sidelights must be used when parked outside a 30 mph limit or in a specified parking area that is within 10 metres of a road junction at night. Dipped headlights should be used in daylight where visibility is reduced by fog, snow or other extreme conditions. High-density rear fog lamps should be used in adverse weather conditions when the driver of a following car might not otherwise see your car. Front fog lights should only be used when visibility is reduced to below 100 metres.

Horn and flashing headlights warn and inform other road users of your presence. Controls vary from car to car (consult the manufacturer's handbook). Use of the horn is not permitted between 11.30 pm and 7.00 am in a built-up area or when stationary (except where there is danger from another moving vehicle). It should be used sensibly to warn others and not as a rebuke. Try to avoid long 'blasts' of the horn in close proximity to pedestrians, but use longer blasts for drivers in motor vehicles. On fast roads, such as motorways, headlamps may be more effective than the horn.

Instrumentation

This group of controls, dials and displays provides the driver with the necessary information on how the vehicle is performing and functioning. Information displays are becoming increasingly more comprehensive. Most of the information is of great assistance to the driver, but some available equipment has yet to be proved useful and may even be found to be counter-productive by causing unnecessary distractions to the driver. This section deals with the essential information that can be justified as necessary to the safe and sympathetic use of a motor car.

Speedometer. This is legally required to be in working order and should be accurate to an error of no more than 10 per cent. Speedometers are usually marked in graduated scales showing both miles and kilometres per hour. They sometimes incorporate a trip recorder switch that can be set and used to record journey mileages or to calculate fuel consumption. Avoid long staring looks at the speedometer when checking your speed, but where necessary take frequent glances to confirm the speed of the vehicle in relation to the speed limit.

Fuel gauge. Check the fuel level at the start of a journey, remembering some gauges may not be fully reliable. Avoid running on less than a quarter tank of fuel if possible. Ensure that, when topping up the tank, only the correct type of fuel is used. Some vehicles are fitted with dual tanks or reserve systems that include 'changeover' switches.

Vehicles fitted with fuel injection systems normally operate more efficiently and return improved performance.

Unleaded fuel causes less pollution, and is generally cheaper than leaded, but consumption can be slightly higher. Petrol engine vehicles can be converted to run on liquid petroleum gas, which requires the fitting of special tanks. When converted, these can run on either petrol or gas. Where a diesel engine is fitted, do not put petrol into the tank, or allow the fuel to run dry, or it may not restart without professional assistance.

If a spare can of fuel is kept for emergencies, it must be suitably marked and have no leaks.

Engine temperature gauge. An internal combustion engine produces mechanical power from controlled explosions (rapid expansion of burning gases) inside the engine cylinders.

At a speed of only 30 mph these controlled explosions can be occurring 60 times every second. This generates a tremendous amount of heat, which, if allowed to build up inside the engine, would melt the pistons and heat other moving parts until they became one solid mass of scrap metal. These high temperatures require an efficient cooling system if the engine is to operate satisfactorily. Most engines are cooled by water. This is pumped through special channels cut into the engine block to carry the heat away to the radiator, where it is then cooled before recirculation.

The driver requires confirmation that this system is functioning normally. The temperature gauge that indicates the normal operating range of temperature provides this. This may sometimes incorporate a separate warning light to provide more visual impact for the driver if the system overheats.

Where an excessive temperature is indicated, the driver should stop and either obtain assistance or rectify the problem before continuing with the journey. The most common causes of overheating are:

- *Broken fan belt*: this normally operates the radiator fan and water pump.
- *Lack of coolant*: water can boil and leak away. Unless the level is checked regularly it may become critical to the cooling system. Also check hoses for leaks and wear.
- *Blocked radiator*: water freezes and will block the radiator with ice during the winter months unless an antifreeze solution is present in the cooling system. Ice also expands and can crack the engine cylinder block during severe conditions. During the normal course of running, limescale from hard water sometimes builds up inside the radiator and can block the water channels.

Oil pressure gauge. Without lubrication, an engine can tear itself apart within minutes of driving off.

An oil pressure failure light and/or an oil pressure gauge provide information about oil pressure. In the event of a drop in oil pressure, pull up as soon as possible and when safe, to check it. Switch off the engine. Obtain assistance or rectify the problem before continuing with the journey.

Before starting an engine, check that the oil pressure warning system is operational. This can be done by switching on the ignition and ensuring the oil pressure warning light activates. The light should switch off within two or three seconds of starting the engine. Oil pressure gauges give a more precise indication of oil pressure when the engine is running, and sometimes help to pinpoint a problem before it reaches a critical level.

Low oil pressure can be caused by *lack of oil, burst oil pipes, inoperative pump*, or a *much worn engine*. Check oil levels regularly, and look for leaks under the car first thing in the morning. Remember too, most cars will use some oil and require topping up between normal servicing.

Brake system malfunction. Vehicles are now being fitted with various kinds of brake warning systems. These can inform the driver of low fluid levels in the system, of uneven pressure in dual-lined braking systems and of worn brake pads. Check these with the vehicle handbook and remember, if the warning systems activate, *stop immediately and obtain assistance.*

Ignition warning light. The ignition warning light is activated when the engine electrical circuits are switched on. Before starting the engine, the system should be checked. This can be done by ensuring that the ignition warning light is illuminated when the circuits are switched on and before the starter motor is activated. As soon as the engine starts, the alternator should generate its own electrical supply and the light should switch off.

The alternator is operated by the fan belt. If this fails, the alternator will cease to provide the electrical requirements for the engine and the vehicle will then be running on battery power alone. In this condition the ignition warning light should activate.

A broken fan belt will also cause the engine to overheat (see 'The cooling system' on page 223).

Other causes of the ignition light switching on are *loose wires, burnt out brushes or diodes on the alternator*, and/or *malfunctions in the voltage regulator.* This does not normally cause any lasting or serious damage to the vehicle, but the journey time will be limited by battery power alone. However, there are safety factors that must be taken into account particularly at night and in cold or wet conditions.

Door and seat belt warning/reminders. Visual/audible warning systems are sometimes fitted to remind the driver that doors are not properly closed and/or the seat belt is not fastened.

Main beam/sidelights/high-intensity rear lights. Warning systems are fitted to remind drivers when these aids are operating.

Rear screen heater. A warning system usually reminds the driver that the screen heater is on. Rear screen heaters consume a fairly large amount of electrical power and can cause a heavy drain on the battery during prolonged periods at tick-over speeds.

Direction indicators and hazard flashers. These are usually fitted with both visual and audible reminders when the aids are in the operating mode. Hazard flashers should not be used on a moving vehicle.

Automatic transmission

A vehicle fitted with automatic transmission should be a safer car to drive than one with manual change, for the following reasons:

- Both hands are free for the steering of the vehicle most of the time.
- Driving an automatic is less tiring, particularly in heavy and slow-moving traffic.
- Because of the human-error factor in driving, to which we are all susceptible, automatic transmission reduces the chances of making an error with a gear or the clutch.

Driving a car with automatic transmission

One of the problems experienced by people wanting to learn on automatics is that there are not widespread facilities available for tuition, with the result that they are not used to their full potential. Driven correctly, automatic cars provide drivers with as much control over the gears as manual-change vehicles. There are certain aspects of driving automatics, however, which the instructor must remember when giving instruction:

- The *handbrake* is generally needed more often and applied more firmly. This is because automatic transmission systems are designed so that the car 'creeps' slowly at tick-over speeds on level ground.
- The *footbrake* should be firmly applied before starting some variomatic transmissions, fitted for example to Volvo cars, where the manufacturer recommends that they should be started in gear. This is particularly true when they are 'on choke'. The footbrake should be firmly applied on other makes of automatic transmissions when they are 'on choke' and before drive or reverse gears are selected.
- The *accelerator* must not be depressed when engaging drive or reverse gears.
- *Right foot only!* It is advisable to use the right foot only for both the footbrake and accelerator. There may be some occasions where it is advantageous to use the left foot for the brake – in some low-speed manoeuvring exercises, particularly if the transmission is not very progressive at low speeds.

Disabled drivers

Where the driver has a right-leg disability, the left foot may be used for both accelerator and brake, but the vehicle may need to be suitably converted. An automatic gearbox is a tremendous help to disabled clients and older people – or in fact anyone finding it difficult to drive a manual gear-change car.

The driving test

Someone who passes the driving test in a car with automatic transmission is issued with a driving licence only for that vehicle category.

Types of automatic transmission

- *Fully automatic* with gear hold position: these have selector positions for forward and reverse with a gear hold for low-speed driving and/or driving downhill.
- *Variomatic transmission:* this type of transmission system is fitted with a hold device that offers a greater degree of engine braking on downhill gradients.
- *Multi-hold systems:* these can retain any particular gear, and are fitted to many makes of vehicle from a Mini to a Rolls-Royce.
- *CVT (constantly variable transmission):* allows for variable gear ratios rather than stepped gear changes.
- *Semi-automatic:* this generally means the vehicle is fitted with a normal gearbox and clutch but without the clutch pedal. The clutch is engaged or disengaged by the movement of the hand on the gear lever.
- *Pre-selector systems:* on these the gear is pre-selected before it is required. The gear is later engaged by means of a foot pedal in place of the clutch.
- *Kick down:* this is a mechanism fitted to many automatics whereby it is possible to change down quickly to a lower gear ratio, usually for overtaking. A sharp depression of the accelerator pedal past the full throttle opening will override the normal gear control system.

Using the accelerator: with manual transmission any fidgeting on and erratic or excessive use of the accelerator burns fuel wastefully in any car, but in an automatic it will lead to changing up and down gears according to changes in this pressure. This causes unnecessary wear and tear on the mechanisms involved, and should be avoided.

Vehicle regulations

There are many laws that specify the way in which cars are to be manufactured, what equipment they must have and the condition of vehicles when used on the roads. Most of these are contained in the Motor Vehicles (Construction and Use) Regulations. Some of the rules apply only to cars first registered after a specified date; older vehicles may therefore not have to include some of the items of equipment mentioned.

Some of the basic rules apply to vehicles of any age. These include the strict rules relating to brakes and steering gear – each part of the braking system and all steering gear must be maintained in good and efficient working order at all times when the vehicle is being used on the road.

The car must be roadworthy. It is sometimes thought the MOT test certificate is a certificate of roadworthiness, but this is not so. The test system looks at the condition of certain main components, but does not necessarily consider the overall roadworthiness of the car.

The regulations contain rules about the dimensions of cars, and about the maximum overhang. The car must have wings or mudguards. The speedometer must work to within an accuracy of plus or minus 10 per cent. Driving mirrors must be fitted, and other compulsory items include safety glass, windscreen wipers, horn, silencer, seat belts and direction indicators.

Lighting

The regulations require that lights and reflectors be kept clean and in good working order. They must be maintained so that the vehicle may be driven during the hours of darkness without contravening the regulations. This chapter includes only a summary of the main requirements, as the original equipment fitted to a modern vehicle will usually comply with the specifications.

Headlamps must be permanently fitted and must have a minimum rating of 30 watts, displaying a white or yellow beam. The lamps must be matched and the beam must be capable of being deflected to the near side so as not to dazzle oncoming traffic.

Sidelamps must be fitted at the front of the vehicle. The two lamps must have a maximum power of 7 watts each (or they may be diffused).

Rear lamps must be visible from a reasonable distance to the rear of the car. There must be at least two lamps, each with a minimum power of 5 watts. Reflectors are also required.

Rear number plate lamp: the plate must be illuminated so that the letters and figures are easily legible from a distance of 60 feet.

Direction indicators on cars registered after 1965 must be the amber flashing type. On older cars they may be either flashing or semaphore arm, and may be white at the front and red at the rear. Flashing indicators must wink at the rate of 60 to 120 flashes a minute. The indicators on both sides of the car must be operated by the same switch, and there must be a warning light or audible warning inside the car to show that the indicators are working.

Reversing lamps may be fitted using one or two lamps of not more than 24 watts each. The beam produced must not dazzle anyone 25 feet away at an eye level of 3½ feet from the ground, and must only be used when the car is reversing. The lights may be operated automatically when reverse gear is selected, or may have a separate switch that includes a warning light.

Fog lamps are to be used as two front fog lamps (or one fog lamp and one headlamp) in darkness and fog, falling snow or conditions of poor visibility. The lights must be placed symmetrically and must be placed more than two feet from the ground unless they are to be used only in fog and falling snow.

Rear fog lamps are obligatory on cars first used on or after 1 April 1980. If one lamp is fitted it must be positioned on the offside of the car, and if two are fitted they must be symmetrical. Rear fog lamps may only be used during adverse weather conditions and when the vehicle is in motion, or during an enforced stoppage.

Stop lamps are compulsory on cars built since 1971. The lamps must be matched and placed symmetrically at the rear of the car. They must operate automatically when the footbrake is applied, and show a steady red light visible from the rear.

During the hours of darkness a vehicle must display:

● two headlamps (when the vehicle is driven on unlit roads);

● two side lamps;

● two rear lamps; two red rear reflectors; one or two rear fog lamps (for vehicles first used after 1 April 1980).

Headlamps must be used when the vehicle is being driven on unlit roads (that is, roads where there are no street lights or where the street lamps are not at regular intervals). Headlamps must be switched off when the vehicle is stationary (except traffic stops). During daylight hours headlamps must be used when travelling in conditions of poor visibility such as fog, smoke, heavy rain, spray or snow. If matching fog or spotlights are fitted, these may be used in the place of headlights.

Parking lights at night: a car or light goods vehicle may park at night without lights if the following conditions apply:

● The vehicle is parked on a road with a speed limit not exceeding 30 mph.

● No part of the vehicle is within 10 metres of a junction.

● The vehicle is parked with its nearside close to, and parallel with, the kerb, except in a one-way street.

The lighting regulations also permit a vehicle to park without lights in a recognized parking area, and within the confines of an area outlined by lamps or traffic signs. If these conditions are not met, lights must be shown (that is, side and rear lights).

Dim-dip lights: new vehicles registered from 1 April 1987 must be fitted with a dim-dip device which causes 10 or 15 per cent of the dipped beam intensity to show when the engine is running (or the ignition is switched on) and the sidelights are on.

Hazard warning lights may be used only when the vehicle is stationary for the purpose of warning other road users that the vehicle is temporarily causing an obstruction, or to warn following drivers on a motorway that there is a hazard ahead.

Parking

Common law states that a public highway is specifically for the free passage of the general public and vehicles, and there is no legal right to park on the road except in specially designated parking places or with the express permission of a police officer or traffic warden. There is no legal right even to park outside your own home. A stationary vehicle in the road or on the grass verge is technically an obstruction, even where no other road user is inconvenienced.

It is a more serious offence to park a vehicle in a position where it might constitute a danger to others (see *The Highway Code* for examples of what might be considered dangerous parking). Parking within the zigzag lines at a pedestrian crossing is an offence punishable by an endorsement. It is illegal to park on an urban clearway at the stipulated times, and on a rural clearway and motorway at any time.

Parking in controlled zones

A controlled parking zone is indicated by waiting restriction signs situated on all entrances, and is marked with yellow lines along the kerb. Restriction times vary from town to town and care should be taken always to read the signs. Parking meter zones are marked with signs 'Meter zone' and 'Zone ends'. It is an offence to park at a meter without paying or to overstay the time paid for, or to feed the meter on return for an extended period.

Use of horn and flashing headlamps

Motor vehicles must be fitted with an instrument capable of giving audible warnings of approach. The tone of the horn must be continuous and uniform, with the exception of emergency service vehicles, which may use a two-tone horn, siren or bell. Some goods vehicles are permitted to use an instrument to announce goods for sale, but the vehicle must also carry the standard audible warning device.

The horn should be regarded as a warning instrument. It should not be used to assert a right of way, and should not be used aggressively. There are some legal responsibilities regarding the use of the horn. It must not be used when the vehicle is stationary on the road, except to avoid danger due to another vehicle moving, and may not be used in a built-up area between the hours of 11.30 pm and 7 am.

The flashing of headlamps has the same meaning as the horn. It is an indication of your presence to other road users. The lamps should not be used to tell other people what you intend to do, or to tell them what to do. Flashing headlamps can be useful in certain driving conditions – high-speed roads and where there is a high level of noise – but should not be regarded as an indication of another driver's intentions. The signal may be directed not to you but to someone else.

Noise and smoke

There are very detailed rules regarding the maximum number of decibels that may be emitted from a car, and it is an offence to drive a car that does not conform to those rules, or to cause a nuisance by making unnecessary noise. It is also an offence to use a motor vehicle that produces smoke, vapour or sparks that may damage or affect other road users and property. Smoke that affects the visibility of other road users is regarded as excessive.

Seat belts

The law requires that seat belts are fitted to all the seats of new motor cars, that they should be maintained in good order, and that they conform to the regulations. The use of seat belts may be an important factor in the assessment of compensation by a court. Recent cases have shown a reduction in the amount of compensation awarded to non-users of seat belts.

Front seat belts are compulsory on cars and three-wheeled vehicles made after 30 June 1964 and first registered after 31 December 1964, and on light vans made after 31 August 1966 and first registered on or after 31 March 1967. Rear seat belts must also be used.

The use of seat belts, where fitted, by drivers and passengers is compulsory. The maximum penalty for failing to wear a seat belt is £500. Drivers are not responsible in law for the non-use of belts by adult passengers.

There are several exemptions provided in the regulations. For example you do not have to wear one under the following circumstances:

- When driving and carrying out a manoeuvre that includes reversing.
- If you are the holder of a valid medical exemption certificate.
- When you are making a local delivery or collection round using a specially constructed or adapted vehicle.
- If a seat belt has become defective on a journey, or previously, and arrangements have been made for the belt to be repaired.
- If an inertia reel belt has temporarily locked because the vehicle is on, or has been on, a steep incline. The belt must be put on as soon as the mechanism has unlocked.
- If you are an instructor supervising a learner who is carrying out a manoeuvre including reversing.
- Driving test examiners need not wear a seat belt if they feel that the wearing of a belt would endanger them or someone else.
- When driving a taxi during normal taxi work, so long as the vehicle displays a plate showing it is licensed as a taxi.
- While driving a private hire vehicle displaying a plate showing it is licensed as such, or that it is licensed at the Hackney Carriage rate and while used for that purpose.
- If you are driving or riding a vehicle displaying trade plates and you are looking into or repairing a mechanical fault.

Other exemptions apply to people in special jobs and in certain circumstances, for example the police.

Child car seats

Children under the age of 14 travelling in the rear of cars should be restrained where an approved restraint is available. The essential point is that the seat belt or restraint should be appropriate for the age and weight of the child. The law does not require that all children in the rear of cars should be restrained, only that if an appropriate device is available it should be used. An appropriate child restraint is deemed available if carried in or on the vehicle, where there is space for it to be fitted without the aid of tools. Children can be exempt from the regulations on medical grounds.

Children up to 3 years old

The child must use the correct child restraint. In the front seat a child must not be carried in a rear-facing child seat where the seat is protected by an active frontal air bag.

For *children aged 3 and above*, until they reach either their 12th birthday, or a height of 135cm: in the front seat, the child *must* use the correct child restraint. In the rear seats, the correct child restraint must be used where seat belts are fitted. There are only three exceptions to this:

1 In a licensed taxi or private hire vehicle.

2 If the child is travelling on a short journey in an unexpected necessity.

3 If there are two occupied child restraints in the rear that prevent the use or fitting of a third restraint.

Only if rear seat belts are not fitted may a child over 3 years old travel unrestrained.

Children over 1.35m in height or who are 12 or 13 years old

In both front and rear seats the adult seat belt must be worn if one is available.

Note: In all cases where a child under the age of 14 is involved, it is the responsibility of the *driver* to ensure that the child is correctly restrained.

Passengers over 14

When travelling in the front or rear seat, an adult seat belt must be worn. It is the responsibility of the individual passenger to ensure that he or she is wearing a seat belt.

Other vehicles

There are separate regulations covering the use of child restraints and seat belts in other vehicles (vans, buses, mini buses and goods vehicles). These details can be found at www.childcarseats.org.uk.

Seat belt pre-tensioner

The front seat pre-tensioner seat belt works together with the seat belt retractor. It helps to tighten the seat belt when the vehicle is involved in certain types of frontal collisions. The front seats are fitted with a sensor that, in the event of an accident or rapid deceleration, will activate an explosive device to retract the seat belt, providing greater support for the front seat occupants.

FIGURE 8.15 The airbag

Supplementary restraint system (airbag)

Many vehicles now have airbags for passengers as well as for the driver. The driver's airbag is designed to supplement the accident protection provided by the seat belt and to reduce the possibility of injury to the head or upper torso in the event of a frontal collision. The seat belt should be worn correctly and the driver should be seated a suitable distance from the steering wheel to enable the system to function effectively.

The airbag is located in the centre of the steering wheel, and will deploy under a moderate to severe frontal collision; minor frontal, side or rear impact, or the vehicle overturning will not activate the airbag. When the airbag system receives a signal from a G-sensor, the airbag inflates as a result of the combustion of a fuel tablet that generates nitrogen gas. The airbag absorbs the impact of the driver's head on the steering wheel and then deflates at a controlled rate. Since the airbag deploys quickly to protect the driver, the force of the airbag deploying can increase the risk of injury if the driver is too close to or against the steering wheel during deployment.

A self-diagnosis system monitors the entire system. If a fault occurs, the self-diagnosis system switches on an SRS function light (red) on the instrument panel or steering wheel. It is absolutely forbidden for unauthorized persons to tamper with, or attempt repairs to, the airbag system.

Mirrors

All new motor cars must be fitted with two rear-view driving mirrors – one inside, the other mounted on the exterior offside. Most vehicles now also have a nearside door mirror. Interior mirrors must have protective edges to minimize the risk of injury in the event of an accident. This regulation also applies to the dual mirrors used by driving instructors.

Windscreen washers and wipers

The law requires that all windows are kept clean so that the driver has a clear and unobstructed view of the road. This includes keeping the windscreen free of stickers, novelties and mascots. There is a legal requirement for automatic windscreen wipers capable of efficiently cleaning the screen. The driver must have an adequate view of the road in front of the vehicle, and in front of the nearside and offside of the vehicle.

There must also be windscreen washers that work in conjunction with the wipers.

Vehicle defects

Under the Vehicle Defect Rectification Scheme (VDRS) some minor vehicle defects such as lights, wipers, speedometer and silencer may not result in a prosecution if the driver agrees to participate in the following procedure:

1 A VDRS notice is issued.

2 The defect must be rectified within a limited time.

3 The repaired vehicle and the VDRS notice are presented at an MOT garage.

4 The MOT garage issues a certification that the defects have been rectified.

5 The certificate is then sent to a local Central Ticket Office.

Failure to follow the correct procedure will normally result in prosecution.

Documents

Registration document

A motor vehicle must not be used on the road until it has been registered by the Driver and Vehicle Licensing Authority (DVLA). When a vehicle is first registered, a registration document (form V5 – occasionally called a 'log book') is issued in which the appropriate details are listed. The DVLA will also issue a 'registration mark' for use on the number plates of the vehicle.

The document should normally be kept in a secure place away from the vehicle. The registration document is not in itself an indication of the ownership of the vehicle. It is issued to the 'registered keeper' of the vehicle. Should a registration document be accidentally lost, destroyed or defaced, a duplicate can be obtained from the DVLA, Swansea, for a fee of £19. Any alterations to the registered particulars of the vehicle should be notified immediately.

Number plates and registration marks

Number plates are now made up of seven characters. There are three parts to the registration mark, each with a separate meaning.

FIGURE 8.16 The number plate format

AB55 DVL

The first two letters show where the vehicle was registered – the *local memory tag*. The first letter of the memory tag represents the region. The second letter relates to a local DVLA office.

The two numbers indicate the age of the vehicle – the *age identifier*. The age identifier changes twice yearly, in March and September. In the example shown in Figure 8.16, '55' represents the six-month period from September 2005 to February 2006. Vehicles registered between 1 March 2009 and 31 August 2009 have '09' on the plate.

The last three letters give a unique identity to the vehicle – the *random letters*. The random letters will combine to make each registration mark unique. A new car purchaser may opt to select these three letters. However, the letters 'I' and 'Q' are to be excluded along with any letter combinations that may be considered offensive. The letter 'Z' may be selected.

The complete list of local identifiers is shown as Figure 8.17.

Vehicle excise licence (tax disc)

Application for vehicle excise licences can be made to the DVLA, Swansea, or to the local vehicle licensing office in whose area the vehicle is normally kept. Vehicles can be licensed for either 12 months or 6 months. A variable rate, based on carbon dioxide emissions, is now in place for newer vehicles. Renewals can be made online at www.direct.gov.uk/taxdisc, by telephone on 0870 850 4444 or at a DVLA local office and most main post offices.

Duty must be paid if you 'keep' your vehicle on a highway, even if the car is never driven. If you do not tax your vehicle on time you will be liable to a financial penalty, which can rise to £1,000 if the vehicle continues to be driven on the roads. The DVLA now carries out monthly checks on its computer for untaxed vehicles.

You must renew the licence before it expires. A reminder is usually sent by the DVLA when the current licence is due to expire, and this reminder may be used as an application form so long as all the particulars shown on the registration document are still correct. When applying for a new licence, in addition to the registration document and the appropriate fee you must provide a valid certificate of insurance and the Department of Transport test (MOT) certificate (if the car is more than three years old).

A vehicle must not be used or kept on the road after expiry unless an application was made before the expiry date of the old excise licence. When the licence disc has been issued, it should be displayed on the nearside of the windscreen so that all particulars are clearly visible from that side of the road.

FIGURE 8.17 Local identifiers

Local Memory Tag	DVLA office	Local Identifier
A	Peterborough	A B C D E F G H J K L M N
	Norwich	O P R S T U
	Ipswich	V W X Y
B	Birmingham	A - Y
C	Cardiff	A B C D E F G H J K L M N O
	Swansea	P R S T U V
	Bangor	W X Y
D	Chester	A B C D E F G H J K
	Shrewsbury	L M N O P R S T U V W X Y
E	Chelmsford	A - Y
F	Nottingham	A B C D E F G H J K L M N P
	Lincoln	R S T V W X Y
G	Maidstone	A B C D E F G H J K L M N O
	Brighton	P R S T U V W X Y
H	Bournemouth	A B C D E F G H J
	Portsmouth	K L M N O P R S T U V W X Y
		HW Reserved for the Isle of Wight
K	Luton	A B C D E F G H J K L
	Northampton	M N O P R S T U V W X Y
L	Wimbledon	A B C D E F G H J
	Stanmore	K L M N O P R S T
	Sidcup	U V W X Y
M	Manchester	A - Y
N	Newcastle	A B C D E G H J K L M N O
	Stockton	P R S T U V W X Y
O	Oxford	A - Y
P	Preston	A B C D E F G H J K L M N O P R S T
	Carlisle	U V W X Y
R	Reading	A - Y
S	Glasgow	A B C D E F G H J
	Edinburgh	K L M N O
	Dundee	P R S T
	Aberdeen	U V W
	Inverness	X Y
V	Worcester	A - Y
W	Exeter	A B C D E F G H J
	Truro	K L
	Bristol	M N O P R S T U V W X Y
Y	Leeds	A B C D E F G H J K
	Sheffield	L M N O P R S T U
	Beverley	V W X Y

A licence may be surrendered for any complete months unexpired and must be posted to the DVLA before the beginning of the month for which the refund is being requested. There is no refund for parts of a month.

The keeper named on the Vehicle Registration Certificate is legally responsible for taxing the vehicle until the DVLA has been notified that it is off the road or has been sold, transferred, scrapped or exported. If you are the keeper of a vehicle but are not using or keeping it on public roads, you must make a statutory off road notification (SORN). If you don't, you could be liable for a penalty of £80.

When you sell, transfer, scrap or export a vehicle, you must notify the DVLA. If you do not, you will continue to be liable for taxing the vehicle and for any other offences committed in the vehicle. When you notify the DVLA it will send confirmation that you are no longer responsible for the vehicle.

MOT test

Most small cars, small goods vehicles and passenger vehicles are subject to an annual test starting three years after the date of the original registration. The car may be taken for test within a month before a certificate is required. If a certificate has expired, the car may be driven to and from a test appointment without a certificate provided that it does not have a serious fault that would contravene the Construction and Use Regulations.

Testing is carried out at designated garages that display the sign of three white triangles on a blue background. The test requirements include brakes, lights, steering, stop lamps, tyres, seat belts (correct fitting, condition and anchorage points), direction indicators, windscreens, windscreen wipers and washers, exhaust systems, audible warning instruments, bodywork and suspension (in relation to braking and steering). A vehicle that passes the test is issued with a test certificate that is valid for one year.

A vehicle failing the annual test but that is left at the testing station for rectification of the faults does not incur a further fee for a re-test. A fee of half the original is charged when the vehicle is removed and then returned for the necessary repairs to be carried out within 14 days of the original examination.

The certificate must be produced, along with the other necessary documents, when applying for a vehicle licence, and on the request of a police officer.

Motor vehicle insurance

Any vehicle being used on public roads must be covered by insurance. For details, see pages 205–08.

Driver Training

09

This chapter deals with the main elements involved in the complex task of teaching people to drive. They include:

- methods of learning;
- teaching and learning;
- coaching methods;
- skill training;
- structuring the learning;
- syllabus for driver training;
- instructions and terminology;
- adapting your instruction;
- assessing progress;
- 'L' driver errors;
- developing safe attitudes.

Methods of learning

The basic requirements for any effective learning to take place are:

- attention;
- activity;
- involvement.

Attention

This is not always a completely conscious activity. Long periods of undivided concentration are difficult to maintain without a break, or at least a change in the type of activity. Periods of concentration, therefore, will need to be shorter in the earlier stages of learning.

Activity and involvement

These elements are vital if the pupil is going to learn efficiently and effectively. Activity should not be thought of as simply the physical activity. For example, although learning to drive a car involves a large degree of physical activity, mental involvement is also necessary to initiate the physical responses.

A saying often used in general education and one that is particularly relevant to driver training is:

What I hear, I forget. What I see, I remember. What I do, I understand!

Keeping the novice actively involved in the learning experience will normally result in more being remembered. However, physical activity alone is not sufficient; learners should also be encouraged to think about what they are doing and why!

Learning by repetition (rote)

Learning by rote, or repetition, is the traditional approach and consists of nothing more than memorizing lists, numbers, facts and formulae and so on, without requiring any understanding. For example, you probably remember learning your multiplication tables by reciting them over and over again.

Most of us have the ability to memorize information 'parrot fashion'. However, the information can only normally be recalled in the order in which it was learnt. Can you say, without thinking about it, which letter of the alphabet comes before the letter 'R'? You will probably have to break into the alphabet a few letters before the 'R' to answer the question.

Rote is the lowest form of learning, and is really only a foundation on which to add more information to give a greater meaning. Some driving skills, such as changing gear, are learnt by rote or repetition – that is, carrying out the physical actions over and over again until they are perfected. These are often referred to in teaching as psychomotor skills – because they involve mainly physical actions.

Learning by understanding (Gestalt)

Learning by the Gestalt method is based on understanding. Understanding can be defined as being able to attach meaning to information. Learning to drive involves combining physical actions with knowledge of the rules and regulations, and is therefore learnt through the Gestalt method and classed as an intellectual or cognitive skill. Effective question and answer (Q&A) routines and feedback techniques will normally be useful tools in the teaching/learning process.

The need for rote and Gestalt

Both methods of learning are important for retaining new information. You may need to teach some basic facts or skills in a rote (memorizing) manner in order to help the learner to acquire the basic competence to handle the car. When these basic skills are mastered, you then need to encourage your pupils to extend their knowledge and understanding by analysing the effect their actions have on the vehicle.

What started out as a memorized list of actions begins to take on some meaning. However, it does not imply that this initial 'meaning' will automatically result in an understanding of how to apply the same information to a new situation. You will therefore have to teach the learner how to adapt the skills for moving off, which were initially learnt by rote, in a wide variety of situations; for example, moving off uphill, downhill and from behind parked vehicles.

As an instructor, you will discover that a mixture of the two methods of learning will be required in most situations. It is poor teaching to over-emphasize the traditional rote learning method without encouraging learners to understand how and why actions need to be taken. It would be equally as bad to over-emphasize progressive learning by allowing them to make and act on their own interpretations of situations before they have an adequate knowledge of the essential rules and skills.

Coaching

For many years driving instruction involved simply 'instructing' – telling the pupil what to do and how to do it without much interaction or pupil involvement. In this method, there would have been an element of 'I'm the expert – do this, do that' and, 'This is what you have to do to pass the test.' As a result, the teaching/learning process was very passive and seen as slightly dictatorial.

Nowadays there is a lot more emphasis on 'coaching' rather than instructing. This move towards coaching techniques involves the pupils in much more decision making and in taking more responsibility for their own learning. Coaching creates an equal partnership between 'coach' and 'coachee', with greater benefits, particularly relating to longer-term and retained learning. Coaching puts pupils in an active role by encouraging them to identify for themselves obtainable goals and objectives. A more effective and efficient performance will normally be achieved by coaching methods, as a result of greater participation and willingness on the part of the pupil.

Coaching involves:

- *Effective questioning*:
  Questions can be used to find out if the pupil knows or understands a particular topic, but there are other reasons for effective questioning.

By asking appropriate questions at the right time you can raise the pupil's awareness and generate in them a feeling of responsibility. Quite often the important questions are those that the instructor does not know the answer to. For example: 'How did you feel about ...?' or 'Had you considered ...?'.

- *Active listening:*
Listening carefully to the pupil's responses will give an indication of how to phrase the next set of questions or to organize the next phase of learning. To make sure you are actively listening, repeating back or summarizing the answer can be an effective way of letting the pupil know that you have taken note of his or her response.

- *Neutral and non-judgemental communication:*
If we concentrate too much on fault-finding we can sometimes create a situation where the pupil will be over-defensive, which then becomes a barrier to learning. To overcome this, we should attempt to balance the positives with the negatives and avoid direct personal criticism of the pupil by using neutral language and by addressing the specific problem with non-judgemental questions such as 'What do you think?'

- *Two-way communication:*
As a professional driver trainer/coach you will develop different ways of communicating effectively with all types of pupil. This will involve varying and adapting your methods and terminology to suit the needs of each individual pupil, making sure that the pupil is involved in the discussion.

- *Motivation skills:*
Coaching involves coaxing, questioning, listening and motivating. Most pupils are mainly concerned with the immediate benefit of passing the test and obtaining a full licence. Part of your role as an instructor is to use your coaching skills to motivate the pupil and encourage longer-term skills and 'safe driving for life'.

All of these topics and skills are discussed in more detail in *Practical Teaching Skills for Driving Instructors;* for details, see page 419.

Developing safe attitudes

As a professional driver-trainer and coach, it will be your responsibility to ensure that the new drivers you are putting on to our roads have the correct attitude towards their vehicle, themselves and other road users. To achieve this, you will need to develop an understanding of the effect their actions have. This type of teaching and learning is called 'affective' because you will be developing safe attitudes through an understanding of the effect that their actions, or lack of them, have on others.

Defensive driving is becoming a necessity on our roads and it is important, if you are to achieve this to any great degree, that your learners understand the need to keep themselves safe at all times.

Learning to drive the car safely and considerately is classed as an attitudinal skill because the phrase 'safely and considerately' describes the attitude of the learner. This makes the difference between merely learning to handle the car(a psychomotor skill) and following the rules of the road (an intellectual skill).

Attitude and behaviour

The attitude of drivers will normally influence their behaviour, and attitudes are formed through personal experiences from an early age. Reckless or unsafe driver behaviour is frequently attributed to negative attitudes. These are often inherent in the person who has always 'done his own thing' without a thought for the consequences on other people, or who has been influenced by sitting for many years next to an inconsiderate driver.

Pupils who have a positive attitude and who have learnt to be more thoughtful towards others, will normally respond favourably as their understanding of correct behaviour and of the consequences of bad driving develops. For example, the person who drives at 30 mph in a busy road, where there are parked vehicles on both sides, with a high volume of pedestrian activity, has a negative attitude. Someone who doesn't understand the risks involved, or simply does not care, may drive in this unsafe manner.

Knowing and understanding the risks may still not have the effect of slowing the driver down if a negative attitude is present. The driver with a positive attitude, however, will normally listen to your reasoning, analyse the effects of the reckless behaviour and work on correcting it.

Road user error

The design of our roads (and sometimes the individual driver's local knowledge) allows for a certain degree of road-user error. This may reinforce wrong actions because drivers with a negative attitude get away with deficient behaviour. It may encourage the development of a feeling of immunity, and eventually result in changing the individual's attitude towards the degree of risk he or she is willing to take. For example:

A driver who lives on a quiet estate may emerge from a junction without taking effective observations because there is usually no other traffic about at that time of the day. No other road user is present and therefore nothing happens. This gives the driver a false sense of security. The same situation may recur a number of times, thus reinforcing this 'safe' feeling. Eventually, and inevitably, other road users will be present and an accident will happen.

It will be your responsibility to try to change negative attitudes. This can be done by:

● explaining the risks involved in any given situation;

- persuading the driver to act safely in order to protect other road users as well as themself;
- setting a personal example.

You may find that some of your pupils will resent your efforts to change their views, remaining subjective and even offering excuses for not complying. Pupils who have a positive attitude will, however, normally listen to your reasoning and become more objective and flexible when they understand the consequences of their actions.

You should recognize that all human beings have their limitations. Try to remember that a driver who is normally patient and tolerant may sometimes, for a variety of personal reasons, such as emotional problems, become hostile. Explain how conflict with others can be avoided if a little time is taken to relax and regain composure.

At the end of their course of training, new drivers should be able to:

- recognize features in the road and traffic environment where accidents are most likely to occur;
- identify the causes of accidents and assess their personal risk of becoming involved in them;
- recognize their own capabilities and limitations;
- apply defensive techniques to minimize the risk of becoming involved in potentially dangerous situations.

Transfer of learning

It is unusual these days for people to present themselves for driving lessons without having some of the basic knowledge or skills required. For example:

- all of your pupils will have been pedestrians and have learnt how to cross busy roads successfully;
- most will have been passengers in cars;
- many of them will have ridden a bicycle;
- some will have had some experience on motorbikes.

Most of them will therefore have developed some skills in the judgement of speed, distance and timing of traffic. As these are among the most essential skills involved in driving, you should be able to take advantage of this knowledge and transfer it to driving.

There are numerous other associations through which you will be able to help your learners relate or transfer existing skills and knowledge to driving.

Interference in learning

Previous learning can sometimes be a disadvantage and interfere with learning a new skill. For example, where people have been passengers over a number of years, they will have probably developed a 'partial sense of speed'. They will have subconsciously learnt an impression of the speed norm of experienced drivers, and this can cause problems if they try to copy them. By driving at what they have learnt to accept as the normal speed, this 'previous learning' can interfere with progress, as, in the early stages, the basic car control skills need to be carried out at slower than normal speeds.

Examples of interference of learning:

- Always change up through the gears as soon as you have moved off.
- Always change down progressively using all of the gears when you are slowing down or stopping.
- Always signal for moving off, passing parked cars and stopping.

If pupils have been previously indoctrinated with certain views, it is likely to cause conflict with the new information you are giving. You must recognize that your pupils are not learning in a vacuum, and will therefore be subject to all kinds of conflicting pressures from other people.

Where this type of interference occurs, you must be tolerant and show an understanding of your pupils' problems during any difficult periods of 'unlearning'. You must also try to avoid saying that the information they have been given is totally wrong.

Motivation

This describes the personal needs and desires of the individual. The fact that someone is prepared to pay for a course of lessons will normally show that he or she is motivated by a desire to learn. The student will normally be alert and keen at the beginning of the course, with a willingness to follow instructions in eager anticipation of the next session. This initial enthusiasm, however, may not always be enough to maintain full interest and attention throughout the entire course, particularly if difficult patches are experienced where very slow progress is achieved.

An important part of your work as a teacher will be to try to maintain pupils' motivation. Help them over any difficult periods by maintaining your enthusiasm and showing that you are interested in their progress. Motivation and interest can be stimulated through success. Even small successes are important to a pupil who is finding the learning hard work.

By creating the right conditions, you can do much to ensure success. This can be done by properly grading the tuition in short, progressive steps. You should then try to maintain this interest by giving suitable encouragement and approval for effort.

Traditional methods of driving instruction mean students are often learning in total isolation from others, and this can frequently cause problems for both the instructor and student. While 'individual' tuition is advantageous, it does limit contact and comparisons with other students. Deprived of the group learning situation, students are unable to measure their progress against that of others. More importantly, if they have no means of assessing their own progress and improvement, they may often feel they are making no progress at all. This may be a result of their instructor not giving sufficient feedback on where improvements have taken place.

If students feel they are making slow progress, encouragement alone from the teacher may not be sufficient to allay their fears of inability. Emphasis needs to be placed on where progress has been achieved, and excess criticism in other areas should be avoided. An unsympathetic teacher may cause students to feel so discouraged, isolated and incompetent, that they become completely demoralized and may even give up the idea of learning to drive.

If you set up easily attainable, intermediate targets, you will help to reinforce your students' feelings of achievement. Intermediate goals also help to organize the learning situation, and do much to prevent pupils from being 'thrown in at the deep end before they can swim'.

One of the first goals to achieve in learning to drive is clutch control. It's important to remember that many of the driving skills are conditioned responses. That is, they not only require the correct system for them to be learnt properly, but they also need continual repetition in order to master them. This basic goal should be attained before students are asked to deal with difficult uphill junctions.

The confidence of some learners is destroyed because they are taken into situations that require good clutch control before they have mastered the basic skill. Imagine how you would feel if you were sitting at a red traffic light on your first driving lesson and you stalled the engine a couple of times!

Clutch control should initially be developed by full talk-through instruction to ensure that confidence is built up. However, in the final analysis, it is only by practice and success that the skill will become 'second nature' as the pupil learns to control it correctly in all situations.

Everyone learns at a different rate. It is therefore important that pupils are allowed to develop at their own individual pace, and setting intermediate goals should ensure that they progress with confidence. This, in turn, will keep the motivation at a good level.

Teaching and learning

You will know from your own experiences that learning is an inconsistent process over which there is little reliable control. Teachers have no mystical power by which to pour knowledge into the minds of their learners, so whatever students learn (whether it is a psychomotor or an intellectual skill), they must learn for themselves. You will merely be providing the circumstances from which learning may occur. These 'learning conditions' may be in the form of practical driving lessons, lectures or discussion; or some other teaching or instructional method.

Your role will essentially be one of establishing the quality of the teaching and of planning and organizing the conditions in which learning can take place. Teachers manage the learning experience by:

- preparing the material;
- organizing the material;
- presenting the experience to the student;
- creating opportunities to practise;
- observing the student's reactions;
- assessing progress.

No matter how carefully prepared and presented the lesson may be, success can be judged only by how much knowledge or skill the learner gains from it.

Teaching driving

The complete experience in learning to drive involves the car, the classroom, or some other location, and the personality and teaching methods of the instructor. It will also be dependent on the attitude, knowledge and skill of the student. Whatever natural abilities and aptitude your pupils have, they will only gain the full benefit of learning if they are actively involved and are attentive. Motivation is vital to students' willingness to learn. You must motivate your students and create an environment and situations from which they can learn.

You should think of yourself as a manager of the learning experience, with responsibilities extending far beyond the act of teaching. You should always be aware that what you are teaching – or are neglecting to teach – could at some time in the future be a matter of life or death to your students.

Apart from the quality and content of your lessons, your responsibilities will range from the organization of the course to the final assessments you will need to make before your students take their driving tests.

The key to the successful management of learning will be your ability to present, adapt and adjust the same basic knowledge and skills for the wide range of learning abilities of the different pupils you will be teaching. You should not only be master of your craft and skills, but you should also have at your command an infinitely variable range of instructional techniques to call on as and when the situation, or your pupils' needs, demand it. Teaching driving is a challenging task that requires thorough training. Make sure you are prepared for it properly.

The learner's needs

The most successful instructors are those who have a concern for their students and are most sensitive to their learning requirements. The needs of the learner driver are as varied and complex as the differences between the students themselves. Avoid grouping people into preconceived categories such as young and old, or quick and slow to learn. Making this type of pre-judgement before you get to know pupils may prevent you from treating them as individuals, and might also prevent you from seeing them with 'open' and 'more sensitive' eyes.

One of your first priorities will be to create a good working relationship with your students. A good test of this will be the rapport that develops between you; and, perhaps more significantly, the level of communication. For example, if a good relationship develops:

- pupils should feel they can readily admit their mistakes without the risk of feeling inadequate;
- they should be able to discuss freely with you their fears and anxieties about their progress;
- you should be able to laugh together about silly mistakes.

In order to develop students' ability and confidence, learning should be founded on mutual cooperation. You can encourage this by structuring the learning so that they are asked only to carry out tasks that can be achieved with some degree of success.

Points to remember about teaching, coaching and learning

- Begin with what the learner already knows or can do and build on this.
- Structure the learning in short progressive steps.
- Be consistent with your instructions and terminology.
- Make sure that your terminology is fully understood.
- Keep your explanations short and simple.
- Emphasize the key points.
- Ensure that your instructions are positive: indicate what to do rather than what not to do.
- Explain the purpose of any demonstration before carrying it out.
- Carry out demonstrations at the correct level according to the ability of the learner.
- Keep initial explanations and demonstration commentaries simple – too many variables will confuse.
- Allow for plenty of practice – people learn by doing things for themselves.
- Ensure that the learner is in no doubt about what is expected.
- Success will stimulate interest and involvement, so try to ensure that initial practice is successful.

- Give praise and encouragement to help stimulate progress – excessive criticism may destroy motivation.
- Give continuous feedback of progress.
- Correct errors positively before they become habitual.
- Positive correction should be made to improve learners' performance.
- Confirmation of minor successes is important to pupils who do not have a natural aptitude.
- Be patient; lack of sympathy for someone who feels he or she is not making progress may demoralize that person.
- Reassure pupils that periods of slow learning are quite natural and common.
- Avoid comparing learners with other students.
- Setting easy-to-achieve intermediate goals may help to promote progress.
- Allow students to learn at their own pace.
- Changes in activity may help sustain interest, so avoid excessive repetition.
- Allow longer periods of training for more mature students.
- Give reassurance and emotional encouragement to avoid the fear of failure.
- Select routes that will ensure, as far as possible, that the learner can cope with the conditions.
- Be prepared to vary your methods of instruction.
- Avoid attempting to expand on variables before the pupil has grasped the key points of a new topic.
- 'Nothing has been taught until something is learnt.'

Skill training

The term 'skill' describes an activity in which the performance should be economical and effective in order to achieve a consistent and satisfactory result. Although it is relatively easy to recognize the skilled performance of an expert driver, it is considerably more difficult to define why it is so. It is even more difficult to analyse (and to give a valid explanation of) the many skills involved in the complete task.

Experienced drivers are often unaware of the numerous individual tasks they are putting into practice because, with experience, these have mostly become subconscious actions. As an instructor you need to be able to analyse each of the skills in detail before being able to teach the complex tasks involved in the process of learning to drive.

As a driver you have to obtain relevant information from the environment, process it, then respond by making decisions and executing the appropriate car control skills. The driving task involves attending to, perceiving and responding safely to driving-related stimuli. The activities involved relate to three different areas:

- psychomotor (or physical skills);
- cognitive (or knowledge-related skills);
- affective skills (or attitude).

When driving, you allocate attention by using your senses to gather information about the performance of your vehicle and also the conditions of the road and traffic environment. As a driver you process the information by comparing it with existing knowledge, memories and previous experiences. You then assess its relevance and either ignore it and do nothing, or decide on a particular response or course of action to be taken to maintain a safe environment.

As an instructor you will have to recognize all of these different aspects and teach your pupils how to drive safely.

Analysing the learning task

To assist your pupils in the acquisition of new skills you need to be able to identify key learning points and to isolate any areas of weakness. To do this you will need to identify the elements of knowledge, attitude and skill involved in a particular learning task.

Essential elements

Knowledge

This describes what you know. It has been found that knowledge influences attitude and assists in the acquisition of skills. Driving involves considerable knowledge of *The Highway Code*, traffic law and the principles of safe procedures. Certain aspects can be learnt more effectively in a classroom or at home rather than in the hustle and bustle of today's road and traffic conditions.

Knowledge, however, is only a basis for 'real' learning. Although it may influence attitudes, in practice knowledge alone is not always sufficient to ensure we have the will or skill needed to behave safely. For example, although most drivers know about speed limits, this doesn't always prevent them from driving at excessive or inappropriate speeds. Legislation and the consequences of being caught, however, place incentives on drivers not to break the law.

Other incentives include the consequences of accident involvement. This knowledge may also help influence our attitude towards alcohol and driving. On this basis, the more we know, the better equipped we are to make our decisions.

Attitude

This describes what we really think, and it usually influences our behaviour. Attitudes are formed over a lifetime of experience and learning. They will not normally be changed overnight! Unsympathetic attitudes towards others, and towards the established principles of road safety, can be contributory factors in causing many road accidents.

You can encourage your pupils to develop safe attitudes towards other road users. You can do this by constantly persuading and providing them with good examples.

In addition to knowledge, an attitude has motivational and emotional elements that influence behaviour. These elements can be so powerful that we may sometimes lose control of our actions. Uncontrolled aggression and love are two extreme examples of this.

Skill

This describes what we can do! There are two main types of skill: *manipulative skills* are physical actions such as turning the steering wheel, pressing the footbrake or operating the clutch pedal; *perceptive skills* are skills associated with awareness, thinking, reasoning and making decisions. They are the predominant skills used in the overall driving task, and rely heavily on visual sense. They include the judgement of:

- reductions in speed caused by differing amounts of braking pressure;
- detecting changes in direction when steering;
- awareness – the general state of mind involving hazard recognition and comparisons with previous experience;
- assessing and predicting risk and making decisions.

Making the driving effective involves the following skills:

- attention – staying alert and concentrating;
- visual search – a systematic scanning of the road and traffic scene;
- responding to situations and taking the appropriate action to control the car;
- using the car's controls smoothly and efficiently.

To make the learning and the driving effective, organize lessons into short progressive steps and let your pupils work through them at their own pace. As aptitudes and abilities vary, you will need to adapt the pace of your instruction to the ability of each individual.

Build on what the pupil already knows and can do, then move on one step at a time. Before attempting a new skill, the pupil will require some basic knowledge upon which to build.

Each physical action has a 'get set' position from which the actual skill commences. This involves preliminary movements and positioning of the hands and/or feet in anticipation of carrying out the skill or sub-skill. This 'get set' position is important for ensuring the efficient and smooth execution of the overall task. For example:

- siting the hand over the gear lever in anticipation of a change, while:
- positioning the foot over the clutch pedal;
- extending the fingers ready to use a signal;
- raising the appropriate hand ready for the first pull movement on the steering wheel.

Teaching a skill

Before you can teach a new skill you have to establish the present standard and abilities of your pupil. You can then decide on the level at which the skill should be introduced, demonstrated and practised. Be prepared to adjust this level, up or down, depending on the pupil's responses and performance.

At the beginning of each session, discuss and agree with the pupil what he or she is going to do and why. The pupil should understand how the skill is to be performed and what is expected of him or her. Relate the subject matter to what the pupil already knows and can do, so that he or she feels the task in hand is attainable. It may be necessary to break some skills down into their component sub-skills to ensure success is achieved.

The generally accepted pattern of skill training is:

1 explanation;
2 demonstration;
3 practice.

1. The explanation

Introduce the topic for instruction and include an indication of:

- what the topic involves;
- why this particular aspect is important;
- when and where it is carried out;
- how it is to be carried out.

Keep your explanations short and to the point. They should be appropriate to each pupil's ability. For example, it would be pointless to go into lengthy explanations on how to exercise clutch control at busy uphill junctions if the pupil cannot move away under control on a level road. Establish and consolidate the main principles of the subject before introducing the finer points and variables. During the explanation make sure you keep the pupil involved – try to avoid a lengthy lecture. Once basic rules and procedures are established, it will be easier for the pupil to understand and retain additional information given at a later date.

There are three main constituent parts to most explanations. These include details and information concerning:

- *control* – of the vehicle's speed;
- *observation* – of hazards and general attitudes towards them;
- *positioning* – of the vehicle by using the steering.

Control Explanations should include the general control of the vehicle for dealing with hazards. Control is mainly a manipulative skill, for example:

- coordination of the car's controls when moving off;
- low-speed clutch control for manoeuvring;
- smooth, gradual use of the steering wheel;
- smooth and progressive use of the accelerator and gears;
- smooth and progressive use of the brakes for slowing down and stopping;
- securing the car when stationary.

Observation Explain about the visual search required to deal safely with any hazard or to maintain safety when manoeuvring. The use of any necessary signals should be included, and any special danger clues the pupil should be looking for.

It is your responsibility to encourage safe attitudes and you should include information on the perceptive skills and safety margins. Explain about the decision-making process required to respond correctly.

Positioning Explanations should include:

- the rules relating to positioning and when to adjust to suit the situation;
- steering – the physical use of the steering wheel;
- maintaining general accuracy throughout the required course;
- lane discipline where appropriate.

Points to remember A general guide for lessons is to:

- discuss with your pupils what they will be doing during the current session;
- explain how to do it;
- allow plenty of time for practising.

It can be totally unproductive to introduce complex procedures until basic car control skills have been adequately developed. Do it with a 'KISS':

Keep It Short and Simple

- Keep explanations as brief as you can for the subject.
- Get straight to the point.

- Use terminology that is straightforward and understandable.
- Use visual aids where they will help your pupil understand what you mean.
- To validate points, refer to official publications such as *The Highway Code* and *The Official DSA Guide to Driving – The essential skills*.
- Emphasize the key points – leaving out any unnecessary detail.

2. The demonstration

The demonstration has a number of applications. It can be used to:

- show pupils how an expert would carry out a manoeuvre or procedure;
- emphasize or reinforce individual components of any skill;
- show the key elements of a manoeuvre prior to giving a more detailed explanation;
- dispel the pupils' apprehension.

To obtain maximum effect from a demonstration it must be preceded by a briefing. You can then emphasize the key points as you give the demonstration by talking yourself through the procedures. Conclude the demonstration with a discussion about the key points, then if necessary give a more in-depth explanation.

Consolidate the explanation and demonstration by giving your pupil plenty of practice under controlled conditions.

Quite often new drivers are genuinely unaware of the mistakes they are making and cannot visualize the correct procedure. A demonstration may help them to 'see' exactly what you mean. This particularly applies where safety margins, hold-back positions and also the use of speed when approaching hazards are concerned. Because of inexperience, pupils can fail to recognize the dangers involved. If you demonstrate safer clearances and speeds, it may result in a better understanding of the problems.

You can tell a pupil to slow down more before a corner and get no result whatsoever. This can mean that the pupil's concept of the word 'slow' is different from your own. Under such circumstances, a demonstration can be invaluable, but use it as part of your explanation and not as a substitute for it.

Points to remember about the demonstration

- It should be at an appropriate level for the pupil's ability.
- It should follow an explanation of the subject.
- It should be a perfect example of the skill or procedure carried out at near normal speed. (Slightly less than normal may be advantageous at times, but it should not be so slow as to become unreal.)
- Commentary should be restricted to the main points using key words (too many variables may confuse).
- It must be consolidated with plenty of practice in controlled conditions.

3. Pupils' practice

Your pupils can only learn practical skills by carrying them out! The practice should, however, be structured and follow a pattern of:

- controlled;
- prompted;
- transferred responsibility; and
- distributed practice.

Controlled practice and talk-through As far as possible try to ensure your pupils 'get it right first time'. Talk them through each action and stage of the operation, skill or exercise until they develop the ability and confidence to do it for themselves. This talk-through technique enables initial practice of new skills or procedures to take place realistically and in relative safety. It also helps to prevent vehicle abuse and inconvenience to other road users. The need for the full talk-through is greatest in the early stages when terminology is least familiar and pupils are more likely to misunderstand the instructions given.

Make sure that pupils are familiar with your terminology and can carry out your instructions before they move away. Instructions should be clear and should be given so that the pupil has plenty of time to interpret and execute them comfortably.

In order to build up confidence, it is essential that initial practice of a new skill should be successful. The talk-through ensures, as far as possible, that nothing goes wrong at this early stage.

While this method of instruction is usually successful for introducing pupils to the basic skills, it does have some complications. Due to the limitations of speech, the timing of some skills is slightly artificial. We can only speak, or give instructions, in a specific order – one at a time. Some skills require perfectly coordinated use of different controls at the same time. It is therefore impossible to give instructions exactly as they should be carried out.

Another problem lies in pupils' speed of interpreting and then carrying out the instruction. There will be a delay of varying lengths for different pupils. They may also temporarily become confused over an instruction, causing even more delay.

New skills should normally begin to develop after two or three talk-through exercises. When you can see that some progress is taking place, encourage your pupils to take some personal responsibility for their actions. There are a number of ways in which development of this responsibility can be encouraged:

- Ask pupils to talk themselves through the sequence. This gives them the responsibility but it may also give you forewarning of any errors. You can then verbally rectify these before they are actually committed.

- Break the sequence into three parts (preparation, observation, and action), and get pupils to talk themselves through each. If pupils become confused with the unfamiliar terminology it is not important as long as they understand what is required. Don't be too particular about making pupils use your precise phrasing. This may result in them feeling inadequate and inhibit their performance of the skill.

- If pupils 'dry up', give a cue or prompt, then let them continue. Practise until the whole sequence can be completed unaided.

- Insist that previously learnt routines are carried out properly, and correct any errors before they become habitual. Excessive criticism, however, should be avoided as it can destroy confidence.

- Encourage improvement by pointing out progress. Identify weaknesses and help pupils overcome them.

- Devise simple exercises to help with any problems.

- Experiment and be prepared to vary your methods of instruction if problems persist.

- Your students should feel that they can approach you without feeling foolish or incompetent. If problems persist, try something new for a while and go back to the subject later.

- Reassure those who find things difficult. Let them know that periods of slow progress are quite common.

At the end of practice sessions, decide if the objectives have been achieved. Ask questions and involve the pupil in a discussion to find out whether the subject has been clearly understood before you proceed to the next. Practice sessions should finish not only with a review of what has been achieved, but also a look forward to what will be covered in the next lesson.

At the beginning of each lesson, revise and reinforce the points learnt in the previous one before going on to new subject matter.

Prompted practice Some pupils may become very good at following instructions, but when left to carry out a skill unaided they are unable to do so. Others who find it more difficult to follow individual instructions are often far more advanced when they are allowed to work on their own initiative. While controlled practice is an essential part of basic training in new skills, it should gradually be phased out when you feel pupils can cope for themselves. Some pupils will require a lot of encouragement to act and think for themselves.

Prompting, where required, is perhaps the natural progression from the controlled practice or talk-through. The amount of prompting required will largely depend on the ability and willingness of pupils to make decisions for themselves. The type of decision required is also significant. For example, if the conditions become too busy for the pupils' ability, there will be a tendency for them to refrain from making any decisions at all. Where these situations arise, you must be prepared to prompt as required. The ultimate objective is to get pupils to carry out all of the skills under normal traffic conditions without any prompting at all.

Revision is important and it requires continuous consideration, particularly in the early stages of establishing a new skill. A true and wholly accurate assessment cannot be made of the driving skill where it is still necessary to prompt.

The use of detailed instructions should be reduced as the pupil's ability increases. For example, at the beginning of a lesson, a pupil hesitates and shows minor signs of distress on being asked to move off. You know that this pupil can carry out the procedure without any assistance, so all you may need to do is give a simple cue such as 'Select first gear.' Normally this will trigger the actions required as the sequence is remembered.

Remember that a simple cue like this is often sufficient to bring back a whole sequence of complicated actions without further instruction. Try not to help too much by giving all the necessary information. If capable, the pupil needs to be given the opportunity of achieving some success independently.

Practice will be required to build consistency, stamina and to reduce the time taken to complete any sequence. When the skill becomes consistent and is carried out in a reasonable length of time, other important aspects can be introduced, with more emphasis being placed on the visual search and timing.

Skills must be applied and practised progressively in more difficult traffic situations: for example, moving off from junctions and traffic lights; moving off and maintaining low-speed control in conjunction with steering.

Transferred responsibility There comes a time when you must hand over to your pupils the responsibility for making their own decisions and acting on them. As control skills develop and confidence grows, you should place more emphasis on the development of perceptive and hazard recognition skills. Point out what pupils should be looking for and where to expect it. Explain the dangers involved and why particular responses are called for.

Encourage pupils to think and to make decisions. Get them to look for information, and encourage them to use their knowledge of the rules and previous experience in order to assess each situation. Build the confidence they need in order to make decisions and to act for themselves.

The Q&A technique becomes very useful in this stage of training. By asking questions relevant to the traffic situation, you can find out what pupils are thinking. How they respond will give you an indication of areas where misunderstandings are occurring and you can then make the necessary corrections.

Distributed practice No matter what skills are being learnt, there is no substitute for practice and this should be organized sensibly. 'Cramming' everything into a few marathon sessions is not an efficient way of learning. 'A little and often' is a more efficient strategy.

Carefully distributed practice, divided evenly over four or five weeks, is more efficient than working for the same amount of hours during an intensive one-week course. For example, one hour of training a day is considerably more efficient than:

- one hour of training twice a day;
- two hours' training once a day;
- two hours' training twice a day.

The general learning curve

You will be able to see the manipulative aspects of the driving task improving by simply watching your pupils execute them. However, prompts and verbal guidance during the early stages of learning will still be necessary. When the skill is sufficiently developed, hints and reassurance should be all that is required. Pupils' progress will vary depending on the type of skill being learnt.

With the learning of some skills, pupils often reach a stage that is referred to as 'the plateau of learning' and progress appears to come to a halt. However, this is not normally the limit of their potential and is usually very short-lived. After a brief while most pupils will overcome the problem and progress to their own personal limits.

Structuring The Learning

There are nine main principles involved in structuring any course of training or instruction. As there is a good deal of common sense involved in teaching a practical skill, most good instructors follow these principles intuitively:

FIGURE 9.1 The general learning curve

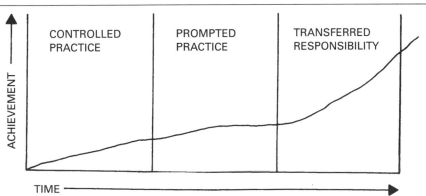

1   The aims and objectives of a course of lessons, and each part of it, should be agreed in advance in terms of observable behaviour

Objectives are statements that describe what your pupil expects to be able to do at the completion of a lesson or a course of lessons. They are normally phrased in terms of observable behaviour. Pupils should be made aware of the new skills they are expected to be able to carry out, or what knowledge they are expected to have gained by the end of the session or each section of learning.

The DSA has published a comprehensive set of objectives in its syllabus for learning to drive, but you will probably want to produce your own supplementary objectives – particularly for the earlier stages of learning.

2   The subject matter to be learnt, and the training routes used, should be appropriate to achieving the specified aims and objectives

The content of each lesson, together with your support materials and the training routes used, should ensure that the aims and objectives are achievable by the pupil. You should classify the matter to be learnt in order of importance as follows:

- *essential material* – what the learner *must* cover in order to achieve the course objectives;
- *desirable material* – what the learner *should* cover, but is not absolutely essential to achieve the objectives;
- *useful material* – what the learner *could* cover, but it is not completely relevant to the objectives.

3   The course content, and individual lessons, should be organized in short progressive steps that follow a logical sequence

Intermediate targets will help to stimulate interest and progress. They can help to reinforce learning by providing positive evidence of progress through each section and also organize the learning situation.

Considered as a whole, driving is a complex task. It is made up of many sub-skills such as moving off, steering and stopping. The whole should be analysed and organized into short progressive units of instruction taking the acquisition of these sub-skills into consideration.

A course of driving lessons should be structured to proceed from:

- the known to the unknown;
- the simple to the complex;
- basic rules to the variations;
- concrete observations to abstract reasoning.

Once pupils have grasped the basic rules and concepts, it becomes easier for them to develop new skills and understand the variables.

4   The content of lessons, and the routes selected, should be graded in difficulty so that your pupils will make as few mistakes as possible, especially in the early stages

Make sure students experience success during the early stages of their training. To do this, avoid setting standards that are too high. Be prepared to accept some technical inaccuracies and deficiencies until they have developed more confidence in their ability. Initial failure may deter pupils and inhibit progress. Build confidence and understanding on a firm foundation of practical skills.

Progress from what students know and can do, working up to the unknown and the new. Simple skills should be taught before complex procedures are introduced. For example, it is unreasonable to expect pupils to deal with right turns at busy traffic-light controlled junctions before they can control the vehicle properly.

5   Your pupils should be introduced to new materials and skills at a level of difficulty that relates to their ability, previous experience and attainments

There are considerable variations in the rate at which students learn. This should cause few problems when giving one-to-one tuition because the course can be tailored to suit the needs of each individual. Pupils should be allowed to work through each unit of learning at their own pace. New skills and techniques can then be introduced at a level commensurate with ability, knowledge and achievement.

One of your first tasks when meeting new students is to find out what previous experience they may have had, and how much they know and can do. In order to plan the level of training, it is necessary to establish the pupils' current knowledge and ability. Use Q&A with pupils to find out what they already know, then encourage them to take some responsibility for the decisions you will be making together.

As skills develop, and mastery of the controls is attained, keep pupils informed of what they are doing and why. They should never be left confused or in doubt. However, some of the basic skills must be taught as simple conditioned reflex procedures. Initially, it is more important for pupils to respond correctly to an emergency than to understand why the particular response was required.

6   Pupils should be allowed to proceed through the course at their own pace

The amount of time devoted to each element of training will vary from one pupil to another. Learning is more efficient when pupils are allowed to proceed at their own pace, as slowly or as quickly as they are able. This allows the learning to be most effective.

7   Keep pupils 'actively' involved in the learning process

Keep your pupils physically and/or mentally involved in the learning experience. Whatever the task under instruction, learning can only be achieved by pupils thinking and doing things for themselves. Activity will help to hold pupils' attention.

Where students may be sitting passively in a classroom, supposedly listening to a necessary, but boring, lecture, it is easy to see how they may become 'switched off'. This may happen where the students do not think the content of the lecture is particularly relevant to their personal needs.

Observing the physical activity of the pupil is relatively straightforward. Recognizing what the pupil is thinking, however, is a rather more difficult problem. An active mind on the part of the pupil is essential to learning and is an important part of driving.

For example, driving at 40 mph along a quiet road with relatively little traffic requires little physical activity other than controlling the steering. The problem in this situation is that there is very little to occupy the mind, so it may not be involved in the driving at all. These situations provide ideal conditions for you to develop the pupil's visual search and observational skills and to relate them to the decisions of an experienced driver.

In the earlier stages of learning a task, keep the pupil's mind active – ask questions about the relevant road features, or of any intended actions. For example, if you see a bus with a left signal on, you could ask what the pupil expects it to do. However, when using this technique, make sure the questions are not too technical and likely to distract the pupil's concentration.

8   Give your pupils continuous feedback of progress

Learning should be reinforced through feedback of progress, helpful comments and a balance of constructive criticism and encouragement. Active involvement facilitates learning. However, this does not ensure that the learning is of the right kind, or that the pupil is making progress towards the final performance as stated in the objectives.

Make sure that pupils are not just perfecting existing faults. Reinforce learning and improve performance, by giving continuous information on progress. Feedback should occur as soon as possible after an event, or between each step in an exercise or manoeuvre. This will help prevent further faults appearing. Comments such as 'good' or 'well done' may be useful as an indication of progress where there is insufficient time to give more detailed information. These comments do not, however, tell the pupil anything about the actual performance. Comments such as the following are all more helpful because they give information on the actual performance:

Our position was a little wide on the approach to the turn.

The gear change was left a little late.

The approach speed needs to be a little slower.

Positive comments that indicate what action must be taken to correct an error are even more beneficial. For example:

Position about a metre from the kerb when turning left.

Slow down earlier before reaching the corner.

Change down to second a little sooner next time.

Short comments and corrections made on the move will be of great value in improving your pupil's performance. However, avoid giving detailed verbal corrections on the move. When they are required, give them as soon as practicable after the incident when a suitable parking position is found.

9 Pupils should master each skill and section of the course before you go on to the next stage

There is sometimes confusion over what is meant by 'complete mastery', and some instructors argue that this cannot be attained until a very advanced stage is reached. Do not expect 'total mastery of the full task' during the intermediate stages. Reduce the demands placed on your pupils by setting properly structured objectives and choosing your routes carefully.

If a course is properly structured, mastery can, and should, be attained in each sub-skill, technique or procedure before introducing new and progressively more complicated variables.

Consistency is an essential feature of good driving. To achieve it, each skill or task should be 'over-learnt' before proceeding to the next. Progress based on mastery of each phase of learning will do much to develop a sense of achievement and confidence. Staging the course into a number of progressive learning units also helps to increase pupils' motivation to learn by sustaining a continuous sense of urgency.

Driver training syllabus

The DSA officially recommended syllabus (which you will find in its publication *The Official Guide to Learning to Drive*) covers the complete range of driving skills and is not restricted simply to 'learning to pass the "L" test'. The syllabus therefore provides a basis for structuring courses for:

- pre-driver training;
- learner driver training;
- post-test training under the Pass Plus scheme;
- advanced/defensive/fleet training.

The main elements of the syllabus include:

- legal requirements;
- car controls, equipment and components;
- road-user behaviour;
- vehicle characteristics;
- road and weather conditions;
- traffic signs, rules and regulations;
- car control and road procedure;
- motorway driving;
- riding mopeds and motorcycles;
- towing larger trailers or caravans.

When structuring your own course you should use this syllabus in conjunction with *The Official DSA Guide to Driving – The essential skills*, *The Highway Code*, and any other material that will help develop and reinforce safe procedures and attitudes.

As well as the skills in which your pupils must achieve basic competence in order to pass the driving test, they must also have a thorough knowledge of *The Highway Code* and the motoring laws, and understanding of the driver's responsibilities. It is your responsibility to influence safe attitudes. You must teach your pupils to have real concern, not just for their own safety, but for the safety of all road users, including pedestrians.

You should be able to teach your pupils most of the subjects listed in the DSA syllabus during their practical on-road lessons. However, some may be difficult for you to cover because of the road and traffic conditions in your area. You may not, for example, be able to give practical experience at dealing with level crossings, floods or dual carriageways, because these situations do not exist locally. However, it remains your responsibility to ensure your pupils have sufficient knowledge on all of the subjects. You can do this by various means. Some of these are:

- teaching pupils in groups;
- spending time in the car going over the rules and procedures;
- setting homework based on the official publications and asking relevant questions on subsequent lessons.

The four phases of skill development

New drivers normally progress through four phases of learning before reaching a competent standard.

1   Dissociated passive

This phase of learning is very superficial. Pupils are only passively attending to the driving task, while you will be playing a dominant role in talking them through the basic routines and procedures. Novice drivers are usually visually inactive, slow to respond, and hesitant, with a tendency to make sudden unexpected moves. You will need to use the basic principles of 'controlled practice' outlined earlier in this chapter and give pupils full instruction through each routine or skill.

'*Controlled practice.*' During this phase of giving full instruction through each routine or skill, tuition should be restricted to developing car control skills. Although the carrying out of the routines may be superficial at this stage, you can still try to develop good habits such as the M–S–M sequence.

The aim of the first lesson is to familiarize pupils with the car's controls. It will also give them an opportunity to get a feel for these by practising some simple exercises while stationary. When you have explained the terminology you will be using, make sure your pupils understand, and are able to carry out, basic instructions before moving away. For example:

Handbrake ready.

Cover the clutch.

Clutch down.

Set the gas.

Find the holding point.

Cover the brake.

In order to develop pupils' car control and steering skills, talk them through the routines and allow plenty of practice on the nursery routes. You will need to tell them exactly what to do and when to do it. This should help them to get things right first time and build up their confidence. Let them practise each step of each exercise separately until they have mastered it reasonably well. Keeping to the quiet routes, use step-by-step exercises to encourage your pupils to do more for themselves.

2   Dissociated active

At this stage your pupils will become more 'active' in the manipulative skills but will still be visually inactive, with slow perceptive responses. You will often need to prompt them into action. (For future reference this phase is referred to as 'prompted practice'.) Near misses, sudden unusual manoeuvres and late over-reactions tend to be the norm, and pupils seem to actively take risks. During this phase you need to use the 'prompted practice' routines described earlier in this chapter.

Your pupils will initially require considerable prompting. Progression through the phase should be structured within their capabilities. First teach them to deal with static hazards. The circumstances of routes and movement of pedestrians and traffic, however, will sometimes create unforeseen situations with which they are unable to cope. When this happens, reassure the pupil and talk him or her through the situation.

To develop skills, use quiet estates with wide roads, rounded corners and as few parked cars as possible. Practise simple M–S–M routines, turning left and right into side roads. Once pupils have mastered this, practise the system approaching and emerging from roads. At first, only practise on junctions that provide clear views into the main road.

When pupils can cope with the quiet estates, give them the opportunity to practise on sharper corners and major roads with more traffic. Avoid very busy junctions and those on uphill gradients. As mastery of the system of car control is achieved at basic junctions, and confidence increases, practise on busier roads, uphill junctions, and those with restricted sightlines.

Introduce the manoeuvring and parking exercise when control skills are adequately developed to ensure initial success. As pupils improve towards the end of this phase, encourage them to assess situations, take on more responsibility for themselves and begin to make their own decisions.

3   Injudicious

Your pupils will now start to become 'visually aware', developing perceptive responses and actively attending to driving the car. They should become more responsible for their own actions. (For future reference this phase is referred to as 'transferred responsibility'.)

At this stage pupils will:

- make some false assumptions;
- be prepared to take risks;
- make occasional misjudgements;
- suffer near misses;
- still make some unusual manoeuvres.

This phase will usually involve some 'transferred responsibility'. Once pupils have mastered the car control skills and the basic rules and routine procedures, give them some experience on busier roads and in traffic. Try to keep them calm and build their confidence in these conditions by giving them plenty of practice. Provide them with plenty of experience on a wide variety of roads and junctions, for example:

- in laned traffic;
- on one-way streets;
- turning on to and off dual carriageways;

- negotiating roundabouts;
- turning right at busy traffic-light controlled crossroads.

Avoid heavy, fast-moving traffic and multi-lane roads containing combinations of parked vehicles, pedestrians and complex junctions until the final stages of training, when they will be able to cope with these situations.

Remember, excessive criticism will destroy pupils' confidence. A little praise will encourage them to do better next time. Tell them when they carry out procedures well, commend them for making good decisions, and give praise for their concentration and effort.

4 Independent

By the time your pupils reach this phase of learning they should be more visually active and aware. They should be developing a quick perceptive response to recognized risks and be able to react in an unhurried and skilful manner. There should no longer be any near misses or unusual reactions. It is your responsibility to teach pupils to recognize and accept that other road users make mistakes. By doing this you can teach them to avoid accidents by compensating for other people's mistakes.

Carrying out assessments and mock tests at this stage should be constructive. They should help to provide your pupils with evidence of progress as well as any weaknesses still to be worked on. Before presenting pupils for the test, ensure, as far as you possibly can, that they are able to cope with busy road and traffic conditions. It is not sufficient for them merely to satisfy the minimum standard required by the examiner.

These four phases of learning are not necessarily independent of each other; they are often interlinked and the pupil may waver from one phase to another depending on the topic under instruction, the level of difficulty of the task, the amount of traffic or the complexity of the route.

You will find more information about structured learning and the importance of coaching in *Pratical Teaching Skills for Driving Instructors*. In particular, there is detail about how people learn, what motivates them and how to overcome perceived barriers to learning.

Route planning

Route planning is an essential element of lesson preparation. It requires a thorough knowledge of local geography and traffic conditions. When planning routes you must take into consideration any specific driving skill or procedure that is to be practised. An inappropriate route can have disastrous consequences when novices are unnecessarily exposed to conditions with which they are unable to cope. In extreme cases, and with particularly nervous pupils, it may even make them give up the idea of learning to drive at all.

Ideally, a fairly wide selection of planned routes containing various types of traffic hazards and conditions will be required. You should not consider them as being rigidly fixed routes from which there must be no deviation.

Flexibility is an important consideration when planning a route, because it allows for changes to be made midway through a lesson. This may become necessary to allow more time to be spent on an area of driving which may be proving unexpectedly troublesome, and yet still allow the lesson to be completed on time for your next appointment.

Excessive repetition over the same routes will often prove counter-productive. It frequently leads to a reduction in the pupil's interest. This in turn may result in boredom and slow progress. Some repetition, however, can be helpful at times when carried out deliberately for a specific purpose relevant to the lesson. For example, practising control skills on the approach to uphill junctions might need to be restricted to a localized area where the same junctions might have to be used several times. This will give pupils more opportunity to practise their skills.

Training routes

Training routes and areas fall loosely into three groups:

- nursery routes;
- intermediate;
- advanced.

There is no definite dividing line between these groups, and there may frequently be considerable overlap between them. On occasions there is justification for incorporating all kinds of route on one lesson: for instance, when making an initial assessment of a new client with previous driving experience.

Starting with the nursery routes, introduce new traffic situations at a controlled rate that is sensitive to the needs of your pupils and sympathetic to their ability. However, in reality, the nature of traffic conditions can be very erratic. Even the most carefully planned route may suddenly prove unsuitable, and the pupil will be faced with new situations he or she cannot yet cope with. Route preparation will, however, help keep these incidents down to a fairly isolated and acceptable level.

Training routes are often a compromise between the ideal and the reality of local geography and traffic conditions. In general, instructors working near the centre of a large city may experience difficulty in finding suitable nursery routes. However, their counterparts, operating in isolated rural areas, may experience problems in finding suitably varied conditions for the advanced routes. Extending the length of some lessons may be a satisfactory answer in both instances, by allowing more travelling time to training areas that are more suitable to the needs of the pupil.

Nursery routes

Various kinds of roads are required, but in general, 'nursery' routes should avoid areas with a high proportion of turns and junctions. Remember too, that apart from not wanting to worry your pupil, you are your own best advert – select routes to allow minimum interference with the flow of traffic and inconvenience to other drivers.

You should progressively use routes that incorporate:

- fairly straight, wide roads that are long enough to allow uninterrupted progression through the gears;
- quiet, fairly wide roads on up/down/level gradients on which to practise the manipulative skills;
- roads containing right/left-hand bends, allowing practice at slowing down, using the gears and steering;
- simple left turns from main into side roads;
- simple left turns into main roads;
- right turns from main into side roads and right turns into main roads;
- some routes containing parked vehicles will be necessary towards the end of the initial stages.

As far as possible avoid:

- busy roads;
- areas where there are lots of parked vehicles;
- pedestrian crossings;
- traffic lights;
- busy roundabouts.

Intermediate routes

There will be some overlap between these routes and the more advanced nursery routes. They should include:

- junctions with 'Give way' and 'Stop' controls;
- all types of basic rule crossroads;
- uphill 'Give way' junctions at which to practise first gear hold and control;
- traffic-light controlled junctions;
- roundabouts that conform to basic rules.

Roads selected for the initial practice of the turn in the road and reversing exercises should be reasonably traffic-free, and roadside furniture such as post boxes and telegraph poles should be avoided.

Routes should, wherever possible, be planned to avoid:

- dual carriageways;
- multi-lane roads;

- one-way streets;
- junctions that do not conform to basic rules;
- right turns on to very busy main roads;
- any other particularly difficult situations;
- driving test routes.

Because of the length of the tuition periods, you should take into account any special features of local geography and road design. If complicated situations cannot be avoided, you may either have to drive pupils to more suitable areas, or give them full instruction and talk through.

Advanced routes

These will incorporate most of the intermediate routes. They should be progressively extended to include as many variations to the basic rules as possible. Where possible include:

- dual carriageways;
- multi-lane roads;
- one-way streets;
- level crossings;
- busy shopping streets;
- all types of pedestrian crossing;
- rural roads providing an opportunity to practise overtaking.

Advanced routes will provide an opportunity for you to conduct 'mock' tests in conditions similar to those used for the driving test. It is stressed, however, that you should avoid actual test routes.

Points to remember

When selecting routes, you should give consideration to:

- the standard and ability of the pupil;
- disruption and inconvenience to other traffic;
- what specific skills you wish to practise;
- which particular hazards you wish to include or avoid;
- how much time is available;
- what danger or inconvenience might be caused to other road users;
- whether any excessive nuisance is likely to be caused to local residents;
- excessive repetition of routes causing boredom;
- test routes and areas used by driving examiners for manoeuvre exercises during their testing hours.

Giving route directions

The quality of a pupil's performance can be totally destroyed if you give late or unclear directions. You must give pupils sufficient time to interpret and respond to any request. You should also bear in mind that inexperienced pupils will take a long time to react to your instructions.

Instructions must be given clearly and concisely. Most directional instructions contain three basic ingredients. These are:

- Alert – draw your pupil's attention to the imminent request.
- Direct – the instruction to turn or pull up.
- Identify – confirm where the instruction is to be carried out.

Examples:

Alert:	*I would like you to …*
Direct:	*… turn left …*
Identify:	*… at the junction ahead.*

Alert:	*Would you …*
Direct:	*… take the second road on the right …*
Identify:	*… this one being the first.*

Alert:	*At the roundabout, I'd like you to …*
Direct:	*… take the road leading off to the right …*
Identify:	*… That is, the third exit.*

Alert:	*I want you to…*
Direct:	*… take the next road on the left, please.*
Identify:	*It's the one where the post box is.*

Confirmation can be given where required by adding further information such as 'It's just out of sight around the bend' or 'It's just before the telephone box, bus stop'.

Instructions and terminology

General instructions

Be consistent and standardize your instructions. If you use terminology similar to that used by DSA driving examiners, your pupils will be familiar with it when they take their test. The following are general instructions for normal driving and special manoeuvre exercises:

General route brief

I want you to follow the road ahead unless otherwise directed by road signs or markings.

When I want you to turn, I will ask you in good time.

Drive on when you are ready, please.

Stopping – parking – angled start – moving off

I want you to pull up and park on the left at the next convenient place, please.

I want you to pull up just behind the stationary vehicle, but leaving yourself sufficient room to move out again.

Drive on when you are ready.

Emergency stop

Shortly, I will ask you to stop the vehicle as in an emergency. The signal will be 'Stop'. When I give this signal, stop immediately and under full control, as though a child has run off the pavement.

After the exercise is completed, let the pupil know exactly what is happening next by saying:

Thank you! I won't/will be asking you to do that exercise again.

Drive on when you are ready, please.

Left-hand reverse exercise

The road on the left is the one I want you to reverse into. Drive past it and stop, reverse in and continue back for some distance into the side road. Keep reasonably close to the kerb.

Right reverse

The road on the right is the one I want you to reverse into. Drive on the left until you have passed it, then move across to the right and stop. Reverse in and continue back for some distance down the side road, keeping reasonably close to the right-hand kerb.

Turn in the road

I want you to turn the car round by means of forward and reverse gears. Try not to touch the kerb while turning.

Reverse parking

Pull up on the left in a convenient place, please. This is the parallel parking exercise. Will you drive forward and stop alongside the vehicle ahead. Then reverse in and park reasonably close to, and parallel with, the kerb. Try to complete the exercise within about two car lengths from the vehicle.

Lane selection Wherever possible you should encourage your pupils to make lane selection decisions for themselves. During early practice in new situations, however, and at more complex junctions, assistance may still be required. For example:

Approach in and maintain the left-hand lane through the roundabout.

Select and maintain the centre/right lane.

Route confirmation When confirming a straight-ahead direction, use the phrase, 'Follow the road ahead' at a junction or roundabout. Avoid terms such as 'Go straight on' or 'Carry straight on' as they may be taken literally resulting in the pupil ignoring traffic signs, give way markings, or stop rules.

Directional errors

Giving clear directions in good time may not always guarantee the correct response. People are often confused between left and right, particularly when under stress, and this problem can be embarrassing for them. Providing no danger or inconvenience is caused to other road users, if a pupil is not going where you have asked, it may be advisable to let him or her continue in the chosen direction – as long as he or she is signalling to go that way. Try not to over-emphasize the problem as this will only make the pupil feel more foolish.

Obviously you should try to cure this problem as soon as possible. One way of helping a pupil who is right-handed is by saying 'I write with my right and what's left is my left.' Another is that most people wear their watch on the left wrist; similarly, wedding and engagement rings are worn on the left, so this could also be used as a point of reference.

Although candidates are not tested on their ability to distinguish between left and right, excessive errors of this nature could prove very difficult for the examiner.

Encouraging independence

When giving directional instructions to pupils who are near test standard, it is important that these are as neutral as the circumstances allow. While they should always be clear and precise, guard against giving pupils too many reminders of what they should be observing for themselves. For example, telling an advanced pupil to turn left where there is a sign giving this order will not encourage independence, nor will it test his or her observation, knowledge or planning.

Extra information, however, may be justified in special circumstances at a particularly complex junction. In certain areas it may be virtually impossible to ascertain which lane will subsequently be required without some knowledge of the area. Under such circumstances you may have to tell your pupil which lane to select and give a reason for doing so.

Points to remember

- Late instructions are likely to cause:
  - rash, hurried decisions;
  - poor control;
  - poor observations;
  - erratic steering;
  - lack of confidence;
  - difficult/dangerous situations arising;
  - over-use of the dual controls.
- Avoid using the word 'Stop', except in an emergency. This could result in the pupil stopping in a dangerous position. If you want the pupil to hold back, or avoid moving away unsafely, the word 'Wait' can be used quite effectively.
- Avoid beginning an instruction with the words: 'Turn' or 'Pull up'. You could get an immediate and incorrect response.
- Try not to use the word 'right' for anything other than a directional change. For example, using the instruction 'Right, turn left at the crossroads please' could cause obvious confusion; as could saying 'That's right!' when in fact you mean 'That's correct!'

Giving instructions and using terminology

Any instructions you give while the vehicle is in motion should be firm, concise and clearly understood. Your terminology should be consistent, particularly in the early stages of tuition. For example, if, after mostly referring to the 'holding point', you change your wording to the 'biting point', there is a possibility of confusion.

Similarly, if, after giving frequent instructions to 'signal' right or left, you change your terminology to 'indicate', it could lead to momentary hesitation, which could lead to serious consequences if there are other road users about. If you wish to instigate correct and immediate response, your pupils must be able to recognize and interpret your terminology.

The need for most instructional jargon is at its highest during the early stages of tuition. However, this is when pupils are least familiar with it. A new pupil should, however, in a short time, become accustomed to your style of terminology.

Pupils who come to you after having had lessons with another ADI may be used to a completely different style of instructional language. In order to make life easier for them, it may help if you can adapt to the difference rather than expect them to learn new vocabulary. This is not always easy, or successful, but it should help you appreciate the difficulties caused by using unfamiliar phraseology.

Terminology

'Koplings' – 'Bremse' – 'Girkasse'

Unless you are familiar with Norwegian, these words for three of the car's controls will be strange to you. When talking to an absolute novice about the clutch, brake or gearbox, you might as well be speaking in a foreign language, so when you introduce these controls, give your pupils sufficient time to assimilate the new words.

Wherever possible, your terminology should be in simple and consistent language that will be easily recognized and clearly understood.

Standard instructions

The following instructions can be used to instigate set responses from your pupils. Make sure you give adequate explanation and practice at using them before expecting pupils to remember them. In most cases the basic responses can be practised while the car is stationary.

Get to know your pupils and vary the tone of your voice according to their personality and the nature or speed of the response required. For example a short, firm 'Brake harder' is far more likely to achieve a positive effect than the same instruction given in a very quiet and slow manner.

Make sure your pupils can understand and carry out the following instructions before attempting to move off:

The instruction	What it means
'Handbrake ready.'	Hand on the handbrake, ready to release it.
'Set the gas.'	Increase the engine speed to a faster tickover.
'Find the holding point.'	Clutch up until the engine is slowed down at the point of clutch take-up. This is often called the 'biting point'.
'Cover the clutch.'	Foot over the clutch pedal.
'Cover the brake.'	Foot over the brake pedal.

Instructions used for moving off and increasing speed

Make an initial check all around.

Clutch down; hand on gear lever, palm towards me, and select first gear.

Set the gas.

Find the holding point and keep your feet still.

Check the interior and door mirrors.

Look over your right shoulder to check the blind spot.

Signal if helpful to warn or inform others.

Handbrake off; hand back to the wheel.

Increase the gas slightly; and slowly raise the clutch.

Cancel the signal (if used).

Instructions used for changing up the gears

Hold the wheel firmly with your right hand and cover the clutch.

Hand on gear lever, palm towards me.

Push the clutch down and come off the gas.

Move the gear lever into second.

Clutch up smoothly; increase the gas gently.

Hand back to the wheel; rest your left foot.

For changing into third and fourth use the same instruction. If the palming method of gear selection is used, you should say 'palm to you'.

Instructions used to change down the gears

Keep both hands on the wheel; off the gas and cover the brake.

Brake gently; off the brake but keep it covered.

Hold the wheel firmly with your right hand and cover the clutch.

Hand on gear lever, palm towards (whichever direction is appropriate for the gear).

Push the clutch down.

Move the gear lever into ... gear.

Clutch up smoothly.

Further instructions will then depend on whether you wish the pupil to keep slowing down or to speed up again. For slowing down more, it would be:

Keep the brake covered; clutch down, etc.

For building up the speed again, it would be:

Increase the gas so that we can change up again.

After any gear change, make sure the left foot is clear of the clutch and the hand returned to the wheel.

Instructions used in normal driving

Hold the wheel firmly.

Look well ahead; look where you want to steer.

Prepare to turn the wheel left/right.

Check the mirrors.

Signal left/right.

Increase the gas/off the gas.

Brake gently/brake harder/ease off the brake.

Clutch down.

Handbrake on and select neutral.

Instructions and prompts used to alert drivers to risks and hazards

Look for pedestrians/cyclists/animals/vehicles moving into/across your path.

Look for and act on things which restrict your view, such as parked cars.

Look for and act on signs/signals/road markings.

Look for and act on bends/junctions/obstructions.

Look, and keep looking both ways.

Instructions to reduce speed

Hold back for …

Once explained and demonstrated, the 'hold back' procedure provides a usefully abbreviated expression. It can be used to replace abstract instructions relating to braking pressure. It also involves the pupil in learning how to judge speed and timing, and helps to develop accelerator sense. It does, however, require considerable practice.

The procedure involves slowing down early enough in order to give the situation more time to clear. Thus it reduces the likelihood of having to bring the car to a complete stop. Once understood, this procedure will give your pupils more freedom and help them develop a sense of responsibility for their own actions in good time to avoid last-minute decisions.

The hold-back position describes that in which drivers would normally:

● wait behind parked vehicles or other obstructions for oncoming traffic;
● follow behind cyclists when waiting for oncoming traffic to clear.

The following are positive commands that should leave pupils in no doubt as to the action that you require of them:

Slow down for …

Give way to …

Both of these instructions should encourage pupils to take some responsibility for their own actions in order to avoid unnecessary stops.

The command 'Stop!' should only be used in an emergency. It is the verbal equivalent of using the dual controls. The tone of your command will normally affect how pupils respond. Used in a careless manner, this command could result in an emergency stop, particularly if the learner is under stress.

Instructions and prompts used to stimulate thought New drivers, because of their inexperience, often fail to recognize or anticipate danger in many common 'high risk' situations. Short comments or questions, directed at drawing their attention to the danger, can help to improve anticipation and responses. Provided that the prompts are used in plenty of time for pupils to respond, this technique helps to make them think about and consider the consequences of their own inaction. For example:

I would approach much slower than this.

I would give way to the oncoming driver!

Are you ready to move away when it's clear?

What's happening behind?

Is it safe to go yet?

Can you see properly?

How far can you see?

Is it clear?

Do you need to signal?

Do you know how much clearance you should give to a parked car?

Can you tell me what the normal driving position is?

What's the speed limit on this road?

Approaching a row of parked vehicles at an excessive speed, ask:

What will you do if a child runs out?

What will you do if a car moves out?

What will you do if a car door opens?

What will you do if the cyclist pulls out?

What will you do if the oncoming car keeps coming?

Approaching a pedestrian crossing at excessive speed, ask:

> *What will you do if that pedestrian steps onto the crossing?*

> *Do you know what's behind us?*

Driving too close to the vehicle ahead, ask:

> *What will you do if the car in front has to stop quickly?*

> *Do you know how close the car behind is?*

> *What is the stopping distance at x mph?*

Approaching a bend or corner at excessive speed, ask:

> *What will you do if there is a car parked just around the bend?*

> *What will you do if there is a pedestrian crossing the side road?*

Corrections on the move

Under normal circumstances, detailed explanations should be avoided while the vehicle is in motion. This applies particularly if your pupil is concentrating on something else, such as when emerging from a junction or waiting at red traffic lights.

However, most incidents involving minor errors may not be recognized by the learner at the time they are committed and 10 minutes later, those that were recognized will have been forgotten. Some brief feedback, therefore, should be given at the time errors are committed, or as soon as possible afterwards. This will draw attention to them, making incidents easier to recall when later referred to and corrected in detail.

You can use short comments as cues to help pupils deal with difficult situations, or as minor rebukes for errors that may have been committed. Where corrections are made, they should be of a positive nature and ideally state the action that is required to cure the error. For example, it is better to say 'Hold the clutch still' rather than 'Don't let the clutch up', or 'Drive about two or three feet from the kerb' rather than 'Don't drive in the gutter'.

Serious errors, or repeated minor ones that appear to involve misunderstandings, should be corrected as soon as reasonably possible after they have occurred, when a suitable parking place has been found.

Intervention and dual controls

Because of their inexperience, new drivers lack anticipation and will fail to recognize or respond to potentially dangerous traffic situations. You should never completely trust them to follow your instructions or to do the correct thing.

Make sure they are aware of their legal responsibilities. Remember too that you could be jointly responsible for any offences committed by them. You must sometimes be firm and take whatever action necessary to protect your pupil, the car and other road users. Look, think and plan well ahead. Get to know individual pupils and watch them. You will soon learn to predict how they are likely to respond in given situations.

You must anticipate changes in the traffic situation and give instructions early enough for pupils to react. If anticipated early enough, most awkward situations can be avoided by giving verbal commands or, if it becomes necessary, taking action with the dual controls. Uncorrected errors will lead to the development of potentially dangerous and frightening situations.

There are four main reasons for intervening:

- to prevent risk of injury or damage to persons or property;
- to prevent an offence against the law;
- to prevent excessive stress to the learner in certain unplanned circumstances;
- to prevent mechanical damage to the vehicle.

A verbal command is often sufficient if given in time. However, if your pupil does not react to this, you will need to act. For example, you might:

- sound the horn;
- turn the wheel;
- switch off the engine;
- select a missed gear;
- release a partially engaged handbrake;
- prevent an unsympathetic gear change by covering the lever.

If it becomes necessary, you must be ready to use the dual controls. However, they should not be used as a matter of routine and when you do use them, you should discuss with the pupil the reasons why you took action.

Continual steering corrections and excessive use of the duals do little to build pupils' faith in their instructor. It could also lead to resentment, particularly if they do not understand why you used them.

There are various ways in which you can maintain a safe learning environment.

Verbal intervention

The verbal command is the most common form of intervention. It will usually work if you are concentrating properly, planning well ahead and giving instructions early enough for your pupil to respond. Commands range from a mild memory prompt to a more positive command for a specific and immediate action.

The prompt is usually associated more with the earlier lessons, but may be extended to more positive instructions such as:

Use the mirrors before changing direction.

Brake harder (or, Ease the brake off).

Clutch down (or, Hold the clutch still).

Increase the gas (or, Off the gas).

The more positive commands needed to relieve potentially dangerous traffic situations are usually those needed when you want your pupil to slow down earlier on the approach to hazards. 'Hold back' or 'Give way' are positive commands requiring a specific reaction, but these also leave the pupil with some freedom of judgement.

'Stop' is the final and absolute command. It should generally only be used in a situation that is fast getting out of control and/or where other instructions have been ignored or are unlikely to achieve the desired response.

Physical intervention

Physical intervention should normally be restricted to situations when it is necessary to avoid danger. This occurs when verbal intervention has not worked or where there is insufficient time to give it. The main methods of physical intervention are use of the dual footbrake, and steering corrections.

In any situation you will need to consider the method of intervention best suited to correcting the problem. There are occasions when both steering and braking corrections may be required. For example, you may need to control the steering wheel while using the dual footbrake. This is to resist the tendency the pupil may have to swing on the wheel. In order to generate more time for you to intervene and turn the wheel it may be necessary for you to control the speed of the car with the dual brake, particularly if the pupil has 'frozen' on the accelerator.

Using the dual footbrake

The procedure is as follows:

- Keep your foot near the brake to allow for its use with the minimum amount of movement.
- If you see a potential need for using the brake, have your foot ready over the pedal.
- Avoid fidgeting with the brake – this is likely to unnerve the pupil.
- If your pupil becomes frozen on the accelerator, it is generally not advisable to use the dual clutch as well as the brake. This could result in a 'blown' engine.

- Sometimes when pupils see a sudden movement towards the pedal, or where they feel a pressure change on theirs, they may react instinctively by braking harder. This double pressure can be dangerous to following traffic or may possibly lock the wheels. Be aware of this possible reaction.
- Before using your brake, check on what's happening behind.
- After using the dual controls, explain to the pupil why it was necessary.
- Reducing the speed with the dual brake sometimes allows pupils more time to turn the wheel.

The steering wheel – points to remember

- Turning the wheel from the passenger seat is generally more difficult than using the dual footbrake, but in certain circumstances it may be the only safe or practical method of intervention.
- The need for your taking the wheel can be kept to an acceptable minimum by ensuring that the route and conditions are suitable and appropriate for your pupil's ability.
- Other than for minor course corrections, if you intend turning the wheel left, go for an initially high position – this will give more leverage. For turning it right, go for a lower position which is more suitable for pushing the wheel.
- When turning the wheel, try to avoid physical contact with the pupil, though circumstances may make contact with the hands or arms inevitable.
- When 'frozen' on the wheel, even a very frail person can become immensely strong and may resist any attempt you make to turn it.
- Minor corrections with the steering to adjust the course are frequently more practical and safer alternatives to using the dual footbrake: for example, if a pupil is steering towards the kerb or too close to oncoming traffic, parked vehicles, cyclists or pedestrians.
- Use the top of the steering wheel to help maintain a steady course, particularly if the pupil has made an incorrect decision to proceed through a narrowing gap.

The dual clutch

Assisting pupils by using the dual clutch should be done sparingly. It should, of course, be used where there is potential danger or risk of damage, but try to avoid over-use as it can lead pupils to think that they have better control than they really do.

The dual clutch could also be used in relatively extreme circumstances when it is necessary to get away from a situation with which the pupil cannot cope. Covering the clutch so as to avoid an unexpected and potentially dangerous move off is one of the more important 'uses' of the dual clutch.

The dual accelerator

Dual accelerators are not normally fitted to driving instruction cars. If one is fitted, it must be removed while the vehicle is being used for a driving test. This is for safety reasons, so that the examiner does not use this pedal by mistake.

Its main use is to accelerate out of danger.

The horn

This should be used sensibly. It is better to remove a danger at source by giving a warning, than to find later that more drastic intervention has become necessary.

Other forms of intervention

- Engage a missed gear at a critical time or place.
- Switch off the engine – as long as you can reach the key.
- Put on or cancel an indicator at times when the pupil is unable to attend to it.
- Correct a mistake in the use of the handbrake, for instance by releasing it properly or applying it when needed.
- Prevent unsympathetic gear changes by covering the lever until the appropriate speed has been reached.

Dual eye mirrors

An extra rear view mirror will help you to keep in constant touch with the all-round traffic situation, and a dual eye mirror, strategically placed and focused on the pupil's eyes, will enable you to monitor his or her mirror use.

Mirrors should be placed fairly high on the windscreen so as not to impede the pupil's view, but low enough to provide you with an adequate view to the rear. They should be correctly adjusted and perfectly directed for you to check just as you would adjust your driving mirror. They should give maximum vision with the minimum of movement.

Some instructors adjust the nearside door mirrors so as to use them. This can be counter-productive and defeats the commonsense purpose of encouraging pupils to make all-round observations.

Avoiding problems

Safety is no accident! It is your responsibility to maintain a safe learning environment by:

- planning routes to suit each pupil's level of ability;
- looking and planning ahead and concentrating on the traffic situation all around;

- being alert to, and anticipating, pupils' actions and reactions in response to moving traffic situations;
- giving directions and instructions clearly and in good time to encourage pupils to think, respond and act accordingly.

Popular belief is that learner drivers are far more likely to have accidents than experienced motorists. However, the novice who is learning in a dual-controlled car under professional supervision is far less likely to have one.

If a driving school car is involved in an accident it is most likely to be a 'rear end shunt'. There are two main reasons for this. First, most novices are reluctant to slow down, give way or stop because of their inexperience at hazard recognition, and because for them, it's easier to keep moving. This initial reluctance to deal with a hazard may subsequently develop into an emergency. Where the situation is allowed to reach this critical level, there are two possible unwanted reactions from the learner:

- do nothing, remain frozen on the controls and proceed on a collision course;
- over-reaction – this can often result in harsh unregulated braking, that will usually bring the car to an uncontrolled and abrupt stop some distance before it's necessary.

Whether it is the instructor or pupil who stops the car under these circumstances, the result is likely to be the same if the driver behind is not concentrating or is following too closely!

The second reason is the 'false start', or 'stall' when moving into a roundabout or pulling out of an 'open' junction. Often, as the learner starts to pull out, the driver behind is looking to the right while moving into the space he or she thinks has been vacated. Unfortunately, and without the driver realizing it (usually because of a lack of observation in both directions), when attempting to move, the learner has stopped or stalled the engine (or the instructor may have stopped the car because of approaching traffic). This emphasizes the need for proper route selection according to the student's abilities.

How to avoid rear end collisions

First, keep your distance, slow down earlier and allow the car to run gently to a halt.

Second, act promptly to prevent a pupil from trying to move off at the wrong time. To allow a pupil to move off in this manner, necessitating a stop within a few feet, is potentially dangerous because it also encourages the following driver to move.

Other accident-prone situations

Pay special attention when approaching traffic lights. Because of a lack of understanding of the meaning of the light sequence and colours, some pupils are apt to stop abruptly if the lights change. This can sometimes happen when they have already crossed the stop line.

The right turn at traffic lights is a particularly dangerous manoeuvre, and careful attention should also be paid when emerging from blind junctions, or where parked vehicles or other obstructions restrict visibility. As well as checking on your pupil's observations, look for yourself and be sure it is safe to proceed before allowing the pupil to go.

You must remember that inexperienced learners will not be as quick off the mark as experienced drivers. This can make emerging into busy roads and roundabouts potentially dangerous manoeuvres. Again, choose your routes to match your pupil's ability.

Be ready to compensate for any sudden movement of the car during low-speed manoeuvre exercises. A slight error on the part of your pupil could have disastrous consequences.

When emerging from junctions, pay particular attention to the blind areas behind your pupil's head. At the same time, position yourself so that you do not restrict the pupil's sightlines. Always make sure for yourself that your pupil is emerging safely.

Assessments and standards

To be able to judge how effective your teaching is, you will need to be able to properly assess your pupils' performance as they progress through the different stages of learning to drive. The elements you will need to be able to assess are:

- knowledge;
- skill;
- attitude;
- personality.

The different methods of assessment needed to keep a check on progress are:

- interviews/oral (Q&A);
- written tests/examinations;
- objective tests;
- aptitude tests;
- practical tests.

As an instructor you will mainly be concerned with assessing the practical skills involved in the driving task. However, because effective driving needs an understanding of the rules and regulations, you will also need to test your pupils' knowledge of *The Highway Code* and other relevant motoring matters, either orally or by setting written papers at intervals throughout the course.

To assess the effectiveness of your training you will need to:

- ascertain the level of the pupil's ability at the beginning of his or her course;

- discuss what the pupil should know and be able to do as he or she progresses through each stage, by specifying objectives for each topic;
- assess the pupil's ability at the end of the course.

Initial assessments

To make an initial assessment of current knowledge and skill, you will need to use a mixture of interview technique and aptitude testing. From information gained, you will then be able to establish a base from which to commence your tuition.

Adapting your instruction

As a driving instructor you need to be able to adapt the style of your teaching methods to suit the ability of the person you are teaching. Your instruction and approach with someone who has never driven before should be totally different from that applied to a driver with years of experience. You should find it much easier to develop efficient skills and safe attitudes in the new learner than in trying to change the style of the experienced driver who has recently been ordered to take an extended test.

Dealing with new pupils

The first lesson It can be helpful to find out a little about pupils prior to their first driving lesson, particularly if they have any disabilities that could mean you need to adapt your teaching methods. You can do this by asking a few relevant questions when you are making the booking.

If you are picking up the pupil, it is important that you look professional. Be punctual and make sure your car is clean and tidy.

Use this lesson as an opportunity to get to know each other, establish a form of address (this is often dictated by the age and background of each pupil), and find out what the pupil already knows and can do. It's important that you use a first meeting to build up pupils' confidence in you and to get them used to your style and terminology. Reassure them that learning to drive can be enjoyable, and motivate them by confirming that driving is an asset, and also that if you work together it will be much easier.

Pupils with no experience For pupils with no previous experience, drive to a quiet location and explain how to get into the car safely, and about the function and use of the main controls. Depending on the pupil's ability and the length of the lesson, by the end of it the pupil should have had some experience in moving off, stopping and changing gears. This initial success will go a long way to satisfy his or her expectations.

Pupils with some experience For those with previous experience, use Q&A to confirm the standard they have reached. However, do not rely entirely on what you are told – some learners are not as good as they think, others understate their ability. It's vital that you make your own assessment by asking a few relevant questions and then select an appropriate route so that you can validate what you have been told. Confirm, and make allowances for, the differences in your car and the one the pupil has been driving.

During the drive, be prepared to adapt your terminology if the pupil appears not to understand you. Only when you have carried out this process can you establish the level of instruction to be used and the point in your syllabus at which to begin.

Dealing with full licence holders

When assessing or training experienced drivers you need to exercise a great deal of tact and diplomacy. Do not make the mistake of treating them as learners – treat them as equals. For example, if habits such as crossing hands on the steering wheel have been practised for 20 years, you should not expect to completely eradicate this style. As long as the car is under control, and is in the correct position on the road, try not to over-emphasize the fault. You may find the driver feels you are 'nit-picking'. This could result in resentment to the point where no learning or improvement takes place in more important areas such as forward planning, hazard awareness and anticipation. This is where your coaching skills will be important.

Where weaknesses in style of driving and knowledge are apparent, advise and give valid reasons for adapting and changing. A very common example is where drivers change down through all of the gears because this is how they were originally taught. Give them a few reasons for 'selective' gear changing, such as:

- it involves less work using the controls, which allows more attention to be paid to the all-round situation;
- your hands are on the wheel longer, especially when braking;
- it saves wear and tear on the clutch and gearbox;
- it's better for fuel economy.

You should find that reasoning is a more positive way of changing attitudes!

Licence and eyesight check

No matter what the level of experience of your client, it's your responsibility to ensure that they are legally entitled to drive your car. Check the licence details. If the licence is not produced for any reason, ask for it to be brought on the next lesson. If you are in any doubt, it may be advisable to postpone the lesson.

You should also check for yourself that the pupil can read a number plate at the prescribed distance. If he or she cannot read it, or has problems with some letters or numbers, try several plates. If difficulties persist and you are not satisfied, postpone the lesson and advise the pupil to have an eyesight test.

Getting to know your new pupil

During the drive to a suitable training area, establish previous experience and other details. Avoid long periods of silence as these can increase tension, particularly if the pupil is already feeling a little apprehensive. An informal chat will help the pupil to relax, and it can also:

- help break the ice by relieving initial tension;
- help keep the pupil's mind occupied if he or she is anxious;
- provide you with some outline information on which to base your objectives.

Do not press too hard if pupils are reluctant to talk about themselves. Other opportunities will arise later. On the other hand, some pupils will be more talkative – this could be to cover up anxiety on their part. In any case, keep the conversation professional, polite and sympathetic.

Try to keep your questions relevant. You could include:

- Are you still at school or college?
- What kind of work do you do?
- What interests or hobbies do you have?
- Why do you want to learn to drive?
- Do you have any previous experience in driving a car, riding a bicycle or motorcycle?
- Do you have any particular worries about learning?

Outline the course objectives

Outline the progressive stages of learning to drive. Explain that everyone is different and reassure your pupil that the course will be structured to suit his or her own capabilities.

Selecting a suitable route

When choosing a route for initial assessments, as far as the local road layout will allow, the following should be taken into consideration:

- It should be suitable for the absolute novice.
- It should be flexible enough to allow for progression to intermediate routes where pupils' ability to cope is satisfactory.
- For those with previous experience, the route should begin in a quiet area, affording the opportunity of familiarizing them with your car. It should then become progressively more difficult. Make sure, however, that it is possible to escape from the more difficult areas if the pupil is unable to cope.

Driver's record

To be completely professional and to retain credibility, it is increasingly important to keep accurate records of pupils' progress and achievements in line with the industry code of practice. For this reason, the DSA has introduced a 'Driver's Record' system. The Driver's Record has been designed and produced by the DSA to help instructors and pupils keep a check on progress during a course of training, and to provide an accurate record of the pupil's level of ability.

The system is based on the official syllabus for learning to drive. It covers all the skills required for safe driving, and should be completed by instructor and pupil on each lesson. A personalized booklet for the pupil and a set of record sheets for the instructor are included. Additionally, the instructor is provided with a set of guidance notes and details of the competencies required for each item in the syllabus.

The Driver's Record is a way of helping both you and the pupil to identify areas where the pupil's skills and understanding need to be developed. It includes a list of 24 skills that are normally covered in the practical driving test and spaces for you to fill in as the pupil progresses through five levels of ability.

The five levels are defined as:

- Level 1: the skill is introduced;
- Level 2: it can be carried out under full instruction;
- Level 3: it can be carried out correctly when prompted;
- Level 4: it rarely needs to be prompted;
- Level 5: the pupil can carry it out all the time without any prompting.

The record helps to remind the pupil about what they are trying to achieve, how to get there and how far they have got.

Copies of the complete system for both pupils and instructors are available from test centres, or may be downloaded from www.direct.gov.uk/en/Motoring. An integral part of the Record allows the pupil and instructor to monitor progress on each topic through the various stages of learning:

- topic introduced;
- pupil under full instruction;
- prompted practice;
- seldom prompted;
- independent.

The main advantages of a Driver's Record (or 'log book') include:

- It enables a structured approach to training and skill development through a written record.

- Both the instructor and the pupil are focused on the need to combine structured formal training and private practice where appropriate.
- Pupils and instructors are encouraged to expand on the learning process beyond the requirements of the 'L' test.
- Pupils are encouraged to gain experience in a wide variety of road and traffic conditions until each part of the syllabus has been achieved.

The inclusion of a 'declaration of test readiness' raises the pupil's awareness of the need to be fully prepared before taking the test.

Patterns of errors

A properly kept progress record will show where any distinct patterns of errors are developing that might otherwise not be so obvious. If allowed to go unchecked, these errors could eventually mean the difference between a pass or a fail of the driving test.

Assessment reports

Where relatives or employers are paying for lessons/assessments you may be required to provide reports. These need not necessarily include detailed information on faults, but they should give a clear and honest outline of the pupil's performance. In certain cases a prospective employer may require a more in-depth assessment before employment is granted.

The following general headings may assist in formulating your reports:

- Knowledge of *The Highway Code* rules and driving procedures.
- Attitude to speed and the safety of other road users.
- Attitude to lessons and the driving test.
- Vehicle control skills.
- Vehicle sympathy.
- Visual and perceptive ability.

Pass Plus syllabus

Pass Plus consists of six separate training modules covering:

- town driving;
- all-weather driving;
- driving out of town;
- night driving;
- driving on dual carriageways;
- driving on motorways.

Town driving

After an introduction to Pass Plus and an explanation of the aims and objectives of the course, you should include in the practical session:

- observations, judgement and awareness;
- eye contact;
- consideration for vulnerable road users;
- keeping space around your car.

All-weather driving

This section should include:

- correct speed;
- safe stopping distances;
- seeing and being seen in:
  - rain
  - sleet, snow and ice
  - mist and fog
  - bright sunshine;
- skidding:
  - causes and prevention
  - correcting slow-speed skids
  - braking on poor surfaces
  - aquaplaning.

Driving out of town

This module, which would be on country roads, will deal with the main differences between town and country driving including:

- observation of the road ahead;
- making progress safely;
- bends, hills, uneven roads, dead ground;
- keeping a safe distance from the vehicle ahead;
- overtaking safely;
- being aware of and showing consideration for:
  - pedestrians, horse riders and animals in the road
  - farm entrances
  - slow-moving vehicles.

Night driving

For this section of the syllabus, you need to cover the main aspects of driving at dawn and dusk, as well as in the dark, and in particular:

- the importance of the correct use of headlights;
- adjusting to dark conditions;
- judging speed and distances;
- correct use and care of lights;
- dealing with dazzle;
- road users who can be difficult to see;
- parking.

Driving on dual carriageways

Driving on this type of road requires particular skills:

- effective observations;
- use of mirrors and checking blind areas;
- judgement and planning well ahead;
- safe separation distances;
- joining and leaving dual carriageways;
- lane discipline;
- overtaking;
- correct use of speed.

Driving on motorways

Ideally, this module should be a practical session on a motorway. If this is not possible, then a theory lesson is acceptable, but the pupil should have a motorway drive as soon as practicable so as to put the theory into practice.

Either way, the training should include:

- planning journeys in advance;
- joining and leaving motorways;
- using slip roads properly and effectively;
- safe speeds for varying circumstances;
- effective all-round observations;
- signs, signals and markings;
- overtaking and lane discipline;
- courtesy towards other road users;
- motorway fatigue;

- breakdown procedures;
- use of lights and hazard warning lights;
- debris on the carriageway;
- crosswinds.

Pupils are allowed to take Pass Plus within a year of passing the driving test to qualify for reduced rates of motor insurance from several companies.

For details of the Pass Plus scheme, see page 21.

'L' driver errors

Driving errors range from those with sometimes very simple causes, to those caused by the pressures and stress built up by driving in complex traffic conditions. Simple causes can range from unsuitable shoes being worn to an incorrect seating position. Both of these could make control of the pedals extremely difficult and result in loss of concentration. Make sure your pupils seat themselves correctly when they get into the car.

The tensions caused by driving in difficult conditions can sometimes result in unusual and possibly dangerous decisions or actions being taken. Avoiding road and traffic situations with which pupils are not yet able to cope should, in most cases, solve this problem.

Poorly developed perceptive skills frequently result in inexperienced drivers approaching hazards at excessive speed. This usually results in rushed actions when carrying out the manipulative skills, and this in turn will result in errors in vehicle control. This problem can be avoided by your giving your instructions early enough for pupils to respond, and encouraging them to slow down sufficiently to maintain control.

The types of errors committed vary considerably according to the particular stage of learning reached. The aptitude and attitudes of pupils also influence the mistakes made. Most errors in the early stages of learning cannot seriously be considered as driving faults as they are usually caused through lack of knowledge or practice. However, unless nipped in the bud, they may well develop into driving faults.

A lack of understanding of new information may also cause errors. Many such problems are intensified by lack of sufficient practice in basic car control skills. This initial 'familiarization' should be carried out in relatively safe surroundings on suitably quiet routes.

You must remain acutely alert for any unusual, sudden or excessive movements with the steering or other controls, particularly during the initial stages of learning. No matter how good your instructions may be, you should not assume that the pupil will carry them out. Initially, most learners have difficulty in co-ordinating their hands, feet, steering and observations. You must allow for this and give full talk-through until these skills develop.

Some of the main causes of basic driver error are:

- lack of knowledge;
- conflicting knowledge;
- underdeveloped perceptive skills;
- lack of or inadequate observations and/or misinterpretation of visual information;
- deficiencies in the basic manipulative (car control) skills;
- deficiencies in behaviour caused by timidity or aggressive and irresponsible attitudes;
- poor health, fatigue, drink, drugs, emotional stress.

Note: the learner driver may often be subject to considerable pressure when having to interpret verbal directions while, at the same time, attempting to assimilate other instructions on the move. Do not overload the pupil with too much information, as this can result in lack of attention to the task in general.

General errors

Poor car control Inadequate car control can usually be traced to insufficient practice at a basic skill, incorrect training and the interference of previous knowledge or practice, lack of knowledge, poor coordination, hurried movements, and excessive speed.

Persistent excessive use of speed Excessive speed is often attributable to an unsafe attitude, incorrect use of the footbrake, lack of awareness of potential or actual danger, or poor perception of speed.

Lack of awareness of potential or actual danger This fault is very common and generally caused by a lack of experience, knowledge, imagination or visual scanning. If a pupil is passively observing a traffic scene, it does not imply that he or she will take any action on a developing traffic hazard.

Indecision This can be associated with lack of confidence, poor control skills, lack of knowledge, timidity or the conditions being too busy for the pupil's ability. Indecision and/or an unwillingness to give way, slow down or stop for a hazard is often caused because pupils lack confidence in their basic ability to move off again. They often fail to recognize that slowing down early will alleviate the situation by creating more time for it to clear, thereby often reducing the need to stop.

As a driving instructor, it is your responsibility to ensure that your pupils attain as high a standard as possible, taking into consideration their own individual abilities. You need to aim for a high standard of driving at all times and at all levels. Try to offer as wide a scope of driver education as possible. This will mean that your work is more interesting, varied and satisfying.

Assessing progress

Question and answer (Q&A) technique

It is your responsibility to produce responsible drivers who will be able to cope safely and effectively with today's complex road and traffic conditions – and also to share the road with all of us. To do this you will need to learn how to use the Q&A technique to encourage pupils to look and plan well ahead, and respond early to developing situations.

Teaching usually involves a progression from the known to the unknown. At the beginning of each lesson recap on what a pupil already knows and can do, then introduce new information at a level to suit his or her knowledge and ability. By asking relevant questions throughout their training, you will discover whether pupils are learning the appropriate rules and procedures outlined in *The Highway Code* and other official publications.

Questions should be short, to the point and phrased in a way that encourages the required response. Begin questions with 'How', 'Why', 'What if', 'When', 'Where' or 'Which'. Sometimes questions will only have one correct answer. If this is the case, make sure the question is phrased so as not to mislead.

'Do you know the main causes of skidding?' A correct response could be either 'Yes' or 'No'.

'What do you know about correcting skids?' This could result in the pupil saying 'Nothing'.

Neither of these responses would be what you were looking for. The questions would have been more direct if phrased as follows:

What is the main cause of skidding?

How would you correct a skid where the rear of the car is sliding to the left?

Allow pupils time to think when using more open-ended questions, such as 'When driving along, what kind of things should you be looking out for in this situation?' Don't worry about short silences – your pupil will need time to interpret the question, search for the answer and then find the words with which to express the answer.

If the pupil is having obvious difficulty in responding, phrase the question differently or give some clues about what you are looking for. For example you might add, 'Think about the movement of other road users' or 'What about the restrictions to your sightlines?'

Listen carefully to what the pupil is trying to say and make the most out of incorrect answers! Give a little praise for partially correct or thoughtful answers before discussing any further information.

Avoid questions that go far beyond what the pupil is likely to know. You could easily cause embarrassment if he or she is never able to give you a correct answer.

The timing of questions can be as important as the wording. While the car is on the move, avoid asking questions that need a lot of thought. This can be a distraction and cause the pupil to lose concentration on the driving task.

If you want to find out what your pupil is thinking about a particular situation, keep your questions simple. For example, if you see a dog wandering about near the pavement edge you could ask, 'What can you expect that dog to do?'

Each learning session should conclude with a few questions to ensure the student understands the main points. Q&A can be very effective for a 'recap' at the end of the lesson. It can also be useful as revision on subsequent lessons.

Throughout their training, students should be encouraged to ask you questions relevant to the points under instruction. If irrelevant ones are asked, rather than giving no response at all, answer them simply and confirm that you will cover this subject in detail at a more appropriate time.

Highway Code and driving-related questions

New drivers generally need some kind of motivation to get them to read the official publications. Continually verbally emphasizing the importance of *The Highway Code* and other publications and their relevance is not always enough. Asking questions that relate directly to the topic under instruction can do much to change attitudes towards learning the rules and procedures. Explaining what should be done and, most importantly, why it should be done, will encourage a better understanding.

A few simple questions and words of encouragement will also help to arouse a degree of interest and a willingness to work with you. You could organize between-lesson projects and provide self-test exercises consisting of multiple-choice objective questions. Supply an answer code to enable students to check their scores.

Objective questions

These are designed so that pupils have to select a response from several answers. For example:

1 Triangular signs usually give:
  (a) orders
  (b) warnings
  (c) information

2 Tyres must have a minimum legal tread depth of:
  (a) 1 mm
  (b) 2 mm
  (c) 1.6 mm

Short-answer questions

These require a specific answer and can be used to reinforce particular learning points. For example:

3 Give reasons for each of the following. Drivers:

(a) must allow adequate clearance for parked cars

(b) should reduce speeds in busy shopping areas

(c) should take extra care on country roads without footpaths

Examples of questions more commonly used in driving instruction and testing are:

What is the stopping distance when driving at 30 mph in good conditions?

Give six examples of places unsuitable for parking.

What are the characteristics of a safe parking position?

Designing questions

Questions should be written simply, so as not to mislead. For example, 'What must you not do before turning right?' is a negative question. After considering this question, you should find two basic flaws which could prove counter-productive if put to a novice:

- Because the question asks what not to do, the learner will probably go up a number of 'blind alleys' prior to reaching the correct answer. There are literally dozens of correct and sensible answers. While occasionally there may be justification for this type of question, it is normally far better to use questions that require a positive and constructive response.

- Changing the question to 'What must you do before turning right?' narrows down the field of correct answers. Remember, while this is a better question, the word 'what' still implies that a specific answer is required. However, there is not one specific answer as the full procedure for turning right involves several actions.

If you require a short, exact response then more information should be included in the question. For example:

What must you do before signalling to turn right?

When turning right into a side road, what must you particularly look out for just before turning?

What position should you be in for turning right on a wide road?

If a more general answer is required, the question could be phrased as follows:

Outline the basic procedure for turning right into a side road.

While this kind of question may frequently be necessary, one of the problems is that it also puts on trial a pupil's ability to communicate. The procedure may be understood but the pupil may have difficulty in explaining the details. Patience and understanding should be exercised, and where necessary, give further help by asking different questions of a more specific nature.

Practical assessments

To assess progress, you need to take pupils into traffic conditions appropriate to their experience and then observe their behaviour. This type of assessment is mainly of a visual nature and consists of watching the pupils' actions in the car. You need to constantly be monitoring their use of the controls, instrumentation, mirrors and ancillary equipment, and behaviour towards the external traffic situation.

You should guard against watching the pupil too intently, as this may result in your missing important changes in the situation to which your pupil should be responding; and against watching the road and traffic too intently, as you may miss faults of a physical nature inside the car, such as an incorrect signal being given, riding the clutch, poor mirror use, or attempting to select a gear with the clutch engaged.

You will need to divide your attention over a wide range of your pupil's activities in fairly rapid succession, and in order to maintain safety, you also need to be reading the road and traffic conditions.

There are some areas where prolonged observation of the pupil will be required so that a thorough assessment may be made. These are observation of his or her use of all mirrors, and the pupil's pattern of observations on the approach to, and emerging from, different types of road junctions. In order to limit the time required to check on mirror use, and also to leave you with more time to keep in touch with the all-round traffic situation, an additional mirror can be discreetly focused on to the pupil's eyes. This extra mirror does away with the need to look directly at pupils at appropriate times when a check would be required.

Looking at pupils often serves as a prompt for them to check mirrors or make some others form of visual check they might otherwise have forgotten to do. Reducing these prompts will allow you to make an entirely objective assessment. Similarly, unless they are intended to be prompts, you need to be extremely discreet with your observations of the road and traffic situation at junctions and during any of the manoeuvre exercises.

Intermediate assessments and tests of students' knowledge and ability are an integral part of a teacher's work, and a considerable amount of your time will be involved directly in this ongoing process.

Mock tests

An objective assessment is one that measures a learner's actual performance against a pre-fixed standard. For the ADI, this pre-fixed standard is the 'perfect driver'. It is a satisfactory yardstick by which any level of driving can be measured.

The perfect driver can be defined as one who:

- is in complete harmony with the vehicle and traffic conditions;
- is always in the correct position on the road;
- is travelling at a safe speed for the conditions and visibility;
- has the ideal gear engaged to suit the varying speed and power requirements.

This 'perfect' driver is totally aware of the surroundings and shows consideration for the rights of other road users. Technically, anything that detracts from this perfection is an error. However, perfection to this degree is extremely rare, even in an experienced driver and it would be unrealistic to expect an inexperienced learner to achieve this standard. It is therefore necessary to devise some means of grading faults whereby significantly more importance is attached to serious and dangerous faults than to those of a minor nature.

You should try not to class driving errors as either 'black' or 'white'. There are many shades of grey, and when assessing the seriousness of a fault, you need to bear in mind that an error can involve varying degrees of importance, and that some errors are of a more serious nature and can result in more severe consequences than others.

Continuous assessment

This type of assessment is more sensitive to the needs of the learner progressing through a course of lessons than is the more decisive objective assessment previously discussed. During the early stages of learning, it is unreasonable to compare the performance of the novice with the 'perfect driver'. Although assessments should be objective, they should also take account of previous experience, practice and general progress, as well as the learner's capability. They should take into consideration the reasons that faults may be occurring.

Continually look for ways to correct faults and encourage your pupils to have a greater understanding of their causes. If you do this, the pupils' overall knowledge and driving performance should improve.

When a learner makes a mistake there is usually a valid reason for it: for instance there may be a basic misunderstanding of what is required. If there is a recurrence of errors you will need to cure them at source rather than superficially treat the symptoms.

There are literally hundreds of different errors waiting to be committed by the learner. Their causes are fewer. If you concentrate therefore on curing the cause, improvement should result in other areas where similar mistakes may be occurring. For example, if a pupil is having difficulty steering around a corner because of lack of time, it is the speed on approach that needs to be worked on.

The 'halo effect'

It isn't possible to remove the human element from driver assessments! If you develop a particular regard for a pupil with whom you get on well, it's possible to subconsciously ignore minor errors. You may even gloss over those of a more serious nature. Without realizing it, you may even select an easier route for the pupil by avoiding some of the more difficult situations. Acceptance that this phenomenon, known as the 'halo effect', exists is in most cases sufficient to guard against it. Try to remain objective, otherwise your pupils may suffer in the long term.

To a certain extent the opposite can also occur with an unpopular client. In this case you may subconsciously treat relatively minor errors as more serious ones; and perhaps fail to notice improvements in performance and give credit where it's due.

Disabilities and Impairments

10

As a professional driving instructor you will need to have a working knowledge of how to teach people with disabilities to drive. This chapter outlines some of the things to consider when teaching people with disabilities to drive. It covers topics such as making preliminary assessments, vehicle modifications and adaptations, methods of teaching, notes on some disabilities, how to apply for the driving test, how the test differs, and driver licensing. We will also deal with factors that might affect the driver's performance, including learning difficulties, physical stature, ill health, drugs, stress, illness and ageing.

The present standards for driving instructor training[1] do not include a practical assessment of your knowledge and abilities in dealing with disabilities and impairments. However, according to the Disability and Equality Act 2010, adjustments have to be made for people with disabilities when accessing services where it is reasonable for the service provider to make these adjustments.

Previously, adjustments to policies, practices and procedures had to be made by service providers only where it would otherwise be 'impossible or impracticable' for someone with a disability to use the service. Now, under the new Act, adjustments have to be made where disabled people experience a 'substantial disadvantage'. This means that you may have to make more adjustments and may be legally obliged to provide driving lessons to someone with an impairment when asked because training is a reasonable adjustment, as is the provision of minor adaptations.

Getting further training in this field will enhance your CPD[2], give you a wider client base and will also give you alternative methods for overcoming difficulties your more regular pupils may be having.

1. 2010. Under the 'modernizing driver training' programme the DSA are currently reviewing driving instructor training.
2. CPD: Continuing Professional Development. For details see Chapter 1.

Assessing the needs

Many thousands of people with disabilities have passed the driving test and are regular, safe and competent drivers. Teaching driving to people who have disabilities is essentially the same as teaching anyone else. The subject matter is exactly the same – you merely have to adapt how you teach it, and take into consideration each individual pupil's needs and their medical conditions.

This type of driving instruction can be extremely rewarding. Very often pupils with some form of disability are highly motivated to do well and gain or regain their independence. You are also likely to be teaching experienced drivers to adapt to a different method of car control; this may involve a different style of teaching/coaching than with novice drivers.

You will need to assess your pupil's personal requirements with regard to any necessary vehicle adaptations. For many, all that may be required to control the car effectively could be:

- a car with automatic transmission;
- a steering ball on the wheel;
- power-assisted steering;
- wedge-style cushion.

Adapting your car will mean that you can attract a wider range of clients. Some of the more common modifications include:

- hand-operated accelerator and brake;
- accelerator pedal swappable to the left side of the brake pedal;
- bolt-on extensions to the pedals;
- panel attached to a steering aid for operating secondary controls.

For those with more complex conditions, a range of high-tech adaptations may need to be considered. Recent developments in technology, such as joystick steering and remote control devices, have given the freedom of driving to those with little movement or strength.

Preliminary assessments

There are many centres in the UK offering advice, information and assessments. A list of these is given in the 'Useful Addresses' section of this book. These centres offer advice on the different vehicle adaptations available to compensate for physical limitations.

Car adaptations may be all that are required for people with physical disabilities such as arthritis or those caused through spinal injuries. However, if there is a possible difficulty with a person's learning capability or ability to cope with the cognitive demands of driving, then a more comprehensive assessment will be required. This type of assessment may be particularly appropriate for people diagnosed with:

- stroke;
- hydrocephalus;
- cerebral palsy;
- head injuries;
- marked general learning difficulties (even in the absence of physical disability).

Several specialist assessment centres around the country offer 'medical fitness to drive' assessments. This type of assessment forms an invaluable information resource for the pupil and the instructor, providing information on relevant aspects to be especially aware of during tuition.

Most centres offer a free advice service; however, there is normally a charge for the assessments. This will depend on the scope of service and facilities required. It is sometimes possible to obtain a subsidy for these fees from an appropriate disability group, for example ASBAH (Association for Spina Bifida and Hydrocephalus). The Department of Social Services at your local council, or a fundraising organization such as the Rotary or Lions Clubs, may also be able to help.

It is certainly sensible to invest in a professional assessment to find out probabilities of driving, prior to investing large sums of money in a vehicle and adaptations.

An assessment centre should provide information on:

- eligibility to apply/reapply for a provisional or full driving licence;
- possible learning or other difficulties during the learning/retraining period;
- suitable cars and adaptations;
- conversion specialists and local driving instructors registered to teach those with disabilities.

Notes on disabilities

Cerebral palsy   This condition, present from birth or infancy, can be caused by birth injury or by the baby and mother having incompatible blood groups. It can lead to stiffness, clumsy movement and difficulty with walking and expressive or receptive language difficulties. Speech problems sometimes mask an alert and lively intelligence. Extra work may be needed in practising coordination of car controls.

Spina bifida   This is a failure of the spine to form normally, and involves the spinal cord. At its most severe it can mean deformity of the spine, loss of feeling from the waist downwards and inability to control the bladder and bowels. Gaining independence as a driver may involve the need for assessment at a specialist mobility centre for advice on transferring into the vehicle and wheelchair stowage methods. Sitting height and sitting balance may need attention. Reduced sitting balance can affect coordination of the controls.

Hydrocephalus This means 'water on the brain' and may be associated with spina bifida. It will have been treated medically by the time people are mature enough to drive. It sometimes leads to damage to parts of the brain dealing with concentration, memory and perception, this may make learning slower and more challenging.

Stroke This is caused by a bleed or clot in the brain that interrupts the blood supply to part of the brain. It is common to assume that the resulting physical paralysis of one side of the body is the only problem. The brain damage causing the paralysis can also cause visual perceptual disturbance (affecting vehicle positioning skills) and information processing difficulties (affecting quick thinking and decision making). Loss of visual field can cause lack of visual awareness on one side. Expert assessment is needed to ensure that the legal standards for driving are met and that difficulties can be overcome. An assessment at a specialist mobility centre prior to rehabilitative tuition is recommended.

Paraplegia This affects the lower half of the body. It is nearly always caused by damage to the spinal cord from an accident. The level of the injury determines the amount of weakness and whether the result will be a spastic (stiff) or flaccid (floppy) weakness. Transfer methods, sitting balance, pressure care and wheelchair loading as well as the choice of hand control styles will need assessing.

Parkinson's disease Reduced coordination and ability to use the car controls efficiently is the presenting problem. Initiating a movement is often difficult, making reaction times too slow. Later in the course of the disease, thinking processes can become slow and some dementia-like changes can occur. The involuntary movements of Parkinsonism can be controlled with medication, but it is imperative that the driver takes the medication at the correct time as physical performance can deteriorate immediately prior to a dose being due. Reducing the physical coordination required by selecting a car with automatic gears and driving it with only the right hand (on a steering aid) and the right foot on pedals can help someone with Parkinson's disease to maintain control more easily.

Cerebellar disease This leads to difficulties with coordination: patients may stagger and lurch when walking, have difficulty with speaking and are clumsy in movement. It is caused by a problem in the cerebellum such as a tumour, or can result from conditions such as multiple sclerosis.

Multiple sclerosis This is a condition in which the insulating cover of the nerves of the central nervous system and brain is damaged. Once the cover (myelin sheath) is destroyed, conduction down the nerve is impaired. It can cause alteration of feeling, loss of balance, difficulty with vision and, in the later stages, deterioration of the mental processes. It is a disease that 'comes and goes', so thorough and frequent assessment is needed for driving. MS can cause loss of position sense in a limb. It is common for the driver to have good sensation and action in the feet, but to have trouble in finding the pedals accurately. Coordinating feet and hands on the controls can be an issue. Nystagmus (eye wobble) can cause intermittent blurring of vision. Optic neuritis (inflammation of the optic nerve) can cause other temporary visual problems. Some people experience cognitive problems affecting speed of thinking and decision making. Denial of symptoms is a common coping strategy, making tuition more difficult.

Arthritis This means inflammation of the joints, there are two common forms. Osteoarthritis implies premature ageing and degeneration of the joints, which may be precipitated by an injury in earlier life. In rheumatoid arthritis the lining of the joints and other tissues deteriorates with specific injury. There are many conditions allied to, though not identical with, rheumatoid arthritis. It is important to preserve the joints by not straining them at all. If the hands are affected all controls should have chunky grips, steering wheel cover and easy operation. Parking brake and gearshift releases are advised. Lightened power steering can help.

Myopathies This means disease of the muscles, and covers conditions in which there is progressive weakness. Most of these conditions are inherited. Often there is weakness round the shoulder and hips, so aids such as power-assisted steering may be needed. Frequent assessments are needed to make sure a person has not become unfit to drive. There are not usually learning problems with this type of disability.

Time of day for driving lessons and the driving test may have an impact on your pupil's performance. For example, a person with osteoarthritis would probably perform better in the mornings because their joints are usually more painful later in the day. Fatigue and energy conservation can be important factors to take into consideration. Find out from your pupil what suits them best.

Vehicle adaptations

A wide range of modifications is available for drivers with disabilities. In all instances, selecting the correct adaptation to suit the particular qualities of the physical limitation is a specialist exercise. A referral to an assessment centre such as QEF Mobility Services at Carshalton is strongly recommended. Mobility centres are able to offer advice on where to purchase the correct products. The controls available have been categorized under headings to explain the use of these controls. Many adaptations, however, will need to be fitted to cars with automatic transmission.

Seating

A wedge-style cushion is a useful item in your training vehicle. It brings the eye level up without lifting the feet away from the pedals. Any cushions used should always be securely fastened to ensure they do not move when your pupil is driving. Care with seating and posture will ensure your pupil has a good view of the road; they are stable when turning corners and fatigue should be minimized. There are small adaptations that can make getting into and out of the car easier; the seatbelt easier to reach; the parking brake easier to operate; and a simple attached bar to enable the indicators to be operated with the other hand. If necessary, an assessment is available to ensure awareness of correct seating and posture and exact positioning of appropriate cushions and wedges.

Steering

Power-assisted steering can be tailor-made to match the strength of the driver of the particular car; certain manufacturers have this built into the car. For other makes this can be a specialist job. Other vehicles have options such as a 'city button'. This allows the driver to lighten the steering with the press of a button. Most pupils who use one hand to steer need standard power-assisted steering to help them in various exercises; for example, turning the car round in the road or reversing.

If only one hand is used for steering, various modifications are available. Remember that the one hand must also operate secondary controls, so a steering aid alone is insufficient for the one-handed driver. (See 'Secondary controls' on page 324.)

Steering ball for either right or left hand. This is usually placed at 10 o'clock for the left hand or 2 o'clock for the right hand, but it can vary, depending on the pupil's sitting position.

Steering aids come in various shapes and sizes to suit the pupil, such as:

- mushroom grip – this has a broader flat top and usually suits people with smaller hands;
- tulip grip – this is the most common style and suits most people;
- quad grip – this is used by pupils who do not have any finger grip, but have sufficient strength in their wrists to turn a steering wheel;
- glove and peg – this is used where gripping the steering wheel is not possible;
- T bar – this is often useful for drivers with cerebral palsy who have high muscle tone and flexed wrists, they can comfortably hold the grip with the back of the hand towards the steering wheel.

A joystick system may be fitted to an automatic vehicle if a pupil is unable to turn the steering wheel. This can be fitted either to the right or left side of the steering column, and will turn the steering wheel without actually touching it.

Foot steering may be used by pupils who have no useful function in their arms, but have full use of both legs. Shoulder or foot steering can steer the vehicle. The size and angle at which the steering wheel is placed can also be altered.

Brake and accelerator modifications

Foot pedals Both the accelerator and the brake pedal can be levelled to make pedal operation easier; or the pedals can have raised edges to keep the feet in place if using one foot over the brake and one over the accelerator. Foot pedals can be extended for a driver of short stature. A floor raiser would also be required. For those who cannot use the right foot on the accelerator/brake pedals, the accelerator may be moved over to the left of the footbrake on a car with automatic transmission. The use of flip-up pedals or bayonet or wing-nut fitting allows the accelerator to be switched back to the right. For a driver who is used to driving a manual car, the left foot will have a clutch reflex, this causes the potential danger of pressing the left accelerator pedal when intending to press the brake pedal to slow down or stop. Several hours of tuition with a considerable amount of manoeuvring are needed to retrain the driver. For this reason, a person with experience of driving manual transmission cars is usually advised to use alternative controls. An assessment centre would be a good place to seek advice.

Knee controls If the feet are not reliable, but the hip and knee joints are functional, adaptations can be fitted to allow a driver to operate the accelerator/ brake controls with the in and out movement of the thigh.

Hand controls If the lower limbs cannot be used to accelerate/brake, then either hand can be used. The most popular modification is the single combined lever for accelerator/brake. This is placed near the steering wheel and the hand normally pushes away to brake, using the driver's body weight. The accelerator is controlled by pulling towards the steering wheel. There are, however, various types of hand control such as a radial accelerator and a trigger or satellite accelerator. These usually require some form of steering aid. A ring accelerator allows the use of both hands for steering; with a split control the driver pulls the separate levers towards the steering wheel for accelerating and braking; and in a radial servo vacuum unit the driver pushes down towards the floor to brake and pulls up to accelerate. The last two systems mentioned have power-assisted braking. An automatic clutch button on the gearshift would enable the driver to use hand controls in a car with manual transmission.

Joystick   A joystick can also be placed either side of the steering wheel, if the driver is unable to use other methods mentioned for accelerating/ braking. There is also a four-way joystick system for use in an automatic vehicle, which enables a disabled pupil with only one usable limb to drive, these are extremely sensitive controls and specialist training and an off-road track for initial training is necessary before teaching someone to drive using this type of system. The joystick can be placed either side of the steering wheel, and the driver pushes the stick to the right or left for steering and pushes forward and backwards for the accelerator/brake.

Tiller   This system combines steering, accelerating and braking. The steering wheel is replaced by two handles either side of the steering column, and is steered like a motorcycle. Acceleration is achieved by twisting one of the handles, and braking is achieved by pushing the whole steering unit downwards.

Gear selector   This can be modified to suit a driver's restricted movement, either by extending the lever, removing the depressant button or lightening the tension required to move the lever. If this is not possible, an electric system can normally be fitted anywhere in the vehicle.

Parking brake   This can be moved to the right-hand side of the vehicle if the left hand cannot be used. If the left hand can reach the parking brake, but the button cannot be depressed, various aids can be fitted to assist with this. There is a parking brake that is like a stick without a button. This is called a CAM handbrake. It is pushed forward to release or pulled back to secure. Electric parking brakes are available and can be placed anywhere within the car. An extension to the parking brake can be made for convenient use. A foot-operated parking brake can also be fitted to suit the driver.

Secondary controls

Indicators   The driver must, of course, be in complete control of the car and must be able to operate all secondary controls while maintaining efficient, coordinated control of the primary controls.

The minimum requirement, when using the single combined-lever hand control, is a trafficator thumb switch attached to the top of it. Some drivers also have the horn and headlamp-beam control fitted.

For the one-handed driver, an infrared or radio-controlled/Bluetooth switch panel attached to the steering aid is essential. Up to 18 secondary functions can be operated using press buttons or flick switches on the panel while still holding the steering aid.

Both of the above systems are very important from the driving instructor's point of view, as they enable the driver to indicate correctly and in good time. All secondary controls, however, can be placed anywhere in the car to suit the driver's ability, including in the head restraint using the head to operate.

Mirrors

Additional mirrors can be placed in or on the vehicle to suit a pupil who has restricted neck movement. A panoramic mirror is most frequently used. This is fitted over the normal rear view mirror and gives more visibility, especially when reversing. This mirror, used properly in conjunction with the two side mirrors, will satisfy safety standards. Other mirrors can be mounted internally or externally to enable safe observation at various types of junction and blind spot areas.

Impaired vision

Distance vision

The driver must be able to read an old-style number plate from a distance of 20.5 metres, or a new-style plate from 20 metres. If a person has a defective or lazy (amblyopic) eye, at no time should he or she attempt to drive with his or her good eye covered (occluded).

When assessing whether a driver can read a standard number plate, it is advisable to note the following:

1 Whether the eyes are being screwed up noticeably. If so, this may indicate the need for glasses or a change of lenses. The driver should be referred to an optician. If glasses cannot bring the vision up to the required standard, sometimes contact lenses can.

2 Whether the driver is adopting a noticeable head posture, which may be:

(a) chin elevation or depression

(b) face turned to one side

(c) head tilted to one side.

A head posture may be adopted for the following reasons:

(a) to help overcome double vision (diplopia)

(b) to bring a reduced field of vision to the central position

(c) to steady a fine wobble in the eye (nystagmus) if this reduces the vision

(d) to try to improve vision when incorrect glasses are worn.

If the head posture is significant, it is advisable to suggest that the driver seeks the advice of an ophthalmologist regarding the cause and possible treatment.

3 Whether there is a tendency to close one eye. This may indicate diplopia (double vision). If so, and treatment cannot be given to eliminate it, the driver is permitted to cover one eye, provided the visual field in the uncovered eye is sufficient. For driving in the UK, we advise covering

the left eye when the vision in the right eye is satisfactory, as the field of vision to the right is the more useful.

Sometimes only partial occlusion of one lens is all that is needed, but the advice of an ophthalmologist should be sought. The presence of a squint does not necessarily mean that diplopia is likely to be a problem.

Squints   These present no problem to driving, provided that a person sees adequately and that there is no double vision (diplopia).

Double vision   There are varying degrees of diplopia depending on the level of vision in each eye and the separation of the images. Diplopia is usually at its worst when drivers are tired and therefore, if control of the diplopia is possible, they should be instructed when feeling least tired. Prisms are often used to correct this, and if recently given, the driver may need a little time to get used to them. In all cases with constant diplopia, one eye must be covered (occluded) for driving.

Colour vision   Defective colour vision is no bar to driving in most countries. However, it is always advisable to check that a person can assess traffic lights correctly by the position of the colours. Traffic signs are designed to be readable even with no colour vision; however, particular attention should be paid to *Highway Code* studies so that the pupil can recognize all types of signs.

Visual fields   People with constricted vision may drive, provided that there is at least 120° in the horizontal field and that it spans the central area. No one may drive with homonymous hemianopia (half the field missing with a vertical or horizontal cut-off through the centre of the field), or with a total quadrant loss (quarter missing).

Monocular vision   These drivers have no depth perception (stereopsis). Forty degrees of their visual fields will be missing on one side and night-time driving may prove more difficult. They may also find it difficult to judge the speed of approaching vehicles.

Impaired hearing

Deafness is not classed as a driver disability. No restrictions are placed on a full licence when a deaf driver passes the driving test. It will be of benefit for those with any hearing problems, especially the profoundly deaf, to disclose this on the Driving Test Application form (DL26). This will ensure that the driving examiner is properly prepared. Some mobility centres, such as QEF Mobility Services, offer training for teaching deaf pupils to drive. There is also training for teaching driving instructors how to teach deaf pupils.

Other impairments and distractions

Illiteracy, dyslexia and non-English-speaking pupils

Some pupils have difficulty with reading – some may not be able to read at all. This is not a disability and does not necessarily mean that they will have difficulty with learning to drive. There are various ways in which you can help these pupils and these are discussed in the 'Methods of teaching' section of this chapter.

Autism

There is a range of disorders in this spectrum. Symptoms can include difficulty communicating and relating to other people. There is often a tendency to work by rules and an inability to work out the more abstract concepts of driving, making it difficult for such pupils to deal with unusual driving situations. This might include situations where *The Highway Code* rules need to be supplemented by you when you are teaching with situational analysis and a reading of other drivers' non-verbal responses or possibly an unusual response, for example when cars from all directions meet simultaneously at a mini-roundabout or simple use of the English language literally.

Physical stature and ill health

Physical discomfort such as toothache, cramp and natural functions can distract drivers. The performance of even the most skilful of drivers can deteriorate when they are feeling unwell. Alcohol and drugs affect every aspect of the driver's physical and perceptive processes, and some simple cold cures contain drugs that affect driving performance. Some common drugs to be avoided while driving are:

Sleeping pills	Tranquillizers	Antihistamines
Amphetamines	Anti-depressants	Pain killers
Opiates	Belladonna	

Drivers with the following conditions may be taking the above drugs:

Anxiety	Depression	Insomnia
Asthma	Toothache	Indigestion
Headaches	Hay fever	Period pains and premenstrual tension
Colds/flu		

One of the difficulties with helping clients with some of the less obvious difficulties is that they can often go unnoticed for a long time, throughout which period the learners simply struggle on as best they can. Some people with a relatively minor disability may be embarrassed by it and so don't mention it. Others may not admit to having one through ill-founded fears that the instructor might be reluctant to take them on or simply through self-denial. Tact and understanding must be used when dealing with these problems.

In some cases a properly secured cushion may be all that is required. Pedal extensions can be used for people with short legs or small feet. The floor of the car can be easily raised, by placing a board (or similar object) under the heel of the foot (make sure it cannot interfere with the pedals). Mirrors can often compensate for trunk and neck restrictions of movement.

None of us feel well all the time, and your pupils will be no exception. Women in particular may feel less well one week in every four due to the menstrual cycle. Mothers-to-be are not invalids and most of them will not appreciate being treated as such. However, they must be given some consideration, particularly with regard to ensuring the happy event does not occur during the driving test (or, for that matter, during a lesson!). Plan the lessons and test sensibly. Opinions in this respect vary considerably, and the final discretion must be exercised jointly by the instructor and pupil in relation to both lessons and test. Where there is any doubt, the client should seek her doctor's advice.

Alcohol

Alcohol is a drug and was a contributory factor in over 14 per cent of road accidents in the UK in 2007. After just one drink a driver is less able to make decisions quickly or react promptly in an emergency.

After the second drink a driver will become more relaxed, with less concern for normal restraint and attention to detail. There is a further deterioration in mental responses and physical reactions, combined with a slight degeneration in coordination and the execution of manipulative skills.

After the third drink a driver's emotions become more extreme and behaviour exaggerated. The driver becomes more confident, talkative, noisy or morose and there is a further deterioration in reactions, coordination and manipulative skill. Perceptive responses become slower and impossible feats are far more likely to be attempted.

Following the fourth drink there is still further deterioration in coordination to the point of clumsiness. Confidence continues to increase while perceptive skills are unknowingly deteriorating. The driver's levels of attention and powers of discrimination and normal restraint are rapidly disappearing. Impossible feats are even more likely to be attempted.

After the fifth drink normal perception of moving and static objects becomes blurred. It takes longer for the eyes to focus, and speeds and distances are severely misjudged. The driver's ability to make sensible decisions, and react promptly, is totally unreliable, resulting in high-accident-risk manoeuvres being unknowingly attempted.

Some mobility centres, such as QEF Mobility Services, offer a 'Fun Young Drivers' Day' where young drivers are made aware of this drug, together with other dangers such as speeding and lack of responsibilities on road use.

Prescription and non-prescription drugs

Drugs impair driving ability by reducing attention levels, the perception of risk and the ability to make sound decisions quickly and respond promptly to the road and traffic scene. Instructors should be particularly cautious when clients have some temporary illness for which they may be taking drugs. They should be advised to ask their doctors whether any prescribed drug will affect driving ability. They should carefully read instructions on the labels of non-prescribed drugs. It may also be appropriate to offer advice on the use of illegal drugs and their effect on driving.

Amphetamines speed up the nervous system and help users to keep going. While taking this type of drug, users may feel more alert and confident, but when the effect wears off they are likely to feel very tired and depressed.

Barbiturates are used to calm the nerves. They have an effect similar to that of alcohol, but when the effect wears off depression may follow. A combination of barbiturates and alcohol can cause severe depression. Tranquillizers are used by people with nervous and emotional conditions. They cause drowsiness, and the people who take them often combine their use with alcohol, with the likelihood of severe or even fatal consequences.

Marijuana is an hallucinogen which can act as either a stimulant or depressant. It slows mental responses and physical reactions, affects the judgement of time and space, and limits the ability to concentrate on more than one thing at a time.

Fatigue

Fatigue is a temporary condition that impairs the ability of all drivers. It reduces the ability to concentrate, impairs vision and the other senses, makes decisions more difficult, and makes drivers more irritable and so less tolerant with other road users. Fatigue can be caused by a medical condition or as a side effect from medication, constant pain, hard work, lack of rest, emotional stress, boredom, or carbon monoxide poisoning. Contributory factors may include illness, overeating, an overheated car, driving for long distances without rest, bright sunlight or glare from oncoming headlights. Fatigue of physical action and of thinking skills can occur in many neurological conditions, particularly common in a driver with, for example, multiple sclerosis.

Carbon monoxide is discharged by the car's exhaust system. If this is leaking, or if boot seals are not effective, or if the tailgate of an estate or hatchback car is not fully closed, carbon monoxide may find its way into the passenger compartment. It is colourless, odourless, tasteless and poisonous. Keep plenty of fresh air circulating through the car.

The effects of fatigue on driving performance are not always obvious to the driver. They are:

- concentration becomes more difficult;
- the eyes become less active;
- decreased thinking time;
- a slowing of physical reactions;
- increasing difficulty with making decisions.

Symptoms for the instructor to be aware of are:

- consistent late braking;
- slow or erratic decision making;
- reduced hazard awareness and anticipation;
- a general impression of the driver driving on the brake lights of the vehicle in front.

Emotions and stress

Extremes of emotions, such as fear or anger, affect attention levels, perception and response to everyday traffic situations. They limit the driver's ability to reason quickly and logically.

Some medical conditions such as a brain injury have effects on personality, mood and emotional control. Aggression, impulsivity or a volatile nature can be symptomatic. Lack of appreciation of danger is common. Driving is in itself a stressful activity. High levels of frustration or stress can be felt because of the vehicle and traffic environment. Stress can cause excessive overreaction, and this adds even more fuel to the fire. On the other hand, these overreactions may (particularly in the case of new drivers in situations they are not yet competent to deal with) be associated with poorly developed hazard recognition skills, resulting in additional stresses due to late reactions and lack of confidence due to deficient car control skills.

Aggression is characterized by the hostile feelings or behaviour that some drivers display towards others. Mentally healthy people are able to tolerate a degree of aggression towards themselves without retaliation. Some experts claim aggression is linked to an individual's desire to dominate another and to compensate for feelings of inferiority or inadequacy. Others describe it as a surge of destructive feeling provoked by frustration. It is unlikely that aggression can be completely suppressed, and when it manifests itself in new drivers, instructors should direct their attention towards their own driver error rather than other road users.

After brain injury, aggression can be a contra-indication to driving. A specialist assessment is recommended. Young people are generally more at risk because they are less able to control hostile feelings. However, aggressive behaviour is not restricted to any particular age group or gender if drivers are pushed beyond their limits.

Anxiety

Most people get upset and anxious from time to time, particularly when faced with a threat of some kind. Anxiety describes the psychological disturbance characterized by feelings of apprehension. Some people are more susceptible to anxiety than others. This may be due to feeling helpless and alone, or experiencing a deep sense of inadequacy. These feelings are all normal in themselves but they can become over-obtrusive. Anxiety ranges in intensity from a vague restlessness to extreme uneasiness, and is usually accompanied by some kind of physical distress such as a tightness of the chest, dryness of the throat, sweating, trembling or tears.

Anxiety can be caused by financial or business difficulties, uncertainty about how to behave in some circumstances, fear of failure or fear of the consequences of an action. Intense anxiety can sometimes result from seemingly insignificant matters: for example, having dirt on one's shirt or blouse when meeting a stranger. Such exaggerated cases may indicate some subconscious cause relating to forgotten experiences. Anxiety makes it difficult for learners to think, reason or make judgements. It reduces their level of awareness and makes it difficult for them to concentrate on driving or any point under instruction. It results in a low level of retention of new information and skills, panic, reduced physical coordination, forced errors and a high degree of risk taking (to flee the situation). Instructors can assist over-anxious students by:

- creating a confident but relaxed and caring atmosphere;
- giving more reassurance and encouragement;
- using common sense over the task demands to help build up confidence – for example, letting them drive more slowly on routes with reduced task demands until confidence grows;
- seeing if shorter training periods and frequent breaks help;
- ensuring students understand what is expected and why;
- following the structure in Chapter 9 under the heading 'Structuring the learning';
- demonstrating and presenting information as graphically as possible.

Illness

From time to time, everyone has a temporary minor illness such as colds, toothache, headache or stomach upsets. Any of these can reduce attention; impair vision and upset judgement, timing and coordination.

Ageing

Ageing can reduce perception. Thinking processes become slower and manipulative coordination can be impaired. Older people are more set in their ways and will generally find learning to drive more difficult. They tend to be more anxious and their reactions are generally slower. Instructors should not place them under too much pressure or compare their progress with that of younger learners.

Regular eyesight tests are necessary, as deteriorating visual acuity can be so gradual that the driver does not notice. Difficulty dealing with headlight glare at night is common in the older driver, and many give up driving at night as a coping strategy. Choosing quieter times of the day to drive and avoiding right turns are other common strategies for continuing to drive safely up to an older age. Most mobility centres, such as QEF Mobility Services, offer assessments not only of the people with disabilities, but also the elderly who may have concerns with their driving safety as a result of ageing.

Methods of teaching

The rules, regulations and subject matter of driving remain the same (see Chapter 9). However, you will need to adapt your teaching methods and lesson programmes to suit the needs of each of your pupils.

Physical disabilities

For those with mobility difficulties, you may need to allow extra time for getting into and out of the car, and for finding the most comfortable driving position.

Some conditions cause people to tire during the day. It is important for you to discuss this with your pupil and arrange lessons at times of the day when he or she is likely to achieve the best results. This should also be taken into consideration when you apply for the driving test so that his or her concentration and confidence will be at a peak. Consider shorter lessons for people with pain or fatigue or longer lessons for people with learning needs.

Hearing problems

The following is an extract from *Teaching the Deaf to Drive* and is reproduced with the kind permission of the Institute of Master Tutors of Driving:

As the age of 17 must have been reached before a provisional licence can be issued, deaf youngsters, having received their education mainly in special schools or units, have some speech, although this may be difficult to follow. Usually sign language is used, and in addition they will be able to lip-read to a certain extent.

Lip-reading, however, depends as much on the clarity of the speaker's lip movements as on the ability of the deaf person. Young people may have a reading age much lower than the natural age. Consequently, the ability to read and write may be limited. They can, however, be just as bright and intelligent as their hearing peers, and with understanding and patience from the instructor will assimilate all that has to be learnt to drive a motor vehicle.

The problem for the instructor is to learn the best way to impart the knowledge and the skill to the pupil. The essential is, what is the best way of communication?

You do not need to learn the sign language, but it is necessary to use simple, straightforward words, which only have one meaning. For example, 'Do not hug the middle of the road'. The word 'hug' to the deaf has only the literal meaning of someone putting arms round another. Again, 'traffic jam' would not be understood; 'jam' is something one spreads on bread and butter.

It is essential to speak slowly and distinctly, and move the lips to form each word. Do not talk through your teeth. It will be appreciated that this approach means it has to be a face-to-face conversation and can therefore only be utilized in a stationary situation. Never shout – the pupil is deaf.

Due to the lack of hearing, it is vital that all 'conversations' be reinforced by demonstrations. Always be patient. Unsatisfactory response is likely to be the fault of the teacher rather than the pupil.

People who are deaf can normally speak, but it is not always easy for the hearing to understand what they are saying. It is difficult for them to make the sounds which we are used to, as they are unable to hear their own voices. Always have a writing pad ready to hand, and ask the student to write down questions.

Learning the *Highway Code* can be helped if you simplify your language. Formulate questions in written form and have the answers following in the same easy wording.

You may benefit from getting in touch with local associations for deaf people or the Royal National Institute for Deaf People (RNID), 19–23 Featherstone Street, London EC1Y 8SL (tel: 020 7296 8000). They are always very ready to help with any difficulties which may arise.

There are DVDs available with sign language translations of the Multiple-choice Theory Test questions and explaining the Hazard Perception Test. Various courses can be found to help you teach people with hearing difficulties.

Reading and understanding problems

If you have any pupils with difficulties such as dyslexia, or pupils who are non-English speaking, there are various ways in which you can help. Making more use of visual aids during in-car training sessions will help pupils to understand when introducing new topics. Showing them pictures of road signs and markings and explaining their meaning should also help. They will understand *The Highway Code* rules better if they can apply them to on-road situations as soon after learning them as possible. It can be helpful to discuss with family or close friends the subjects currently under instruction, and encourage them to help the pupil by giving some in-between lesson revision and learning exercises. If a student's command of English is inadequate for both training and testing purposes, try to develop some comprehension of the 'key words' described in Chapter 9.

Keep your terminology as simple as possible, and to avoid confusion, make sure you are consistent with the words and phrases you use. It may be advisable to obtain the services of someone known to the pupil to act as interpreter. This can be particularly useful during the training stages because, when the pupil attends the driving test, you will not be able to act in this capacity and the person who has already been present on lessons would be familiar with what is required. Try to give as much encouragement as possible to all of your pupils, perhaps by emphasizing their successes at the practical skills. In no way should you embarrass them or make them feel inadequate – this will do little to gain their confidence in you or themselves. You should introduce independent driving as early as practicable during the training so that this is not a surprise during the driving test. Speak with your local examiners to find out how they can help your candidate through this part of the test.

Applying for the driving test

The procedure outlined in Chapter 11 should be followed when applying for tests for people with disabilities, taking into consideration the following notes. When completing the application form DL26, try to give as much information as possible about the disabilities. If there is not enough room on the form to explain the disability and how the candidate is affected by it, write out the extra information and attach it to the application form. Supplying this information in advance will avoid any possible embarrassment to both pupil and examiner by questions that have to be asked on the day of the test.

When booking a practical test, please let the DSA know if your candidate:

- is deaf or has severe hearing difficulties;
- is in any way restricted in their movements;
- has any physical disability.

No matter how complex a disability might be, the pupil will still be taking the same driving test as every other test candidate. However, more time is allocated for the test. This is to allow the examiner to talk to the candidate about his or her disability and any adaptations fitted to the vehicle. If the candidate is dyslexic, supplying this information beforehand will allow a suitable means of communication to be devised. The senior examiner at the test centre should be informed at least two days before a test appointment where any of the following exist:

- impaired hearing;
- minor restrictions are experienced;
- abnormal stature;
- any disabilities not noted on the application form.

Providing such information may explain to an examiner why certain actions are taken by the candidate and allowances can therefore be made for them. For example, if an examiner knows in advance that a candidate has restricted neck movement, not classed as a disability, and uses the mirrors for making rear observations when manoeuvring, this will be expected and allowed for. If the information is not volunteered, then the examiner can only assume that correct observations are not made and there is no reason for it.

When preparing for the test

By this time you should have ensured that the adaptations used by each individual pupil overcome his or her disability as far as possible. If they do not, then you should advise on any further adaptations that you think are necessary, allowing plenty of time to get used to them. The time allotted for the examiner when testing people with disabilities spans two normal test periods. You should bear this in mind when entering the appointment in your diary.

Attending for the test

Make sure you allow plenty of time for getting to the test centre if the candidate has difficulty getting out of and into the car. Where it is not practical for the candidate to go to the examiner, you may go into the waiting room to inform the examiner that the pupil has arrived. The content and length of the driving test are the same as for standard driving tests but allow more time in your diary for the examiner to complete paper work with the candidate. At the beginning of the test, the candidate will be asked if there are any additional disabilities that are not noted on the application form. Encourage your pupils to be frank about this as it will help the examiner to make an effective and objective assessment. The examiner will also ask about the vehicle's adaptations. Where there are hand adaptations, more emphasis will normally be placed on downhill junctions to check that control is adequate. If a candidate has neck or vertebrae problems, emphasis is normally placed on the ability to make frequent observations at those junctions where sightlines are restricted.

At the end of the test

The examiner has two decisions to make: Does the candidate have the ability to drive? And do the adaptations overcome the disabilities? If the examiner is satisfied that the candidate is competent to drive all unadapted vehicles in the category on which he or she was tested, and in any additional categories covered, a normal pass certificate for that category is issued. If the examiner considers that the candidate can drive unadapted vehicles only of the category on which he or she was tested, but not the additional categories covered, then the pass certificate is issued for that category (eg category B) and a D255 should indicate that the candidate should be restricted to category B vehicles. If the examiner considers the candidate can drive only a vehicle with suitable adaptations, this is indicated on the pass certificate. The appropriate EU code (listed on page 189) is entered on the DSA10. All candidates, whether they pass or fail, are given a copy of the Driving Test Report Form DL25. If a candidate fails and the examiner feels that some other adaptation might enable him or her to pass, an indication of this may be given.

The reporting of driving test results

The results of all tests are reported to the DVLA at Swansea. Any restrictions noted by examiners are then itemized on candidates' driving licences.

Instructor courses

If you are interested in teaching people with disabilities, training courses are available at QEF Mobility Services, Damson Way, Fountain Drive, Carshalton, Surrey SM5 4NR (tel: 020 8770 1151; fax: 020 8770 1211; website: www.qef.org.uk/our-services/mobility-services).

For details of other centres, see pages 413–15.

With grateful thanks to Chris Kingsley and his colleagues at QEF Mobility Services for their assistance in updating and revising this chapter.

The Driving Test

11

The 'L' test for new drivers is conducted in two parts – the theory test (including hazard perception), followed by the practical driving test. Candidates must pass the theory test before they can apply to take the practical driving test. After passing the theory test, the candidate has a maximum of two years in which to take and pass the practical test.

Theory and hazard perception test

Administration

The Theory and Hazard Perception Test is available at about 150 test centres throughout England, Scotland and Wales. The candidate can take the test at any of these centres.

In Northern Ireland the theory test is conducted by the Driver and Vehicle Agency at six locations.

All test centres in Wales, and some in England, are equipped to conduct the test in Welsh. For candidates with special needs such as dyslexia or reading difficulties there is a facility to listen to the test being read in English. Candidates who are not able to read or understand English or who want to take their test in their first language can listen to the test in one of 20 other languages.

For people who have learning difficulties, arrangements can be made for a showing of an 'on screen' video of the test in British Sign Language. Candidates with any other special needs can apply for more time to complete the multiple-choice part of the test.

Booking the test

The test can be booked online, by phone, fax or post.

Online booking

Log on to www.direct.gov.uk. This is probably the quickest and easiest method of booking. You will need the candidate's personal details and credit or debit card details. Confirmation of the date and time of the test is available immediately.

By phone

Applications can be made by phoning the DSA on 0300 200 1122. If you or the pupil need to change or cancel the test the appropriate link is: www.direct.gov.uk/changetheorytest. If you are ringing on behalf of a pupil, you will need to have his or her personal details and driver number. If you are using the pupil's card for payment, he or she must be present when you make the call.

The advantage of this method of booking is that you can discuss alternative dates and times and receive immediate confirmation of the appointment. The disadvantage is that it can sometimes be quite time-consuming to get through the DSA telephone menu system to talk to a booking clerk.

By post

Application forms are available from test centres or from the DSA. Payment can be made by credit or debit card or with a cheque or postal order. The completed application form should be sent to DSA, PO Box 148, Salford M5 3JY. It normally takes about 10 days to receive a reply, and there is no guarantee that you will get the date requested.

By fax

The form should be faxed to 0300 200 1177 together with credit or debit card details. Again, the response time is normally about 10 days.

'Trainer booking'

As a registered driving instructor you can make your test applications online. To do this, you need to register with the DSA for an 'online profile', indicating which test centres you expect to use and up to five credit or debit cards you will use for payment. The website for bookings is available 24 hours, but you can only assign pupils to a test at times when their licence entitlement can be verified by the DVLA.

To register for this service, visit the DSA website at www.dsa.gov.uk/tests.

Test fees

The theory test fee (at January 2011) is £31.
In Northern Ireland the application fee is £30.

Cancelling tests

To cancel or postpone a theory test, at least three clear working days' notice must be given. This period of notice does not include:

- the day of the test;
- the day that the notice of cancellation or postponement was made;
- Sundays;
- public holidays.

This means that you need to give more than six or seven days' notice if there are weekends and holidays involved.

Attending for the test

Your pupils must produce both parts of their photo-card driving licence as visual proof of their identity. In the unlikely event that pupils have the old-style paper licence instead of a photo-card licence, a valid passport must be produced. Pupils should also take with them the appointment card or booking reference details.

The format of the test

The test involves multiple-choice questions, followed by a hazard perception test.

The multiple-choice questions

This part of the test involves answering 50 questions that are displayed on a computer screen. A number of correct and incorrect responses are shown, and the candidate selects his or her choice by touching the screen. To pass, 43 questions must be answered correctly within 57 minutes.

Only one question appears on the screen at a time, and candidates can move backwards or forwards through the questions. This means that they are able to recheck or alter any answers. The system also alerts the candidate if any questions have not been answered.

There is no requirement for the pupil to be computer literate, as members of staff are on hand to assist with any queries or difficulties. A practice session of up to 15 minutes is allowed to enable candidates to familiarize themselves with the system before starting the actual test.

The theory test syllabus

The pupil's knowledge of the following subjects is tested:

- *Alertness:* observation, anticipation, concentration, awareness, distraction.
- *Attitude:* consideration, safe distance, courtesy, priority.

- *Safety and the vehicle:* fault detection, defects, safety equipment, emissions, noise, vehicle security.
- *Safety margins:* stopping distances, road surfaces, skidding, weather conditions.
- *Hazard awareness:* anticipation, attention, speed and distance, reaction time, alcohol and drugs, tiredness.
- *Vulnerable road users:* pedestrians, children, elderly drivers, new drivers, people with disabilities, motorcyclists, cyclists, animals, horse riders.
- *Other types of vehicle:* motorcycles, lorries, buses, trams.
- *Vehicle handling:* weather conditions, road conditions, time of day, speed, traffic calming.
- *Motorway rules:* speed limits, lane discipline, stopping, lighting, parking.
- *Rules of the road:* speed limits, parking, lighting.
- *Road and traffic signs:* road signs, speed limits, road markings, regulations.
- *Documents:* licence, insurance, MOT certificate.
- *Accidents:* first aid, warning devices, reporting procedures, safety regulations.
- *Vehicle loading:* stability, towing;
- uninsured and unlicensed driving;
- eco-driving and environmental issues;
- new motorway signage;
- first aid;
- health and driver licensing.

Case studies

Some of the multiple choice questions are given as case studies. The subject matter of the case study focuses on real-life examples that drivers could come across in normal driving, with five separate questions based on that scenario.

Hazard perception test

After completing the multiple-choice questions the candidate is given a three-minute break before starting the hazard perception test. The test consists of 14 video clips featuring various types of hazard, with each clip lasting about a minute. The candidate has to respond to each hazard by clicking on a computer mouse as each hazard develops. Up to 5 marks can be scored for each hazard; the earlier a response is made, the higher the score. On this part of the test it is not possible to go back to change a response, as the object is to recognize hazards as early as possible.

The hazards depicted are those that would need a response from the driver such as changing speed or direction, or by taking some other form of action.

Sample questions

Q   You are the driver of a car carrying two adults and two children, both of whom are under 14 years of age. Who is responsible for ensuring that the children wear seat belts?

(Select one answer)

a   the children

b   their parents

c   the driver

d   the front seat passenger

A   The correct answer is
c   the driver (*Highway Code*)

Q   You are driving towards a zebra crossing. Pedestrians are waiting to cross. You should:

(Select one answer)

a   slow down and prepare to stop

b   give way to the elderly and infirm only

c   use your headlamps to indicate that they can cross

d   wave at them to cross the road

A   The correct answer is:
a   slow down and prepare to stop (*Highway Code* and *The Official DSA Guide to Driving – The essential skills*)

Q   On which three occasions must you stop your vehicle?

(Select three answers)

a   when involved in an accident

b   at a red traffic light

c   when signalled to do so by a police officer

d   at a junction with double broken white lines

e   at a pelican crossing when the amber light is flashing and no pedestrians are crossing

A   The correct answers are
a, b and c

Candidates are not penalized for clicking on insignificant hazards – they are only marked on the designated developing ones. However, if too many unnecessary responses are made in a very short space of time, a score of 0 might be allocated for that clip. This is to stop the candidate randomly clicking or guessing.

The pass mark for this part of the test is currently set at 44 out of a possible 75, but the DSA constantly review the results and adjust the requirement.

At the end of the test

Candidates are given the result of both parts of the test within a few minutes of completing the HPT test. Feedback is given on any incorrect answers.

Successful candidates are issued with a pass certificate that is valid for two years. The practical test must be passed within this two-year period, otherwise a further theory test needs to be taken.

When applying for the practical test the theory pass certificate number should be quoted.

Test training

To prepare for both parts of the Theory and Hazard Perception Test your pupils will need to study:

- *The Highway Code;*
- *The Official DSA Guide to Driving – The essential skills;*
- *The Official Guide to Learning to Drive;*
- *The Official Theory Test for Car Drivers;*
- *Know Your Traffic Signs.*

For details of these books and other resource material see page 419.

You need to have a thorough knowledge of the contents of all these books to prepare yourself for the ADI theory test. You also need to have an understanding of the syllabus and the various topics so that you can help your pupils prepare for their own theory test.

Your own knowledge and teaching skills will be even more relevant if you are dealing with pupils who have learning difficulties. In these circumstances you will need to use plenty of encouragement, and might involve the pupil's family or friends to assist.

There are many books and CD-ROMs on the market to help with theory training. Some of these materials contain the entire DSA question bank and can be used to aid the learning process. However, you will need to check, by the skilful use of your question and answer technique, your pupils' understanding of the rules and regulations if they are to be able to apply them to the on-the-road situation. Other CDs are aimed at the practical side of the ADI's job, and relate to hazard recognition and awareness.

The DSA has produced programmes for all types of learner, including car, motorcycle, large goods vehicle (LGV) and passenger-carrying vehicle (PCV) drivers. Even if you do not have computer skills or access to a PC yourself, you should make sure that you are able to offer the appropriate CDs to your pupils. Most of them will have these skills and be able to use a computer at home, school or college.

Good instructors will automatically be incorporating hazard perception into their practical training courses. This helps learners to understand how to apply the rules and procedures. After all, how can you teach driving without teaching the rules and regulations and encouraging safe attitudes?

For more information about both parts of the theory test, visit the website at www.direct.gov.uk or phone the DSA on 0300 200 1122.

Preparation for the theory test

The DSA book, *The Official Theory Test for Car Drivers*, offers advice on how to prepare for the multiple-choice part of the theory test and recommends that pupils study the various books from which the questions are taken. You should also use the other resource materials as teaching and study aids. These include:

- *The Highway Code*. Contains the laws that apply to all road users and up-to-date advice on road safety.
- *Know your Traffic Signs*. Contains information and explanations of most signs and road markings.
- *The Official DSA Guide to Driving – The essential skills*. Explains the best driving practices in detail.
- *The Official DSA Theory Test CD ROM for Car Drivers*. Contains all the questions and allows your pupils to practise for the multiple-choice part of the theory test.

All of these books and materials can be obtained from The Stationery Office by telephoning 0870 600 5522 or at www.tso.co.uk. Other suppliers of books and training materials are listed on page 419.

Remember that the theory test questions change from time to time. This can sometimes be as a result of revisions to legislation or because of customer feedback. Make sure that you and your pupils are using the most up-to-date versions of any publications.

Your pupils can also take a mock theory test online at www.theory-tests.co.uk. For a fee of £6.99 you can practise taking the multiple-choice part of the theory test as often as you like within a 30-day period.

Practical test

Administration

This test is administered by the DSA, which is an executive agency of the Department for Transport. The DSA conducts about 2 million 'L' tests on cars and motorcycles every year, as well as administering the vocational tests for LGV and PCV drivers. (Vocational tests are dealt with in Chapter 12 of this book.) In Northern Ireland driving tests are conducted by the Driver and Vehicle Testing Authority.

To ensure uniformity in the conduct of practical driving tests, all the DSA's driving examiners are trained at the Training Centre at Cardington, Bedford. They are monitored regularly and are sometimes accompanied on test by a senior member of staff.

Application

The practical test can be booked online at www.direct.gov.uk/practicaltest. Tests can also be changed or cancelled by using this same website address.

The 'L' test syllabus

You will find the test syllabus in full in *The Official Guide to Learning to Drive*, which is available from most good bookshops. Alternatively, it can be purchased in bulk from Desk Top Driving and other suppliers for selling on to pupils. The book describes in detail:

- the requirements of the test;
- the types of vehicle suitable;
- different categories of driver, such as those with disabilities, hearing and speech problems;
- general road procedures;
- the manoeuvring exercises;
- what the examiner will be looking for;
- the recommended syllabus for learning to drive.

The 'L' test syllabus covers the following main points.

Eyesight test

At the start of the test the examiner will ask your pupil to read a car number plate at the prescribed distance. (To avoid any potential problems on the day of the test, make sure by checking that your pupils can do this a few weeks prior to the test and then check again a couple of days before.)

Safety questions

Before starting the on-road part of the test the examiner will ask the pupil two vehicle safety questions. The subjects covered in this part of the test include:

- tyres and wheels;
- brakes;
- steering;
- engine oil and cooling fluids;
- lights and reflectors;
- direction indicators; and
- audible warning devices.

One of the questions will be a 'show me' type and the other will be 'tell me'. Example questions include:

- *'Tell me* how you would check that the engine has sufficient oil.'
  The pupil would need to be able to open the bonnet, identify the oil indicator level or dip stick and describe how to check the oil level against the minimum/maximum marker.
- *'Show me* how you would check that the headlights and tail lights are working properly.'
  The pupil should operate the appropriate switches (by turning on the ignition if necessary) and walk round the vehicle.
- *'Tell me* how you would check the tyres to ensure that they have sufficient tread depth and that their general condition is safe to use on the road.'
  The pupil would need to explain to the examiner about 'no cuts or bulges' and about '1.6 millimetres of tread across the central three-quarters of the breadth of the tyre and round the entire circumference'.
- *'Show me* how you would check the parking brake for excessive wear.'
  The pupil would need to demonstrate to the examiner that the brake secures itself when it is applied and that it is not at the end of its working travel.
- *'Show me* how you would check that the power-assisted steering is working before starting a journey.'
  The pupil's explanation should cover the two checks that can be made. Gentle pressure on the steering wheel when starting the engine should result in a slight movement. Turning the steering wheel just after moving off will give an indication that the power assistance is working.
- *'Tell me* how you would check that the brakes are working before starting a journey.'
  Brakes should not feel slack or spongy and should be tested when setting off. The car should not pull to one side.

Safety precautions

Driver checks are carried out including doors, seat, mirrors, seat belts and head restraint. The pupil should adjust these so that he or she is comfortable and can reach all the controls. Before starting the engine, the doors should be shut properly, the handbrake should be on and the gear lever or selector in neutral.

Controls

All the main controls should be handled smoothly. This includes use of the accelerator, clutch, gears, footbrake, handbrake and steering.

Moving away

Moving away safely, under control, on the level, from behind a parked car and, where practicable, on a hill, with correct observations.

Emergency stop

Even and progressive braking is required, avoiding locking the wheels. In wet weather pupils should be aware that it could take twice as long to stop. The emergency stop exercise is conducted randomly on about one test in three.

In Northern Ireland the emergency stop is carried out on all tests.

Reverse to the left or right

Under full control and with reasonable accuracy. Good all-round observations and correct response to others.

Turn in the road

Smooth control with full all-round observations. Correct responses to other road users.

Reverse parking

Either reversing behind one car, between two cars, or the manoeuvre may be carried out in the test centre car park, reversing into a bay. This exercise may be done at the start, during or at the end of the test.

Note: Only one of the three manoeuvring exercises – reverse, turn in the road and reverse parking – is conducted on any particular test.

Use of mirrors

Mirrors should be used regularly and pupils should be aware of the presence of others in their blind spots. Pupils' response to the all-round situation is tested. Early use of mirrors should be made before signalling; changing direction and/or speed; and as part of the mirror–signal–manoeuvre routine.

Signalling

Give signals clearly and in good time to warn other road users of intentions in accordance with *The Highway Code*.

Response to signs and signals

Understand and be able to react to all traffic signs and road markings; check when proceeding through green lights; and respond to signals given by police officers, traffic wardens, school crossing patrols and all other road users.

Use of speed

Safe and reasonable progress should be made according to the road, weather and traffic conditions, the road signs and speed limits. Candidates should always be able to stop within the distance they can see is clear.

Following distance

Maintaining a safe distance from the vehicle ahead in all conditions, including when stopping in traffic queues.

Maintaining progress

Driving at appropriate speeds for the type of road and the speed limit; the type and density of traffic; the weather and visibility. A safe approach to all hazards should be demonstrated without being over-cautious. All safe opportunities to proceed at junctions should be taken.

Junctions

Apply the correct procedure to all types of junctions, including applying the mirror–signal–manoeuvre routine and using the correct lanes. Good all-round observations should be made and safe response to other road users demonstrated.

Judgement

Correct responses when dealing with other road users including overtaking, meeting oncoming traffic and turning across traffic. Other road users should not be made to slow down, swerve or stop.

Positioning

Maintain correct positioning at all times according to the type of road, the direction being taken and the presence of parked vehicles.

Clearance to obstructions

Allow plenty of room when passing stationary vehicles and other obstructions that may be obscuring pedestrians.

Pedestrian crossings

Recognize and respond correctly to the different types of crossing.

Position for normal stops

Choose safe and legal places to stop without causing inconvenience or obstruction to others.

Awareness and planning

Think and plan ahead and anticipate the actions of other road users. Demonstrate safe attitudes when dealing with vulnerable road users such as pedestrians, cyclists, motorcyclists and horse riders.

Ancillary controls

Understand the function of all the controls and switches, especially those that have a bearing on road safety. Appropriate use of indicators, lights, windscreen wipers, demisters and heaters.

Eco-safe driving

During the test the examiner assesses candidates on their ability to drive in a way that shows eco-safe driving techniques. In particular, the examiner assesses control and planning and gives feedback on the efficiency of the driving at the end of the test. This is purely for guidance and does not form part of the criteria for a pass or fail.

Two main areas are assessed. First, control: using all the vehicle controls as smoothly as possible, particularly when starting and moving away, accelerating, using gears and driving at an appropriate speed. Second, planning: anticipating road and traffic conditions and acting in good time, particularly when approaching potential hazards; making use of engine braking when appropriate; and switching off the engine during lengthy stops.

Applying for the practical test

When you feel your pupils have reached a fairly consistent standard, you will need to advise them on applying for their driving test. It is important that you make the decision and the application jointly. This avoids problems arising such as pupils:

- applying independently before they are ready;
- not informing you of the date until it is too late to be postponed;
- being reluctant to delay the test once they have an appointment;
- obtaining an appointment at a time when you may already have another test booked.

Whether or not to apply for the test is one of the most difficult and subjective decisions you may have to make. There are a number of reasons for this:

- From a business point of view, to make sure pupils stay with your school, you may often feel obliged to apply for tests early on during their training.
- Because of pupils' wishes, you may often be put under pressure to apply at the earliest possible date.
- If there is a particularly long waiting list for test appointments in your area, a combination of this with the above two reasons may also affect your decision. However, sometimes an early application might act as an incentive and increased motivation for the pupil.

Where none of these pressures exist to any significant degree, your decision may still not be easy. You must be fair to pupils and not impose standards so high as to absolutely guarantee a pass. It could well mean that pupils feel you are delaying the decision for purely monetary reasons. Apart from this, you can never actually guarantee they will pass!

Pupils will make varying rates of progress at different stages of their training. For example, some make very rapid progress in the early stages, and later, when a higher degree of understanding is required, progress may slow down considerably. Others make very slow progress at first, then make very rapid headway after better understanding is achieved.

Although the DSA try to ensure that tests are usually available within six weeks, the waiting time is occasionally unpredictable in its length. Sometimes, for example if a new examiner is appointed to a centre, you may receive an appointment much more quickly than you anticipated. To ensure that you do not arrange one before the pupil is ready, make sure you specify an earliest date on the application.

It is as well to remember that if you apply for tests too early:

- The test may subsequently have to be postponed. This means extra administration, expense, time and possible ill-feeling, since pupils generally do not like having tests deferred.
- The pupil may not be ready and will probably fail. This may reflect back on you since you were saying, in effect, that when you applied you considered that the pupil was ready for the test.
- Your efficiency record of passes and failures on the DSA statistics will be affected.

If you are applying for a test where there is a long waiting list, you should emphasize to the pupil that the booking is made on the assumption that a reasonable rate of progress will be maintained and that his or her driving will have reached a suitable standard.

Having taken all of this into consideration you can make the application by phone, fax, post or online as shown on pages 337–38. Make sure you give your driving school number as this will avoid problems with double-booked appointments. Most pupils and instructors these days prefer to book online, as it is now possible to use a 'trainer booking' facility and the opportunity to book, cancel or change a booking.

The current fees for 'L' tests (at Jan 2011) are:

Weekday test	£62.00
Saturdays and weekday evenings	£75.00

It is important to keep a record of test applications. For postal applications if an appointment is not received within three weeks, contact the DSA booking clerk to check. Make sure pupils inform you immediately they receive appointments so that the date and time can be entered into your diary and the school car reserved accordingly.

If you are posting the application, it is advisable to accept only cheques and postal orders payable to the Driving Standards Agency. This will ensure that no misunderstanding occurs over the fees paid.

When the appointment card is received you should reserve the time in your diary. It is usual to give pupils a lesson immediately prior to the test. Ensure that on the day they know that payment normally has to cover both the lesson and use of the school car for the test. Some pupils may think that payment of the test application fee also includes your fees.

Application forms (DL26) are available from driving test centres or in bulk from the DSA. Make sure all of the requested information is included to avoid any delays in the allocation of appointments.

The same application form is used when applying for tests for people with disabilities and for drivers who have been ordered to take extended tests. It should be noted that the time for extended tests is double the length of the 'L' test and the fees charged are higher.

For more information on how to apply for tests for people with disabilities see Chapter 10.

Driving test times

Practical tests are normally available at most test centres from about 7.30 am to 4 pm Monday to Friday. The application form allows you to request preferred days of the week and morning or afternoon appointments. If you apply for an evening or weekend test, make sure that your pupil understands that there is a higher fee.

Cancelling and postponing tests

If you feel that the pupil is not yet ready to take the test, make sure he or she understands that it is in his or her own interests as well as those of other road users that you postpone it. Remember, though, that the booking is a contract between the pupil and the DSA – you should not cancel without the pupil's agreement.

The DSA require at least three clear working days' notice for a cancellation; otherwise the fee is lost. You should advise the pupil of the need to cancel at least two weeks before the day of the test and certainly not less than 10 days before.

The pupil may offer resistance to your advice. Be sympathetic and tactful, but firm. Be objective and give the pupil a realistic 'mock test'. This will usually convince even the most adamant that you are acting in their best interests. If the pupil still insists on going against your advice, then all you are entitled to do is withhold the use of your car.

It should be noted that driving examiners may not use the dual controls to avoid an accident unless there is a risk of danger – and then it may only be a last-second decision. Your car may be at risk! The school car is the 'tool of your trade'. It is imperative, therefore, that it is not off the road for unnecessary repairs because you let someone attend for a test too soon.

There are also other considerations. You are depriving other candidates of an appointment, and, more importantly, your reputation could be at risk if you regularly present candidates for test when they are not up to standard.

When you and your pupil have come to a joint decision to postpone a test, you will need to give three working days' notice to avoid forfeit of the fee. Remember that this period of notice does not include Sundays, public holidays, the day of the test and the day of the cancellation. In practice this means that more than a week's notice has to be given – especially if any public holidays are involved. You may simply defer the test to a later date or you may cancel it. If a cancellation is made by telephone and a further appointment is not required, it must be followed up with a request in writing for a refund of the fee. The fee will be withheld pending receipt of this request, which should be made within one week of the cancellation.

Driving test cancellations: the DSA's Compensation Code

Occasionally tests have to be cancelled by the DSA at short notice: this means with less than three clear working days. The DSA will refund the fee or another test will be arranged at no further cost if the test:

- is cancelled by the DSA;
- is cancelled by the candidate and the above amount of notice is given;
- is cancelled by the candidate for medical reasons and a doctor's letter or certificate is provided;
- does not take place or is not finished for a reason other than the candidate's fault, or the fault of the vehicle, for example bad weather conditions.

Certain expenses incurred on the day of the test will also be refunded to the candidate if the DSA cancel at short notice, unless it is for bad weather or poor light conditions. Reasonable claims for the following will be considered:

- any standard pay or earnings lost through taking unpaid leave (usually for half a day);

- the cost of travelling to and from the test centre if a theory test is involved, or the cost of hiring a vehicle for the test, including travelling to and from the test centre if a practical test is involved (generally up to one and half hours of vehicle hire).

The DSA will not pay for the cost of driving lessons arranged prior to a particular test appointment, or for extra lessons taken while waiting for a rescheduled appointment.

Application forms, giving full details of the above and how to apply for compensation, are available from the DSA in Nottingham.

Attending for the test

To ensure that everything goes smoothly on your pupil's test day:

- Check that the pupil has a valid, signed driving licence, his or her Theory and Hazard Perception Test pass certificate and some form of photographic identity if necessary.
- Take the test appointment card in case any errors have been made.
- Make sure your car is clean and tidy and has sufficient fuel.
- Clean the windows, leaving one slightly open if there is a risk of condensation.
- Make sure that the pupil knows where the ancillary controls are and how they work.
- Make sure that your car is:
  - roadworthy and has a current MOT certificate if applicable;
  - fitted with front and rear seat belts in working order, and adjustable head restraints;
  - fully insured for the pupil to drive while on the test;
  - properly taxed with the disc displayed in the correct position;
  - displaying 'L' plates clearly visible to the front and rear;
  - fitted with a rear view mirror for the driving examiner.

The car must meet the minimum test vehicle requirements. For a car first registered after 1 October 2003, this means that it must be capable of reaching 100 kph (62 mph).

You should leave your ADI Registration Certificate or Trainee Licence in the windscreen when your car is being used for a test.

If any of these points are overlooked, the test may be cancelled and the pupil will lose the fee. As these requirements are your professional responsibility, you will then be obliged to pay for another appointment.

At the test centre

Take your pupil into the waiting room a few minutes prior to the time of the appointment, making allowances for toilet requirements. Try to maintain a relaxed atmosphere by chatting to your pupil.

Documents

The examiner will come in to the waiting room and ask for your pupil by name, request some form of identification and ask the candidate to sign the DSA 'Driving Test Report' form. This signature will serve as a declaration that the vehicle presented for test carries valid motor insurance in accordance with the Road Traffic Act.

A reminder is given to candidates about motor insurance responsibilities on their test appointment card. However, it is sensible to remind your pupils, before they go into the waiting room, that this formality will take place. Confirm with them that your car is properly insured. If, for any reason, the candidate does not sign the declaration, the examiner will refuse to conduct the test and the fee will be forfeited.

Observer on test

At the start of the test the examiner will ask the pupil if he or she would like his or her instructor (or another observer) to sit in on the test. As well as accompanying the pupil on the practical part of the test, the observer can listen in to the examiner's feedback at the end of the test. It is purely the candidate's decision whether to have an observer with them.

The opportunity to go along on a test as an observer gives you, particularly if you are new to the job, a clearer idea of what is required by examiners.

Introduction

Examiners are trained to use their discretion about introducing themselves either on the way to, or in, the car. They will also decide whether or not it is appropriate to use first names.

Driving test examiners are sympathetic towards candidates. They understand 'test nerves'. You should realize, however, that while nerves are frequently used as an excuse for failing, they are rarely the real cause. Provided your pupils are properly prepared, and know what to expect, nerves should not be too much of a problem. Conducting a realistic 'mock test', to give pupils an insight into what will happen, can do much to allay these fears.

Eyesight

The eyesight test will be conducted outside the test centre. The legal requirement is for the candidate to be able to read, in good daylight, a car number plate from a distance of 20 metres (or 20.5m for the old-style plates). If the candidate fails this, the test will not be conducted.

FIGURE 11.1 The Driving Test Report form

DECLARATION

I declare that my use of the test vehicle for the purposes of the test is covered by a valid policy of insurance which satisfies the requirements of the relevant legislation. Signed...

Driving Test Report

Candidate's Name

Vehicle Type

Registration No.

Driver Number

	S	D			S	D
1(a). Eyesight			12. Use of speed			
1(b). Highway Code (Categories F/G/H)			13. Following distance			
2. Precautions						
3. Control :- accelerator			14. Maintain progress by :-			
clutch			driving at an appropriate speed			
gears			avoiding undue hesitation			
footbrake						
handbrake			15. Junctions :- approach speed			
steering			observation			
balance m/c			turning right			
4. Move away :- safely			turning left			
under control			cutting corners			
5. Emergency stop :- promptness			16. Judgement when :- overtaking			
control			meeting traffic			
making proper use of front brake (m/c)			crossing traffic			
6. Reverse to left or right :- control			17. Positioning :- normal driving			
observation			lane discipline			
7. Turn in the road / control			18. Clearance to obstructions			
'U' turn (m/c) :- observation						
8. Reverse parking :- control			19. Pedestrian crossings			
R C observation			20. Position for normal stops			

9. Use of mirrors / rear observation (m/c) well before :-

	S	D			S	D
signalling			21. Awareness and planning			
changing direction						
changing speed			22. Ancillary controls			

10. Give appropriate signals :-		Visitor		Total driving faults :-	
where necessary					
correctly		23. Result of test	Pass	Fail	None
properly timed					

11. Response to signs and signals :-		Route number	Examiner's signature	
traffic signs				
road markings		Extended test	Examiner's name	
traffic lights				
traffic controllers		1 3		
other road users		2 4	Supervision.SDE	SE	AOM	ACDE

Test Terminated in the Interest of Public Safety		Pass certificate No.	ADI Number	Category
Test Terminated at Request of Candidate			Test Centre	
Examiner Took Action	Verbal	Physical	Staff number	Date	M
Oral Explanation Given	Yes	No		Time of Test	F

| DL25A | DSA - An executive agency of the Department of the Environment, Transport and the Regions | 2/00 |

Ⓧ Crown Copyright 2000

PCN17147168

Vehicle safety questions

Before starting the on-road part of the test the examiner will ask two questions on vehicle safety. Details of this part of the test, including sample questions, are given on page 345.

The pupil is not expected to physically check fluid levels, or to touch a hot engine, but may be required to open the bonnet to show the location of the various items.

Directional instructions

At the start of the test the examiner will explain to the candidate that he or she should 'follow the road ahead unless directed otherwise'. Any instructions to turn off to the left or right will be given in plenty of time.

The directions and instructions described in Chapter 8 are general guidelines, and examiners may use slightly different terminology where appropriate to suit a particular candidate.

Independent driving

Since October 2010 a new 'independent driving' element has been included in the practical driving test. For this phase candidates are asked to drive for about 10 minutes or so without any specific turn-by-turn instructions from the examiner. The pupil is expected to follow a series of directional instructions, following traffic signs or a combination of the two. To help the candidate understand exactly where he or she is expected to go the examiner may show them a diagram of the route.

If the candidate goes off-route it will not affect the result of the test as long as there no actual driving faults.

If the pupil has special needs the examiner uses an appropriate method of directions, taking into account the particular needs of the individual candidate.

For candidates who speak little or no English, the examiner will use diagrams and/or written place names so that the driver can visualize the route to be taken.

Independent driving is designed to test the candidate's ability to drive unsupervised and to make decisions without guidance.

Marking system

Driving examiners are trained to look for the 'perfect driver'. At the moment of getting into the car every test candidate is considered to be perfect. Any deviations from this perfection are graded into three categories of fault: driving, serious and dangerous.

Faults are graded and recorded on the Driving Test Report form (DL25C), as they occur. Before any minor deviation from perfect is marked on the form, the examiner must consider its significance to the overall performance.

The Driving Test Report explained

Please note that the following is a direct extract from the DL25, using DSA terminology.

1(a) The eyesight test

At the start of the test the examiner asked you to read a vehicle registration number. If you required glasses or contact lenses, you must wear them whenever you drive. If you had problems with the eyesight test, perhaps you should consider consulting an optician.

1(b) Highway Code/safety

If you didn't need to take a separate Theory Test, for example to obtain a licence for a tractor or other specialist vehicle, you will have been asked questions on the *Highway Code* and other related motoring matters. You will also have been asked to identify some traffic signs. If you had difficulty with these questions make sure that you study properly by reading as wide a range of publications as you can to increase your understanding. If you have already passed a theory test you will not have been asked *Highway Code* questions at the practical test stage; but you should still have a thorough knowledge of it.

Safety questions (if applicable) – you should know the location of, and be able to operate, safety components such as fire extinguisher, fuel cut-off switch and emergency door.

2 Controlled stop

You will need to be able to display a high level of skill in bringing your vehicle to a stop, safely, promptly and under full control avoiding locking the wheels.

Remember that in wet weather it can take twice as long to stop safely.

3, 4 and 5 Reverse exercises

You will need to display the ability to control the vehicle safely whilst reversing to the left, right, when parking on the road or into a parking bay.

You must take good effective all round observation throughout the manoeuvre and show consideration to other road users.

6 Turn in the road

You will need to display the low speed control and observation skills necessary to carry out this exercise safely with due regard for other road users and pedestrians.

7 Vehicle checks

You will need to display to the examiner a basic knowledge of the fundamental safety checks applicable to your vehicle. For example safe fluid levels, lighting and tyre checks.

8 Taxi manoeuvre

You must be able to display the ability to turn your car around by whatever means available, making sure you take effective, all round observation showing consideration to other road users and pedestrians.

You should control your vehicle smoothly making proper use of the clutch, accelerator, brakes and steering.

You should not use a driveway or allow your vehicle to mount the pavement as this could damage your vehicle.

9 Taxi wheelchair

You should be able to

- securely erect wheelchair ramps,
- safely install the wheelchair and an imaginary occupant into your vehicle,
- ensure the wheelchair and occupant are secured in readiness for the journey, and
- reverse the entire process.

10 Vehicle and trailer combinations. Uncoupling /recoupling

You will need to demonstrate the skills necessary when uncoupling and recoupling your vehicle, driving the towing vehicle to a designated position prior to recoupling safely.

11 Precautions

Before you start the engine make sure that you are comfortably seated and all controls can be safely operated.

12 Control

This section covers, where appropriate, the safe and controlled use of accelerator, clutch, gears, footbrake, parking brake and steering.

Additional specific control elements apply to the drivers of different vehicle categories.

Always try and use the vehicle controls as smoothly as possible. This means less wear and tear on your vehicle and a smoother ride for your passengers.

Make proper use of your accelerator and clutch to make a smooth start.

Always depress the clutch just before you stop.

Select the correct gear to match the road and traffic conditions.

Change gear in good time but not too soon before a hazard.

Do not allow the vehicle to coast by running on in neutral or with the clutch depressed.

There should be no need to look down at the gear lever when changing gear.

Use the footbrake smoothly and progressively.

Brake in plenty of time for any hazard.

Make full use of the parking brake whenever it would help you to prevent the car from rolling backwards or forwards, and if you are parking.

Steer the vehicle as smoothly as possible.

Avoid harsh steering, or steering too early or too late as it may cause you to hit the kerb or swing out towards another road user.

If you are riding a motorcycle slowly, maintain a straight line and do not allow the machine to wobble towards other vehicles.

13 Move off
You will need to demonstrate your ability to move off smoothly and safely on the level, on a gradient and at an angle taking the correct precautionary observations.

14 Use of mirrors – rear observations
Use all the mirrors fitted to your vehicle safely and effectively.

You must always check carefully before signalling, changing direction or changing speed.

Use the Mirrors Signal Manoeuvre (MSM) routine effectively.

15 Signals
You must signal clearly to let others know what you intend to do. You should only use the signals shown in the *Highway Code* if it would help other road users (including pedestrians).

Always signal in good time and ensure that the signal has been cancelled after the manoeuvre has been completed.

Do not beckon to pedestrians to cross the road.

16 Clearance to obstructions
Allow plenty of room to pass stationary vehicles, obstructions and be prepared to slow down or stop. A door may open, a child may run out or a vehicle may pull out without warning.

17 Response to signs and signals

You should understand and be able to react to all traffic signs and road markings.

You must act correctly at traffic lights, and check that the road is clear before proceeding when the green light shows.

Obey signals given by police officers, traffic wardens and school crossing patrols.

Look out for signals given by other road users, including people in charge of animals, and be ready to act accordingly.

18 Use of speed

You should make safe, reasonable progress along the road bearing in mind the road, traffic and weather conditions and the road signs and speed limits.

Make sure that you can stop safely, well within the distance you can see to be clear.

Do not speed. Remember that as a new driver, your licence will be revoked if you accrue six or more penalty points during the first two years, and you have to retake and pass both theory and practical tests.

19 Following distance

Always keep a safe distance between yourself and other vehicles.

Remember, on wet or slippery roads it takes much longer to stop.

When you stop in traffic queues leave sufficient room to pull out if the vehicle in front has problems.

20 Maintain progress

In order to pass your test you must show that you can drive at a realistic speed appropriate to the road and traffic conditions.

You should approach all hazards at a safe, controlled speed, without being over cautious or interfering with the progress of other traffic.

Always be ready to move away from junctions as soon as it is safe and correct to do so.

Driving excessively slowly can create dangers for yourself and other drivers.

21 Junctions (including roundabouts)

You should be able to judge the correct speed of approach so that you can enter a junction safely and stop if necessary.

Position your vehicle correctly.

Use the correct lane.

If you are turning right, keep as near to the centre of the road as is safe.

Avoid cutting the corner when turning right.

If turning left, keep over to the left and do not swing out.

Watch out for cyclists and motorcyclists coming up on your left and pedestrians who are crossing.

You must take effective observation before moving into a junction and make sure it is safe before proceeding.

22 Judgement

Only overtake when it is safe to do so.

Allow enough room when you are overtaking another vehicle.

Cyclists and motorcyclists need at least as much space as other vehicles. They can wobble or swerve suddenly.

Do not cut in too quickly after overtaking.

Take care when the width of the road is restricted or when the road narrows.

If there is an obstruction on your side or not enough room for two vehicles to pass safely, be prepared to wait and let the approaching vehicles through.

When you turn right across the path of an approaching vehicle, make sure you can do so safely. Other vehicles should not have to stop, slow down or swerve to allow you to complete your turn.

23 Positioning

You should position the vehicle sensibly, normally well to the left.

Keep clear of parked vehicles and position correctly for the direction that you intend to take.

Where lanes are marked, keep to the middle of the lane and avoid straddling lane markings.

Do not change lanes unnecessarily.

24 Pedestrian crossings

You should be able to recognize the different types of pedestrian crossings and show courtesy and consideration towards pedestrians.

At all crossings you should slow down and stop if there is anyone on the crossing.

At zebra crossings you should slow down and be prepared to stop if there is anyone waiting to cross.

Give way to any pedestrian on a pelican crossing when the amber lights are flashing.

You should give way to cyclists as well as pedestrians on a toucan crossing and act correctly at puffin crossings.

25 Position/normal stops
Choose a safe, legal and convenient place to stop, close to the edge of the road, where you will not obstruct the road and create a hazard.

You should know how and where to stop without causing danger to other road users.

26 Awareness/planning
You must be aware of other road users at all times.

You should always think and plan ahead so that you can

- judge what other road users are going to do
- predict how their actions will affect you, and
- react in good time.

Take particular care to consider the actions of the more vulnerable groups of road users such as pedestrians, cyclists, motorcyclists and horse riders.

Anticipate road and traffic conditions, and act in good time, rather than reacting to them at the last moment.

27 Ancillary controls
You should understand the function of all the controls and switches, especially those that have a bearing on road safety. These include

- indicators
- lights
- windscreen wipers
- demisters
- heaters.

You should be able to find these controls and operate them correctly when necessary, without looking down.

Boxes 28 and 29 on the marking sheet are normally used by the examiner for any faults relating to eco-driving and for the fleet training test.

As a professional driving instructor you should be completely familiar with the DL25 and the above detailed explanations.

Fault categories

Faults committed during driving tests are assessed under the following categories:

- *Dangerous fault:* recorded when a fault is assessed as having caused actual danger during the test. A single fault in this category will result in failure.
- *Serious fault:* recorded when a fault is assessed as potentially dangerous. A habitual driving fault can also be assessed as serious when it indicates a serious weakness in a candidate's driving. A single serious fault is an automatic failure.
- *Driving fault:* a less serious fault, which is assessed as such because of the circumstances at that particular time. Driving faults only amount to a failure when there is an accumulation of 15 or more.

There is an obvious need for a degree of standardization between the consistency of assessments made in training and those used for the driving test. It is essential therefore that you become familiar with this grading system.

There are, of course, other types of errors that you will be dealing with during a pupil's training. These include marginal errors that could develop into more serious faults or that could lead to bad habits being formed, and they are dealt with in more detail in Chapter 8, Driver Training.

Driving test faults

Driving fault

The pupil is approaching a junction to turn right into a fairly wide side road. Visibility into the road is good and, after ensuring it is safe to turn and the side road is free of traffic movement, the learner turns into the side road, cutting the corner very slightly. No potential danger was caused to other road users because the pupil had checked the situation before turning. On a driving test this would be recorded as a driving fault. It would not result in failure.

Serious fault

The pupil is approaching the same right turn. This time visibility into the side road is severely restricted by parked vehicles, making it impossible for the pupil to see whether or not there is traffic approaching the end of the new road. The pupil blatantly cuts the corner into this unknown situation. No actual danger occurred because no other road user appeared from the side road. This, however, was purely good luck and not an assessed judgement. The incident involved potential danger and the learner would fail the test.

Dangerous fault

In exactly the same circumstances as the example above, the learner cuts the corner. This time, another vehicle appears approaching the end of the side road. The other driver has to brake to avoid a collision. This incident involved actual danger and, of course, the learner would fail the test.

Driving, serious or dangerous?

It is not necessary for you to be able to grade errors exactly to DSA Driving Test criteria. While some degree of standardization is desirable, it is not absolutely essential to get it right all the time, and you need not worry unduly over this matter. In any event, the difference between serious and dangerous is purely academic, because in both instances the result is the same – failure.

The difference between a driving fault and a serious fault in this situation, however, could mean the difference between pass and fail. Using again the above examples, for comparison, we can define the errors in a different way. The essential difference between the two incidents is that the driver committing the driving fault in the first example was able to see that the new road was clear. In the second example the fault was a serious fault because the driver was unable to see if the new road was clear, but was prepared to take a risk or was completely unaware of any risk.

The fault really is not a difference between two people cutting a corner with one of them getting away with it. One of them was able to see and might well have acted differently had the visibility been restricted; the other proved to be totally unaware of the danger caused by the parked vehicles. It is only possible to assess the actions of a driver in the light of the prevailing situation.

Summary of 'L' driver faults

According to the DSA driving skills book, *The Official Guide to Learning to Drive*, some of the most common causes for driving test failure are:

- **Eyesight test:** unable to read a vehicle number plate at 20.5 metres (67 ft) or 20 metres (66 ft) for the new-style plate.
- **Highway Code:** knowledge of the Highway Code (and application of it during the drive) weak or wrong.
- **Precautions before starting engine:** handbrake not applied, neutral not selected, when starting or restarting the engine.
- **Make proper use of:**
  - **accelerator:** erratic, fierce or jerky use; poor coordination with clutch;
  - **clutch:** not depressed far enough, causing noisy changing or stalling; poor coordination with accelerator;
  - **footbrake:** not used when needed; used late, harshly or erratically;
  - **gears:** incorrect selection; coasting; not in neutral when needed; harsh control of the gear lever; looking at lever; reluctant to change; incorrect use of selector on automatic;

- **handbrake**: not applied when required; not released when moving; used before stopping;

- **steering** (position of hands on wheel): one hand off; both hands off; hands on spokes, rim or centre; hands crossed unnecessarily; elbow on window ledge;

- **steering** (oversteer): erratic control of steering; wandering on wheel; late correction; over- or understeering; jerky or fiddling movements.

- **Moving off – angle, hill, level, straight**: not done smoothly; not safe; not controlled; causing inconvenience or danger to others; not using mirrors; not looking round or not acting sensibly on what is seen; not signalling when needed; incorrect gear; lack of coordination of controls.

- **Emergency stop**: slow reactions; like a normal stop; footbrake/clutch used in a manner likely to cause a skid; handbrake used before stopping; both hands off the wheel.

- **Reverse, left/right**: rushed; stalling; poor coordination of accelerator and clutch; incorrect course; mounting kerb; steering wrong way; too wide or close (not realized); not looking around before/during reverse; not acting on what is seen.

- **Turning in road**: rushed; stalling; poor coordination of accelerator and clutch; not using handbrake; incorrect steering; mounting or bouncing off kerb; uncontrolled footbrake or accelerator; more moves than needed; lack of observation before or during manoeuvre; danger or inconvenience to others; looking but not acting sensibly on what is seen.

- **Reverse park**: rushed; poor coordination of controls; incorrect course; too wide or too close to parked car; lack of effective observations before/during exercise; poor response to other road users; not using handbrake; not finishing exercise correctly.

- **Effective use of mirrors**: not looking in good time; not acting on what is seen; omitted or used too late; used as or after movement is commenced; not used effectively before signalling, changing direction, slowing or stopping; omitting final look when necessary.

- **Give signals correctly**: signals omitted; given wrongly, or given late; too short to be of value; not cancelled after use; not repeated when needed; arm signal not given when needed.

- **Prompt action on signals**: failing to comply with signals or signs – stop, keep left, no entry, traffic lights, police signals, school crossing wardens, signals given by other road users.

- **Use of speed**: not exercising proper care in use of speed; too fast for conditions or speed limits; too close to vehicle in front in view of speed, weather, road conditions.

- **Making progress**: not making normal progress; too low speed for conditions; crawling in low gear; no speed build-up between gears;

speed not maintained; undue hesitation at junctions; over-cautious to the point of being a nuisance.

- **Crossroads and junctions**: incorrect regulation of speed on approach; late appreciation of, or reaction to, junctions or crossroads; not taking effective observation before emerging at a crossroad or junction; not being sure it is safe to emerge before doing so; incorrect assessment of speed and distance of other vehicles, including cyclists; incorrect positioning for right turns, at or on approach; position taken late, too far from centre, wrong position out of narrow road, or from one-way street, wandering, wrong position at end of right turn; incorrect positioning for left turns, at or on approach; too far from near kerb; swinging out before turning; striking or running over kerb; swinging out after turn; cutting right turns when entering or leaving.

- **Overtaking/meeting/crossing other traffic**: overtaking unsafely; wrong time or place; causing danger or inconvenience to others; too close or cutting in afterwards; inadequate clearance for oncoming traffic, causing vehicles to swerve or brake; turning right across oncoming traffic unsafely.

- **Normal position**: unnecessarily far out from kerb.

- **Adequate clearance**: passing too close to cyclists, pedestrians or stationary vehicles.

- **Pedestrian crossings**: approaching too fast; not stopping when necessary, or preparing to stop if pedestrian waiting; overtaking on approach; not signalling (by arm if necessary) when needed; giving dangerous signals to pedestrians.

- **Normal stops**: stopping unsafely or in inconvenient place; not parallel to kerb; too close to other vehicles or hazards, compounding hazards.

- **Awareness and anticipation**: lack of awareness or anticipation of others' actions. (This is marked when the result of bad planning or lack of foresight involves the test candidate in a situation resulting in late, hurried or muddled decisions.)

- **Use of ancillary controls**: not using equipment that is necessary for the conditions.

At the end of the test

Driving Test Report – DL25 (DL9A in N. Ireland)

During the test the examiner uses this form to record any driving errors. Other information regarding the conduct of the test is also itemized. At the end of the test a copy of the marking sheet is given to the candidate. The examiner may also discuss the reasons for failure with the candidate and the instructor. The form lists the main subjects outlined in *The Official Guide to Learning to Drive*. It should be used as a guide for both you and your pupil. For more detail see pages 356–61.

When your pupil passes

The examiner will record all driving faults on form DL25, and a duplicate is handed to the candidate. The examiner will discuss any relevant points and the instructor will be invited to listen to this explanation.

A Certificate of Competence to Drive (D10) will also be issued. This allows the candidate to drive unaccompanied on any type of road, without 'L' plates. You should advise your pupils to apply for a full licence as soon as possible, and in any case within two years, otherwise the D10 will become invalid.

The examiner will hand the pupil a copy of the DSA magazine *Drive On*, which contains useful information and advice for new drivers; and a leaflet describing the Pass Plus scheme. This is your opportunity to encourage him or her to take further training in those areas of driving not already covered within your syllabus. See pages 21–22 for information on the scheme. Details of the Pass Plus syllabus are given in Chapter 9.

In Northern Ireland the successful candidate receives a pass certificate that is sent, together with the provisional licence, to the licensing department for processing. For the first year after passing the test the driver is restricted to 45 mph and must display R plates on the front and rear of the vehicle.

If your pupil fails

As well as giving the pupil a copy of the Driving Test Report form, the examiner will give a verbal report on the reasons for failure. You may sit in and listen to this explanation if you wish – it may help you advise the pupil on any further training requirements. The reverse of the form gives an explanation of the markings, and an outline of the appeals procedure.

Application for a retest can be made immediately, but the test must not be taken within 10 working days. Book the pupil a lesson as soon as possible so that your analysis and correction of weaknesses is more valid. This also allows the current standard of driving to be maintained and improved where required.

After the test

Whether the pupil has passed or failed, it is usually appropriate and advisable for you to drive the car away from the test centre as soon as practicable.

There are several reasons for this:

- You can vacate the parking space for candidates who are preparing for the next test time.
- The pupil will be feeling very elated if he or she has passed and will not be able to concentrate properly on his or her driving.
- The pupil will be disappointed, angry or upset if he or she has failed – none of which is conducive to driving.
- The test centre is not the ideal time for carrying out a post-mortem.

Finally, as soon as possible after the test make sure that your pupil signs up for his or her first session of Pass Plus training.

Car and trailer test

From time to time you may need to train a pupil in a car towing a trailer. This is because the current regulations allow a new driver to tow a trailer where the nett weight of the car exceeds the gross weight of the trailer, and if the total weight of the outfit is under 3,500 kg. For heavier trailers, or where the trailer weighs more than the car (a horsebox, for example), an additional test will be needed for category B+E.

To take this test, the pupil must:

- already hold a full category B licence;
- be over 21;
- be accompanied by a person who has held (and still holds) a full licence for B+E for at least three years.

The vehicle must carry 'L' plates (or 'D' plates in Wales if you prefer).

Minimum test vehicles

The vehicle to be used for the test must conform to the minimum test vehicle requirements. For vehicles first registered before 1 October 2003 the vehicle must be capable of 100 kph (62 mph) and the trailer must be at least 1 tonne maximum authorized mass. For a vehicle first registered after 1 Oct 2003, there is an additional rule: the trailer must be 'a closed box trailer – slightly less wide than the towing vehicle, but rear view must be by external mirrors only'. (Test fee: £115; evenings/weekends: £141.)

Test centre

Vehicle and trailer tests are conducted at LGV/PCV testing stations, where there are special facilities for maneouvring and for braking exercises.

Safety questions

At the start of the test the examiner will ask five questions on vehicle safety. As with the car test, these questions are based on the 'show me'/'tell me' principle.

The subjects covered include:

- tyres and wheels;
- brakes;
- steering;

- engine oil and fluid levels;
- lights and reflectors;
- direction indicators;
- audible warning devices;
- loading;
- trailer body condition.

Sample questions include:

- '*Tell me* the main safety factors in loading this vehicle.'
- The trainee's explanation should include 'even distribution throughout the length of the vehicle', 'securely stowed, within the size and weight limits' and 'secured so that there is no danger of the load moving or falling off when cornering or braking'.
- '*Show me* how you would check for air leaks on this vehicle.'
- The pupil would need to show the examiner the location of the air tanks and how to check the gauges for a drop in pressure, and would need to walk round the vehicle to listen for obvious leaks.

Test syllabus

Reversing

This exercise is carried out at the test centre, using an area that is set according to the size of the vehicle and trailer combined. The candidate has to reverse to the right and then to the left between cones, finishing in a simulated loading bay. The maneouvre must be done:

- under control and in reasonable time;
- with good observation;
- with reasonable accuracy;
- inside a clearly defined boundary.

The extreme rear of the trailer should finish within a yellow painted box area at the end of the marked bay.

Braking exercise

The braking exercise takes place on the special manoeuvring area rather than on the public roads. The examiner travels in the vehicle during the exercise. The candidate is asked to achieve about 20 mph in a distance of about 200 feet, and then stop the vehicle on reaching a set of markers. The vehicle should be stopped:

- as quickly as possible;
- under full control;

- as safely as possible;
- in a straight line.

The candidate should avoid:

- driving too slowly;
- braking too soon;
- taking too long to stop.

On the road

The test is about one hour long. Because the braking and reversing exercises are carried out at the test centre, the candidate is not required to do any other manoeuvres, such as turning in the road, reversing round a corner, or emergency stop. There is, however, a requirement to move off:

- at an angle;
- on an uphill gradient;
- on a downhill gradient.

The route includes dual carriageways, one-way systems, and where possible, motorways.

Uncoupling and recoupling

At the end of the test the candidate is expected to park the outfit and uncouple the trailer. The towing vehicle is then parked safely alongside the trailer before recoupling the trailer. Some of the key points:

- Jockey wheel lowered correctly.
- Electric lines disconnected and stowed safely.
- Stabilizing equipment removed.
- Safety chain or coupling removed.
- Coupling removed and trailer moved clear of the towing hook.
- Check that the coupling is secure by using an appropriate method.
- Wheels, legs, etc are raised.
- Operation of the lights and indicators.
- The pupil should be able to uncouple and recouple the vehicle and trailer confidently and without any unnecessary delay.

Medium-sized goods vehicles (Category C1)

It is now illegal to act as an accompanying driver in a Category C1 (medium-sized lorry), C1+E, D1 (minibus) or D1+E vehicle unless you have passed a driving test for the category of vehicle concerned.

A supervising driver in category C1 or D1 vehicles (including vehicle plus trailer combinations) must:

- hold a full (post 1997) licence for the category of vehicle that is being driven by the learner;
- have held that licence for the relevant period of time – usually three years.

Drivers who hold category C1, C1+E, D1 or D1+E entitlements that were obtained before 1997 ('implied rights') and who passed the appropriate driving test in one of those categories before 1 May 2010 are given 'credit' for the time they held implied rights entitlement. This means that they would have held the entitlement for long enough to be allowed to accompany a learner.

If you pass the relevant test from now on, you would have to wait until you have held the new entitlement for the relevant period, usually three years, before you would be able to act as an accompanying driver in a vehicle covered by that entitlement.

These arrangements apply to accompanying or instructing on these types of vehicle and do not affect your entitlement to drive a medium-sized lorry or a minibus.

Extended driving test

If a driver is convicted of an offence of dangerous driving the court will impose an Extended Driving Test as part of the disqualification process. Similarly, courts have discretion to order an Extended Test for other offences that involve obligatory disqualification.

The Extended Test is much longer than the ordinary test, lasting about 70 minutes, and is much more demanding. During the test a wide variety of different road and traffic conditions are covered, including dual carriageways. As the candidate will hold a provisional licence, motorways are not included. Because of the extra duration of the test a higher fee applies.

The test includes all the exercises that are part of the normal 'L' test, but with particular emphasis on whether the candidate is able to concentrate for the duration of the test and whether his or her attitude to other road users is satisfactory.

DSA service standards

Full information about complaints is given in the DSA's Service Standards leaflet, available from the Head Office in Nottingham. The contract for driving tests is between candidates and the DSA. If you have a pupil who has a complaint to make about any of the following, he or she should write to or telephone the appropriate DSA section:

- test cancellations;
- compensation;

- lost applications;
- delays in providing tests or results;
- Theory test results;
- the conduct of a practical test.

The DSA will forward the complaint to the appropriate area customer service unit. The complaint must be set out clearly, including any redress the client is seeking.

You should note that if a pupil has a complaint about the conduct of a practical driving test, the result of the test cannot be overturned. However, if it is felt that the test was not conducted according to the relevant regulations, the pupil should contact a magistrates' court, or sheriff's court if he or she lives in Scotland, which can order a retest.

Driving Large Vehicles

12

Passing the ordinary 'L' test gives full licence entitlement for category B, that is goods vehicles up to 3.5 tonnes gross weight and for passenger vehicles with up to eight passenger seats. If your first full licence was issued before January 1997 you will have additional entitlement for category C1 and D1 vehicles. These categories cover goods vehicles up to 7.5 tonnes and passenger vehicles (not used for hire or reward) with up to 17 passenger seats.

However, under the new licensing arrangements that came into force in 2010, you are not allowed to instruct or act as an accompanying driver unless you have passed a driving test in that type of vehicle and have held the licence for the appropriate qualifying period (normally three years). These changes do not affect your existing entitlement to drive this type of vehicle.

This chapter covers licences, tests and instructor qualifications for large vehicles in general terms, but for detailed information you need to refer to the official DSA and DVLA publications. These include:

- *The Official DSA Guide to Driving Goods Vehicles.*
- *The Official Theory Test for Drivers of Large Vehicles.*
- Leaflet D100, *What you need to know about driving licences.*

Other books that you might find helpful include David Lowe's *Transport Manager's and Operator's Handbook* and *The Professional LGV Driver's Handbook*, both published by Kogan Page. For details of books see page 419.

The drivers of some large goods vehicles are exempt from the requirements of the LGV driver licence. These exemptions include:

- steam propelled vehicles;
- road construction vehicles;
- engineering plant;
- works trucks;
- industrial tractors;

- agricultural vehicles;
- digging machines;
- vehicles hauling lifeboats;
- vehicles manufactured before 1960 used unladen;
- articulated vehicles under 3.05 tonnes;
- military vehicles;
- vehicles being used by the police;
- vehicles that only travel very short distances on public roads.

Full details of the exemptions can be found on the DVLA website www. dvla.gov.uk and in the leaflet D100.

LGV driving licences

To apply for a provisional LGV driving licence you must first hold a full UK car licence. The provisional licence will be for rigid vehicles only, as you must pass a test on this type of vehicle before moving on to vehicles with a trailer (including articulated vehicles and drawbar outfits). This system of 'staged testing' means that in order to eventually drive an articulated vehicle or large drawbar outfit, you must progress through the following sequence:

TABLE 12.1 Driving licence categories

Type of vehicle	Category	Min. age
Goods vehicle with a maximum authorized mass between 3.5 tonnes and 7.5 tonnes	C1	18
Goods vehicle and trailer As above, with trailer more than 750 kg – total weight not more than 12,000 kg	C1 + E	18 or 21
Large goods vehicle with a maximum authorized mass of more than 7.5 tonnes	C	21*
LGV with draw bar trailer Rigid vehicle with trailer of more than 750 kg	C + E (restricted to drawbar trailers)	21
Articulated vehicles	C + E	21

NOTE Whether or not you have C1 entitlement on your licence it is permissible to progress straight from category B to C to C + E, subject to the minimum age requirements being met. However, an 18-year-old would need to take the category C1 Theory and Practical Tests before moving on to category C at 21.
*A category C licence can be obtained at 18 if the driver is tested for the initial Driver CPC (for details see page 385).

- Provisional driving licence for rigid goods vehicles.
- LGV Theory and Hazard Perception Test.
- LGV Rigid Vehicle Practical Test.
- Full rigid vehicle licence (with provisional trailer entitlement).
- Artic or Draw Bar LGV Practical Test.

Full details of all licence requirements and the exemptions are in the DVLA booklet, *What you need to know about driving licences* (D100), or at www. direct.gov.uk/en/motoring/driverlicensing.

Health and eyesight

To obtain a licence for LGVs you need to undergo a stringent medical examination by a doctor who must complete the medical certificate form D4. You have to pay for the medical privately, but the cost is normally allowed against tax as a business expense. If you are unsure about any aspect of health or eyesight, or your eligibility for a licence for health reasons, you should consult your doctor or discuss the details with the Drivers' Medical group at the DVLA. It can be contacted on 0870 240 0009.

The eyesight standard for driving large vehicles is much more demanding than that of the 'L' driver test where the requirement is simply to be able to read a car number plate at the appropriate distance. To qualify for a licence for large vehicles you must have visual acuity of at least 6/9 in the better eye and at least 6/12 in the weaker eye. If corrective lenses are worn, the uncorrected acuity must be no less than 3/60 in each eye.

The health standards are also much higher for drivers of large vehicles. This is mainly because the responsibilities of handling a large vehicle are much greater, and because accidents involving LGVs are often more serious than those involving cars. A medical report is required with each application for a licence and with each renewal. The law does not allow for a new PCV or LGV licence to be issued to anyone who has had an epileptic attack since the age of five or who is being treated by insulin for diabetes.

Some of the other conditions that might make it unsafe to drive larger vehicles (and which might cause the DVLA to refuse a licence) include disorders of the heart, epilepsy, alcohol and drug dependency, psychiatric illnesses and eyesight defects. A full list of the relevant medical conditions is available from the DVLA.

Applying for a licence

Application forms (D2) are normally available from main post offices or from commercial LGV driving schools. The form and other documents should be sent to the DVLA at Swansea SA99 1AD. Before applying for provisional entitlement for LGVs you must already hold a full car licence. Your application must be accompanied by the full car licence (or a provisional licence together with a pass certificate) and a completed medical report form (D4). There is no fee for vocational licences, including renewals.

A first provisional LGV licence is valid for category C (rigid) vehicles only. A full category C licence is needed before you can apply for a provisional licence for artics or trailers. The Theory and Hazard Perception Test must be passed before taking a Rigid Vehicle Practical Test, but this is not necessary for upgrading from rigid to artic vehicles.

The licence application is normally processed by the DVLA within about 10 days, and you have to wait for the licence to arrive before you can drive the larger vehicle. Licence entitlement is normally valid until the driver's 45th birthday. For drivers over 45, the licence lasts for five years. From the age of 65 the licence has to be renewed annually. A medical report is required with each application or renewal.

When driving an LGV, the learner must:

- hold provisional licence entitlement for that category of vehicle;
- be supervised by a driver who has held a full licence for that type of vehicle for at least three years;
- display 'L' plates (or 'D' plates in Wales, if preferred) on the front and back of the vehicle.

LGV theory test

The two-part Theory and Hazard Perception Test is a multiple-choice paper followed by a hazard perception test. The two parts can be taken on separate occasions, but both parts must be passed within two years to obtain the overall test pass. The pass certificate is valid for two years to allow the learner time to take and pass the practical test.

Syllabus

- *Vehicle weights and dimensions*:
  - vehicle size;
  - stowage and loading;
  - vehicle markings;
  - speed limiters.
- *Drivers' hours*:
  - driving limits;
  - keeping records;

- – tachograph rules;
- – tiredness;
- – vehicle security.
- *Braking systems*:
  - – types of brakes;
  - – maintenance and inspection;
  - – connection and proper use of brakes;
  - – tailgating;
  - – freezing conditions;
  - – anti-lock brakes.
- *The driver*:
  - – consideration;
  - – courtesy;
  - – priority;
  - – vehicle safety equipment;
  - – tiredness;
  - – drugs and alcohol.
- *The road*:
  - – anticipation;
  - – hazard awareness;
  - – attention;
  - – speed and distance;
  - – reaction time;
  - – risk factors.
- *Accident handling*:
  - – reducing risk;
  - – injuries;
  - – casualties.
- *Vehicle condition*:
  - – wheels and tyres;
  - – principles of construction;
  - – function of larger vehicles;
  - – vehicle coupling mechanisms;
  - – breakdowns.
- *Leaving the vehicle*:
  - – the driver's cab;
  - – your own safety and that of others.

- *Vehicle loading*:
  - loading;
  - safety;
  - types of load.
- *Restricted view*:
  - mirrors;
  - signals;
  - parking;
  - moving off;
  - blind spots;
  - observation at junctions.
- *Documents*:
  - for national and international carriage;
  - when receiving, carrying and delivering goods.
- *Environmental issues*:
  - vehicle noise wind resistance;
  - fuel consumption, refuelling.
- *Other road users*:
  - vulnerable road users;
  - other vehicles.
- *Traffic signs*:
  - road signs;
  - speed limits;
  - regulations.

The procedures for the multiple-choice part of the exam are much the same as for the L-driver test (see page 339).

For the LGV theory test you are allowed 115 minutes to complete 100 questions. To pass you must achieve 85 or more correct answers.

Most of the questions require one correct answer from four alternatives, but with a few questions having two or three correct answers from five alternatives.

The current theory test fees (January 2011) are £35 for the multiple-choice and £15 for the hazard perception test.

To prepare thoroughly for the test, the DSA recommend that you should study *The Highway Code, Know Your Traffic Signs, The Official Theory Test for Drivers of Large Vehicles* and *The Official DSA Guide to Driving Goods Vehicles.* All of the questions and answers are included, together with an explanation for each one. The books also give a complete, detailed breakdown of the test syllabus, as well as a list of all theory test centres.

The theory test must be taken if you are applying for a category C or C1 licence, but is not required when upgrading from C1 to C, or from C to C+E.

Sample questions

1. Under EC rules, when may you interrupt the daily rest period?

(Mark one answer)

When part of it is to be taken on board a ferry or train.
When loading or unloading a vehicle.
When there is a gap of not more than one hour between rest periods.
When your journey involves night driving.

2. You are driving a lorry with a wide load. The width of the load is between 3.5 metres (11 ft 6 in) and 4.3 metres (14 ft 2 in). Which three of the following apply?

(Mark three answers)

Side markers must be shown.
The police must be notified.
An attendant must be carried.
Reduced speed limits apply.
Department for Transport approval must be obtained.

3. An LGV is found to be overloaded. Who is liable to be prosecuted for the offence?

(Mark one answer)

The person who loaded the vehicle.
Both the driver and the operator.
The operator only.
The driver only.

4. What could prevent air pressure building up in the air brake system in cold, frosty weather?

(Mark one answer)

Moisture in the air may form bubbles in the brake fluid.
The air will contract, reducing the pressure.
Moisture drawn in with the air may freeze and cause a blockage.
The dampness may cause valves to rust.

5. How far can a load overhang at the rear before you must use triangular projection markers?

(Mark one answer)

1 metre (3 ft 6 in).
1.5 metres (5 ft).
2 metres (6 ft 8 in).
2.9 metres (9 ft 6 in).

6. **You are uncoupling a trailer. Before disconnecting any of the air lines, you MUST .....**

   (Mark one answer)

   Drain the air tanks.
   Apply the trailer parking brake.
   Lower the landing gear.
   Disconnect the electrical line.

7. **You have been driving non-stop since 5 am. It is now 9.30 am. Under EC rules you must have a break of at least:**

   (Mark one answer)

   15 minutes.
   30 minutes.
   45 minutes.
   60 minutes.

8. **Exhaust brakes give greatest efficiency when used:**

   (Mark one answer)

   At high engine speed in low gear.
   At low engine speed in high gear.
   On stop–start town work.
   On high speed motorway runs.

Hazard perception test

The second part of the Theory and Hazard Perception Test is 'hazard perception' and can be taken immediately after the multiple-choice test or on a separate occasion. As with the 'L' driver test (page 340), HPT consists of a series of video film clips showing potential driving hazards on screen. The test requirement is to 'spot' these hazards by clicking on a computer mouse as soon as the potential hazard is recognized. You are shown 19 film clips, with one hazard on 18 clips and two hazards on the other one. Each hazard is given a maximum of five points – the earlier you spot the hazard, the more points you achieve. Out of a possible 100 points, you need to obtain 67 to pass.

You must pass both parts of the theory test within a 24-month period to obtain a valid theory test pass.

To prepare for the hazard perception test, the DSA recommend that you train with a professionally qualified instructor using a properly structured course. This training should be supplemented by studying the relevant DSA books and the DSA video or DVD *The Official Guide to Hazard Perception*, which is the official guide to the hazard perception test for all drivers.

Once you have passed both parts of the test you can apply for the practical test.

LGV practical test

Application for a test can be made by post, fax, phone or online. Forms are normally available from the DSA or most commercial LGV driving schools. If you are having training with a recognized school it will normally make the arrangements for your test by using the 'trainer booking' system.

To book online, go to www.driving-tests.co.uk. You will need details of your licence, your theory pass certificate and payment by credit or debit card.

If you apply by post you will need to send a cheque or postal order. Applications by phone or fax can be made using a credit or debit card. In either case, your driving licence details are required unless the application is made under the trainer booking system. With this system the test is allocated to the training organization, with the candidate's details given at a later date. The current fee for a weekday test (Jan 2011) is £115. For evening and weekend tests the fee is £141.

LGV driving tests are conducted by a team of experienced examiners who are specially trained for the specific requirements of larger vehicles. A list of test centres is given on the application form. The candidate has to provide a suitable vehicle that complies with the following requirements:

- The vehicle must be unladen and of the correct category for which the licence is required.
- It must display 'L' plates (or 'D' plates in Wales if you prefer) on the front and rear.
- It must have sufficient fuel for the test, which lasts up to 1½ hours.
- It must be in good roadworthy condition with all stop lamps and direction indicators working properly.
- Proper seating and a seat belt for the examiner must be provided.
- The vehicle must not be operating on trade licence plates.
- It must not exceed 60 ft in length.
- Nearside and offside mirrors for use by the examiner.

Practical test format

The DSA book *The Official DSA Guide to Driving Goods Vehicles* is available from most bookshops and training organizations. It explains the contents of the LGV test and how to prepare for it. You should read it in conjunction with *The Official Guide to Learning to Drive*, which gives advice on correct vehicle control and road procedures for candidates on both car and lorry tests.

In order to pass the LGV test you must:

- demonstrate to the examiner that you can handle the vehicle safely and competently in all types of road and traffic conditions;

- show courtesy and consideration for other road users, no matter what the situation;
- show that you have complete control of the vehicle throughout the test, whatever the weather and road conditions.

The test is in several parts:

1 A series of safety questions based on 'show me' or 'tell me'.

2 A test of the driver's ability to control the vehicle in a confined space. This part of the test is conducted at the test centre on a special area of about 300 ft × 60 ft.

3 A drive over a route covering various road and traffic conditions. During this part of the test (which lasts about one hour), the candidate has to carry out several special exercises, including uphill and downhill starts.

4 For drivers of articulated vehicles and drawbars, a practical exercise in coupling and uncoupling the trailer is included.

Minimum test vehicle requirements for LGV practical tests

All vehicles must be capable of 80 kph (50 mph) and must be fitted with an anti-lock braking system (ABS) and a fully working tachograph.

1 Safety questions

At the start of the practical test, candidates are asked several questions on vehicle safety. The questions are normally of the 'show me'/'tell me' type. This part of the test includes questions on:

- engine oil levels;
- engine coolant levels;
- windscreen wipers and washers;
- tyres, wheels and mudguards;
- brake lights, indicators and reflectors;
- headlamps, side and tail lights;
- windscreen and windows;
- vehicle suspension and power-assisted steering;
- loading mechanisms and safety factors;
- air pressure and leaks;
- cab locking mechanism;
- tachographs and discs;
- instrument checks;
- audible warning devices;
- vehicle body condition.

TABLE 12.2 Minimum requirement for LGV Practical Tests

Category	MAM	Length	Width	Cargo compartment/ trailer
C1	4 tonnes	5 metres		Closed box cargo compartment at least as wide and high as cab
C1 + E (drawbar)	4 tonnes + 2 tonne trailer	8 metres		Closed box trailer, slightly less wide than the towing vehicle, but rear view must be by mirrors only
C1 + E (artic)	6 tonnes	8 metres		as above
C	12 tonnes	8 metres	2.4 metres	Closed box cargo compartment at least as wide and as high as cab
C + E (drawbar)	Cat. C towing vehicle total –20 tonnes	14 metres Trailer at least 7.5 metres from coupling eye to extreme rear	2.4 metres	as above
C + E (artic)	20 tonnes	14 metres	2.4 metres	as above

NOTE: Category C and C+E vehicles must have at least eight forward gears, taking account of splitter boxes and range changes.

Typical questions

Show me how you would check that the wheel nuts on this vehicle are secure.

Tell me how you would check the condition of the suspension (or windscreen, wipers, reflectors) on this vehicle.

Show me how the cab locking mechanism is secured on this vehicle.

Tell me how you would operate the tail lift mechanism on this vehicle.

Show me how you would replace the tachometer disc on this vehicle.

Tell me how you would check that the power-assisted steering is working.

2 Exercise

Reversing The candidate is expected to drive in reverse along a course marked out by cones, involving the use of right and left steering lock, and finishing in a bay 1½ times the width of the vehicle. The object of the exercise is to complete the manoeuvre smoothly, without touching any of the cones, without going over the boundary lines, and to stop with the extreme rear of the vehicle within a 3-ft marked area and close to a simulated loading platform. Throughout the exercise the driver should maintain all-round observations and complete control of the vehicle.

During this exercise the examiner will be outside the vehicle to check on the accuracy of the manoeuvre and for the driver's observations and vehicle control.

FIGURE 12.1 Reversing exercise

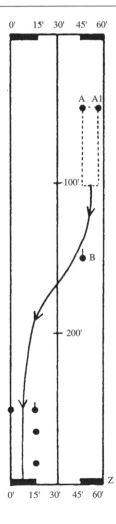

3 On the road

During the 'on-road' section of the test, the candidate is required to carry out several set exercises as well as a normal drive of about 25–30 miles. The set exercises include uphill and downhill starts. In order to show that all gears can be used when necessary, the driver is required to demonstrate progressive upward and downward gear changes. During this exercise it is not necessary to use any auxiliary transmission systems.

Depending on the size of the vehicle used for the test, some degree of tolerance in positioning at junctions is permitted. However, care must be exercised so as not to endanger or inconvenience other road users.

The test route may include a section of motorway driving.

For full details of the requirements of the test, you should take professional tuition and refer to the DSA book *The Official DSA Guide to Driving Goods Vehicles*.

4 Coupling/uncoupling

For tests on category C1+E and C+E (artics and drawbars) there is a requirement to demonstrate uncoupling and recoupling of the trailer or semi-trailer. The candidate is asked to uncouple the trailer and then park the vehicle alongside. The towing vehicle is then realigned with the trailer before recoupling.

During the exercise the candidate is assessed on:

- control of the vehicle;
- accuracy of the maneouvre;
- effective observations.

LGV practical test syllabus

The test covers the following main topics:

- *Vehicle controls:* accelerator, clutch, footbrake, handbrake, steering.
- *Precautions before starting.*
- *Moving off safely and under control.*
- *Use of mirrors:* well before signalling, changing direction or speed.
- *Use of signals:* when necessary, correctly and properly timed.
- *Reversing exercise:* under control and with effective observations.
- *Controlled stop:* promptly and under control.
- *Uphill and downhill starts.*
- *Clearance to obstructions.*
- *Response to signs and signals:* traffic signs, road markings, traffic lights, traffic controllers, other road users.
- *Use of speed.*

- *Maintaining a safe following distance.*
- *Maintain progress:* use of appropriate speed; without undue hesitation.
- *Junctions:* speed on approach; observations; right and left turns; avoidance of cutting corners.
- *Judgement:* overtaking, meeting, crossing the path of other vehicles.
- *Road positioning:* in normal driving; lane discipline.
- *Pedestrian crossings.*
- *Safe position for normal stops.*
- *Awareness and planning.*
- *Ancillary controls.*
- *Uncoupling and recoupling.*

After the test

At the end of the test the successful candidate is given a pass certificate. This entitles the applicant to exchange the provisional licence for full licence entitlement for the relevant category of vehicle. There is no fee for vocational licences.

An unsuccessful candidate is issued with a statement of failure on which the examiner will have marked the points that require particular attention. As with the car test, any serious or dangerous fault or more than 15 driving faults will result in a test fail.

Driver CPC (certificate of professional competence)

A new qualification for professional lorry drivers – the Driver Certificate of Professional Competence – started in September 2009. From now on, simply holding a vocational driving licence for categories C, C1 and C + E is not sufficient for someone who drives a large vehicle professionally.

This new initiative is a direct result of an EU Directive that requires all professional lorry and bus drivers to hold a CPC as well as the basic driving licence. The main aim of the new legislation is to help road safety by producing better-qualified drivers, as well as generating an improved and more positive image for the industry. As a result of raising the profile of the industry it is anticipated that more people (particularly the younger age group) will be attracted to join a much more structured profession.

As well as additional testing for new entrants, part of the new scheme involves refresher training for all drivers every five years. This means that drivers' skills will be developed and maintained on a regular basis.

The normal minimum age for starting to drive large vehicles such as category C and C+E is 21 unless the person is taking a comprehensive training programme under the Young Driver scheme. With the introduction of the new system a vocational driving licence can be obtained at 18 so long as the driver is being trained and tested for CPC.

Exemptions

Some drivers will be exempt from the need to hold the Driver CPC, depending on the actual driving being undertaken. These exemptions include drivers of vehicles:

- that have a maximum authorized speed not exceeding 45 kph;
- being used by, or under the control of, the armed forces, a police force or a fire and rescue authority;
- undergoing road tests for technical development, repair, or maintenance purposes, or of new or rebuilt vehicles that have not yet been put into service;
- being used in an emergency or a rescue mission;
- being used in the course of driving lessons for the purpose of obtaining a driving licence or CPC;
- used for the non-commercial carriage of goods for personal use;
- carrying material or equipment to be used by them in the course of their work, provided that driving is not that person's principal activity.

Initial training

The legislation requires new drivers to have a minimum of four hours of theory testing and at least two hours of practical testing.

For drivers who are not going to be driving for a living the theory and practical tests as outlined on pages 375–85 continue to be the only qualifying exams for the LGV driving licence. For drivers who *will* be driving professionally and who require Driver CPC, there are two additional modules to complete: case studies and practical test.

Case studies

To obtain the Driver CPC you need to pass this part of the theory test as well as the multiple-choice and hazard perception tests. Case studies are used to test your knowledge and how to put that knowledge into practice.

Each test is made up of seven case studies, each one having six to eight questions. The maximum possible score is 50, with a pass mark of 38.

Driver CPC practical test

The final part of the test for Driver CPC follows the practical driving test (see page 380).

This half-hour additional module tests your ability in several key areas:

- ability to load the vehicle with due regard for safety rules and proper vehicle use;
- security of the vehicle and contents;
- ability to prevent criminality and trafficking in illegal immigrants;
- ability to assess emergency situations;
- ability to prevent physical risk;
- demonstrate your ability through a physical, walk-round vehicle safety check.

The test consists of five topic areas covering the Driver CPC syllabus. To pass, you must score at least 15 out of 20 on each topic area and an overall score of 80 per cent.

Driver CPC syllabus

1 Advanced training in rational driving based on safety regulations:
- the characteristics of the transmission system;
- the technical characteristics and operation of the safety controls;
- ability to optimize fuel consumption;
- ability to load the vehicle with due regard for safety rules and proper vehicle use.

2 Application of regulations:
- knowing the social environment of road transport and the rules governing it;
- knowing the regulations governing the carriage of goods.

3 Health, road and environmental safety, service and logistics:
- awareness of the risks of the road and accidents at work;
- ability to prevent trafficking in illegal immigrants;
- ability to prevent physical risks;
- awareness of the importance of physical and mental ability;
- ability to assess emergency situations;
- ability to adopt behaviour to help enhance the image of the company;
- knowing the economic environment of road haulage and the organization of the market.

'Grandfather rights'

Anyone who held a driving licence for Large Goods Vehicles on 10 September 2009 (when the Driver CPC regulations came into force) does not need to take the initial testing requirements for Driver CPC, but will have to fulfil the requirements for periodic training as indicated in the next section.

Periodic training

To continue to qualify for a Driver CPC the driver must undergo at least 35 hours of periodic training in each five-year cycle. The training must be taken in minimum blocks of seven hours, but apart from that requirement there is complete flexibility over the detailed scheduling of the training. For example, it is permitted to take all of the training in the final year of the five-year cycle or to spread the training in several blocks of seven hours over the complete period.

The main intention of periodic training is to build on the knowledge and skills acquired during the initial training and testing period. It is geared to suit the specific needs of the individual driver and includes any changes in legislation or an element of remedial training where appropriate. The training can be conducted at 'approved training centres' which have shown that they can meet the required training standards. The DSA keeps a central record of these centres and the training they provide so that employers and drivers will know what training is available.

Courses for periodic training usually include:

- safe and fuel-efficient driving;
- legal requirements;
- health and safety, service and logistics.

Driver CPC – summary

- Covers all professional drivers of vehicles in categories C1, C, C+E.
- Start date for LGV Driver CPC: 10 September 2009.
- Minimum age for driving lorries for drivers with CPC – 18 years.
- Initial qualification for new drivers from September 2009: four hours' theory test; two hours' practical test.
- Periodic training (for all professional drivers from September 2009): total of 35 hours every five years; minimum of seven hours for each training session; training centres and courses to be specifically approved by the DSA.

By introducing the Driver CPC the government anticipates that there will be several significant benefits, including:

- Having better-qualified drivers will lead to improved road safety standards and a reduction in accidents.

- A more positive image for the industry and a perception of enhanced professionalism.

- Younger people will be attracted to a more structured industry.

- Financial savings as a result of improved environmentally friendly driving techniques.

Full details of Driver CPC, including the complete syllabus, can be obtained from www.drivercpc.direct.gov.uk or from the DSA phone helpline on 0300 200 1122.

LGV Instruction and Fleet Driver Training

13

Instructor qualifications

As a qualified car instructor, and if you have held a licence for large vehicles for some time, you may be considering moving on to training on LGVs. The job of the LGV instructor can be demanding, as you will be in charge of a much bigger and heavier vehicle, with probably two trainee drivers to teach. It can, however, be very rewarding, as you are preparing your drivers for a professional qualification.

In order to accompany a learner LGV driver, the supervising driver must be at least 21 and have held a full unrestricted driving licence for that type of vehicle for at least three years. This is the minimum legal requirement. However, most LGV instructors hold other voluntary qualifications, such as the ADI certificate, RTITB approval, the Voluntary Register of LGV Instructors or a training qualification from the armed forces.

Alternatively you may be considering Fleet Driver Training as an addition to your normal ADI work or as a specialist in this area of training. To qualify for the Fleet Driver Training Register you need to be an existing ADI and then take a separate qualification by exam or by training. Full details of the scheme are included in the second part of this chapter.

Register of LGV instructors

This scheme, which is likely to become compulsory within the next few years, was developed by the DSA in conjunction with various trade bodies, with the aim of improving the standard of training for lorry drivers. It is very similar to the ADI Register in its administration and testing procedures. As with the ADI, there are three examinations – a theory test, a practical test of driving ability and an instructional ability test. An information pack containing the application forms, and the syllabus is available from the DSA.

The register is open to anyone who has held the appropriate licence entitlement for a period of three years and who has not been disqualified from driving at any time in the preceding four years. To qualify for the register, you have to take and pass all three parts of the examination within one year. You are allowed only three attempts at each of the practical tests.

You must take and pass the Theory Test before applying for the practical parts (driving and instructional ability). However, with the practical tests you can decide whether to take them both on the same day or on separate occasions. There are advantages and disadvantages in each case – for instance, if you opt for consecutive tests and fail the driving ability part, you may have to forfeit the instructional ability test. On the other hand, if you take them separately, there may be some delay in booking the third part of the exam.

Training providers

A scheme of accredited training providers has been set up to ensure that the standard of training offered is to a high standard and that all instructors are fully qualified and registered.

LGV Instructor Accreditation Scheme

LGV Instructor Accreditation Scheme

1st Class Trucking Ltd (Enfield)	Enfield	0845 644 808
Ace LGV Training Ltd	Sawbridgeworth	01279 722711
CEVA Logistics Ltd	Suffolk	02476 400308
Driver Training Centre Ltd	Hastings	01424 432200
Highlands & Islands Fire & Rescue Service	Inverness	01463 227111
Kent Fire & Rescue Service	Maidstone	01622 774116
Nithcree Training	Dumfries	01387 256528
Peter Smythe Transport Training	Mansfield Woodhouse	01623 620062
Ritchies HGV Training Centre Ltd	Glasgow	0141 557 2212
Roadtrain	Letchworth	01462 680 100
Roadtrain	West Thurrock	01708 890953
Strathclyde Fire & Rescue	Glasgow	01698 300999
System Training	Carlisle	01228 574000
Wallace School of Transport	Battersea	0845 602 9498 or 020 8453 3440
	Croydon	0845 602 9498 or 020 8453 3440

	Greenwich	0845 602 9498
		or 020 8453 3440
	Park Royal/Wembley	0845 602 9498
		or 020 8453 3440
	Watford	0845 602 9498
		or 020 8453 3440
	Enfield	0845 602 9498
		or 020 8453 3440
	Heathrow	0845 602 9498
		or 020 8453 3440
Widdowson Group	Leicester	0116 232 2666

The theory test (Part 1)

The theory test is in two parts – multiple-choice and hazard perception – and can be taken at any one of about 150 centres around the country. The current fee (Jan 2011) is £63.25.

Multiple-choice questions

In this test there are 100 questions with a choice of three or more alternative answers to each. You are allowed 90 minutes to complete the test. The syllabus for the examination covers:

- principles of road safety generally, and their application in particular circumstances;
- techniques of driving an LGV correctly, courteously and safely, including control of the vehicle, road procedure, recognizing hazards and taking proper action, dealing properly with pedestrians and other road users, the use of safety equipment;
- theory and practice of learning, teaching and assessment;
- tuition required to be able to instruct a pupil driving an LGV, including the items set out above, the correction of pupil errors, the manner of the instructor and pupil;
- *The Highway Code*;
- the DSA publication *The Official DSA Guide to Driving Goods Vehicles*;
- interpretation of the reasons for failure to pass the driving test given in the form DLV 25, the 'Statement of Failure' to pass the driving test.

The questions are grouped into 10 subjects and into four 'bands'. In order to pass you must obtain a minimum of 80 per cent in each of the bands, as well as an overall mark of 85 per cent.

Band 1	Road procedure
	Driving technique
Band 2	Instructional techniques

Band 3   Mechanics
          Vehicle condition
          Drivers' hours and rest periods
          Loading, unloading and load security
Band 4   Driving test
          Environmental issues
          Accident handling

To improve your practical skills in preparation for the exams you will probably benefitr from studying *Practical Teaching Skills for Driving Instructors* – available from Kogan Page.

Sample questions

1. **You must drive your vehicle at lower speed limits when its load is wider than:**

   (Mark one answer)

   2.7 metres (9 ft).
   4.0 metres (13 ft).
   4.3 metres (14 ft 2 in).

2. **When part loading a vehicle with an empty ISO container, you should position the container:**

   (Mark one answer)

   Close to the fifth wheel.
   Over the front axle.
   Close to the trailer edge.
   Over the rear axles.

3. **Your tractor unit has three air lines. You are connecting to a trailer with two air lines. What colour is the line you should leave unconnected?**

   (Mark one answer)

   Red.
   Yellow.
   Blue.

4. **What shape are hazardous cargo labels?**

   (Mark one answer)

   Diamond.
   Triangle.
   Circle.
   Oval.

5. The process of perception can be described as ...

(Mark one answer)

Shrewdness and foresight.
The interpretation of necessary information.
The selective focusing on a given hazard.

6. As a pupil's knowledge and driving competence increases the level of instructor involvement is likely to ...

(Mark one answer)

Remain the same.
Increase.
Decrease.

The complete question bank is available from the DSA.

Hazard perception test

This part of the exam tests your hazard perception skills by using video film clips as in the 'L' and LGV theory tests (pages 337 and 375). You are allowed about 25 minutes for this part, during which you are shown 14 film clips, with 15 scoring hazards. The pass mark for the test is 57 out of a possible 75.

Before leaving the test centre you will be notified of the result for both parts of the test, and will be given information about how to apply for the practical driving ability test.

The practical driving test (Part 2)

The driving test can be taken at about 38 LGV centres around the country. It lasts about an hour and a half over a route that is similar to, but more demanding than, the usual LGV test. The test is of an advanced nature and a very high standard of driving is required.

You must provide a suitable vehicle for the test. Depending on which qualification you need it can be a Category C1, C1+E, C or C+E vehicle. It must, of course, meet the minimum test vehicle requirements that are outlined on page 381 and must have right-hand steering and a suitable forward facing seat for a passenger. 'L' plates should not be displayed.

The syllabus for this part of the examination covers:

- special 'off road' exercises, including braking, reversing and (where applicable) uncoupling/recoupling;
- a wide variety of road and traffic conditions, including dual carriageways, one-way systems and, where possible, motorways;
- gear change exercise, which is normally carried out during the on-road section;

- uphill and downhill starts as well as moving off normally and at an angle;
- meet, cross and overtake other traffic;
- keep a safe separation distance;
- negotiate various types of roundabout;
- exercise correct lane discipline;
- display courtesy and consideration to other road users, especially pedestrians, riders on horseback, cyclists and motorcyclists;
- apply correct procedures at all types of road junctions and hazards, including pedestrian crossings, level crossings, traffic signals;
- effective use of mirrors and signals;
- alertness and anticipation;
- speed limits;
- vehicle sympathy.

You will pass if you commit six or fewer driving faults, and no serious or dangerous faults are recorded. At the end of the test the examiner will give you the result.

Test of instructional ability (Part 3)

This part of the test is an assessment of your ability to give instruction and to pass on your knowledge to a 'pupil'. The test can be taken at certain selected test centres and usually lasts about one hour. As in the driving ability test, you must provide a suitable vehicle that conforms to all the previously listed requirements. 'L' plates (or 'D' plates in Wales if you prefer) should be displayed on the front and rear of the vehicle.

The examiner must be covered by insurance for the time he or she is driving the vehicle. The insurance should not name any particular examiner, but should cover any DSA examiner.

During the test the examiner adopts the role of a learner lorry driver and will simulate faults that are appropriate to the particular role selected. This is done by using a selection from the following nine preset tests:

PST 1   *Safety precautions/controls:*
Accelerator, clutch, footbrake, handbrake, steering, gears
Move off and stop: on level, uphill, downhill, angled
Mirrors, observation, control

PST 2   *Signs, signals and road markings:*
Road signs, markings, traffic lights, controllers, other road users
Recognition, appropriate action
Braking exercise:
Safely, full control, promptly, distance

PST 3   *General driving:*
         Faults – identification, analysis, remedial
         Gear change exercise:
         Control, observations, signals

PST 4   *Use of mirrors:*
         Moving off, signalling, changing direction or lanes, turning,
         overtaking, increasing speed, slowing, leaving vehicle, parked
         vehicles
         Uncouple/recouple:
         Safe place, brakes, landing gear, taps, air lines, coupling
         mechanism, number plates

PST 5   *Judgement of speed:*
         Road, traffic, weather, vehicle speed limits, hazards
         Road positioning:
         Keep left, parked vehicles, weaving, lanes, one-way, road
         markings

PST 6   *Junctions (turning into and emerging):*
         Position, speed, observations, priorities
         Roundabouts and crossroads:
         Mirrors, signal, manoeuvre (MSM)
         Position, speed, look (PSL)
         Gears, observations, lanes, position through, exit

PST 7   *Approaching or turning at crossroads, roundabouts or junctions:*
         MSM, PSL, gears, observations

PST 8   *Meet approaching traffic:*
         Mirrors, signal, speed, gears, position, observation
         Overtaking/anticipating the actions of other road users:
         View, speed, limits, bends, junctions, gradients
         Mirrors, signal

PST 9   *Remedial lesson after test failure:*
         DLV25, assess, faults

During the test you will be assessed specifically on the following:

● Fault assessment, analysis and remedial action.
● Level of instruction.
● Planning the lesson.
● Controlling the lesson.
● Communication.

- Question and answer techniques.
- Feedback and encouragement.
- Attitude and approach to the pupil.
- The method, clarity, adequacy and correctness of the instruction given.

As with the driving ability test, you will be given the result by the examiner at the end of the test.

The cost of each of the practical tests (at Jan 2011) is £119 plus VAT. Registration is for a period of four years at a cost of £100 plus VAT.

To prepare for the voluntary register exams you will need to refer to the official publications:

- *Driving Goods Vehicles – the official DSA syllabus*;
- *The Highway Code*;
- *The Motor Vehicles (Driving Licences) regulations 1999*;
- *The Official theory Test for Drivers of Large Vehicles*;
- *DVL25 – Driving Test Report*;
- *The Official Guide to Hazard Perception* DVD;
- *Know your Traffic Signs*.

You may also find it helpful to use *Practical Teaching Skills for Driving Instructors* (published by Kogan Page), which has a lot of useful information about teaching and learning.

Further details about the examination and registration can be obtained at www.businesslink.gov.uk or by phoning the DSA.

Fleet driver training register

The voluntary register of fleet driver training was started in 2002 for instructors and assessors involved in the training of company drivers in both cars and vans. To qualify for the Register you first need to be a qualified and registered ADI.

There are two separate ways of qualifying. You are allowed to take a set of exams with the DSA or you may complete an approved training course with a DSA accredited training provider. The exams follow a similar format to that of the ADI exams: a theory test, practical driving test and a practical instruction/coaching test. If you decide to qualify by the approved training route, you apply after completing the course.

Full details of the Register, are available from The Fleet Driver Training Register at the Driving Standards Agency. Registration lasts for at least four years (depending on the expiry date of your ADI registration).

The registration of fleet training instructors is part of the DSA policy to of modernizing and upgrading the qualification standards and arrangements for all types and categories of professional driver trainers. The Fleet Driver training and LGV registers are part of the strategy for achieving this aim.

Application

To apply for registration you must be currently registered with the DSA. If you intend to register by taking the DSA exams your application to the DSA has to include the fee for the theory part of the exams. Once your application has been accepted you will be notified about a date for the theory test.

If you have taken an accredited training course, your application for the Register should be accompanied by the registration fee, the processing fee, two passport photos and documentary evidence of having passed the appropriate qualifying course.

Fees

Processing fee	£12
Theory Test	£66
Driving Ability Test	£134.40
Instruction/Coaching Test	£134.40
Registration fee	£120

These fees apply at Jan 2011 and are subject to VAT at the current rates as the Register is not one of the DSA statutory exams.

Qualifying

Anyone who is currently on the DSA register of ADIs can apply for the Fleet Driver Training Register.

There are two options for registration:

1 By taking and passing the three-part DSA exam. This set of exams includes:
   - a multi-choice theory test and hazard perception test;
   - a practical driving ability test;
   - a practical test of instruction/coaching ability.

A maximum of three attempts is allowed for each of the tests. All three parts of the exam must be taken and passed within 12 months. This period of one year starts from the date of the first attempt at the theory test. If you do not pass all three parts in this time you have to start the whole qualifying process again.

The tests are very demanding and the DSA recommends that you should not apply unless you are thoroughly prepared for them. If you are in any doubt, contact the DSA before applying.

After passing all three parts of the exam you have 12 months in which to register.

2   By successfully completing a DSA-accredited training scheme.
With this method you must apply for registration within 12 months of
completing the training course. Courses have been assessed by the DSA
and meet all the criteria for skills and knowledge for the Fleet Driver
Training Register.

Fleet driver training courses

By attending and qualifying on one of the training courses listed below you
will gain entrance onto the Register without the need to take the DSA exam.
These courses have been assessed by the DSA and the content and validation
processes meet the fleet trainer skills and knowledge criteria.

Accredited training providers

AA DriveTech plc	Crowthorne	01344 773144
ADI Federation	Wellingborough	01933 461821
ADIndifleet and Three Shires Fleet	Raunds	0845 437 950
Amber Driver Training	Carlisle	01228 527000
Any Driver	Abercyon	0845 51 90 321
ATC Driver Training	Epping	01992 522287
Bill Plant Fleet Craft Ltd	Ripon	01765 609140
BSM	Bristol	01454 658318
DrivexLtd	Isle of Wight	01983 810012
Driving Instructor Association	Croydon	0208 6655151
Excelsior Training	Uttoxeter	01889 591474
Fast-Trak Driver & Rider Training	Shrewsbury	01743 460460
IAM Drive & Survive	London	020 8996 9700
Inspire Driver Training and Development	Sunderland	0191 5212919
Lancashire County Council	Preston	01772 534525
Learner Driver Centres	Ponefract	01977 691800
Lincolnshire Road Safety Partnership	North Kyme	01526 861170
MAC GB Ltd	Abergele	01745 828180
Pelican Fleet Training Ltd	Rotherham	01226 742950
Professional Driver Services (PDS) Ltd	Barry	01446 722229
RED Fleet Training	Brighton	01273 547900
Somax Accredited Driver Training	Bristol	01275 465 555
The Royal Society for the Prevention of Accidents (RoSPA)	Birmingham	0121 2482124
Total Driving Solutions (UK) Ltd	Harrogate	0800 141 2446
UK Road Safety	Bristol	01454 423164

If you intend qualifying by taking one of these training courses the DSA
recommends that you should contact them before making a commitment
with the individual training organization.

Theory test

The theory test for the Fleet Driver Training Register is currently available at 38 centres around the UK. It consists of 100 questions each with a choice of four alternative answers. Each question has one correct answer.

The complete bank of 365 questions is available from the DSA as part of the starter pack.

The exam syllabus is separated into four groups of subjects ('bands'):

Band 1 – driving practices and procedures
– road and traffic signs
– motorway driving

Band 2 – driver attitude
– driver and the law
– environmental issues

Band 3 – vehicle dynamics and handling
– accident procedures

Band 4 – instructional coaching techniques
– hazard perception

Sample questions:

1 A trainee is making satisfactory progress during his or her training session. A trainer should:
(a) continue with a high level of guidance for all situations;
(b) give only retrospective guidance from this point on;
(c) stop giving feedback until a serious error has been committed;
(d) aim to give the trainee a level of instruction to suit his or her ability.

2 Red diesel is:
(a) only used by private cars;
(b) for authorized purposes only;
(c) available at all garages;
(d) very environmentally friendly.

3 Fatigue-related accidents are *most* likely to occur:
(a) in the reduction of alertness that may occur after a midday meal;
(b) between midnight and 8 am;
(c) between 8 am and midnight;
(d) during the early evening.

To pass the test you must achieve an overall mark of 85 out of the 100 questions and you must also have a minimum of 80 per cent in each of the four topic bands.

The result of the test will be notified to you in writing by the DSA.

It may seem relatively straightforward to memorize the correct answers from the 365 questions in the official question bank. In practice, though, it's not that easy. You should make sure that you fully understand the reasons for each of the answers by preparing yourself thoroughly by using the appropriate resource materials. The DSA recommended reading list includes *Practical Teaching Skills for Driving Instructors* and *The Driving Instructor's Handbook* as well as the official DSA publications.

Driving ability test

The driving ability test is conducted at 48 test centres around the UK.

After passing the theory test you need to send the application form to the DSA at Nottingham. You will then be contacted by them to arrange a convenient appointment date, time and venue.

You can opt to apply for this part of the test individually or linked to the instruction/coaching ability test at the same time or on the following day. There are, of course, some advantages and disadvantages with each of these choices and you can make the decision based on your individual circumstances.

The test lasts about 60 minutes using a route that is very demanding and which will normally include a wide variety of different road and traffic conditions.

During the test the candidate is required to give a talk-through commentary on his or her driving for a minimum period of 10 minutes.

Syllabus

Eyesight test – ability to read a number plate of 3 1/8 ins (70.4 mm) from a distance of 90 ft (27.5 m).

Ability to move off safely and smoothly, uphill, downhill, normally ahead and at an angle.

Ability to:

- meet, overtake and cross the path of other vehicles;
- keep a safe separation distance;
- negotiate various types of roundabouts;
- exercise correct lane discipline.

Display courtesy and consideration to other road users, especially pedestrians, horse riders, cyclists and motorcyclists.

Apply correct procedures at:

- pedestrian crossings;
- level crossings;
- traffic signals;
- road junctions.

Demonstrate:

- effective use of all mirrors;
- correct use of all signals;
- alertness and anticipation;

– observance of speed limits;

– vehicle sympathy.

During the test there will be one reversing exercise selected at random by the examiner. An emergency stop exercise is not carried out.

You will pass this part of the test if you have no serious or dangerous faults and a maximum of four driving faults.

Both practical tests (driving and instructional ability) can be taken in Category B vehicle – either a car or a van. In the case of a car, it must not be a convertible. The vehicle must have right-hand drive, an adjustable passenger seat and an additional rear view mirror for use by the examiner.

Instruction/coaching ability test

This part of the test is conducted at various driving test centres around the country.

The test lasts about 60 minutes and is designed to assess your ability to identify and prioritize areas of risk in the customer's driving and to offer a risk profile for the driver.

Syllabus

- Give a short interactive presentation to raise the customer's awareness of occupational road risk.
- Practical vehicle check, including knowledge of basic mechanical principles and legal requirements.
- Demonstrate pre-start checks.
- Driving assessment.
- Communicate a risk assessment.
- Use appropriate coaching methods to reduce risks.
- Highlight the customer's key strengths and weaknesses.

During the test the examiner tests the candidate's ability by role-playing a particular type of customer with various strengths and weaknesses in his or her driving. The examiner will portray an experienced or inexperienced car or van driver who is attending for driver development as appropriate.

The examiner will simulate one of the following topics to be used during the role-play exercise:

- Attitude and culture:
  - identify weaknesses in attitude towards other road users;
  - demonstrate and discuss the benefits of a considered approach to driving.
- Legal requirements:
  - an understanding of the legal requirements in driving;
  - road traffic accident procedures.

- Driver and passenger safety:
  - understand and discuss issues that affect safety;
  - drink, drugs, illness, fatigue;
  - advantages and disadvantages of ABS and traction control.
- Vehicle safety and sympathy:
  - basic mechanical principles;
  - importance of vehicle safety checks.
- Vehicle loading and security:
  - demonstrate and discuss the correct methods of loading;
  - effects of loads on vehicle handling;
  - security of vehicles and loads.
- Dealing with aggressive drivers:
  - ability to give correct advice on dealing with inappropriate behaviour in other drivers.
- Environment effects:
  - demonstrate and discuss the benefits to the environment of good driving practices;
  - fuel savings.

As with the ADI exams you will be assessed on several main areas of ability including:

- the method, clarity, adequacy and correctness of the instruction or coaching given;
- the observation and accuracy of fault and risk assessment;
- your general manner and attitude when dealing with the customer.

Preparation for the exam

To pass the instruction/coaching ability test you must prepare yourself thoroughly in the following subject areas:

- Core competencies:
  - risk and fault identification;
  - risk and fault assessment;
  - remedial actions.
- Instructional and coaching techniques:
  - presentation;
  - level of coaching and instruction;
  - planning and controlling the training session;
  - communication;
  - question and answer techniques;

- feedback and encouragement;
- trainer's use of controls.
- Trainer characteristics:
  - articulate;
  - enthusiastic;
  - encouraging;
  - friendly;
  - patient.
  - confident.

Registration and check test

After passing the exams, or on completing an appropriate training course, you can apply to have your name entered on the Register. Registration is normally for a period of four years, although the initial registration may be for more than four years – often until the expiry of your ADI certificate.

When giving Fleet Driver training the ADI certificate should be displayed on the vehicle and your Fleet Driver certificate should be available for inspection.

After qualifying for the Fleet Driver Training Register you have an obligation to take a Check Test at regular intervals. For the check test you must bring a pupil who has a full driving licence (or you can ask the examiner to role-play a pupil). If your pupil only holds a provisional licence, the Check Test will only apply to your ADI registration and you would need to take another check test for your Fleet Registration.

Although the basic criteria are similar to those for the ADI Check Test, there are many variations, particularly in relation to coaching. These changes and the higher standards of coaching required are illustrated in the following article by an expert in the field of Fleet Driver Training:

Fleet Check Test

Where an ADI is a DSA Fleet Registered Instructor/Trainer, there will inevitably come a time whereby they will be invited to take a Fleet Check Test. As with all check tests thorough preparation is the key to a good result.

The DSA system does allow that where an ADI is Fleet Registered, then they may opt for a Fleet Register Check Test and that would also be accepted as the compliance with the ordinary ADI Check Test (ie one Check Test instead of two). This is of course where the ADI had notified the examiner before attending at the test centre.

The basic principles of a Fleet Check Test are not dissimilar to that of the normal check test. However, Fleet is based on a much higher level of performance and as such the instructional techniques are based more towards coaching skills as opposed to basic instruction. This is the main difference between the two and it must be remembered that in general terms the delegate chosen to be the driver for the check test, will be a qualified driver as opposed to a learner under formal instruction.

The ADI candidate invited to take the Fleet Check Test may request that the examiner role-play the part of a delegate on the day, provided the examiner was informed of this in advance of the day.

The assessment part of a Fleet Check Test does not differ from that of a normal Check Test, however, there is a vast difference in the structure. Although the examiner will be flexible about this, the trainer needs to consider the following areas for the test itself:

1 A short presentation about occupational road safety may be given either in the examiner's office or in the car. Remember time is very short and any presentation needs to take this into account.

2 With a role-play Check Test it is good to discuss vehicle safety checks and ideally physically carry out these checks on the vehicle itself before going on-road. (The challenge here is that time is short so you will need to be concise.)

3 Driving licence check to demonstrate to the examiner that you know what you are doing. The examiner may have previously stated that all documents were in order therefore it is probably unlikely you will need to go into this much detail.

4 Eyesight test.

5 When on-road the initial drive, lasting about 10 to 15 minutes, would be to assess the examiner's driving standards. (Note that in this situation the examiner is role-playing a delegate.)

6 Pull up in a safe place preferably off-road, to discuss the driving standard and any faults or raised risks associated with the driving style displayed during the initial drive. The trainer will need to set key objectives and prioritize the serious faults.

7 Due to time constraints, it is probably unlikely that a demonstration drive would be accepted at this stage, therefore the trainer should now concentrate on coaching techniques and encourage the examiner role-playing a delegate into better driving habits without being nit-picking or patronizing.

8 At the end of the period, do ensure a full debrief is given on the whole session before concluding the check test.

9 Now discuss with the examiner in the office your performance throughout the test.

The alternative method of carrying out a Fleet Check Test is to take along your own delegate for the test. Remember this would be a qualified driver who needs further development and preferably someone that drives for a living would be ideal.

Whether you accept a role-play check test or take along your own delegate is a matter of choice. However, in either case, where an instructor/trainer is a little unsure of his or her own abilities it is strongly recommended to seek out a professional trainer who will impart the necessary knowledge in order for them to do well on the Check Test.

With qualified drivers and especially the company car driver, there is a wide variation with the style of driving performance. Some may have taken further advanced training or even passed an advanced driving test. Generally speaking, most just drive under pressure to meet deadlines for their company and ultimately drop into bad driving habits over time.

The role of the Fleet Trainer is therefore to observe any risk characteristics that may be apparent and offer advice on how to lower and eliminate that risk altogether. Other factors come into play such as coaching and offering advice on driving more economically while reducing stress and also how to make better progress with total safety in order to reduce journey times without breaking any speed limits.

This multi-tasking role is the essence of a good Fleet Trainer and that is why the higher level of knowledge is accepted if a Fleet Check Test is taken as opposed to the ordinary ADI requirement.

So let us look at a typical Fleet Trainer's day, when for example he or she visits a company that has requested training for one or several employees.

The day would consist of the following components:

1   In-classroom presentation discussing occupational road safety.

2   Driving licence check.

3   Eyesight test.

4   Full vehicle check procedure.

5   Recap on the key objectives for the current training session.

6   An initial driving session by the delegate to benchmark the current driving standard and identify any serious faults.

7   The Fleet Trainer may where necessary provide a demonstration drive with a full commentary.

8   The delegate would then be coached as he or she drove again for the remainder of the session. The emphasis would be placed on reducing the identified risks observed during the initial drive.

9   A full debrief on the objectives achieved and what aspects of driving need more development.

10 Follow-up written reporting for the company records.

As you can see from the above details it is practically impossible to cover all of this on a Fleet Check Test, since the Check Test itself will only last for one hour's duration in total.

That hour will include meeting the examiner and informing them of the intended content for the Check Test about to begin. Unless the option for the examiner was to role play a typical delegate, then it is best to concentrate on item 5, the on-road coaching session, as the basis for the test.

You can have carried out beforehand and before arriving at the test centre, the initial assessment drive and have provided a demonstration drive for your delegate. Once you arrive at the test centre for test, you now have the information documented and available for the examiner to review. This way you are now free to deliver a good coaching session while the examiner sits in the back of your vehicle and observes your performance.

Do always remember to introduce the examiner to your delegate and inform the delegate as to the reason why the examiner is there on that day.

Where a company driver is taken along on the day, every effort will be made by the examiner not to impact on the smooth running of the business. Time allocated for the Check Test should take into account not only the one hour for the test itself, but also arriving on time and allowing time for a discussion of about 15 minutes post-test with the examiner. The examiner will not make any comments to the delegate other than the normal courtesies expected for good manners and politeness.

The criteria for the Fleet Check are based on three areas of expertise:

Core competencies; Instructional techniques; and Instructor characteristics.

It is always a good suggestion for every instructor or trainer to run a self-check on themselves after every training session and consider the following areas where perhaps improvements could be made:

- Did the training session achieve the objectives?
- How well planned was the training session?
- Was the delegate sufficiently involved in the training at the correct level?
- Did the training match the ability of the delegate and was it pitched at the appropriate level?
- Was there sufficient feedback or encouragement?
- In the event of a serious problem being identified, did the trainer deal with that as a matter of priority or offer retrospective advice?
- Was the route selected sufficiently challenging to help develop better driving habits?
- Were the coaching skills adequate?
- Was there anything that could have been done differently?

This self-analysis will help by constantly keeping up your standards as a good instructor/trainer.

Remember that on a Check Test everything you do will be monitored from the time you arrive at the test centre through to the conclusion of the test. It should be obvious that total professionalism will be rewarded with a high score.

Additional training in preparation for the check test is advisable. Many instructors tend to work in isolation and as such may not be familiar with the latest developments. It is essential to remember there is no such thing as a bad student. It is the skills of the teacher that will bring the correct results.

How you choose to prepare and set the objectives will ultimately depend upon the results you seek. The need to determine what is the best way to help your delegate and communicate at the correct level and at the most appropriate opportunity will help to ensure that he or she is willing to learn and is prepared to achieve a much higher level of expertise.

Drivers will reflect on what happened during their time with you long after they have gone away. Your skill is to impart sufficient information so that they willingly want to change and move away from bad habits and ultimately become a more defensive driver.

During your Fleet Check Test you will have the opportunity to shine and show the examiner just how well you know your subject and to leave him or her in no doubt that you have raised the standards and are a true professional.

Good luck with your test.

APPENDIX I

Useful Addresses

Driving Standards Agency (DSA)
The Axis Building
112 Upper Parliament Street
Nottingham NG1 6LP
Tel: 0115 936 6666; www.dft.gov.uk/dsa
For full details of DSA departments, see pages 417–18

Driving and Vehicle Licensing Agency (DVLA)
Longview Road
Swansea SA6 7JL
Tel: 01792 782 341
Drivers' enquiries: Tel.: 0870 240 0009; Fax: 0870 240 1651;
Hearing impaired customers: 01792 766 366;
e-mail: drivers.dvla@gtnet.gov.uk
Vehicle enquiries: Tel: 0870 240 0010; Fax: 0870 850 1285;
Hearing impaired customers: 01792766 426;
e-mail: vehicles.dvla@gtnet.gov.uk

Driver and Vehicle Agency (DVA)
Customer Services
County Hall
Castlerock Road
Coleraine
BT51 3HS
Tel: 0845 601 4094; www.dvtani.gov.uk

ADI consultative organizations

AA Driving School
3rd Floor, St Patricks House
17 Penarth Road
Cardiff
CF10 5ZA
Tel: 0800 587 0086; e-mail: drivings@theaa.com;
www.theaa.com/driving-school

Approved Driving Instructors National Joint Council (ADINJC)
47 Sweetmans Road
Shaftesbury
Dorset SP7 8EH
Tel: 01747 855091; e-mail: liaisonofficer@ adinjc.org.uk;
www.adinjc.org.uk

British School of Motoring Limited (BSM)
RAC Building
2610 Quadrant
Aztec West Business Park
Bristol BS32 4TR
Tel: 0800 0147233; www.bsm.co.uk

Driving Instructors Association (DIA)
Safety House
Beddington Farm Road
Croydon
Surrey CR0 4XZ
Tel: 020 8665 5151 or 0845 345 5151; Fax: 020 8665 5565;
e-mail: DIA@driving.org; www.driving.org

Driving Instructors Democratic Union (A branch of UNITE)
Chairman, DIDU
Transport House
55 Call Lane
Leeds LS1 7BW
Tel: 05602 609125; e-mail: info@didu.org.uk; www.didu.org.uk

Driving Instructors Scottish Council (DISC)
4 Burnside Road
Uphall Broxburn
West Lothian
EH52 5DE
Tel: 01506 855455; e-mail: aeneas.disc@tiscali.co.uk; www.d-i-s-c.org.uk

Motor Schools Association GB Ltd (MSA)
101 Wellington Road North
Stockport
Cheshire SK4 2LP
Tel: 0161 429 9669; Fax: 0161 429 9779; e-mail: mail@msagb.co.uk;
www.msagb.co.uk

Training aids and services

Desk Top Driving Ltd
Unit 6, Gaugemaster Way
Ford
Arundel
West Sussex BN18 0RX
Tel: 01903 882299; Fax: 01903 885599; www.desktopdriving.co.uk

Driving School Aids
Low Lane
Horsforth
West Yorks LS18 4DD
Tel: 0113 258 0688

Driving School Supplies
2–4 Tame Road
Witton
Birmingham B6 7DS
Tel: 0121 328 6226; Fax: 0121 327 1864; www.d-ss.co.uk

He-Man Dual Controls Ltd
Cable Street
Southampton SO14 5AR
Tel: 023 8022 6952; Fax: 023 8033 0132; www.he-mandualcontrols.co.uk

Porter Dual Controls
Impact Business Park
Greenford
Middlesex UB6 7JD
Tel: 020 8601 3566

RCM Marketing Ltd
20 Newtown Business Park
Albion Close
Poole
Dorset BH12 3LL
Tel: 01202 737999; Fax: 01202 735 909; www.rcmmarketing.co.uk

Royal Society for the Prevention of Accidents (RoSPA)
28 Calthorpe Road
Edgbaston
Birmingham B15 1RP
Tel: 0121 248 2000; Fax: 0121 248 2001; www.rospa. com

RoSPA in Scotland
43 Discovery Terrace
Heriot-Watt University Research Park
Edinburgh EH14 4AP
Tel.: 0131 449 9378

RoSPA in Wales
2nd Floor, Cwrt-y-Parc
Parc Ty Glas
Cardiff Business Park
Llanishen
Cardiff CF14 5GH
Tel: 02920 250600

RoSPA in Northern Ireland
Nella House
4 Dargan Crescent
Dargan Wholesale Park
Belfast BT3 9JP
Tel: 02890 501160

SmartDriving
Ballinultha
Boyle
Co. Roscommon
Ireland
www.smartdriving.co.uk

The Stationery Office (TSO)
St Crispins
Duke Street
Norwich NR3 1PD
Tel: 01603 622211; www.tso.co.uk

Wholesale Book Supplies
18 High St
Bala
Gwynedd LL23 7AG
Tel: 0800 195 2208; Fax: 0800 195 2209; www.wholesalebooks.co.uk

Disabled drivers' assessment centres

QEF
Leatherhead Court
Woodlands Road
Leatherhead
Surrey KT22 0BN
Tel: 01372 841100; Fax: 01372 844072; www.qef.org.uk

Forum of Mobility Centres
c/o Providence Chapel
Warehorne
Ashford
Kent TN26 2JX
Tel: 0800 559 3636; www.mobility-centres.org.uk

Local centres

Cornwall Mobility Centre
Tehidy House
Royal Cornwall Hospital
Truro
Cornwall TR1 3LJ
Tel: 01872 254920; Fax: 01872 254921;
e-mail: mobility@rcht.swest.nhs.uk;
www.cornwall-homepage.co.uk/homepages/mobile/index/html

DART Driving Assessment and Advice Centre
Cobtree Ward, Preston Hall Hospital
London Road
Aylesford
Kent ME20 7NJ
Tel: 01622 795719; Fax: 01622 795720; e-mail: janicestannard@nhs.net

Derby Regional Mobility Centre
Kingsway Hospital
Kingsway
Derby DE22 3LZ
Tel: 01332 371929; Fax: 01332 382377;
e-mail: info@derbyregionalmobilitycentre.co.uk;
www.derbyregionalmobilitycentre.co.uk

Hertfordshire Action on Disability Mobility Centre
The Woodside Centre
The Common
Welwyn Garden City
Herts AL7 4DD
Tel: 01707 324581; Fax: 01707 371297; e-mail: driving@hadnet.co.uk;
www.hadnet.org.uk

Kilverstone Mobility Assessment Centre
2 Napier Place
Thetford
Norfolk IP24 3RL
Tel: 01842 753029; Fax: 01842 755950; e-mail: kmacmobil@aol.com;
www.ridgenage.co.uk/mobility

Mobility Centre
Regional Neurological Rehabilitation Centre
Hunters Road
Newcastle upon Tyne NE2 4NR
Tel: 0191 219 5694; Fax: 0191 219 5693;
www.nap.nhs.uk/snrs/index.html

Mobility Service of the Disabled Living Centre
The Vassall Centre
Gill Avenue
Fishponds
Bristol BS16 2QQ
Tel: 0117 965 9353; Fax: 0117 965 3652; e-mail: mobserv@dicbristol.org

Northern Ireland Mobility Centre
Disability Action
Portside Business Park
189 Airport Road
Belfast BT3 9ED
Tel: 028 9029 7880; Fax: 028 9029 7881; Text: 028 9029 7882;
e-mail: mobilitycentre@disabilityaction.org

North Wales Mobility and Driving Assessment Service
The North Wales Resources Centre
Glan Clwyd Hospital
Bodelwyddan
Denbighshire LL18 5UJ
Tel: 01745 584858; Fax: 01745 582762; e-mail: info@drivemobility.org

Regional Driving Assessment Centre
West Heath Hospital
Rednal Road
Birmingham B38 8HR
Tel: 0121 627 8228; Fax: 0121 627 8629

Scottish Driving Assessment Service
Astley Ainslie Hospital
133 Grange Loan
Edinburgh EH9 2HL
Tel: 0131 537 9192; Fax: 0131 537 9193

South Wales Mobility and Driving Assessment Service
Rookwood Hospital
Fairwater Road
Llandaff
Cardiff CF5 2YN
Tel: 029 2055 5130; Fax: 029 2055 5130

William Merritt Disabled Living Centre and Mobility Centre
St Mary's Hospital
Green Hill Road
Armley
Leeds LS12 3QE
Tel: 0113 305 5288; Fax: 0113 231 9291;
e-mail: wmmobilityservices@cwcom.net

Wrightington Mobility Centre
Wrightington Hospital
Hall Lane
Appley Bridge
Wigan
Lancs WN6 9EP
Tel: 01257 256409; Fax: 01257 256409;
e-mail: mobility.centre@alwpct.nhs.uk

Motoring organizations

Automobile Association
Member Administration Contact Centre
Lambert House
Stockport Road
Cheadle SK8 2DY
Tel: 0870 600 0371; Disability helpline: 0800 26 20 50;
Fax: 0161 488 7544; www.theaa.com

Royal Automobile Club
Customer Services
Great Park Road
Bradley Stoke
Bristol BS32 4QN
Tel: 08705 722 722; www.rac.co.uk

APPENDIX II

Driving Standards Agency – Contacts

Headquarters

The Axis Building
112 Upper Parliament Street
Nottingham NG1 6LP
www.dft.gov.uk/dsaCustomer service enquiries:
Tel: 0300 200 1122 (theory); 0300 200 1188 (practical)
Welsh line: 0300 200 1133; Fax: 0300 200 1177 (theory);
0300 200 1155 (practical)
For hearing-impaired customers: (minicom): 0300 200 1144
e-mail: customer.services@dsa.gsi.gov.uk

ADI (Approved Driving Instructor) enquiries:
Tel: 0300 200 1122; Fax: 0300 200 1155; e-mail: adireg@dsa.gsi.gov.uk

CBT (Compulsory Basic Training) enquiries:
Tel: 0115 936 6547; Fax: 0115 936 6582; e-mail: cbt@dsa.gsi.gov.uk

To contact a particular department at the DSA by phone, dial 0115 936,
followed by:
Switchboard: 6666
Testing & Assessment (COB): 6449 & 6514
E-assessment: 6446
Pass Plus: 6504 & 6563
Experienced Driver Assessment Services: 6488
Despatch: 6045

Other sections

Arrive Alive: 0300 200 1122
Technical support: 0300 200 1122
Training centre and Learning materials (Cardington): Tel: 01234 744000
Customer service enquiries and complaints:
London and South-east: Tel: 020 7468 4712; Fax: 020 7468 4550;
e-mail: londoncsu@dsa.gsi.gov.uk
Midlands and Eastern: Tel: 0121 697 6762; Fax: 0121 697 6750;
e-mail: birminghamcsu@dsa.gsi.gov.uk
Wales and Western: Tel: 029 2058 1218; Fax: 029 2058 1050;
e-mail: cardiffcsu@dsa.gsi.gov.uk
Scotland: Tel: 0131 529 8645; Fax: 0131 529 8589;
e-mail: scotlandcsu@dsa.gsi.gov.uk
Northern: Tel: 0191 201 8161; Fax: 0191 201 8010;
e-mail: northerncsu@dsa.gsi.gov.uk

APPENDIX III

Reference Books

Your Road to Becoming an Approved Driving Instructor (ADI 14), Driving Standards Agency (DSA)

The Official DSA Guide to Driving – The essential skills, DSA/The Stationery Office (£12.99, ISBN 9780 1155 31347)

The Official Guide to Learning to Drive, DSA/The Stationery Office (£9.99, ISBN 9780 1155 30913)

The Official DSA Theory Test for Car Drivers and The Highway Code, DSA/The Stationery Office (£12.99, ISBN 9780 1155 31262)

Know Your Traffic Signs, DSA/The Stationery Office (£4.99, ISBN 9780 1155 28552)

The Official Highway Code, DSA/The Stationery Office (£2.50, ISBN 9780 1155 28149)

The Official DSA Guide to Driving Goods Vehicles, DSA/The Stationery Office (£17.50, ISBN 9780 1155 30814)

The Official Theory Test for Drivers of Large Vehicles, DSA/The Stationery Office (£15.99, ISBN 9780 1155 29030)

Practical Teaching Skills for Driving Instructors, John Miller and Margaret Stacey, Kogan Page (£19.99, ISBN 9780 7494 63106)

Practical Business Skills for Driving Instructors, John Miller, Kogan Page (£19.99, ISBN 9780 7494 53947)

Glove Box Guide: Your car, Haynes (£9.99, ISBN 9781 8596 07923)

Instructional Techniques and Practice, Les Walklin, Stanley Thornes (£24.99, ISBN 9780 7487 16319)

The Professional LGV Driver's Handbook, David Lowe, Kogan Page (£29.95, ISBN 9780 7494 51189)

APPENDIX IV

The Official Register of Driving Instructor Training (ORDIT) – Terms and Conditions of Membership

Aims and objectives

The aim of the ORDIT scheme is to maintain, produce and promote the current Register (and work towards a compulsory Register) of driving instructor training organisations and driving instructor trainers that can be relied upon by the public, the driver training industry and the Driving Standards Agency to provide good quality training by qualified trainers, from premises that are ORDIT inspected and meet satisfactory standards and from organisations that have agreed to abide by the terms and conditions of the scheme.

The main objectives of the ORDIT scheme are to ensure that:

- Satisfactory standards of training are available for members of the public wishing to qualify as Approved Driving Instructors (ADIs);
- Satisfactory standards of training are available for ADIs who wish to receive further training or retraining;
- All trainers delivering training under the scheme have been tested by the DSA and accepted as being suitable for entry onto the Register;
- Any person seeking training with an organisation or individual whose details are entered in the Register should be protected from unfair business practices and inferior training;
- Those organisations, premises and trainers that are successfully ORDIT inspected will be promoted through the ORDIT list contained within the DSA's Starter Pack for potential ADIs (ADI 14);
- The DSA and the ADI consultative organisations will only promote those organisations, premises and individual trainers entered on the Register;
- Only those organisations, premises and trainers entered onto the Register are entitled to display ORDIT certificates/badges to help the public recognise them;

- Any course offered by ORDIT Members shall be genuinely adequate for the purpose of enabling a trainee to pass the ADI qualifying examination.

Code of practice

Those on the Register must:

- Clearly inform all prospective Trainees in writing of the services provided, with particular reference to the Trainer's qualification, costs, venue, duration and content in relation to the ADI examination structure.
- Inform prospective Trainees of the Organisation's terms of business and complaints procedure.
- Take all reasonable care, skill and diligence in providing training in all relevant aspects of traffic and driver education needed to pass the ADI qualifying examinations, taking into account individual training needs and safety.
- Not disclose to a third party any information given by a Trainee during training or training progress or driving and instructional ability except where under obligation in Law or with the DSA as part of an ORDIT inspection or with a third party who is paying for a Trainee's training but subject to the Trainee's knowledge.
- Ensure all vehicles used in training are maintained in a safe and satisfactory condition, properly insured, taxed and where appropriate certified as roadworthy.
- Apply an honest, moral and professional approach in all business practice and avoid improper language, suggestion or physical contact with Trainees as well as maintaining proper standards of personal hygiene and dress.
- Comply with all current legislation particularly in respect of business premises and practice, staff, vehicles and public liability.

Advertising and promotional code of practice

- All advertising shall fully comply with the best practice, as defined by current Codes of Practice issued by the Advertising Standards Authority (ASA), in the spirit as well as the letter.
- All advertising shall be legal, decent, honest, truthful and prepared with a sense of responsibility to both trainees and competitors as well as respecting the principles of fair trading and competition.

- Any claim made in advertising shall be able to be substantiated objectively by documentary evidence, which shall be made available for inspection upon request.
- The full terms of any guarantee shall be given in writing before any training course agreement is signed.
- Members of the Register convicted of any trading standards or fair trading offence, or having an adjudication made against them by the Advertising Standards Authority, shall have their continued membership of ORDIT reviewed by the ADI Registrar, who shall have the power to remove that person or Organisation from the Register.
- The ADI Registrar shall retain the right to demand timely changes to the advertising of any Organisation or Trainer following ASA OFT or Trading Standards rulings with the ultimate sanction of exclusion from the Register.
- The ADI Registrar shall retain the right to demand timely changes to the advertising of any Organisation or Trainer in the case of it not being covered by any regulatory body.
- The ADI Registrar reserves the right, but not the duty, to make a complaint about a member's advertising (in whatever form) to the appropriate regulatory body if in his opinion such material does not satisfy the above criteria. As an alternative to such a complaint being raised the member may elect to immediately remove the offending material and thus potentially avoid such action being taken.

Business code of practice

An organisation shall:

- Provide a full copy of their training course contract or agreement and any other associated terms and conditions and give an opportunity for any prospective Trainee to study them away from the Premises and seek independent advice, if so desired, before they are required to sign any document or make any payment.
- Have a refund policy in circumstances where a Trainee cannot continue with the course at the time or at any reasonable time in the future on serious medical grounds confirmed in writing by a doctor that prevents them from being able to drive or instruct and such refund shall be limited to the savings that an Organisation would make by not having to deliver the remainder of the training course in accordance with the Guidance on refunds provided by the Office of Fair Trading.
- Have a refund policy in the event of the Trainee failing three attempts at Part Two of the ADI examination providing that each exam was taken in good faith by the Trainee and provided any free remedial training offered

by the Organisation prior to the failed attempts is taken and such refund shall be limited to the savings that an Organisation would make by not having to deliver the remainder of the training course in accordance with the Guidance on refunds provided by the Office of Fair Trading.

- Have a refund policy in the event of the Trainee being refused their application for registration by the DSA provided the Trainee had not deliberately withheld or falsely stated any relevant information as part of their application to attend the course and provided it was not as the result of any event or incident following commencement of the training course and such refund shall be limited to the savings that an Organisation would make by not having to deliver the remainder of the training course in accordance with the Guidance on refunds provided by the Office of Fair Trading.

- The refund policy must provide for an automatic and prompt refund to the Trainee for any ADI examination, trainee licence or registration fees paid to the Organisation whether identified separately or inclusive in the overall training course fee. The Trainee's entitlement to this money, at any time upon their written request, should be clearly stated in the course contract or agreement. If the fees are paid on behalf of the Trainee by the Organisation it will be deemed that these fees have been collected as part of the fee for the training and subject to the terms of this clause.

INDEX

NB: page numbers in *italic* indicate figures or tables

ADI Register 34–48, 198
  choosing a course 6–10
    course material 9
    course syllabus 9
    making the decision 10
    time taken to qualify 9–10
    tutor 7–8
    types of course 8
  DSA service standards 48
  exam structure 39–47, *see also*
    Part 1: Theory and Hazard
    Perception; Part 2: Driving
    Ability; Part 3:
    Instructional Ability
  exemptions 38
  overview of 6
  qualifications 34–37
    application for registration 36
    candidates with disabilities
      35–36
    criminal history checks 37
    practicing with friend or
      relatives 36–37
    registration in Northern Ireland
      47
    trainee licence 37–38
      conditions for qualification
        37
      in Northern Ireland 38
advanced driving tests 29–30,
  210–17
ageing 332–33
anti-lock braking system (ABS) 64,
  88, 89, 230, *230*
anxiety 331
Approved Driving Instructors
  National Joint Council
  (ADINJC) 13–14

assessments and standards 301–04
  adapting instruction 302
  choosing a route 304
  full licence holders, dealing with
    303
  getting to know your pupil 304
  initial assessment 302
  licence and eyesight check 303
  new pupils, dealing with 302–03
  outlining course objectives 304
Association for Spina Bifida and
  Hydrocephalus (ASBAH) 319
Automobile Association (AA) 192

blind areas 120, 125

car, the 218–55
  documentation 252–55
    MOT test 255
    motor insurance 255
    number plate 252–53, *253,*
      254
    registration document 252
    tax disc 253, 255
  mechanical principles 218–38
    anti-lock braking system
      (ABS) 230, *230*
    automatic transmission
      226–27
    brakes and gears 228–29, *229*
    clutch 225, *225*
    cooling system *223,* 223–24
    differential units 227
    engine 219–20, *219, 220, 221*
    engine lubrication 222,
      222–23
    exhaust system 227–28, *228*
    exhaust turbo charging 228

fuel system 221
gearbox 226
handbrake 229
ignition system 221–22
power-assisted steering 231
shock absorbers 232, *233*
steering 231, *231*
suspension 232
transmission system *224*,
    224–27
tyres 233–35, *234*, *235*
vehicle controls and operation
    238–45
    automatic transmission
        244–45
    driving aids 240–41
    instrumentation 241–43
    main controls 238–39
    starter controls 239–40
vehicle regulations 245–52
    airbag 251, *251*
    child car seats 249–50
    horn and headlamps, use of
        248
    lighting 246–47
    mirrors 251
    noise and smoke 248
    parking 247–48
    seat belts 249
    seatbelt pre-tensioner 250
    vehicle defects 252
    windscreen washers/wipers
        252
see also vehicle safety checks
Cardington Special Driving Test
    29–30, 210–12
    Special Test Certificate 30
    Certificate in Education 31
    Certificate of Competence to
        Drive 366
    Check Test 1, 3, 48, 174–82,
        404
appointment, the 175
the car 176
at the end of the test 182
Fleet Check Test 404–08

instructor grading
    Grade 1 181–82
    Grade 2 181
    Grade 3 180–81
    Grade 4 180
    Grade 5 179–80
    Grade 6 179
instructor's test results 182
presenting the lesson 176–78
test frequency 174
your pupil 176
City & Guilds Further Education
        Teacher's Certificate 31
continuing professional
        development (CPD) 29–32
    BTECs 32
    Cardington Special Driving Test
        29–30
    Certificate in Education 31
    City & Guilds Further Education
        Teacher's Certificate 31
    Credit Accumulation and
        Transfer Scheme (CATS)
        31
    DIAmond Advanced Motorist
        Test scheme 30, 216–17
    Diploma in Driving Instruction
        30–31
    NVQ in driving instruction
        31–32
controls 117–23
    accelerator 121–22
    building up confidence 123
    clutch 122
    doors 119
    engine, switching on the 120
    footbrake 121–22
    gear lever 121
    handbrake and neutral 119, 121
    head restraints 119
    horn 120
    indicators 120
    lesson content 118
    lesson structure 118
    mirrors 119–20
    moving off and stopping 122–23

seat adjustment 119
seat belts 120
steering 120
summary of key points 123
timing your explanation 118–19
Credit Accumulation and Transfer
    Scheme (CATS) 31
crossroads and roundabouts
    146–50
    crossroads
        common faults 148
        experienced pupils 147
        fault assessment 148
        giving feedback 148
        inexperienced pupils 147
        summary of key points 150
    roundabouts
        common faults 150
        experienced pupils 150
        inexperienced pupils 149
        summary of key points 150

Department of Environment ADI
    (DOE ADI) 6
Direct Access 24, 191
disabilities and impairments 185,
    188, 190, 244, 317–36, 350
    ADI applicants 35–36
    application 334–35
    assessing needs 318–19
    autism 327
    disabilities, notes on 319–21
    Disability and Equality Act 2010
        317
    driving tests 335–36
    dyslexia 327
    illiteracy 327
    impaired hearing 326
    impaired vision 325–26
    instructor courses 336
    non-English-speaking pupils 327
    physical stature and ill-health
        327–28
    teaching methods 332–34
        hearing problems 332–33
        physical disabilities 332

reading and understanding
    problems 333–34
vehicle adaptations 321–25
drink- and drug-driving
    alcohol 196, 328
    drugs 329
Driver and Vehicle Licensing
    Agency (DVLA) 183, 184,
    190, 252
    Driver Enquiry Unit 187
    see also driver licensing
Driver and Vehicle Testing Agency
    (DVTA) 344
Driver Certificate of Professional
    Competence (CPC) 24,
    385–89
    case studies 386
    exemptions 386
    grandfather rights 388
    initial training 386–87
    periodic training 388
    practical test 387
    syllabus 387
driver errors 309–10
    car control 310
    excessive speed 310
    indecision 310
    lack of awareness 310
driver licensing 184–92
    health and eyesight 188, 189–90
        disabilities 188, 190
        epilepsy 188
        eyesight 189–90
        medical assessment 190
        pacemakers 188
    licence applications 186–88
        application fees 187
        application forms 186
        and disqualified drivers 187
    licence categories 185, 186
    licence information codes 188,
        189
    motorcycle licences 185, 190–91
    photo card licenses 184
    provisional licences 184–85
    vocational licences 191–92

driver training industry, the 19–24
  defensive driver training 22–24
    company drivers 22–23
    fleet driver training 23
    LGV instruction 24
    lorries 24
    minibuses 24
    motorcycles 23–24
    skills refresher courses 23
    traffic offenders 23
    vocational training 23
  information technology 21
  'L' driver market 19
  number of lessons needed 20
  Pass Plus scheme 21–22
  pre-driver training 22
  theory and hazard perception
    training 20–21
Drivers' Medical Group 374
driver's record, keeping a 305–06
  assessment report 306
  patterns of errors 306
Driving Goods Vehicles – the
  official DSA syllabus 397
Driving Instructors' Accident and
  Disability Fund 16
Driving Instructors Association
  (DIA) 13, 16–17, 183
  DIA Motor Insurance Scheme 17
  DIAmond Advanced Instructor
    17
  DIAmond Advanced Motorist
    Test 17, 30, 216–17
  Diploma in Driving Instruction
    17, 30–31
  Driving Instructor 17
  Driving Instructors' Accident
    and Disability Fund 16
  Driving magazine 17
Driving Instructor's Manual, The
  16
Driving Standards Agency (DSA) 6,
  24, 32, 34, 49, 397
  Compensation Code 351–52
  contacts 417–18
  Despatch 13, 28, 183

Drive On 366
National Driving Standards 3
service standards 48, 370–71
Driving Test Report (DL25) 9, 42,
  50, 64, 72, 73, 336, 355,
  356–61, 365, 366, 397
driving tests 337–71
  car and trailer test
    minimum test vehicle
      requirements 367
    safety questions 367–68
    syllabus 368–70
    test centres 367
  DSA service standards 371
  Extended Driving Test 370
  practical test
    administration 344
    after the test 366–67
    applying for the test 348–50
    attending the test 352
    before the test begins 353,
      355
    booking 344
    cancelling or postponing a test
      350–52
    eco-safe driving 348
    fault categories 362
    fault types 362–65
    fees 350
    if your pupil fails 366
    if your pupil passes 366
    marking system *354*, 355–61
    syllabus 344–48
    test times 350
  theory and hazard perception
    administration 337
    booking 337–38
    cancelling a test 339
    at the end of the test 342
    hazard perception test 340–42
    preparation 343
    proof of identity 339
    test fee 338
    test format 339
    theory test syllabus 339–40
    training for 342–43

dual controls, using 110–11, 295–301
  avoiding problems 299–301
  dual accelerator 299
  dual clutch 298
  dual footbrake 297–98
  dual mirror 299
  horn 299
  other intervention 299
  physical intervention 297
  steering wheel 298
  verbal intervention 296–97
dyslexia 21, 39, 52, 327, 334–35

eco-driving 71–72, 217, 348
emergency stop and using mirrors 123–31
  avoiding conflict 129–30
  avoiding emergencies 130
  fault analysis 129
  lesson structure 129
  maintaining safety 131
  reaction speed 130
  skidding 130–31
  summary of key points 131
European Driving Schools Association (EFA) 15
European Secure Vehicle Alliance (ESVA) 15

fleet driver training 390, 397–408
  accredited training providers 399
  application 398
  Check Test 404–08
    areas to cover 405
    and multi-tasking 406
    self-analysis 407
  driving ability test 401–02
  fees 398
  Fleet Driver Training Register 397–98
  instruction/coaching ability test 402–04
  qualifying 398–99
  registration 404
  theory test 400–01

Green Flag 192

Helping Learners to Practice – The official DSA guide 9, 50
Highway Code, The 3, 9, 26, 50, 61, 64, 70, 98, 99, 103, 120, 123, 125, 126, 128, 130, 133, 139, 143, 149, 152, 194, 195, 214, 216, 247, 269, 271, 280, 301, 306, 311, 312, 326, 327, 333, 334, 342, 343, 347, 363, 377, 392, 397
How to Be an Advanced Motorist 212

Institute of Advanced Motorists (IAM) 29
  special driving test 212–14
Institute of Master Tutors of Driving 332
Instructional Techniques and Practice for Driving Instructors 50, 117
instructions and terminology 287–95
  directional errors 289
  encouraging independence 289–90
  general instructions 287–89
  standard instructions 291–95
  terminology 291
International Association for Driver Education (IVV) 17, 30
International Driving Permit (IDP) 192

junctions, approaching (phase 1) 132–34, 135
  experienced pupils 133–34
  hazard awareness 134
  inexperienced pupils 133
  summary of key points 135
junctions, approaching (phase 2) 132, 134–35
  common faults 134–35
  fault assessment 134
  summary of key points 135

Know Your Traffic Signs 50, 61, 342, 343, 377, 397

large vehicles, driving 372–89
    applying for a licence 374–75
    driving licenses *373*, 373–74
    exemptions 372–73
    health and eyesight 374
    practical test 380–85
        after the test 385
        applying for the test 380
        during the test 382–84, *383*
        fees 380
        format 380–81
        minimum test vehicle
            requirements 381, *381*
        syllabus 384–85
    theory and hazard perception
        375–79
        hazard perception test 379
        sample questions 378–79
        syllabus 375–77
    see also LGV instruction; Driver
        Certificate of Professional
        Competence (CPC)
learning methods 256–63
    activity and involvement 247
    attention 256
    attitude and behaviour 260
    coaching 258–59
    interference 261–62
    learning by repetition 257, 258
    learning by understanding
        257–58
    motivation 262–63
    road user error 260–61
    safe attitudes, developing
        259–60
    transfer of learning 261
LGV instruction 24, 390–97
    fees 397
    hazard perception test 394
    LGV Instructor Accreditation
        Scheme 391–92
    practical test 394–95
    qualifications needed 390

Register of LGV Instructors 24,
    390–91
test of instructional ability
    395–97
theory test 392–94
    sample questions 393–94
training providers 391

making progress, hesitancy and
        road positioning 157–60
    common faults 160
    dual carriageways 158–59
    fault assessment 159
        excessive speed 159
        failure to make progress 159
        positioning 159
    summary of key points 160
meeting, crossing the path of, and
        overtaking other traffic,
        allowing clearance and
        anticipation 141–46
    anticipation 144
    clearances 143
    common faults 145
    crossing other traffic 143
    experienced pupils 145
    following at a safe distance 144
    inexperienced pupils 145
    meeting other traffic 142–43
    overtaking 143–44
    summary of key points 145–46
Ministry of Transport 13
motor insurance 205–08, 255
    accident procedures 207–08, *209*
    comprehensive insurance
        206–07
    compulsory insurance 205–06
    driver responsibilities 207
    EC requirements 207
    third party insurance 206
Motor Schools Association of Great
    Britain (MSA) 14–16, 183
*Motor Vehicles (Construction and
    Use) Regulations* 194, 245
Motor Vehicles (Driving Licences)
    Regulations 1999 50, 397

moving off and stopping 123–28
 coordination of controls 125–26
 experienced pupil 124
 inexperienced pupils 124–25
 lesson structure 124
 making progress 127
 M-S-M routine 125
 precautions 125
 recognizing problems 126
 stop control 126
 stop position 126–27
 summary of key points 127–28

New Driver Act 1, 183, 198
NVQ in driving instruction 13,
  31–32

*Official DSA Guide to Driving –
 The essential skills* 3, 9, 24,
 26, 50, 61, 88, 98, 99, 117,
 120, 128, 138, 149, 217, 238,
 271, 280, 342, 343
*Official DSA Guide to Driving
 Goods Vehicles, the* 372, 377,
 380, 384, 392
*Official DSA Guide to Hazard
 Perception DVD* 9, 50
*Official DSA Theory Test CD
 ROM for Car Drivers, the*
 343
*Official Guide to Hazard
 Perception, the* 379, 397
Official Guide to Learning to Drive
 3, 9, 20, 50, 96, 116, 17, 128,
 138, 149, 279, 342, 344, 363,
 365, 380
Official Register of Driving
 Instructor Training *see*
 ORDIT Register
*Official Theory Test for Car
 Drivers, the* 342, 343
ORDIT register 2, 4, 7, 10–12,
 future development 12
 inspection criteria 12
 membership terms and
  conditions 420–23

training programmes 11
 what is ORDIT? 10
 what the inspector looks for
  11–12

Parliamentary Advisory Council for
 Transport Safety (PACTS) 15,
 17
Part 1: Theory and Hazard
 Perception 39–41, 49–57
 and dyslexia 39
 hazard perception test 56–57
  after the test 56–57
  pass mark 56
  resource materials 56
 test structure
  banding system 40
  hazard perception test 40
  pass mark 40
  results 40–41
 theory test 49–56
  banding system 52
  booking the test 52
  and dyslexia 52
  organising your studies 51
  pass mark 55–56
  resource materials 50
  sample questions 53–55
  special needs learners 52
  studying the syllabus 50–51
  taking the test 55
Part 2: Driving Ability 41–43, 58–92
 application 58–59
 the car 59
 car control 84–90
  brakes and gears 86
  double de-clutch 86
  emergency braking 89–90
  handbrake 85
  skidding 88–89
  stopping distances 86–87, 87
 eco-safe driving 71–72
  marking 72
 eyesight 59–60
 marking system 72–73
  faults, categories of 72

faults, examples 73
on the road 76–84
  anticipation 77
  communication 79
  courtesy 80
  decisions, making 79–80
  defensive signals 80
  eye contact 80
  gathering information 82–83
  hazard recognition 78
  hold-back procedure 83
  implied signals 80
  position 82
  progress 83
  response and control skills
      79–80
  road sense 76–77
  signalling by position 79–80
  signalling by speed 80
  speed adjustment 81–82
  speed control and steering 83
  visual awareness 77–78
'perfect driver', profile of 74–76
  attitude 75
  emotion 75
  hazard recognition 76
  knowledge 74
  motivation 75
  perception 76
  personality 75–76
  skill 74
preparation 61–70
  during the test 64–70
  effective training 62–64
  mock test sessions 62
resource materials 61
syllabus 60–61
test structure
  application fee 41
  driving technique 42
  eyesight 41
  if you fail 43
  if you pass 43
  result 42–43
  test format 41
  vehicle safety questions 41–42

vehicle safety questions 60
Part 3: Instructional Ability 43–45,
    93–173
  ADI certificate 163
  application 93–94
  assessment of instructional
      ability 103–12
    approach to pupil 112
    attitude 112
    communication 107–08
    control of the lesson 107–08
    fault analysis 105
    giving feedback 110
    identification of faults
        104–05
    level of instruction 105–06
    planning 106
    Q&A technique 108–09
    remedial action 105
    use of controls 110–11
  the car 94
  if you fail 162
  fault assessment 116
  fee 94, 95
  key learning points 116
  learning to teach 117
  marking sheet 161, 164–73
    criteria for grading 161
  when you pass 161–62
    registration declaration 162
  pass rate 10
  phase 1 97, 98–101
    demonstrations 99
    developing understanding 101
    establishing the base line 99
    giving feedback 101
    learning through practice 100
    maintaining control and
        safety 100
    positive correction 100
    Q&A on the move 100
    retrospective correction
        100–01
    visual aids 99
  phase 2 97, 101–03
    assessing ability 101

dealing with faults 102–03
establishing problems 101
identifying faults 102
over-instruction 102
recognizing faults 103
preparation 112–14
    DSA tips 114
    pass rate 114
    training and practice 113
preset tests *see* controls;
        crossroads and
        roundabouts; emergency
        stop and using mirrors;
        junctions, approaching
        (phase 1); junctions,
        approaching (phase 2);
        making progress, hesitancy
        and road positioning;
        meeting, crossing the path
        of, and overtaking other
        traffic, allowing adequate
        clearance and anticipation;
        moving off and stopping;
        pedestrian crossings and
        signal use; reverse and turn
        in the road manoeuvres;
        reverse parking;
        T-junctions, emerging
        (phase 1); T-junctions,
        emerging (phase 2)
and seat belts 94
subjects tested 116
test format 94–98
    exam topics 96–97
    key elements 98
    lesson format 98
    phase 1 97
    phase 2 97
    structuring the lesson 95–96
test structure
    ADI Certificate 46
    application fee 43
    asking for further information
        46–47
    displaying your certificate 46
    at the end of the test 45

if you fail 46
    marking sheet 44–45
    in Northern Ireland 47
    if you pass 45
    registration declaration
        45–46
    role play 44
Pass Plus 21–22, 306–09, 366
    all-weather driving 307
    country driving 307
    dual carriageways 308
    motorways 308–09
    night driving 308
    overview of 21–22
    town driving 307
pedestrian crossings and signal use
        150–54
    arm signals 152
    common faults 154
    experienced pupils 153
    fault assessment 153
    inexperienced pupils 153
    lesson structure 151
    pedestrian crossings 152
    practice 154
    sample questions 152–53
    summary of key points 154
    using signals 151
*Practical Teaching Skills for
        Driving Instructors* 1, 2, 41,
        45, 48, 50, 51, 97, 105, 106,
        107, 108, 112, 116, 117, 259,
        393, 397, 401
*Prepare for your practical driving
        test* 50
professional associations 13–19
    Approved Driving Instructors
        National Joint Council
        (ADINJC) 13–14
    Driving Instructor Scottish
        Council (DISC) 17–18
    Driving Instructors Association
        (DIA) 16–17, 183
    Motor Schools Association of
        Great Britain (MSA)
        14–16, 183

Northern Ireland Approved
Driving Instructor
Association (NIADIA)
18–19
SmartDriving 19, 183
*Professional LGV Driver's
Handbook, the* 372
progress, assessing 311–16
continuous assessment 315–16
Highway Code questions 312–14
practical assessments 314–15
Q&A technique 311–12

QEF Mobility Services 321, 326,
328, 332,
qualities, of a good driver and
instructor 24–28
qualities, of a good instructor 5–6

refresher training 23, 48, 216, 385
reverse and turn in the road
manoeuvres 138–41
demonstration 140
explanation 139–40
giving feedback 141
inexperienced pupils 139
lesson content 139
lesson structure 138–39
observations and safety 140–41
practice 140
summary of key points 141
transferring skills 139
reverse parking 155–57
common faults 157
experienced pupils 155
inexperienced pupils 156
lesson content 155
manoeuvre 156
practice 156–57
summary of key points 157
Road Safety Act 2006 24
Road Traffic Act 1991 6, 34, 37,
194, 353
road traffic law 194–205
disqualification 196
and the ADI 198

driver identity 200–01
driver rehabilitation scheme 196
driving offences
careless and inconsiderate
driving 195
dangerous driving 195
drink/drive offences 196
driving other than in
accordance with a
licence 195
offences incurring
disqualification 196
endorsement codes *202–04*
Extended Driving Test, the
196–97
fixed penalties 198–200
extended fixed penalty scheme
199–200
mobile phones, use of 205
national driver improvement
scheme 200
New Driver Act 198
penalty points *197*
Road Traffic Act 1991 194–95
speed limits 201, *204*
Speed Awareness Courses
204–05
Road Transport Industry Training
Board (RTITB) 390
*Roadcraft: the police driver's
handbook* 212, 215
route planning 283–87
advanced routes 286
giving directions 287
intermediate routes 285–86
nursery routes 285
points to remember 286
Royal Automobile Club (RAC)
192
Royal National Institute for Deaf
People (RNID) 333
Royal Society for the Prevention of
Accidents (RoSPA) 15
RoSPA Advance Driving Test
214–16
RSAC 192

skill training 266–75
  essential elements
    attitude 268
    knowledge 267
    skill 268
  learning curve 275
  teaching a skill
    demonstration 271
    explanation 269–71
    practice 272–75
Speed Awareness Courses 204–05
stress 330
supervising drivers, legal
  obligations of 208

Teaching the Deaf to Drive 332
T-junctions, emerging (phase 1)
  135–36
  practice 136
  summary of key points 137–38
T-junctions, emerging (phase 2)
  135–36, 137–38
  fault assessment 137
  summary of key points 137–38
Trainee Licence Scheme 8, 9, 37,
  90–92

Vehicle Defect Rectification Scheme
  (VDRS) 252
vehicle safety checks 235–38
  daily checks 235–36
  periodic checks 237
  seasonal checks 238
  weekly checks 236–37
visitors and new residents, driving as
  designated country nationals 193
  EU and EEA nationals 192–93
  Gibraltar nationals 193
  Jersey, Guernsey and the Isle of
    Man nationals 193
  nationals of other countries 194
  Northern Ireland nationals 193
Voluntary Register of LGV
  Instructors 390

What You Need to Know about
  Driving Licences 50, 185,
  372, 374

Young Driver scheme 185, 386
Your Road to Becoming an
  Approved Driving Instructor
  (ADI 14) 6, 35, 39, 48, 58, 162

INDEX OF ADVERTISERS

AA Driving School	*inside front cover, i–iii*
Adrian Flux	*iv*
DeskTop Driving	*xvi–xvii*
Driving School Supplies	*v*
Grade Six Supplies	*xxii–xxiii*
Hitachi	*xi–xiii*
Motor Schools Association	*xxiv–xxv*

With over 1,000 titles in printed and digital format, **Kogan Page** offers affordable, sound business advice

www.koganpage.com

KoganPage